An American Challenge

A Report on Economic Trends and Social Issues in Appalachia

Commission on Religion in Appalachia

Richard A. Couto

KENDALL/HUNT PUBLISHING COMPANY
4050 Westmark Drive Dubuque, Iowa 52002

This edition has been printed directly from camera-ready copy.

ISBN 0-8403-9481-0

Printed in the United States of America
10 9 8 7 6 5 4 3 2 1

An American Challenge

A Report on Economic Trends and Social Issues in Appalachia

An American Challenge

A Report on Economic Trends and Social Issues in Appalachia

Table of Contents

Foreword

Whether Appalachia is an idea, a nostalgia, a theme park, a literary construct, or many Appalachias, the more we know about its diversity, its injuries, its strengths, tendencies, and its increasingly complex relationships with national and international economies, the more likely our plans, investments, and commitments will be pertinent and helpful to the ones to whom this report is devoted: Appalachian families and communities; their children, their future. We must know as much as we can know and interpret the flow of historical events with as many facts at our disposal, with as much honesty and wisdom as possible. This book is important because we must continue to seek to understand what the situation is, how it came to be this way, and where, possibly, the future is tending. It is urgent. Lives are at stake.

Reinhold Niebuhr reminds us that "...every larger frame of meaning, which serves the observer of historical events in correlating the events into some kind of pattern, is a structure of faith rather than of science." So this important book of very current information is also a "creature of the web of events, in the creation of which it participates." It must be read with critical perspective of its sources and context. The test of the pertinence and usefulness of this book lies not so much in any inherent value of the data but in the commitment, wisdom, and tenacity of the reader. The heights and depths of Appalachia cannot be measured, but clues to its mysteries and its disorders can be ascertained in this book by caring and careful readers.

Economic trends and social issues within Appalachia, which this report describes and analyzes, are not encouraging. They are indicative of serious national economic problems, attendant social changes, and the complexity of selecting appropriate solutions. This report deals with trends, however, not inevitabilities. It assumes that the economy, like politics, is a set of social relationships. Human beings can alter the trends which their actions put in motion. Within Appalachia, there are reasons—spelled out in the lives of children, families, and communities—to alter economic trends.

Appalachia has often been a harbinger of need and a precursor of related change in America. The coal miners of the region provided crucial leadership in the dramatic growth of industrial unions in the 1930s. Mountaineers and the region's economic conditions provided much of the inspiration for the 1960s programs to respond to "the other America." Grassroots efforts of the region in each decade since the

1950s have provided reform movements for labor, occupational health, land use and reclamation, community health centers, environmental quality, maternal and children's services, housing, and a host of other issues and human needs. This report is intended to help existing community change efforts and to stimulate new ones by placing them in a national context of economic changes and related social issues. Now, no less than in the past, the Appalachian region speaks to the nation about itself.

The perspective and advocacy of this report stem from its origins within the Commission on Religion in Appalachia (CORA). The Commission set out, in 1982 when I served as executive director, on a self assessment and regional analysis that included plans for a report to understand the region as a dynamic area undergoing change, to provide more analysis on all three subregions of Appalachia, and to assist CORA to respond more appropriately to emerging needs in the region.

This report substantially revises the one originally completed in 1984. It includes additional and recent information including 1990 economic and census data. It complements CORA's *Atlas of the Church in Appalachia* that provides information on regional church membership.

In preparing this revised report we are deeply indebted to Dick Couto who adhered to the original objectives but has broadened the intended audience and broken new ground. One will find numerous reports on Appalachia and related national conditions reviewed and summarized in this report. Consequently, those unfamiliar with Appalachia and its political economy will find information that relates the issues of the region to national issues with which they may be familiar. Those familiar with Appalachia will find a broad discussion of its political economy and that of the nation as a context within which to place their own information.

This report is intended for those who seek "to deal with the religious, moral, and spiritual implications inherent in the economic, social and cultural conditions in the Appalachian region" (CORA 1992). It is addressed to people who understand or believe that human beings have responsibilities for one another. Our responsibility is expressed, in part, by the political economy that we construct and continue. Human bonds that extend beyond the market place serve as a premise of this study. With this critical base of information, these human bonds form the hope and the promise of mission with which CORA began in 1965 and which this report continues and extends.

Jim Sessions
Director, Highlander Research and Education Center

Preface

A spate of articles in the national media in the early 1990s brought new attention to the Appalachian region. The stories had a formula: a flashback to the 1960s and Appalachia, a frontline in the war on poverty; a list of programs that resulted; a focus on the current difficulties of a particular county and community; a close-up on a particular person or family; a list of staggering figures on current conditions, local poverty, unemployment, and other human needs; a brief inquiry about what went wrong; and, finally, the glimmer of a ray of hope in one group or program trying to make a difference locally (Carlson 1992; Gugliotta 1993; Johnson 1992; O'Brien 1993; Ralston 1993). Each of these articles, others like them, and all of them together suggest how the term "Appalachia," like "the inner city" or "the homeless," portrays the unfulfilled promise of American life.

Other reports and historical, political, and sociological studies of Appalachia provide more context and interpretation than this media coverage. They explain the regional conditions as part of the unfavorable terms of exchange between economic institutions outside the region and local residents for the extraction of the region's resources. In these reports and studies, Appalachia is a stage upon which a famous, familiar, and international cast performs a national drama.

How we interpret the problems of Appalachia affects what we consider appropriate responses. Based on media reports we can interpret severe human need in Appalachia as an unintended problem which we should address and which we can address effectively, should we choose to do so. Broader reports and interpretive studies may lead us to interpret Appalachian problems as a logical, but also an unusual and lamentable, outcome of American economic and political institutions and practices. Thus, we may interpret Appalachia, like the inner city and homelessness, as the unfulfilled promise, the false promise, or an over promise of American life.

This work encompasses all of these interpretations of American promise. Readers will find the unfulfilled promise of American life measured in the severity of particular problems of Appalachia. Readers will also find the over promise of economic trends in many of those same problems. Hopefully, readers will also become adept at recognizing the false promise of American poverty policy proposals that skirt social guarantees of work, income, and other basic needs.

This work differs from media accounts, other reports, and interpretive studies of Appalachia. The specific reports of one instance of Appalachian conditions and the broader interpretive studies, however excellent as many of them are, seldom provide an overview of the thirteen states and 399 counties of the Appalachian region as this work does. Nor do they give adequate attention to public policies to do something about the problems they report and analyze. This report spans the gaps among media reports of a particular community, interpretive studies of Appalachian events, their national contexts, and public policy.

This report complements many studies on Appalachia. Readers well acquainted with particular instances of Appalachian conditions will find a larger context in which to place and compare them. Readers well acquainted with interpretive studies of Appalachia's past will find an interpretation of the political economy with which to compare them. Most of all, however, this report provides common ground for policy analysts and ordinary, concerned citizens, within and outside the region, to interpret Appalachia as part of the social consequences of recent national economic trends.

These purposes and characteristics flow directly from the objectives that the Commission on Religion in Appalachia (CORA) had for this report:

- -- to specify regional economic issues, including employment and developments in big industries, demographic trends, environmental concerns, educational issues, family and gender role changes, and religious trends;
- -- to combine social science, knowledge of the Appalachian region, and ethical sensitivity;
- -- to collect, review, and summarize research and reports of agencies, universities, and organizations within the Appalachian region in a form useful to CORA; and
- -- to note national trends, including federal budget allocations, for their potential impact on the region and on CORA's work.

To pursue these objectives this report modestly emulates and borrows from the towering 1944 study by Gunnar Myrdal of race relations in America. He found a dilemma between the actual conditions of African Americans and the American creed of ideals of democracy, equality, and economic opportunity. The majority of white Americans, Myrdal found, created a set of "valuations," assumptions including pejorative attributes of African Americans, that permitted the white majority to preserve its belief in equality and to tolerate gross racial inequalities. These valuations seemed an obvious defense *of* the apparent inequalities of African Americans. Myrdal pointed out that these valuations also defended white Americans *from* the apparent failure to achieve their ideals or to even pursue them seriously. Many of the interpretive studies of Appalachia deal with valuations about the region and its residents that permit another defense of another set of inequalities and a defense from the same set of American political and economic ideals.

Appalachian conditions challenge the political and economic ideals of America. The acute conditions of unemployment, dislocated workers, low incomes, family changes, and child poverty within large portions of the Appalachian region represent a fundamental challenge to the American creed of some degree of economic equality and an abundance of economic opportunity. Closing the gap between conditions and creed presents a second challenge.

Myrdal placed his faith in the majority of Americans to close the gap of racial inequality. He underestimated the capacity of African Americans to close that gap by their own individual effort and organized action for change. Myrdal was exactly right, however, to place the responsibility for the major shortcomings of American ideals of social and economic equality primarily on those who say they embody them. The inspiring stories of individual and collective efforts for change within Appalachia, the defense of American ideals, are the material for other books. The story of this report is the gap between Appalachian realities and American ideals and the related shortcomings of American policies and practices. This report offers no valuations to defend the nation from its ideals. Instead, it insists that the best defense of our political and economic ideals is their application to social problems and needs such as those we find in the Appalachian region.

This report had far less time and resources than Myrdal and so, not surprisingly, it is far less comprehensive and original than Myrdal's work. It summarizes the work of others to establish the political economy that is the context of Appalachia and provides new measures of census and personal income data. Time and space did not permit the integration of many important studies of local instances of economic trends and social issues. Consequently, this report serves as a companion to the excellent stories regularly reported in journals such as *Southern Exposure, Southern Changes,* and *Appalachian Journal* and the newsletters of several regional organizations like Highlander, CORA, The Brushy Fork Institute, the Appalachian Center of the University of Kentucky, and Kentuckians for the Commonwealth. Likewise, several recent books and articles (Couto 1992; Fisher 1993; Gaventa et al. 1990; Gaventa et al. 1992) convey the flesh and bone, human nature of the numbers and concepts that this report offers. Also, newspaper series such as those of Bill Bishop (1993) and Jeff Fleischman (1994) provide detailed descriptions about the trends and issues of this report and ground them in the lives of specific people and places within Appalachia. It is in the nature of reports like this to cover a wide area. The references of this report will direct those who seek more depth on any of its particular parts.

It is the intention of this report to add to a discussion of the political economy of Appalachia and America but not to have the final say. It also intends to provide base line measures going back to 1970. The opportunity to update these measures, hopefully, will become part of the regular discussion of Appalachia in the future.

The report addresses those in institutions of power and wealth, including churches, who still have social consciences. It adopts the almost tortured prose of policy wonks to present as clearly and dispassionately as possible a case for new and different economic policies and practices. Hopefully, this report will help those within institutions to push their boundaries in the direction of social and economic equity.

Over the course of four years of work on this report, I have presented some of its information to groups throughout the region. At a meeting of church leaders in Berea, Kentucky in October 1991, I presented income data including evidence of a redistribution of income from low-income groups to high-income groups. A minister in that audience came to me later and explained that his church members had wealth and would welcome the news of an upward drift of income into allegedly more productive hands. I have had that minister and his church members in mind while writing this report. I intend that they find here new degrees of inequality and human need that our valuations of poverty, work, and opportunity cannot explain away or justify.

Occasionally, a discovery of Appalachia accompanies American efforts to redress a set of related national problems. In the 1960s, Michael Harrington (1962) discovered poverty for Americans and Harry Caudill (1962) provided a rich, historical account of conditions in one part of the Appalachian coal fields. Something was "broke" in America and providing economic opportunity would fix it. The discovery of Appalachia in the 1930s showed America problems with exploitative labor conditions (Ross 1933; Dreiser 1970rpt). Providing working people legal protection to join labor unions and government regulations to eliminate exploitative practices would make America, in the 1930s, better. Perhaps America will rediscover Appalachia in the 1990s through some future article, some powerhouse work, such as Harrington and Caudill produced, or some cataclysmic event.

If we do discover Appalachia again and Americans begin to search for effective means to redress the problems we find there, this report

suggests that full-scale, redistributive social policies and bold strokes for economic justice are the appropriate response. In Appalachia, in the last decade of this century, we can find the challenges to the promise of American life. What we have yet to find is the renewed determination of Americans to fulfill that promise as we enter the next century.

Acknowledgments

Several people and organizations have helped me in my work on this report. Jim Sessions, then executive director of the Commission on Religion in Appalachia, convinced me to undertake an earlier 1983 report and encouraged me during this work. The Lilly Endowment, Inc., through its Religion Program and its director, Fred L. Hofheinz, provided CORA support for this study. For that support, I am most grateful. Jim, Tena Willemsma, who followed Jim Sessions as acting executive director of CORA, and staff at the Lilly Foundation displayed considerable patience. Delays in getting data meant that deadline after deadline came and went without a final product. The other staff members of CORA all provided me assistance and encouragement in the manner that has made them and CORA admired and respected in the region. Clifford Gramich generously shared with me secrets of mapping software that he uncovered in his own work for CORA. He and I also shared the frustrations of data collection that imposed limits on what we could do and how quickly we could do it.

The Appalachian Studies Fellowship Program of Berea College generously assisted me with financial support several times. Their willingness to provide me several small grants over a short period of time expressed confidence in my work for which I am grateful. Loyal Jones, in particular, showed confidence in my work that provided me a great deal of encouragement.

The University of Richmond Faculty Research Committee provided me additional financial support and support for student assistants. Isaiah Jefferson and Greg Liebe provided initial assistance and helped me to develop formats for tables from the Local Area Personal Income data. This work followed up on the earlier efforts of Lucas Malawe and Hariharan Shankar at Tennessee State University. In the final stages of preparation, Morgan Benton, Cheryl Schott, and Eric Smith assisted in the preparation of tables, graphs, and maps used here. Members of the University of Richmond Computer Center were gracious in providing this project additional access. Bill Hoyt worked diligently and creatively to conduct the computer work on the tables and reports and then to transform them into tables. Members of the University of Richmond Boatwright Library staff, especially William Suddeth, helped us up our learning curve with downloading census data for 1990. Everyone on the library staff whom we approached, helped us in the manner that makes the library an exciting and rewarding place to learn. The provost's office of the University of Richmond provided a subvention for this book that helped reduce the price and make it more available.

The staff of the Appalachian Regional Commission, especially Judy Maher, has helped me to find and verify data. Monroe Newman, who was with ARC at the time, offered a severely critical assessment of my work that informed and cautioned me.

Nancy Simpson assisted me numerous times. The cover art work was contracted by the National Cancer Institute originally and is used here with its permission. Similarly, Appendix B was prepared for the Appalachia Leadership Initiative on Cancer (ALIC) publication, *Sowing Seeds in the Mountains* NIH Publication No. 94-3779. They are used here with the kind permission of ALIC and the National Cancer Institute. Margaret Gregg designed the quilt that appears on the cover. I am endebted to her, like so many others, for her artistic insight and expression.

Scott DeBergh, Chris O'Brien, Wendy Jochum, Vicky Splinter, and their associates at Kendall/Hunt smoothed the way for a rapid transition from manuscript to book.

Ron Eller, Steve Fisher, Helen Lewis, and Tena Willemsma took time to read a nearly completed draft of the manuscript. All of them made valuable suggestions for changes that improved the report. Unfortunately, a lack of time did not permit me to incorporate as many changes as they suggested and that I would have otherwise. Ben Poage, who is with the Kentucky Appalachian Ministry, pointed out to me the relationship between the counties beyond distress and the estimates of real unemployment by the Appalachian Center of the University of Kentucky. Jamie Harris copyedited the manuscript with diligence and skill.

My wife, Took, conjured up skills from a previous work life and entered and revised several drafts of the entire manuscript. Everyone knows how difficult and tedious that work is. No one does that work for nothing. So I presume she did it for love. For the work and for the love I am most grateful.

With all these people I share what is good about this report. Despite their assistance, mistakes may remain. If so, they are my responsibility alone.

An American Challenge

A Report on Economic Trends and Social Issues in Appalachia

Introduction

There is no single Appalachia. There are several. The Appalachia we discuss here industrialized the United States and now leads the American transition to a deindustrialized and postindustrial society. This Appalachia instructs the nation on the costs and benefits of large scale economic transformations.

Defining the Geographic Region

Different researchers have used various geographic boundaries for the region. Early sociologists, like John C. Campbell and Horace Kephart, established boundaries, Southern Highlands, that united a group of people with common cultural characteristics. In 1962, Thomas Ford, another sociologist, rearranged preexisting boundaries and organized a region primarily by needs and problems as well as common cultural characteristics (Ford 1962:1-8; Raitz and Ulack 1984:9-33).

In addition to varying geographic definitions, writers, journalists, and video and camera crews have set down in specific places within Appalachia's boundaries to define the people. Once there, they explain how the characteristics of the people found there express a variation of American experience: dialect, rural lifestyle, subsistence agriculture, Godlessness, Godliness, violent family feuds, excessive parental affection, industrial work, exploitation of labor, the organized resistance of workers to exploitation, or poverty, in large amounts and severe forms. Because of varying definitions and studies, Appalachia conjures up clear images in the popular mind of mountains but conflicting images of the people who live there (Shapiro 1978; Batteau 1990). We had the Waltons, offered as a model in the 1992 Republican campaign on family values, although the Waltons were New Deal Democrats. On the other hand we have the Hatfields and the McCoys, commercialized as bumbling bumpkins or as cruel and calculating cutthroats. Similarly, popular images suggest both the indolence and innocence of Li'l Abner and Snuffy Smith and the grueling work and union militancy of nameless coal miners. Whatever their cultural distinctions, the residents of Appalachia share no cultural trait to explain the economic condition of the region. We will not be concerned with cultural definitions of Appalachians (Couto 1994).

The geographic definition of Appalachia we will use extends far beyond the bounds of earlier studies to include thirteen states and 399 counties. The 1962 study of Thomas Ford, by contrast, included only 190 counties in six states. The geographic bounds of Appalachia expanded with the inception of the Appalachian Regional Commission (ARC) in 1965.

However much the boundaries vary, every definition has sought to encompass a problem area within the national economy (Ford 1962:3). The current definition came from a national sense of acute need within the Appalachian region and a national commitment to do something about it. It also resulted from an effort of state and congressional leaders to include their jurisdictions in an area of special federal initiatives. The desire of federal administrators to curry as much political support for the fledgling regional development efforts of the Kennedy and Johnson administrations also expanded the boundaries. These efforts anticipated other Great Society programs of the 1960s. Ironically, the Shenandoah Valley of Virginia, home of the Waltons, did not make it into the official government definition of Appalachia.

Any geographic definition of Appalachia encompasses areas with diverse economies and populations. This diversity makes generalizations difficult. The ARC definition compounds this difficulty. ARC's region extends from Southern New York to Eastern Mississippi and has over twenty million people residing within it. It has areas with a concentration of past and present industrial activity such as steel, coal mining, and textile and apparel, and automobile manufacturing. Other areas have a concentration of agriculture and tourism. The region includes many rural counties with populations less than ten thousand. On the other hand, these rural counties lie between two major metropolitan areas with economies built from steel and coal, Pittsburgh and Birmingham. Appalachia is next to other major metropolitan areas including Atlanta, Cincinnati, Harrisburg, Lexington, and Montgomery. Other nearby major cities, including Albany, Baltimore, Buffalo, Cleveland, Columbus, Memphis, Nashville, New York, Philadelphia, and Washington, D.C., are within an hour's drive of Appalachia's boundaries. Obviously this geographic region as defined by the ARC is not the hidden, socioeconomically homogeneous, remote, and distinct region that may remain in the popular imagination.

ARC and many other analysts break the region into more homogeneous subregions, Northern, Central, and Southern Appalachia. The Northern subregion takes in the Appalachian portions of New York, Ohio, Pennsylvania and Maryland. All of West Virginia falls within the boundaries of Appalachia, the only state that does, and most of West

Map I - 1
Counties, Subregions and Metropolitan Counties of Appalachia

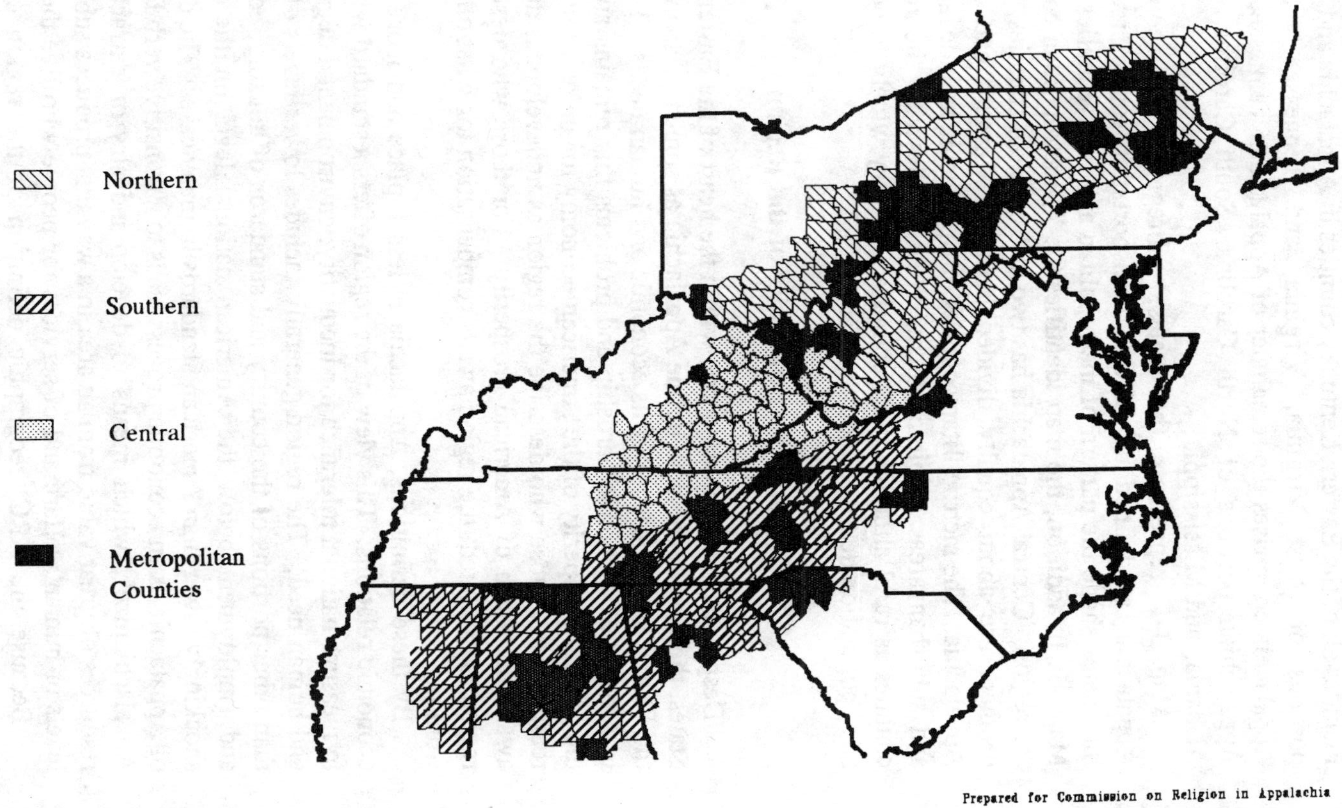

Virginia's counties are in the Northern subregion. The Central subregion includes all of the Eastern Kentucky counties in Appalachia and adjoining portions of West Virginia, Virginia, and Tennessee. Southern Appalachia comprises the remainder of Appalachian Tennessee, and the Appalachian portions of North Carolina, South Carolina, Georgia, Alabama, and Mississippi.

Map I-1 represents the states, subregions, and counties of Appalachia, as defined by ARC. Transportation routes, rivers, and interstates shape the pattern of metropolitan and rural counties found in Map I-1. In addition, the map identifies the 77 metropolitan counties of the region. Central Appalachia has two metropolitan counties. The rest of them are about equally divided between Northern and Southern Appalachia. The metropolitan counties of Appalachia include large cities and suburban areas adjoining them. We shall describe the remaining counties as rural although these counties also vary widely in population size, population density, and other factors.

Defining the Economics of the Region

Despite its geographic bounds within the heart of the Eastern United States, there are some who define Appalachia as somehow anomalous to the United States because of its economic and human needs. To them it is a region of economic hardship and problems that remains apart from the general prosperity of the American economy for unique and peculiar reasons. For those who describe the region as undeveloped, the region awaits the touch of American prosperity. For those who describe the region as exploited, the region awaits compensation for what others took from it.

By these definitions, Appalachia is less a place and more a set of economic relations. This view of the region offers a standard with which to measure national tolerance for inequality, environmental degradation, and human need. The region generally includes lower levels of income than other portions of the country and standards of housing, education, and employment below the American national level on the average, shockingly lower than American standards in many cases. The definition of Appalachia as an economic process leads to a transitive verb form, "to Appalachianize", which means to develop industry or extract natural resources of great value from an area in a way that produces substandard levels of human welfare and of services for people who live there.

Because the ARC geographic definition of the region expanded beyond previous boundaries, even generalizations of economic need within the Appalachian region need qualification. The geographic diversity of the region encompasses many economic and human conditions: prosperity and poverty, decline and growth, all of which vary by kind and degree. Most counties of the Appalachian region lag the nation and their individual states in economic prosperity. However, the region also includes counties, especially metropolitan counties, that exceed the nation in terms of per capita income, employment, and other measures of prosperity. Winston-Salem, North Carolina and suburban Atlanta, for example, have higher than national average per capita incomes. They have also enjoyed economic growth and increased prosperity for two decades.

The region is a central part of the political economy of the United States. Coal and steel forged the industrial revolution and textiles provided an early industry of mass production. The industrial revolution brought profound change and conflict that served as a backdrop, too often undiscerned, of events in the Appalachian region from the Civil War to the Depression. Indeed, recent scholarship permits us to understand how the transference of ownership of the region's coal resources from local landowners to absentee corporate owners fueled a portion of the conflict of the Hatfields and McCoys (Waller 1988). Appalachia and its relation to the development of several industries portray the American industrial revolution, the changes it brought, and the present course of American industrial history.

The Appalachian region also expresses the postindustrial revolution in the American economy. Each subregion has experienced different economic changes since 1969, and different human consequences. The Northern Appalachian subregion, with the decline of the coal and steel industries and changes in the manufacturing sector of its economy, has lost population. Many of the people who remain have seen their economic position diminish. The Southern Appalachian subregion, on the other hand, increased in population and improved in per capita income from 1969 to 1989. Central Appalachia, the core of all definitions based on geography and economic need, had severe decline in its coal industry. This meant a decade of outmigration and increased poverty in the 1980s that was reminiscent of the 1950s.

These regional differences articulate current American economic and social changes even more clearly. Within the region we find part of the "rust belt," areas of decline in America's traditional heavy industry. We also find some of the "sun belt," areas of economic growth in new industries and the expanding service sector of the economy. We find in Central Appalachia areas of chronic economic need comparable to "inner cities." The eastern and southern edges of Appalachia even touch the

"Gun Belt" of the U.S. economy, a concentration of military contractors which extends from Boston down the east coast and then west across the South to Texas.

Besides these subregional distinctions we will report on metropolitan and rural counties. The region's population is about equally divided between them but the prosperity and needs are not. In every subregion the rural counties generally have more needs than the metropolitan counties and less economic prosperity and growth. The differences between metropolitan and rural counties highlight the issues of polarization, the distribution of economic benefits and costs in different portions to different sets of Americans. The analyses of subregions and of metropolitan and rural counties permit us to get behind averages. These either disguise or distort the uneven development within the region and the severity of problems in some places.

Other distinctions remain to be made within the averages given here. For example, the averages of the region's poorest counties do not suggest the range within those counties between residents in the county seat and those in the remainder of the county. This level of analysis offers us distinctions with which to probe regional averages. It should also sensitize us to the need to probe even the averages we use to make further distinctions. There are concentrations of wealth and poverty and patterns of uneven development within each county and also within the region among subregions and between metropolitan and rural counties.

Outline

The first three chapters, Section I, discuss changes in the national economy that have shaped the political economy of Appalachia. Chapter 1 reviews the findings of several economic and social analyses of the United States since 1970. It focuses on studies that have examined the decline in real wages of the American worker, the changes in the nature of employment, and changes in the industrial sector of the economy. In addition, this chapter reviews what has happened nationwide as a social consequence of these economic changes. As one consequence, Chapter 2 discusses the distribution of wealth and new forms and degrees of poverty in America. Following this, Chapter 3 focuses on national changes for their impact on the Appalachian region. In particular, the chapter reviews changes in the industries concentrated in the Appalachian region.

The chapters of Section II discuss changes in the social capital of the Appalachian region related to the broad economic changes. Chapter 4 explains changed employment and income patterns since 1969. Chapter

5 examines the changes in the population in the Appalachian region over the past 20 years. Chapter 6 discusses the poverty of individuals and families. Chapter 7 reports on measures of specific sectors of social capital, education, health, and the environment.

Section III offers an overview of policies recently proposed to address the human needs of income, work, and family maintenance evident in some portions of Appalachia. Chapter 8 reports policies proposed at the time of the 1992 presidential election. Chapter 9 reports on long term reforms that supersede any particular reform measure.

Social Capital

Poverty awakens some people from the American dream rudely. For example, no other advanced industrial nation permits so many of its children, more than one in six in 1990, to grow up in poverty (Children's Defense Fund 1992). Similarly, the increased number of homeless people seems incongruous given the economic boom of the 1980s. We struggle to explain and address these apparent anomalies to affluence. The programs of the 1960s assumed that poor people needed more preparation to take advantage of existing opportunities (Marris and Rein 1967). The cutbacks of the 1980s assumed that the programs of the 1960s were a cause of poverty (Murray 1984), not a cure. Perhaps both approaches miss the mark because of their emphasis on economic roles. Perhaps, as we will assume here, Appalachia shows the need for new approaches in social capital and the need to invest in people for their worth that extends beyond their economic value.

The human problems of the Appalachian region, and other areas of economic and social need, are, at root, problems of social capital: the investments a political body makes to produce and reproduce human beings in community. Private capital is the means by which we produce and distribute goods and services for individual and private profit. Social capital is the investment we place in health care, education, housing, culture, the environment, and other factors to produce and reproduce people and their community.

In general, investment in social capital comes from private sources, follows upon the needs of private capital, and has as its central purpose the production, reproduction, and distribution of a labor force for private capital. When groups of people have subordinate roles in the economy, the social capital invested in them is modest. When people have no role in the economy, even less social capital is invested in them. Similarly, when a community's economic condition changes, so will the social capital invested in it.

American public policy has a strong emphasis on the private provision of social capital. We look to the laborer's wage as the first and primary source of social capital and then to the employer as the secondary source of social capital. Public provision of social capital, such as education, is linked to the needs of local employers and the local economy. We spend most social capital to produce and reproduce people as a labor force and smaller amounts on people as citizens, parents, community members, or other public roles. Our public policies also depend upon work-related social capital—primarily the wage—to provide the financial means to get housing, transportation, and cultural and recreational opportunities. Health care insurance is another work related form of social capital dependent upon a person's place in the economy.

The coal towns and the steel towns and textile towns that dot the map of Appalachia graphically depict the relation of social capital and the work place. For the first half of this century, private capital produced and reproduced a work force for the industries it created through social capital investment (Serrin 1993; Shifflett 1991). When the need for this labor force diminished, social capital dried up and coal towns began a decline that is apparent in the region. Steel towns (Serrin 1993) and some textile towns have followed that decline.

The shifts in private capital investments, which Robert Reich and others discuss (Fisher 1992), have their parallels in the shifts in social capital. In areas of private capital investment and increased demand for skilled labor, we find a corresponding investment in schools and education programs. For example, in Appalachian South Carolina counties, new investment by German automobile manufacturers provides new facets of a familiar role for education, e.g., preparing and upgrading a work force for new local employment opportunities. Consequently, those counties in the region enjoying relative and absolute increases in employment and per capita incomes also enjoy the best forms of social capital: schools, medical systems, and housing. This is not to say they have no problems but only to assert that the problems of the poorest and wealthiest counties in the region vary in degree and in kind.

Where the demand for a skilled labor force declines so does incentive to invest social capital. In West Virginia, Appalachian Ohio, and Eastern Kentucky, for example, schools are more likely to face the prospect of preparing a work force for either distant employment opportunities or for changed and declining employment opportunities at home.

An unregulated market is likely to treat social capital goods as any other commodity, according to Adam Smith. In his exposition of the tenets of capitalism, Smith related the cost of labor to its supply. When wages dropped below the subsistence level, working class people died. The supply of workers declined. The cost of labor increased. Wages increased to a level above subsistence. The number of workers increased. More workers, without a corresponding increase in demand for workers, depressed the wages of workers. This drop in wages, naturally, set off another effort of the market to adjust the supply and demand for people as workers by their wages. Smith concludes, in understated and morbid tones, "It is in this manner that the demand for men, like that of any other commodity, necessarily regulates the production of men; quicker when it goes on too slowly, and stops it when it advances too fast" (Heilbroner 1986:204). The housing crisis, the education crisis, and the health crisis are related. They are part of a deficit in the budget of social capital that has increased as public policy entrusted the distribution of economic benefits and costs to the "invisible hand."

The human problems of the Appalachian region are rooted in the American policies of social capital and their intrinsic relation to employment and the market. The evidence of this report is that private capital has withdrawn from some parts of the region, that social capital investment has decreased there, and that the wage is providing inadequately for the social capital needs of increasing numbers of individuals and families who remain in portions of Appalachia and the United States.

Problems, Policies, and Prospects

In the 1980s, some analysts and policy makers devised supply-side economics as a means to deal with economic development and the distribution of wealth. This theory simply restates a belief in an invisible hand as the prime mechanism of the distribution of social and economic benefits. Two centuries after Adam Smith, American economic policy was still premised on the hypothesis that people pursuing the maximization of their own utility will bring about maximum common benefit.

Appalachia, generally, and Central Appalachia, in particular, are regions where the sleight of the invisible hand left large portions of the residents of the Appalachian region impoverished, with human services far below national standards, and with more than their share of enduring and new economic problems. As Barbara Greene, who has been a staff member of several community groups in Central Appalachia, explained,

"We've had lots of trickle down but I don't feel wet yet." Frequently, economists simply have no remedy for economic improvement other than the individual solution of migration. This remedy reduces hope for stable communities in areas of acute economic hardship and defines human communities and the welfare of human beings in terms of profit and loss, primarily if not exclusively. As we shall see, some of Appalachia's needs come from economic policies that should be changed because they do not provide adequately for people and the communities that give their lives meaning, dignity, and value.

Section I

The American Political Economy and Appalachia

Chapter 1

National Economic Trends and Social Issues

A pundit observed that economics is the one field in which people make wrong predictions for a lifetime without losing their stature as experts. Relatedly, expert opinions and diverse prescriptions for the ailing American economy abound. This chapter selects a few economic analyses, reviews them, and combines them into an overview of the American economy and the recent changes it has undergone. The analyses selected have three common characteristics. They portray economics as a social relationship. They agree that the American economy has changed radically since the early 1970s. And they express concern for the social consequences of disparities in income and changed employment opportunities that resulted since those changes. To illustrate these analyses, this chapter reports on changes in income, work, and labor union memberships.

Problem and Policies

After 1972, growth in output, productivity, real wages, profit rates, and investment rates in the American economy declined (Bowles et al. 1990:6). This meant a gradual shift from the American dream. Working class Americans found it increasingly difficult to find steady employment at wages that permitted a middle class life style, e.g., home ownership, health care, and higher educational opportunities for children. The working middle class had far brighter prospects from World War II to 1972 than it had after 1972.

By the late 1960s and clearly by the early 1970s, America and the world had changed. The economies of Japan and Germany, shattered by World War II, were restored. American political and military interventions in the affairs of other nations, such as oil-rich Iran in the 1950s, were stymied by the national revulsion with the Vietnam war and the increased cooperation among other nations, like the Organization of Petroleum Exporting Countries (OPEC), formed in 1973. The peaceful industrial relations, which accords between workers and managers and among managers had brought after World War II, began to unravel in the late 1960s. Labor costs re-entered the calculation of profit and competition (Bowles et al. 1990:47-79).

Wages, adjusted for inflation, began a steady decline. Congress's

Joint Economic Committee estimated that a 30-year-old male with a high school education made $3,500 less in 1989 than he had in 1979, adjusting for inflation, and $5,000 less in 1989 than he had in 1969. Men 25 to 34, in 1989, regardless of education had declined earnings compared with men of the same age in 1969. Only the same age cohort of men with graduate school education had an increase in income from 1979 to 1989 (Greenhouse 1992:1). Comparable figures for women were not available because questions of equality had not broken the gender barrier sufficiently to stimulate attention to measures of income. The incomes of college graduates and the hourly wages of workers declined by equal amounts, slightly more than 3 percent, in the last part of the 1980s. The recession made bad matters worse and exacerbated a decade of decline for workers that followed a decade of slower improvement.

Robert Kuttner (1991:287) suggests that our recent economic quandary comes directly from our political preference to maintain inequality. The idealization of laissez-faire economics includes winners and losers. Its political utopia gives everyone a chance to gain wealth with little care for those who do not. Kuttner criticizes this view, which became increasingly popular since 1968 and pervasive in the 1980s. It holds that the wisdom and discretion of the wealthy drives economic progress. Thus the more resources that can be allocated to the wealthy the faster the economic engine is likely to run.

Benjamin Harrison and Barry Bluestone (1988) examine responses of corporate America to increased international competition for their impact on the American economy. First, corporations have attempted to reward and expand management to supervise and profit from global activity while "downsizing" their American work force and demanding decreases in labor costs as the condition for continued employment. Second, they have shifted investment from productive capacity, which creates jobs, to speculative ventures, which create profits, for increased returns on their money. Harrison and Bluestone assert that corporate America has the assistance of the federal government in making this "U-turn" in the American economy.

John Kenneth Galbraith (1992) places responsibility for current economic conditions in much larger political and social characteristics of a culture of contentment. The majority of members in such a culture, who are fortunate and favored or who hope to be so, act on behalf of their own immediate short-term benefit. Policies of equity in this culture follow the path of more resources to the fortunate and favored so that they can do more for those who are not fortunate and favored.

Derek Bok (1993) examines the fortunate and favored. He studied patterns of compensation for business executives and five professions. Like the others, Bok begins in 1970. He found that earnings in the professions remained at about their 1970 level for the decade. In the 1980s, earnings of corporate executives increased rapidly along with corporate lawyers and surgeons. Three other professions, teachers, professors, and federal career officials made small increases or lost ground (Bok 1993:66). The increased disparity in income raises issues of equity for Bok. It also means difficulty in convincing young talented people to pursue careers with explicit public and social purpose because there is less income, much less income, in them. Finally, Bok observed the highest compensations go to those who produce immediate results. This only increases the emphasis on the short-term in American life and economic activity (Bok 1993:1-5).

Robert Reich, Secretary of Labor in the Clinton administration, distinguishes among the new jobs of the American economy and sees another form of polarization. Some of those jobs, especially information processing, will be organized like industrial manufacturing. Data processors, like the diminishing numbers of assembly line producers, will work in large groups and perform the same or similar tasks over and over. Like assembly line workers, these new routine producers of the information age, e.g., telemarketers or 800 number telephone operators, will be linked world-wide and in competition with other producers anywhere with access to a telephone or modem. A second set of new service sector employment will be in-person services such as retail sales, waiters and waitresses, hotel workers, janitors, hospital attendants and orderlies, child care workers and security guards, the fastest growing service sector employment category. Finally, there will be symbolic-analytic services or the problem-identifying, problem-solving, and strategic-brokering work of research scientists, public relations executives, investment banks, and an array of engineers. Reich places paramount importance on preparing this last group of workers and on this sector as the driving force of the economy for the twenty-first century.

Disparities remain among these employment prospects. Routine producers of the information age, like the producers of in-person services, will be predominantly female and African American or Latino. Symbolic analysts will be predominantly male and white. The former groups will receive low wages with few benefits and the latter group will make large salaries with excellent benefits. Routine producers will be faced with foreign competition and the elimination of their jobs, while symbolic analysts will compete in the global economy as a routine aspect of their work.

Reich hopes that public policies can mitigate existing polarities in the work force and society. "What do we owe one another as members of the same society who no longer inhabit the same economy?" That central question, evidently, is one symbolic analysts will work on from their separate economy because of their sense of being part of the same society (Reich 1991:303). It will not be their first concern, however. Reich overlooks the task of the symbolic analysts to put people out of work in order to reduce production costs in a competitive, global economy. Primarily, the social division of work that Reich envisions will mean more pressure on employment and wages of routine producers and in-person service producers. Symbolic analysts will aid the transition from labor intense to capital intense service production that we have seen in manufacturing (Reich 1991:171-84).

Others have paid more attention to the social disparities of current and coming economic trends. By 1990, women made up two-thirds of the annual labor force growth. Women are also participating differently in the labor force. They are staying in the work force through child-bearing and -rearing ages. By 1990, the nature of participation in the work force for women ages 20 to 40 became approximately the same as that of men of the same age in 1970. Thus, young women in 1990 participated in the labor force differently than women did before them and like men did in 1970 when the economy was expanding (Masnick and Bane 1980:69).

The economy in which women enter today is far different from 1970, however. Jobs are increasing either in management, the high paying end, or in service and less skilled manufacturing, the low paying end. As women enter the labor force in larger numbers than before, the job market will have fewer high paying opportunities and more competition for them. This compounds the problem for women of attaining well-paying positions. It also provides grounds for new work arrangements such as flexible work schedules and day care (Choate 1983:3).

In addition to changes in the rate and nature of work force participation of women, women have a changed status as primary wage earners. Women who are heads of households continue to earn necessary income for their families. In addition, women with spouses have increased their labor force participation and in 12 percent of American male-female households women earned more than their spouses in 1982. Some of these women were dubbed "female superstars" in the Census Bureau study reporting this finding. But they were only about 14.5 percent of the six million women who had higher earnings. The more common case is one in which a woman works in a non-professional job and her spouse has "labor force difficulties." Women with spouses have increased their status as wage earners, in general, because the status of men as wage earners has declined. In some cases the men were retired. But in more than half the cases where men and women in the same household both worked and a woman earned more than her spouse, the husband worked less than full time. Unfortunately, wages for men are falling and thus equality is developing among men and women at lower wages (Marshall 1983:6).

At the same time, African Americans made up 1 in 4 of new entrants into the labor force (Norwood 1987:19). Most of the new African-American workers are women and by the year 2000 they should outnumber African-American men in the work force. African-American men will see their portion of jobs decline, it is estimated, from 4.9 percent in 1985 to 3.8 percent in the year 2000 (Johnston 1987:102).

Young people entering the work force without education beyond high school have had seriously declining fortunes also. Fewer of them find full-time work. The rate of men with high school diplomas and full-time employment dropped to 48.9 percent from 72.7 percent, a rate of change of 33 percent, from 1968 to 1986. At the same time, the comparable rates for women declined from 57 percent to 41.9 percent, or at a rate of 26 percent. Obviously, these changes had impact on incomes as well. The average annual earnings of men, 20 to 24 with high school educations, declined by 28.3 percent. African-American and Latino men in this category had declines of 43.8 percent and 34.5 percent respectively (Grant 1988:19-28).

Workers entering the work force in the 1990s can expect to need higher qualifications and to meet more competition for lower lifetime earnings than the previous highly educated generation of workers who entered the labor force before 1972. Only Reich's "symbolic analysts" and a segment of professionals can expect, on average, increased earnings.

Social Consequences of Economic Trends

Changes in work opportunities and wages coincide with changes in the distribution of income. Both are increasingly polarized. After-taxes household income figures indicate a redistribution of wealth from low-income groups to high-income groups from 1977 to 1988. The poorest fifth of households lost 10 percent of their average after-tax income in that period. At the same time, the wealthiest fifth of households increased their income by 34 percent. The wealthiest households, the richest 5 percent and 1 percent, increased their average after-tax incomes by even larger amounts, 60 percent and 122 percent respectively (Shapiro and Greenstein 1991:3). From 1980 to 1988, the middle class, the middle 60 percent of households, lost 7.8 percent of their share of the nation's after-tax income. This loss indicates the much heralded decline of the middle class.

The economic recovery of the 1980s is remarkable for the shift in incomes from lower income groups to higher income groups. In 1988, the top one percent of households had average incomes of $451,000. This group's share of national income equalled the share of the lowest 37 percent of households. In 1980, the portion of the wealthiest one per cent of households' income equalled the share of the lowest 25 percent. Similarly, in 1980 the middle 60 percent of households had a larger share of the national income than the top 20 percent of households. In 1988, they had less. By 1988, the top 20 percent of households had after-tax incomes about equal to that of the other 80 percent households. Table 1-1 provides figures on the division of national after-tax income by households.

Table 1-1
Changes in Portions of American After-Tax Household Incomes, 1980-1988, By Income Groups

	Share of National After-Tax Income		
Income Group	1980	1988	% Change
Poorest Fifth	5.4%	4.3%	-20.4%
2nd Quintile	11.4%	9.8%	-14.0%
Middle Quintile	16.2%	15.1%	- 6.8%
4th Quintile	22.6%	21.4%	- 5.3%
Wealthiest Fifth	44.9%	49.8%	10.9%
Middle Three-Fifths	50.2%	46.3%	- 7.8%
Top 5%	19.7%	25.2%	27.9%
Top 1%	8.4	12.8%	52.4%

Source: Center on Budget and Policy Priorities, Selective Prosperity, p. 4.

This change has created the most unbalanced distribution of wealth in fifty years, or since the New Deal. The poorest fifth of American families has the lowest share of national family income since 1954. The richest fifth has the highest share ever recorded. The remaining three-fifths of American families has the lowest share of family income ever recorded, 46.3 percent (Center on Budget and Policy Priorities n.d.).

Many factors have contributed to this trickle-up redistribution of wealth. Changes in the nature of employment and compensation for lower income groups have left them with less income. The average wage and salary income of the bottom 90 percent of American households fell by 3.5 percent in constant dollars from 1977 to 1988. At the same time, wages and salaries of the wealthiest one percent of American households increased by 121 percent (Shapiro and Greenstein 1991:3).

Federal tax reforms of the 1980s increased the tax burden on low-income groups, reduced it on high-income groups, and thus exacerbated changes in before-tax income. The one percent of wealthiest American households were projected to receive $175,000 in capital gains income in 1990, more than twice the amount they received in 1980, $83,000. The bottom ninety percent were expected to receive $300 in average capital gains income in 1990 or $12 more than they received in 1980 (Greenstein and Baranick 1990:1).

The tax reform measures of the 1980s shifted the tax burden downward to the low-income groups, as Table 1-2 shows. The burden of the richest one percent of American households declined almost as much as the burden of the lowest 20 percent increased, 14.4 and 16.1 percent respectively. These figures account only for the changes in federal taxes. As federal spending declined, state and local governments increased their sales and property taxes, which add disproportionately to the burdens of low-income groups. Increases in these regressive state and local taxes contributed to additional shifts in after-tax household incomes, as well.

Table 1-2
Average Tax Burdens of American Households, 1980-1990,
By Income Groups

Income Group	1980	1990	% Change
Poorest Tenth	6.7%	8.5%	27.7%
Poorest Fifth	8.4%	9.7%	16.1%
2nd Quintile	15.7%	16.7%	6.0%
Middle Quintile	20.0%	20.3%	1.2%
4th Quintile	23.0%	22.5%	-2.2%
Wealthiest Fifth	27.3%	25.8%	-5.5%
Top 5%	29.5%	26.7%	-9.5%
Top 1%	31.8%	27.2%	-14.4%

Source: Center on Budget and Policy Priorities, Drifting Apart, p. 17.

Analysts differ on the portions of the redistribution of wealth that occurred in the 1980s and the degree to which policies of the Republican administrations since 1980 are responsible. Incomes of households and individuals can vary widely from year to year. By 1992, for example, the recession affected the income distribution once again. Comparing different years produces very different gaps between income groups but all comparisons show gaps and increased gaps over any five year period of the 1980s. Whatever years we choose, there has been a trickle of income up, rather than down, that began in the 1970s with the broader economic changes already discussed. That trickle became a steady stream in the 1980s with the tax reform measures of the Reagan administration. A Republican political commentator, Kevin Phillips, described the 1980s as "a Republican conservative-capitalist overdrive period, sharing ten common characteristics [with the 1870s and 1920s] that ranged from tax cuts and deregulation to surges in debt and speculation" (Phillips 1990:x).

The result, according to Phillips, was that "among major Western nations, the United States has displayed one of the sharpest cleavages between the rich and the poor." In fact, Phillips's figures show that the low-income households of the United States have a smaller portion of national income and the high-income households have a larger portion of national income than Germany and Japan, America's most often cited industrial competitors. While the top-income households in America generally enjoyed twelve times the share of wealth of the low-income households, the ratio in Germany was 5 and in Japan only 4 (Phillips 1990:9). Our competitors among advanced industrialized nations in the global economy seem capable of competing with far less economic disparity and polarization.

Other comparisons are equally instructive. The share of income among the lowest 40 percent of American households, in 1985, places the United States behind every one of the 25 nations with high-income economies except for Australia and Singapore, according to the World Bank. Of the twenty-one low- and moderate-income nations reporting income distribution, the United States falls behind nine of them, including Bangladesh, Ghana, India, and Pakistan. The United States' income distribution is more "equitable" than only its client states of Central and Latin America: Guatemala, Peru, Colombia, Jamaica, Costa Rica, Venezuela, and Brazil (World Bank 1990:Table 30). Phillips expected the "excesses" of the 1980s to place strains on the continuation of Reagan's policies and on the political coalition that put them in place and sustained them.

The federal policies of the 1980s exacerbated the social consequences of the changing American economy and of the recession of the late 1980s. Obviously, the changes in income among groups of Americans have meant the rich got richer and the poor got poorer and increased in numbers. Similarly, incomes and income shares of most Americans declined. The economic experience and prospects of the working and professional middle class declined from 1970 to 1990. It may not have been a fall to poverty but most middle income earners and families have "fallen from grace" in the phrase of Katherine S. Newman (1988), an anthropologist, who chronicled and documented the downward mobility of the American middle class.

In her work, Newman drew a lesson from Appalachia. She cited mass layoffs, the closing of the Singer sewing machine factory in Elizabeth, New Jersey and the air traffic controllers, for their impact on the income and community of the middle class. She found that "fellowship is an inexplicable source of comfort in the midst of economic dislocation" (Newman 1988:235). The air traffic controllers had a "community of experience" and the Singer workers a community of people who live in close proximity. She observes, "For the better part of a century, the Singer Company was to Elizabeth, New Jersey what coal mining is to Appalachia" (Newman 1988:235). Not just coal mining but steel making and textiles and apparels created communities of proximity throughout Appalachia. The unions of these industries created communities of experience as well. Such communities may grow up around economic activity and find sustenance within it but they are incidental to the central purposes of capital. Profit making and return on investment come far above community, of any sort, in the conduct of capital.

Social Capital and the Economic Transition

Changes in income and change in work meant less social capital. The wage declined for those in work and meant less social capital to maintain people in community. In 1973, 20.1 percent of white, hourly wage workers in full-time, year-round work earned too little to keep a family of four out of poverty. This figure increased to 23.6 percent in 1979 and 25.4 percent in 1989. After the "boom" of the 1980s, a larger portion of white, American hourly wage workers were unable to keep their families out of poverty than before the "boom." The ensuing recession made matters worse. In 1991, 28.1 percent of white, hourly wage workers made too little to keep a family of four out of poverty. Matters were worse for other groups. For African-American workers comparable rates started at 27.3 percent in 1973 and rose to 41.1 percent in 1991. For Latino hourly wage workers the rates increased from 29.7 to 45.9 percent over this same period (Shapiro 1992:27-28).

Those without work had less access to wages that were declining in real value terms. Thus, basic forms of social capital, food and shelter, became more difficult to acquire for some. Access to health care became a crisis precisely because medical insurance was tied to employment for most Americans and the terms of compensation for work declined.

Before the recession of the late 1980s brought these problems into sharp focus, they were already apparent as a general trend dating back to the economic transition that was discernible by 1972. In an 1987 assessment of the future of employment, Janet L. Norwood, U.S. commissioner of labor statistics, suggested that "we have passed through a period of tremendous demographic and industrial change and see still more ahead." By the mid-1980s, 7 out of 10 Americans worked in the service-producing sector that had expanded by 30 million jobs from 1969. In contrast, the number of manufacturing jobs in 1987 was approximately the same as in 1969. Nine out of every 10 *new* jobs in the first half of the 1990s are expected to come from the service-producing sector, especially business and health services (Norwood 1987:18-19). By 1985, the economy increasingly polarized new job creation. Professional, managerial, and technical jobs, the work of symbolic analysts in Robert Reich's terms, grew. These jobs require high skills and provide ample compensation. Unskilled, subordinate, and repetitious jobs also grew, the work of mass produced services in Reich's terms. These jobs required few skills and provided minimal compensation. The middle ground of employment opportunity eroded, leaving college educated youth and other high-skilled people in oversupply (Norwood 1987).

Analysts agree that the vast majority of new jobs will be in the service sector. A projection in 1981 of the twenty occupations with the highest growth rate (Carey 1981:48) listed seventeen service occupations and three categories of symbolic analysts, computer systems analysts, aero-astronautic engineers and architects. These three accounted for 13 percent of the estimated increases in high-growth occupations. Eight of the service occupations were in-person services that require some form of face-to-face, hands-on exchange. Two of these categories, fast food restaurant workers and nurse orderlies, accounted for slightly more than one-half of the more than two million new jobs predicted for the decade among these twenty high-growth occupations. Five occupational categories were routine service producers or related to information processing machinery. Four categories spanned routine and in-person services, for example, travel agents and paralegal personnel may be either routine or in-person service providers. In terms of absolute growth, not rate of growth, the twenty occupations projected to have most growth were all in-person services and accounted for 7.8 million projected new jobs.

The decline in the goods-producing sector of the economy brought on several problems. New jobs developed at a very slow pace and in places distant from where old jobs declined. Thus mining, construction, and automobile manufacturing declined in former centers of production and new mines and plants, with new employment opportunities, developed in new, distant places. Workers in formers places of production were displaced from their industries.

Migration to jobs in the same industry in new places was possible in some instances, but new jobs did not keep pace with old jobs, and the new jobs came with lower social capital. In particular, the goods-producing sector of the economy had the largest and strongest labor unions that had gained high wages and benefits for their members. The changes in the goods-producing sector of the economy has meant a decline in union membership, 3.1 million fewer union members in the private sector between 1980 and 1985. In this same five years, employment increased by 7 million people. This increase in total employment and decrease in union membership dropped the portion of wage and salary workers who were union members to 18 percent in 1985. This is the lowest level in 50 years since the Wagner Act, the New Deal, and a period of increased public provision of social capital, including the strengthened position of labor unions. By 1992, union representation in the private sector dwindled to 12 percent (Brody 1992:33).

Unions reacted to the decline within their industries and their own bargaining position. They reluctantly reintroduced labor costs into the calculation of competition. Unions participated in labor cost cutting in their industries in an effort to save jobs. In addition, new compensation systems established lower wages and fewer benefits for workers hired after certain dates, and thus established two-tier compensation systems. Benefits schedules changed for union and non-union employees, as well. Most notably, as health care costs increased employers modified health benefit plans to limit the set of providers or to shift some of the costs of medical care to the employee.

The declines in the numbers and wages and benefits of union workers suggest that the social contract that emerged after World War II between labor and management is now undone. Government deregulation, foreign competition, technological changes and capital mobility are some of the forces that transformed the American economy and reintroduced competitive labor markets after 1972 (Troy 1993; Brody 1992). America's primary competitors among advanced industrial nations, Germany and Japan, have managed to acquire and keep their place with a work force with a larger portion of union members. As we have seen, U.S. union membership among active workers declined. From about 30 percent in 1970, union members by 1990 made up only 16 percent of workers in the private and public sector. During the same time, union members among Japan's workforce dropped from 35 to 26 percent. Germany's unionized labor force remained the same, 33 percent, from 1970 to 1990 (Chang and Sorrentino 1991). In contrast to the United States, most industrialized countries had an increase in the portion of labor force in labor unions between 1970 and 1985. Apparently, competition in the global economy explains only part of the decline and magnitude of decline of U.S. labor unions. Public policy and union busting also contributed to the changes the United States has seen (Chang and Sorrentino 1991; Brody 1992).

The decline of employment opportunities and the reduction of unions and workers' wages have stimulated a perverse economic growth. Corrections officers and jailers were projected as eleventh in the rate of new jobs (Carey 1981:48). For Samuel Bowles and his colleagues this growth indicates a "garrison economy." It suggests that in a declining economy more people find employment as enforcers of the formal and informal rules that govern economic life. These rules enforce scarcity in declining economies. In times like the 1980s, which were times not of economic decline but of redistribution of wealth, the rules protect those who are getting more from those who are getting less. Behind these rules are powerful myths of ample opportunity for employment with adequate compensation and the personal nature of the failure to reach economic subsistence. These myths establish the right of society to punish those who fail to support themselves and to protect some of its members from those who cannot support themselves. Many people secure employment to provide those rights.

These same economists specify two forms of enforcement employment: guard and threat labor. Among guard laborers they list workplace supervisors; police, judicial, and corrections employees; private security personnel; the armed forces and civilian defense employees; and producers of military and domestic security equipment. Among threat laborers are the unemployed, the discouraged workers—unemployed but not counted—and prisoners. Threat laborers make the peril of job loss exacting and credible. By 1987, these authors estimate that guard labor amounted to 22.5 percent and threat labor amounted to 10.4 percent of non-farm civilian employment. By this estimate, guard and threat labor equaled almost one-third of the civilian workforce and all of the military. Between 1979 and 1987, these forms of labor increased by 7.6 million jobs and employed a total of almost 34 million people. Bowles and his colleagues contrast employment in the garrison economy, with employment in the investment-goods sector of the economy which is more productive employment and relies more on carrots than sticks for economic incentives (Bowles et al. 1990:194-96;1992).

Adam Smith referred to the garrison state, which was recognizable even in the formative stages of capitalism. He explained that the "strong arm" of the law maintains disparities between the rich and the poor. In contrast to the "invisible hand", which allegedly distributes benefits from the wealthy to the poor, the "strong arm" receives less attention in treatments of market economies. The strong arm of the law imposes threats about unemployment. For example, American public policy ties a substantial number of social capital needs to employment, precisely as Smith understood the market economy to work in regulating supply and demand for labor.

The lack of employment threatens adequate amounts of social capital. Most obviously, people without employment lose wages. To mitigate the harsh and fatal consequences of wageless unemployment, which Smith described, Americans instituted unemployment insurance. In the 1980s, as part of our infatuation with free markets, Americans introduced gaps in the coverage of the unemployed. In 1979, for example, 42 percent of unemployed Americans received unemployment insurance. In 1990, a year of economic slowdown when rates of the unemployed insured generally increase, there was a decrease in coverage of the unemployed to 36.8 percent. An even more instructive comparison takes two years of peak unemployment—1975, with 8.5 percent unemployment and 1983, with 9.7 percent. The rates of the unemployed receiving unemployment insurance dropped from 75.5 percent in 1975 to 45.3 percent in 1983. The rates of the unemployed insured dropped below 40 percent consistently in the 1980s. Previously, that rate had dropped below 40 percent only once since World War II (Shapiro and Nichols 1991).

Even for those with work, the levels of social capital dropped. During the 1980s, the numbers of working poor people increased as did the numbers of Americans without medical insurance. Outside of metropolitan areas, especially, workers found it increasingly difficult to earn wages to keep their families out of poverty. In 1978 and 1987, two years with low unemployment and in advanced stages of economic recovery, the rates of rural families with poverty incomes and a wage-earner increased from 7.6 percent to 10 percent. More importantly, nearly two-thirds of all poor families in rural areas had at least one worker in 1987 (Shapiro 1989:xi,7). The rates for working poor families in rural areas are higher than those in metropolitan areas, as one might expect. Unexpectedly, levels of educational attainment have improved for these wage earners. The formula of more education and work does not equal family incomes above poverty for many Americans.

In part, this is because we have entered new variables into the formula. The nature of work has changed and the compensation for that work has declined. The increase in service sector work and the decrease in manufacturing jobs mean less income for families. In 1987, 27 percent of rural family heads who worked in the service industry reported family incomes below the poverty level. Farming, forestry and fishing were the next highest category of employment and poverty, 19 percent. More people are working at minimum wage jobs, such as service, where employment growth resides. Rural industries which had high rates of employment, resource extraction and routine manufacturing, employed far fewer people (Shapiro 1989:18-19,33).

Changes in federal policies during the 1980s contributed to the increase in the working poor, as well. The minimum wage rate did not increase in the 1980s, so that families with wage earners working for minimum wage fell farther and farther behind in the decade. Federal changes in 1981 of eligibility standards for Aid to Families with Dependent Children (AFDC) eliminated 440,000 low-income working families from benefits through this program and reduced the benefits to others. These families were naturally at the upper end of income eligibility, precisely the low-income families most likely to have a working member (Shapiro 1989:35-40, 47-49).

As the working poor underwent new hardships in the 1980s, other Americans began to understand what it is to have compensation erode. Employer-provided medical insurance declined in scope and in breadth. Fewer jobs provided medical insurance as a benefit and those that did provided less coverage. Moreover, changing jobs threatened health coverage because of provisions that excluded coverage for some conditions in the initial periods of the contract (*Richmond-Times Dispatch* 1992). A Census Bureau study in 1992 found that 14 percent of Americans, 35.4 million people, had no medical insurance in 1991. This was an increase of 4.4 million people from 1987. In addition, the report found that 61 million Americans had no medical insurance for at least one month from 1987 to 1989. As expected, Latinos and African Americans had more frequent gaps and whites, middle-aged men and women, and suburbanites had the fewest gaps. Thanks to Medicare, the elderly had the most consistent coverage. Because of Medicaid, only 28.6 percent of those in poverty had no medical insurance.

Other vagaries persisted, however. Because Medicaid is tied to AFDC, members of female-headed families were more likely to have medical insurance than members of two-parent poverty-income families. On the other hand, members of all female-headed families were more likely to lack coverage than members of other families. In 1991, 72.2 percent of Americans were covered by employment-related medical insurance, a decline from 75.5 percent in 1987 (Summer 1992). Half of those without medical insurance, for at least a portion of this two year period, were under twenty-five years old (*Richmond Times-Dispatch* 1992).

Conclusion

American economic trends since 1972 have created changes in the nature, amount, and compensation of employment. These changes are related to each other. Jobs in high-paying manufacturing and blue collar occupations declined, and jobs in the low-wage service sector increased. These changes are also related to the redistribution of wealth since then. Without access to high-paying jobs, the majority of Americans have problems attaining previous levels of middle class incomes. These economic changes, coupled with federal tax reforms and social program cutbacks of the 1980s, fostered a redistribution of wealth that brought us back to the most skewed income structure since before the New Deal.

Chapter 2

Poverty in the New American Economy

The changes in the American economy in the 1970s and later meant less demand for unskilled and low-skilled workers and decline in workers' income among the working classes. They also meant increased numbers of poor people and the increased severity of their conditions. Adam Smith related low wages and poverty to the supply and cost of labor within a market economy. The enchantment of policies of the United States with the free market includes a tolerance for social deprivation. The valuation of the free market leads some Americans to substitute characteristics of the poor for economics as an explanation of poverty and the income inequalities in American society. Work and income are the primary determinants of poverty. How they are distributed are social and not merely individual decisions.

New Perspectives on Poverty

As the 1980s brought a new emphasis on free markets, the human costs of market economies were not only ignored but very consciously avoided. One survey of poverty policy from the mid-60s to the late-80s described a change from a War on Poverty to a War on Welfare (Katz 1989). Although the War on Welfare had many antecedents, the clearest expression of reaction to the policies of the 1960s and a call for further reversals of those policies than the 1970s provided came in Charles Murray's book, *Losing Ground*.

Murray went further than most critics' position that social welfare policies do little good. He contended that social welfare policies do harm and that they are the cause of new social problems. His suggested solution was a radical cutback in social welfare policies that would leave working-aged people "with no recourse whatsoever except the job market, family members, friends, and public or private locally funded services." Gone would be "AFDC (Aid to Families with Dependent Children), Medicaid, Food Stamps, Unemployment Insurance, Worker's Compensation, subsidized housing, disability insurance, and the rest" (Murray 1984:227-28).

In effect, Murray suggested a free market approach to labor. This assumes that poor people must be threatened with severe need to insure that they will work; that there is work for all those who are willing to work; and that work eradicates financial need. The fundamental problem of American social welfare policies, according to Murray, is that they tried to remedy assumed failures of economic and political systems. He proposed scrapping this approach and replacing it with a system premised on individual compliance with sound market principles in the economic and political realms (Murray 1984:218).

Adam Smith was less judgmental about poor people, and his analysis did not make Murray's assumptions. In fact, Smith was clear that there were times that people would neither find work nor sufficient wages to provide for freedom from need. There were systemic economic factors—supply and demand for labor—to explain poverty and need, according to Smith. Smith wrote, half-approvingly and half-resignedly, of the oppression of the poor by the rich through laws and government. In the 200 years since Smith and since the onset of democratic political practice, only Smith's conservative side is discussed. Murray thus reiterates Smith's belief that "the peace and order of society is of more importance than even the relief of the miserable." The unfettered operation of the market, including poverty, is, according to Murray, the surest path to peace and order of society.

Murray's position has its critics. Robert Kuttner, for example, describes "utopian laissez-faire," like Murray's, as a "spiral of self-deception and decline" that permits us to ignore important national questions of distributive justice, including poverty (Kuttner 1991:286-87). William Julius Wilson's (1987) treatment of inner-city poverty emphasized systemic factors of employment, income distribution and discrimination as causes of social needs and problems. His analysis focused on inner-city poverty, specifically in Chicago, and popularized the term "underclass" to describe a set of low-income individuals who are not one-time or sometime poor but are trapped in neighborhoods depleted of organizations, commerce, and institutions that had previously sustained a group with a broader range of income and education. Poverty, as manifested in the underclass, is increasingly concentrated and removed from buffers that previously mitigated its consequences.

These analyses indicate the increased specificity of discussions of American poverty and social problems. An industry of information and research has developed around poverty It is fueled by competing definitions of poverty, each of which is based on different assumptions, and each of which leads to different policy implications. In 1984, the range of different definitions produced poverty rates from a high of 18.6 percent to a low of 5.9 percent. These rates varied because different analysts used different government figures on income; included or excluded duration of poverty as an element of the definition, e.g., in poverty for all 12 months of a year; and included or excluded noncash benefits, e.g., food stamps, or Medicare and Medicaid payments, in calculating income (Sawhill 1988:1075-82). The rate of poverty, as defined by the Census Bureau, declined modestly from 1965 to 1985. By 1989, the rate of poverty exceeded the 1969 level and grew over the next two years. By 1991, a record number of Americans, 35.7 million, were in poverty. The poverty rate reached 14.2 percent. One in every seven Americans was officially poor (Pear 1992). Relative poverty, those with less than one-half of the median income, also increased since 1965 (Sawhill 1988:1083).

Poverty not only increased in the 1980s, it took on a new, more severe character. In 1965, when Americans began to measure poverty, the poverty line equalled 46 percent of median income of a family of four. By 1986, the level of poverty income had fallen to 32 percent of the median income (Sawhill 1988:1076). Americans not only instituted a more severe test of poverty income, we watched as the visible conditions of the poor deteriorated. By 1988, the National Alliance to End Homelessness estimated that 735,000 people were homeless in America on any night and that between 1.3 and 2 million Americans would be homeless at least one night that year. In addition, the Alliance estimated that 6 million Americans were at risk for homelessness because of the high portion of their incomes that they paid for rent. The increase in homelessness that these figures represent is not known. Before the 1980s we paid little attention to the numbers of homeless people. We started noticing them as their number increased and as they became more visible. As with all social problems, advocates and bureaucrats wrangled on the nature and extent of homelessness. Estimates of the homeless problem varied from 300,000 to 2.2 million (Katz 1989:186-87). Ironically, as this nation hurtled into the "information age" and lauded information services as a growth sector of the new economy, its counts of the homeless varied by a factor of seven. Americans did know that women and children accounted for the fastest growing segment of the homeless in the 1980s.

Hunger indicates severe poverty but is also a very elusive measure. A Physicians Task Force on Hunger visited different sections of the United States in 1985 and estimated that 20 million Americans were hungry. A Louis Harris poll, in 1984, estimated that 21 million Americans did not have enough to eat at some time in a year. A replication of that study in 1992 estimated the number of Americans who did not have enough to eat at 30 million. Two other methods arrived at the same estimate (Brown 1992).

Hunger is implicit in the definition of poverty. The federal government's initial definition of poverty was premised on the cost of a food plan for "temporary or emergency use when funds are low." This emergency food plan reduced a low-cost food plan by 20 percent. The low-cost plan provided nutritionally adequate diets for one-fourth of those who used it. Thus, the estimate of the cost of a food plan, which was inadequate for 75 percent of the people using it, was reduced by 20 percent to establish poverty level incomes. Food stamps now supplement the income of poor and low-income individuals. The food stamp program is partial admission of the link of poverty and hunger and the inadequacy of poverty incomes to provide adequate nutrition from a theoretical assessment of the caloric requirement of an emergency need diet and its corresponding cost (Couto 1975:17-20).

The American public also felt that poverty had become more severe. Official definition erred on the conservative side. In a Gallup poll taken in 1988, Americans estimated that poverty, in their community, began with an income of $15,017 for a family of four or 24 percent higher than the government's poverty line. This higher income figure would naturally increase the number of poor Americans, especially among the elderly.

The estimation of poverty varied among the different groups of Americans polled. Those in poverty suggested levels 110 percent of the official government figure while those with incomes $50,000 or more suggested levels at 139 percent. Similarly, Americans with less education proposed lower standards than those with more. Latinos proposed much lower rates, 103 percent, than other racial groups, 125 percent to 130 percent. Likewise, people in rural areas of the South and Midwest offered the lowest estimations of poverty income, 107 and 104 percent, while residents in urban areas of the West offered the highest estimates, 142 percent. By any estimate, American public opinion on poverty incomes is higher than the official standard and increases the rate of poverty of Americans in all categories, e.g., age, education, gender, and race. This is true even when non-cash benefits are figured in as income for the poor (O'Hare et al. 1990).

In the 1960s Americans discovered "the poor." By the 1990s, social analysts had refined the poor into sets and subsets of people in poverty. Some of the poor did much better than others. For example, America made dramatic progress in reducing poverty among the elderly. Instead of one in four of the elderly living in poverty as in 1970, by 1990 the percentage of poor among the elderly was cut in half to one in eight. At the same time, the percentage of children in poverty increased. Female-headed families changed little in their rate of poverty. These families remained about three times more likely to be in poverty than other family types. Similarly, although more white people are in poverty than black people, the rate of poverty among blacks remained almost three times the rate for white people. Table 2-1 presents poverty rates for different groups.

Table 2-1
Characteristics of the Poverty Population 1970, 1980 and 1990

	1970	1980	1990
Total Persons in Poverty (%)	13.3	12.4	13.1
Age			
Elderly	25.3	15.7	12.2
Adult	8.7	8.9	10.7
Children	14.8	16.0	17.6
Household Status			
Female-head	32.5	32.7	33.4
All	10.7	9.6	10.0
Race/Ethnicity			
White	9.9	10.2	10.7
Black	33.5	32.5	31.9
Latino	na	25.7	28.1

Sources: U.S. Bureau of the Census, *Current Population Survey*, and *Poverty in the United States: 1991*; Sawhill. "Poverty in the U.S.," Table 2; calculations based on U.S. Dept. of Commerce, *County and City Data Book.*.

Reports from the Center on Budget and Policy Priorities measure the different impacts of economic change, decreased earnings and increased poverty among different groups. For example, in 1987, 11 percent of rural households had incomes in the top fifth of households compared with 23 percent of urban households. On the other hand, a majority of households in rural areas had incomes in the lowest forty percent of all households compared with 37 percent of urban households. Although three out of four poor Americans live in metropolitan areas, the rates of poverty are higher in rural areas where nine million American poor live, only 10 percent of them on farms.

This gap of rural and urban poor narrowed when rural households areas were compared with households in central cities. The poverty rate in rural areas in 1987 was 16.9 percent compared with 18.6 percent in central cities. Rates of poverty for whites in rural areas and in the central city are about equal, but rates of poverty are higher for African

Americans and Latinos in rural counties than in central cities. These rates are much higher than those of whites, regardless of location. Similarly, poverty rates for female-headed households in rural counties and central cities were about identical in 1987, 44.8 and 44.4 percents. Two-parent families have a slightly higher rate of poverty in rural areas than central cities. African-American two-parent families in rural areas have a poverty rate of 27 percent, which is more than twice the rate of poverty for African-American families in the central cities, 12.3 percent.

In addition, long-term poverty, eight out of ten years, seems to be more common among the poor in rural areas, 52 percent, than among the poor in central cities, 39 percent. The South has the highest rate of poverty in rural areas, while the rate of poverty in metropolitan areas is more evenly spread across the nation. Slightly more than half of the rural poor, 53.6 percent, lived in the South in 1987 (Porter 1988).

Per capita income in rural areas dropped from 77 percent of per capita income in urban areas to 73 percent between 1979 and 1987. In addition, the recession of 1979 to 1982 brought swifter decline and slower recovery to rural areas than metropolitan areas. Most telling of all, in 1987, 42 percent of rural workers and 29 percent of urban workers earned wages too low to keep a family of four out of poverty with full-time, year-round work (Barancik 1990).

The rates of poverty among African Americans remain much higher than the national rates. Figures for any particular year will offer slight variations in the gaps. In general, however, the rate of poverty among African Americans, 31.9 percent in 1990, fluctuates from 2.5 to 3.5 times the national rate. The rate for African-American children reached 46 percent in 1987 and has increased since then. Beyond considerations of poverty, the economic situation of African-American households has declined severely. Their number among the poorest of the poor, those with incomes below half the poverty income line, increased from 33 percent in 1978 to 45 percent in 1987, an increase of 69 percent.

The political economy of American poverty means that it has spatial concentrations and racial, gender, and age correlations. Poverty is concentrated in rural and inner-city areas. African Americans and Latinos have poverty rates higher than the national averages. Female-headed households are more likely to be poor than other households. Children are poor at very high rates. Combining some of these factors gives us the startling consequence of public policies of social capital investment. The majority of children under 18 in female-headed families were in poverty in 1987, 60.3 percent and 60.7 percent in rural and central cities. These poverty rates went higher for African Americans: 76.7 percent of African-American children in female-headed families in rural counties were in poverty in 1987 and 68.9 percent of those children in central cities (Porter 1988:28).

The Persistent Problem of Poverty

In sharp contrast to the simple optimism of eliminating American poverty by 1976, which was expressed as the War on Poverty began, Americans now emphasize the persistence of poverty and specific reasons for that persistence among different groups. As we understand the diversity of poor people, we also understand better the causes of poverty. True, one may still find interpreters of poverty who focus on the traits of poor people as explanatory causes of poverty, Murray among them. In general, however, Americans have improved their understanding of poverty and its complexity. In addition, we also find far more sophisticated analysis of the effective means of addressing poverty and of poverty's underlying causes. Isabel Sawhill (1988) reviewed recent work on poverty and divided it into five areas of emphasis: demographics, economic performance, human capital investments, income transfers, and the growth of an underclass.

Demographics: One increase in the poverty rate came from the increased number of families headed by women. This segment of American households increased from 10.8 percent in 1970 to 16 percent in 1990. As Table 2-1 indicated, female-headed families are much more likely to have a poverty income. Thus, as the number of female headed families grows, as it has in the past twenty years, the number of people in poverty increases. On the other hand, the portion of Americans who are over 65 years of age declined between 1969 and 1989, and so did their rate of poverty. Between these upward and downward pressures on the numbers of the poor are the children of America. One in six is likely to be poor, in general, and of those in female-headed households six of ten are likely to be poor (Porter 1989:28). The demographics of poverty suggest that poverty persists and has increased because increased numbers of children grow up in poor households. (Sawhill 1988:1086-88).

Economic Performance: A Kennedy-era premise about poverty asserted that a rising tide lifts all boats or that economic growth would increase the incomes of the poor and improve their condition. The economy affects poverty profoundly because most poor people work and earnings are the dominant source of income for the poor. Studies do suggest that economic growth reduces the number of white, male-headed households. Other households are either not affected or less affected by economic growth. Economic recessions, however, impact the poor disproportionately and widen the income gulf between rich and poor. In particular, unemployment drives the rates of poverty up. Annual poverty rates indicate increases in poverty during the recessions of the mid-1970s and from the late 1970s to the early 1980s (Pear 1992). However, even in good economic times inequality in earnings has increased among all demographic groups and among occupational and industrial sectors (Sawhill 1988:1088-92).

We are not dealing with tides but with locks in a dam. Water from some low-income locks either leaks or flows rapidly to float the boats of others.

Human Capital Investments: Investments in education, job training, and other human services to improve the skills of the poor and prepare them for jobs are another enduring legacy of recent efforts to eliminate and reduce poverty. The increased rates of poverty would suggest that such efforts have failed. The relation of poverty to employment, however, qualifies that negative assessment. Job-readiness does less to eliminate poverty than a job, and some jobs eliminate poverty better than others. Among the most prominent human capital investments to address poverty are compensatory education, e.g., Head Start; job training, e.g., Job Corps, CETA (Comprehensive Employment Training Act), and JTPA (Job Training Partnership Act); and health care, e.g., Medicaid, Medicare, and community health centers. Programs in all these investment areas can boast of accomplishments and important outcomes. As a means to reduce poverty, however, they have a mixed record of individual successes but aggregate stalemate or failure (Sawhill 1988: 1092-97).

Human capital investment remains popular as a means to reduce poverty and to reach several related goals. This strategy reflects the adage of teaching people to fish rather than giving them a fish. The transfer of skills enables people to feed themselves for a lifetime rather than feeding them for only a day. Lisbeth Schorr, who helped fashion Head Start and the federal program of community health centers, placed new emphasis on human capital investment. She asserted that we know what works and that we have lacked the political will to allocate the resources to support successful programs and to expand their enrollments (Schorr 1988). Her analysis deals with improving social conditions, reducing infant mortality, school dropouts and teen pregnancy, on the one hand, and increasing school performance and health status on the other. While obviously related to eliminating poverty, Schorr's analysis also deals with improving the conditions of the poor. On the other side of the human capital investment ledger, Robert Reich (1991) promotes educational reform, in particular, as a means to economic growth and high tides to lift all boats. Schorr's broader approach would expand our social capital policies while Reich's approach ties social capital to work and thus reinforces the short tether of the economy, work, and poverty. Reich does not take into account that we may have to stock the pond if we are to encourage people to fish for themselves.

Income Transfers: Human capital investment's popularity has its mirror image in the unpopularity of income transfer. People are expected to work their way out of poverty and not to be supported within it. In fact however, spending on social welfare programs—AFDC, General Assistance, Medicaid, Medicare, food stamps, school lunch and breakfast programs, public housing, social services, unemployment insurance, railroad retirement, workmen's compensation, and government veterans' pensions and other programs—has increased enormously since 1960. Total social welfare expenditures increased to $476 billion dollars in 1984 or almost four times its 1960 amount, adjusting for inflation. The expenditures grew from 5.2 percent of GNP to 13.4 percent. This growth of an unpopular approach creates attentive audiences for calls for "welfare reform" from about every candidate for office of whatever party or political leaning. However, almost 80 percent of social welfare expenditures goes into social insurance spending or money used to prevent people from becoming poor, the benefit of which is seen in the reduced rates of older people in poverty. The benefit is less obvious, but real, in keeping a portion of disabled and unemployed working-age people out of poverty. The remainder of social welfare expenditures goes to assist people who have incomes often far below the poverty level. Moreover, research indicates that transfer payments reduce the amount of wages recipients might have otherwise worked for by only 23 cents for every dollar of transfer income. or an average of 4.8 hours of work per welfare recipient. Welfare does not provide the unemployed poor a financial alternative to work. Similarly, other research suggests that transfer income has no more impact on the composition of families or the attitudes of welfare recipients than it has on the willingness to work (Sawhill 1988:1097-1105).

Recent analysis also suggests that transfer payments not only go to white Americans in larger portions than to African Americans and Latinos but that transfer payments, Social Security, unemployment compensation, and benefit programs like food stamps and cash assistance, are twice as likely to lift white Americans out of poverty than they are other groups. In 1991, 14.6 million white Americans, or 45 percent with poverty incomes, avoided poverty because of government transfer income programs compared with 20 percent of African Americans and 19 percent of Latino Americans (Shapiro 1992:xi).

The Growth of the Underclass: The clearest generalization possible about the underclass is that the portion of poor people living in poor areas has increased. This is not self-evident. It suggests a concentration of poverty in specific areas: inner cities and rural areas in regions of Appalachia and the rural South (Sawhill 1988:1106-1109).

Sawhill ends her review of poverty studies with several conclusions pertinent to our analysis. First, the poor are a diverse group about whom generalizations are difficult. Differences among the poor, not similarities, permit us more accurate generalizations. For example, we know that people's chances of being poor greatly increase if they are African American, in a female-headed household, or under 18 years of age. We know that income poverty is temporary rather than permanent, although people born into a poor family are likely to remain poor for a longer period than those who are not. We also know that poverty is increasingly concentrated in low-income, urban areas even though the majority of poor people do not live in such areas. Second, poverty income has decreased in relative and absolute terms since the mid-1960s, although some basic needs, like health care, are better met now than before. Finally, the decline in real income and increased unemployment have largely eliminated the benefits of human capital investment and income transfers in reducing poverty. Income transfers have been effective in reducing the poverty of the elderly through social insurance programs (Sawhill 1988:1112-13).

The clearest correlation Americans have about poverty is that it increases and becomes more severe as unemployment increases. In the simple terms of Adam Smith, the market makes an adjustment for the oversupply of labor: the incomes of people decline.

The recent increases in poverty are one manifestation of the role of social capital in the American economy and public policy. We have improved on the harsh market forces of reducing the income of some people below subsistence to reduce the number of workers. We have not confronted the human consequences of tying social capital to employment as much as other industrial nations. Indeed, the reports on homelessness and hunger in America are actually an indication of the remnant of Adam Smith's market correction of the supply and demand of labor. Even more graphic and tragic, the 1980s brought about the first period of time in which the infant mortality rate stopped declining and the infant mortality rates of some groups increased. As the theory of social capital would lead us to predict, the groups with increased infant mortality rates were low-income minorities whose labor is in oversupply.

Even though white Americans benefit more from social capital than other groups of Americans, their benefits fall short of social capital in other nations. The poverty rate among white Americans is higher than the poverty rates of the populations of Australia, Canada, France, Germany, the Netherlands, Sweden, and the United Kingdom. A comparative study of 1986 income figures established as a poverty measure 40 percent of each nation's median disposable income, adjusted for family size. Almost 16 percent of white Americans had incomes below this level compared with an average of 22.8 percent among the other seven nations. After including government benefits into income, however, the rate of poverty among white Americans dropped to 9.1 percent while the average poverty rate among the other nations dropped to 4.9 percent. In other words, other nations do a far more effective job of keeping their low-income citizens out of poverty than the United States does. As with other groups, the children are affected most. More than 13 percent of white American children are in poverty, after benefits are calculated in income, compared with an average of 5.5 percent of the children of these seven other nations (Shapiro 1992:10,24-25).

Conclusion

The economic transitions that have occurred since 1972 changed the amount and nature of work. Less work and lower wages, the material of Chapter 1, connect recent economic changes to the new and increased poverty of Americans, which we have just examined. The return to the laissez-faire of the 1980s brought new levels of poverty to American life and a greater severity of poverty. Poverty is not random. In the 1980s, we became particularly aware of its geographic concentration and its characteristics of race, age, and family.

Chapter 3

Appalachia in a National and International Economy

The broad changes in the national economy and income distribution that we discussed in Chapter 1 and new levels and forms of poverty that we discussed in Chapter 2 have affected various parts of Appalachia differently. As the industrial sector of the American economy declines, the industrial centers of Northern Appalachia decline as well, especially coal and steel. Central Appalachia, with concentrations of the coal industry, had serious setbacks after the energy crisis brought a temporary boom in the 1970s. By 1990, serious economic decline reminiscent of the 1960s was evident in Central Appalachia. Southern Appalachia has shown economic growth and improvement for two decades. Consequently, within the Appalachian region we find the costs of deindustrialization, in different degrees, and the prospect of prosperity of postindustrialization.

Appalachia and National Economic Recovery

The economic success of the 1980s highlights the nation's and the region's economic problems. For example, the year 1983 ended with conflicting economic messages for the American public. On the one hand, there was the good news that inflation came down, interest rates declined, unemployment dropped slightly to 1980 levels, and the leading economic indicators confirmed that the economy was making a modest recovery from the recession that gripped it since 1979. We were on the eve of what Reaganomics' advocates would later describe as the greatest peacetime economic boom since World War II. More people were working, but there were fewer high-paying manufacturing jobs and basic industries, like steel, were in drastic decline. Recovery came about nationally by high rates of unemployment in the manufacturing sector of the economy, which slowed inflation, and higher amounts of government spending on defense, a pump priming measure. Different regions benefitted from this twin approach to economic recovery. The "Massachusetts miracle" provided Michael Dukakis a chance to run for president in 1988. Some parts of Southern Appalachia thrived as well in the 1980s. Much of the Northern and Central Appalachian regions felt the inflation control of manufacturing unemployment but not the economic stimulant of deficit spending on the military.

Other events suggested profound changes at the end of 1983. General Motors agreed to build small cars jointly with Toyota in California and to build jeeps on its own in the Peoples Republic of China. Bus drivers, miners and auto workers conducted strikes to limit the concessions in wages and benefits they were asked to make. Steel workers in Weirton, West Virginia, on January 11, 1984, purchased the mill at which they worked to continue its operation. The economy exuded increased internationalization, increased labor productivity, a decline in basic industries, a decline in the wages and benefits of many American workers, and a search for economic alternatives.

Appalachia's Industrial Base

Mining, primary metals, textiles, apparel, and wood products have dominated the economy of the Appalachian region. Employment in the region has been concentrated in these industries in excess of the portion of the U.S. labor force. For example, in 1980, 8.5 percent of Americans lived in Appalachia, 7.7 percent of the American labor force worked in Appalachia, but 73.7 percent of all coal miners could be found there; 28.1 percent of all textile workers; 20.3 percent of primary metal workers; 18 percent of apparel workers; and 18 percent of lumber and furniture workers.

Appalachia has had a spatial concentration of industry as well as a concentration of employment in specific industries. Map 3-1 identifies the areas of concentration of major industries within the Appalachian region in 1970. It uses a measure of concentration of 10 percent or more of personal income from an industry. This is approximately the level of personal income from government employment, including the school system, in most counties. This measure indicates the economic dependence of a county on a particular industry. Surrounding counties were likely to have high levels of concentration of employment in the industry but less dependence. The northeast corner of Ohio, for example, has extensive coal mining but the map shows only one county with heavy reliance on the industry. Primary metal production centers were located in Northern Appalachia—West Virginia, Pennsylvania, and New York—as well as in Southern Appalachia around Birmingham. Textile and apparels, in 1970, were concentrated in Pennsylvania, North Carolina, South Carolina, and all other Southern Appalachian states. Coalmining activities were, and remain, predominantly in Central Appalachia, West Virginia, and the Appalachian portions of Alabama, Pennsylvania, and Ohio. The coal counties run roughly from Pittsburgh to Birmingham and shape the spine of the Appalachian region. Alabama,

Map 3-1
Concentration of Appalachian Industries by Personal Income, 1969

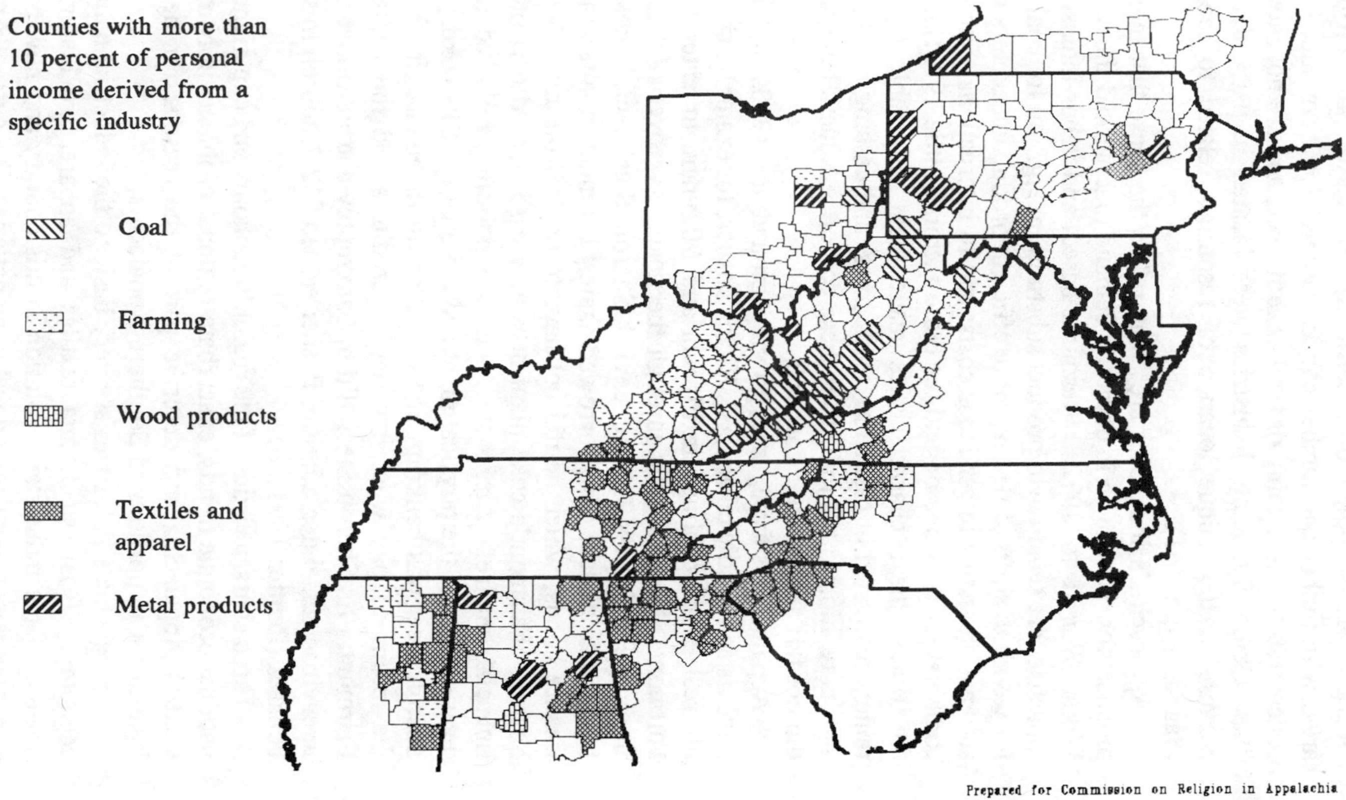

Georgia, Mississippi, North Carolina, Tennessee, and Virginia were areas with timber and lumber concentrations. Some counties had higher concentrations in farming or textiles, however, and are not shown on the map. Obviously, some industries were located in particular counties because of the unique location of resources related to the industry (Saunders n.d.: 61).

Appalachia's industries are "mature" in the sense that there is little prospect for the growth in domestic demand that marked the period from World War II to 1972. Resource-based and labor-intensive, these industries are sensitive to product substitution, e.g., oil for coal or plastic for wood; to shifts to newer, more efficient production centers with more automation and/or lower labor costs; and to international competition in combination with one or both of these factors (Little 1982:1). Later in the 1980s, these characteristics made them vulnerable to corporate raiders interested in cash flow, cash cows, and cashing in. Community and its relation to the industries these corporate raiders bought and sold did not fall among their concerns.

Appalachia served as a proving ground for 1980s and leveraged buyouts and hostile takeovers. Victor Posner, for example, stepped from his real estate dealings in Florida and Maryland to enter the life of Fairmont, West Virginia through the hostile takeover of Sharon Steel Corporation in 1969. He envied Sharon Steel's cash position and freedom from debt. He borrowed against his much smaller company to finance bonds, which he did not have to pay off on until 1994, to buy Sharon. Fairmont's coke plant became a cash-starved part of Posner's financial empire. Air, water, and soil pollution followed the steady deterioration of the physical plant and the quality of its coke. By 1987, Sharon Steel was bankrupt and defaulted on its bonds. It did not have the means to pay what it owed its creditors and the community of Fairmont. As Sharon Steel slid to bankruptcy and Fairmont slid lower in environmental degradation, Posner earned $12.7 million in salary and bonuses (Reutter 1991).

These characteristics of the region's economy and experience, within national economic trends, exacerbate regional problems in Northern and Central Appalachia and describe part of the reasons for new capital investment in portions of Southern Appalachia.

Appalachia's industries are very basic to the industrial nature of any economy. Coal, steel, and textiles and apparel are historically the essence of the industrial revolution in this country and now play a role in expanding economies of developing nations. The current Appalachian economy is in trouble because the industrial economy of America and the globe is changing. America's manufacturing industries are in decline,

Figure 3-2
Employment Changes in National Industries Concentrated in Appalachia, 1959 to 1990

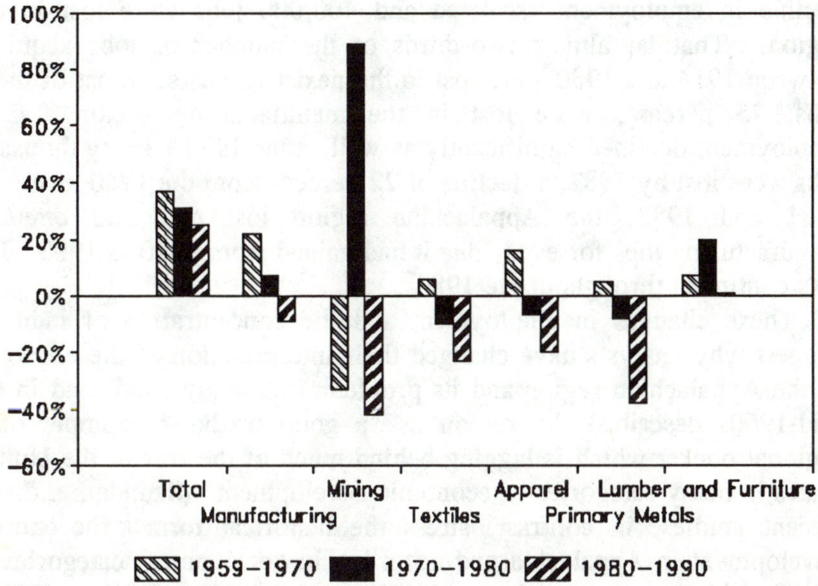

especially those that are predominant in Appalachia, steel and textiles. Coal mining's pattern of boom and bust has entered a new round of employment decline in the Appalachian region spurred by new capital intense production methods, e.g., longwall mining and a shift to new areas of production, e.g., Western states.

Figure 3-2 illustrates employment changes in the industries dominant in Appalachia from 1959 to 1989. As Chapter 1 indicated, the U.S. economy developed fewer new jobs after 1970, as the measures of total employment indicate. In general, U.S. manufacturing industries have had employment growth rates significantly lower than national employment growth rates and a loss of jobs, after 1980. At the same time, the growth of new jobs overall has declined. Among Appalachian dominant industries only coal mining and lumber have had employment growth rates equal to or better than the national figures for manufacturing for any period of time. The graph indicates the "boom and bust" nature of coal employment. Bust in the 1960s as mechanization eliminated jobs. Boom in the 1970s with the energy crisis. Bust again in the 1980s because of falling prices and increased mechanization. Employment losses in textiles and apparel and primary metals are significantly greater than the national employment loss in manufacturing.

Thus, mature industries mean slower growth rates at best and declines in employment ordinarily.

With the exception of mining, the major industries of Appalachia employed fewer people in 1980 than in 1974. In 1981 and 1982 the decline in employment escalated and 400,000 jobs were lost in the region. That is, almost two-thirds of the number of jobs acquired between 1974 and 1980 were lost in the next two years. Most of these jobs, 75 percent, were lost in the manufacturing sector. Coal employment declined significantly as well, after 1980. Forty thousand jobs were lost by 1982, a decline of 22 percent from the 1980 level. In 1981 and 1982, the Appalachian region lost *two and one-half* manufacturing jobs for every *one* it had gained from 1970 to 1980. Job loss continued throughout the 1980s.

These changes in employment and the concentration of industry suggest why analysts have changed their interpretation of the economy of the Appalachian region and its problems. A study conducted in the mid-1960s described the region as "a good textbook example of a regional pocket which is lagging behind much of the rest of the United States in many categories of economic development" (Saunders n.d.:1). Recent studies, in contrast, stress the historical form of economic development in Appalachia and not a lag in development categories to explain, in part, economic conditions in the region (Billings; Eller; Gaventa; Lewis; Gaventa, et al; and Walls).

Extending the history of economic development to our own time suggests that Appalachia evidences the brunt of decline in American basic industries. It also evidences the trio of factors that have changed those industries—product substitution, international competition, and shifts from labor intense to capital intense production methods.

Appalachia's Mature Industries

In general, the mature and dominant industries of Appalachia were hit harder by economic recessions and recovered slower, if at all, than the rest of the nation's economy. Textile, steel and furniture employment regularly declined more sharply in each recession than employment generally. The coal industry boomed strongly during the earlier recession that was caused, in part, by the increase of energy prices that fostered a general economic decline. After 1979, employment in the coal industry declined, especially in metallurgical coal.

Coal

The Appalachian coal industry illustrates well the end of the labor-industry accord after World War II. The United Mine Workers of America (UMWA) passed through a strike prone period immediately after the war to an accord that established higher, industry wide wages and benefits for fewer workers. This accord provided managers the confidence to invest heavily in capital equipment that improved productivity vastly during the 1950s but permanently displaced a huge portion of miners. By the early 1970s, miners were making new demands at the same time that coal industry representatives sought competitive advantages through lower labor costs. In reaching labor and management accords and then running their course, the coal industry was the precursor of other smokestack industries (Couto 1987; Maggard 1993).

By the 1970s, the industry had grown and become concentrated in the West. The founding members of the 1950s Bituminous Coal Operators Association (BCOA), steel-related coal mines, played a smaller role in the changing coal industry. Some companies in the BCOA, like the new companies of the West, became subsidiaries of parent corporations with less stake in industrywide agreements and stable floors of labor standards in the industry. Initially, oil corporations bought into the coal industry. As oil profits dwindled and cash flow problems beset these companies, they sold assets, including coal companies, to prevent being bought themselves (Couto 1987). This infusion of capital from outside the coal industry unraveled the frayed remnant of the UMWA-BCOA understanding.

Ironically, new capital managers enthroned "return on investment" (ROI), an acronym of the French word for king, as ruler of Appalachian economics where coal had been "king", in plain English. New coal companies had less stake in a high-wage, stable coal industry and greater concern for return on investment in any field. Amoco's coal operations, for example, were profitable but fell below the company's goal of 13 to 15 percent of return on investment. Consequently, the operations were put up for sale in 1985. Under the rule of ROI, coal companies competed with other investment opportunities of their parent companies and not only with other mining ventures. This new competition placed new downward pressure on wages and benefits of miners. New managers proposed to reintroduce labor costs into the calculation of competition. Their proposed action repeated the historic tendency of management to create surplus capacity and then to cut costs by paying less to fewer miners. The accord of the UMWA and the BCOA coincided with the post-war prosperity. Its end, in the 1970s, heralded the changes in the American economy and labor relations (Couto 1987).

Map 3-3 illustrates the consequences of this downward pressure on wages and shifts in production. The map indicates the decline in personal income from coal employment from 1979 to 1989. Central Appalachia had the largest decline, 7.0 percentage points or a rate of 51.5 percent. Many counties lost more than 10 percentage points of their coal-based personal income. This drastic decline left Central Appalachia with 3 percent less in coal-based personal income than it had in 1969. Map 3-3 provides a picture of coal income and dependence in an expanded market. This map uses 1979, a boom year, as a base. Map 3-1 used 1969 as a base and showed far fewer heavily dependent counties because of the decline in production at the time.

While employment and income have declined, production remains high and Appalachian coal supplies markets around the world. The coal industry is instructive because it shows how increased mechanization leads to dislocated workers, declining incomes, and unemployment.

Two strikes in the 1980s, at the Massey and Pittston mines, illustrated the problems that coal miners faced in a changed industry. The international coal industry stimulated new competition and a production capacity that exceeded demand. At the same time, new managers of the American coal industry, like Pittston, had little commitment to an industrywide standard for health care benefits, retirement pensions, or wages for coal miners, or memories of their origins and the sacrifices made by miners and managers to achieve them (Couto 1992).

Coal companies in an industry changed by mergers and diversification use increased savings and higher profits not for reinvestment but to pursue higher rates of profit in or outside of an industry at home or abroad. Big coal companies took over small ones; oil companies took over coal companies; conglomerates took over oil companies; and multinational corporations erased national, state and local boundaries and redrew all geographic locations with the "bottom line" of return on investment.

Managers of Massey Coal Group invoked competition from foreign, western, and non-union producers to justify the need for company by company agreements in its dispute with the UMWA that led to the strike of 1984-85. Yet, the corporate structure of Massey illustrated the confusion of "competition" in the industry. The Massey Coal Group was literally a subsidiary of a joint venture of joint ventures of subsidiaries of parent corporations, Fluor and the Royal Dutch/Shell Group. The Royal Dutch/Shell Group owned mining interests in South Africa, and Fluor was developing coal mining in China with Massey's assistance.

Map 3-3
Change in Personal Income from Coal Employment, 1979 to 1989

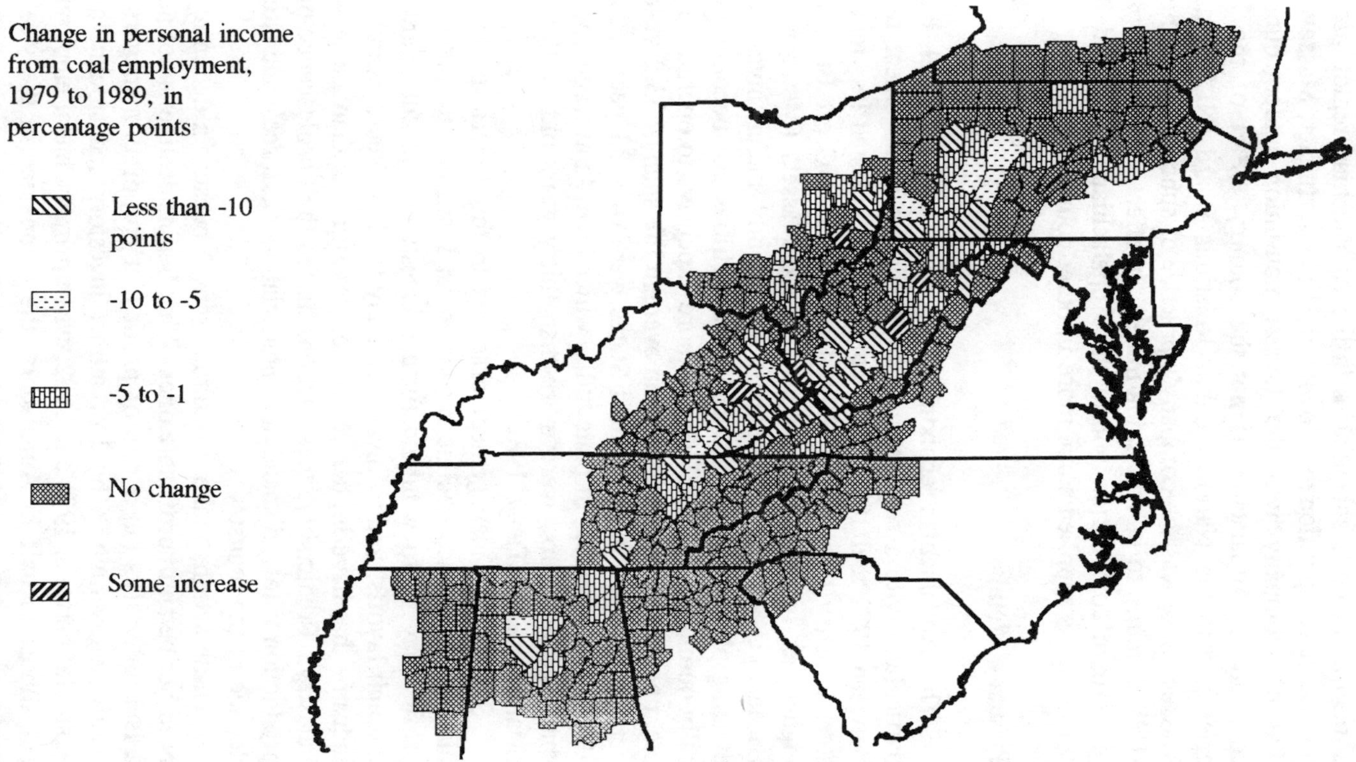

Prepared for Commission on Religion in Appalachia

Some of Massey's subsidiaries in the Appalachian region provided the non-union competition to its own union mines. In fact, Massey estimated that his company was the largest non-union underground mining company in Appalachia, if not the country. Part of the UMWA's grievance to the National Labor Relations Board (NLRB) during the Massey strike was the company's practice of subcontracting the work of UMWA mines to its non-union mines. In effect, Massey supplied some of its own competition within the Appalachian region and its parent corporations supplied some more in other countries.

Primary Metals

The Appalachian economy in general and the steel industry in particular invite a reassessment of American management techniques. Between 1972 and 1977, U.S. companies reinvested less money in the steel industry than Japan, West Germany, and Great Britain and had higher net incomes as a percent of fixed assets (Metzgar 1983:35). Because U.S. steel companies consistently under invested in their existing plants, many American steel facilities had become technologically outmoded in the 1970s and more expensive to operate. For example, openhearth furnaces have an average life span of 33.2 years, yet 43 percent of those in the United States were over 33 years of age as of 1979. Forty percent of plate mills, which have an average operating life span of 25.6 years, were more than thirty years old in 1979, as well (Marchione and Tabac 1982).

Simply put, management practices in the American steel industry illustrate that once decline begins in an industry, the means to make profits may be to withhold further investment, to cut operating costs through layoffs, and to invest company funds in ventures outside of the industry that have higher returns on investments than those within the industry. Predictably, these actions hasten the obsolescence of existing production sites, disband an industrial work force, and steepen the decline of the industry.

These actions make economic "sense" because a declining industry need not be an unprofitable one. What begins decline is not necessarily a lack of profits but a rate of profit that corporate managers consider insufficiently high to hold or attract investors and stockholders. For example, between 1974 and 1982, when primary metal employment was cut almost in half in Appalachia, the companies in the steel industry recorded average profit rates of 8 percent. In particular, 1974 and 1981 were record years for profits. Steel production fluctuated from a high of 145 million tons to a low of 110 million tons from 1974 to 1981

(Metzgar 1983). The fundamental problem was that companies were not making *enough* profits to keep up with reinvestment requirements. While the steel industry averaged 8 percent profit annually from 1974 to 1981, all manufacturing industries averaged 15 percent and the general economy averaged 18 percent. The rate of profit of the steel industry was not high enough to hold or attract the capital of even the steel companies. Consequently, as the *Wall Street Journal* reported, "Retirement of aging and technologically obsolete capacity has emerged as a prime element of domestic steelmakers' strategy to firm up prices when a recovery does come" (DuBois 1983:13).

The experience of U.S. Steel indicated the conflict between profit and employment in the economy. On December 27, 1983, U.S. Steel announced cutbacks that eliminated 15,400 high paying, union jobs. On the same day its stock rose five-eighths of a point to 29 7/8 in active trading on the New York Stock Exchange. Investors anticipated increased profits as the company diminished its payroll. This restructuring of U.S. Steel provided a small portion of the decline in employment in established industries with high wages, high benefits, and union membership. However, it made clear that corporate profitability no longer implied secure employment for large numbers of workers. Corporations had found and would pursue new avenues to profit that would satisfy investors but cost workers their jobs. Corporate managers correctly assessed the response of investors to layoffs.

American steel companies also diversified in search of profits. This prompted the often cited comment of U.S. Steel Chairman David Roderick, "U.S. Steel is not in the business of making steel. It is in the business of making money" (Metzgar 1983:26). To prove the point, U. S. Steel used record 1981 profits, which were acquired through tax cuts and generous depletion allowances as well as labor concessions, to purchase Marathon Oil in 1982. U.S. Steel changed its name to USX to further distance itself from its own history. Only two of the top seven steel companies increased their investments in steel in 1982 (Metzgar 1983:32).

The cost of competing in the steel industry presently can be measured by the price the 10,000 steel workers in Weirton, West Virginia paid. They bought out the company for $386.1 million, in 1984, assumed $192 million of the company's liabilities, such as pensions, cut wages 18 percent and agreed to no wage increase for six years. They hoped to keep the mill operating, to make and share profits, and most importantly to keep their jobs. After almost a decade, these actions have succeeded but only by attrition and labor cost reductions.

Map 3-4 portrays changes in the amount of personal income from employment in the primary and fabricated metal industry from 1969 to 1989. This share of personal income declined, in the region, by almost two-thirds dropping from 5.8 percent of total personal income to 2.1 percent. Hardest hit were the metropolitan counties of Northern Appalachia. Metals employment there went from 10 cents of every dollar of income to 3.4 cents from 1969 to 1989.

The closing of steel mills meant serious decline for the communities that grew up around them and that drew their social capital from them. Several studies have documented the decline of the steel industry (Hoerr 1988) and its impact on one particular community (Serrin 1992; Ruetter 1988). William Serrin makes three central points during his examination of the impact of U.S. Steel's decision to close the Homestead Works in Homestead, Pennsylvania. First, the "go-go years" of robust economy of the 1980s ignored "the men and women in the steel towns, the mining towns, the auto towns, the farm towns, and the poultry producing lines, in the back offices—working-class people across the country" (Serrin 1992:xix). Second, Homestead was "Every Town." Traveling to Homestead meant passing through "the slums of Newark and Philadelphia, the deserted mining towns of central and western Pennsylvania, and...the shuttered steel mills and electrical plants" and a time line of 150 years of industrial activity. Third, the change at Homestead was partially attributable to macro economics. In addition, however, it was the "small stuff...going on in the plants, in the corporation, in the union" that provided the basis for the upheaval in the steel industry, other troubled industries, and "other troubled institutions of American life." Homestead suggested a strange way to run a country, "use things up, people and places, and throw them away" (Serrin 1992:xix-cciv).

By 1990 the American steel industry had recovered. Cost per ton of cold-rolled sheets of steel was 10 percent lower than any import and about one-fourth lower than Japan and Germany's prices. Profits began to appear in 1987 and imports' share of the American market receded. Automation in joint-venture plants with Japanese manufacturers reduced the labor hours in a ton of steel by more than half. Automation also reduced the $28 per hour jobs, including benefits, of union workers in the industry (MacLean 1992). Employment in basic steel production in the "recovered" industry was 120,000 jobs in 1990 compared to 500,000 in 1975 (Brody 1992:33).

The shifts of capital in the metals industry gave union members and leaders new challenges. The new managers, encouraged by President Reagan's action against the air traffic controllers, quickly hired replacement workers in response to strikes. This action in Ravenswood, West Virginia meant 1,700 union workers were locked out of the

Map 3-4
Change in Personal Income from Metals Employment, 1969 to 1989

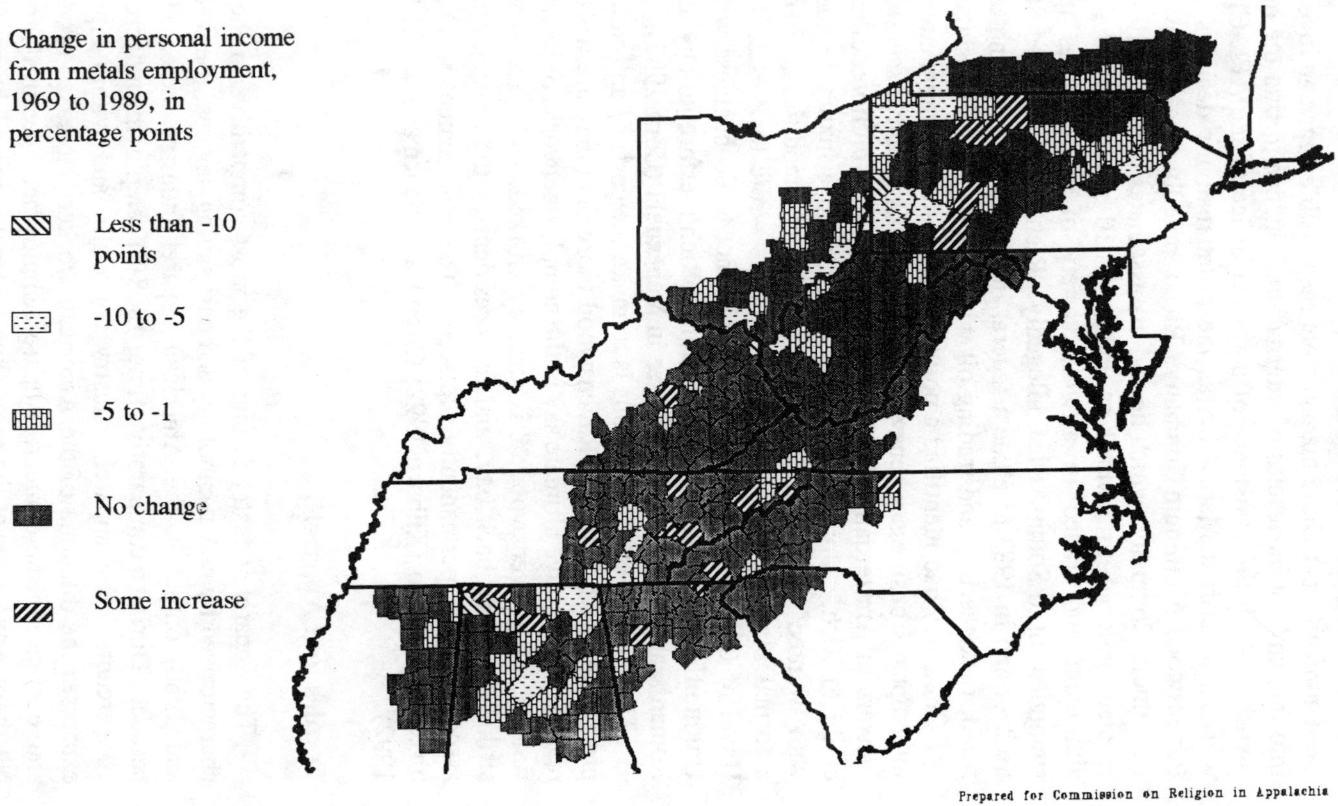

aluminum plant there for 18 months.

Union efforts to hold management responsible began an investigation into the baffling intricacies of international finance to find the burrowed owners. With the assistance of a special office of the AFL-CIO, steel workers identified Marc Rich as the point man for dealings with the Ravenswood Aluminum Company. Rich reputedly runs the Ravenswood Aluminum Company, which he and his associates bought in 1989. Rich is also believed to control as much as 10 percent of the world's aluminum and traded in a wide variety of commodities including smuggled oil to South Africa, allegedly. Rich fled the United States for Switzerland in 1983 to elude a federal indictment for evading tax laws, fraud, racketeering, and trading oil with Iran during the hostage crisis.

Once they had identified a point man, the steel workers attempted to interrupt his business whenever possible. This meant discussions with bankers in Amsterdam who had extended a multi-million dollar line of credit to Rich. Union members also leafletted a luxury London hotel with "wanted" posters of Rich as the London commodities exchange held a formal black-tie dinner. Union officials wrote to President Vaclav Havel of Czechoslovakia and urged him not to do business with Rich. Union efforts also extended to muddling Rich's efforts to buy a hotel in Romania and an aluminum smelter in Venezuela (Corn 1992).

The purpose of these actions is to make the costs of anti-union labor practices in such places as Ravenswood more than they are worth to the managers who have ultimate say in the complex networks of international finance. In Ravenswood, this strategy worked. The union won the strike, including back pay, and the president of the company and two associates were permanently replaced. The replacement workers they hired were let go (Kilborn 1992; Cimini and Behrmann 1992; Spencer 1992).

Textiles and Apparel

The apparel industry is one of the most competitive in the world, characterized by new technology and cost saving devices. Between 1970 and 1980, output in the American apparel industry increased by 30 percent. During a comparative time, 1968-81, employment decreased by 10 percent. The apparel industry nationally and within Appalachia expresses the dilemma of the American worker: increased productivity and decreased employment. Apparel employment declined greatly in Northern Appalachia at the same time it increased in Alabama, Georgia, and North Carolina. This shift provided an early indication of the movement of capital from one production center to another.

What remains of the American apparel industry is under severe pressure from imports. Like many other industries within the region, textiles and apparel reflect the increased internationalization of the American economy so that textiles are exported and apparel made from the same materials are imported.

Textiles accounted for 12 percent of all manufacturing employment within the region in the early 1980s. Most of the textile plants within the region are small and employ 250 people or less. Only 2.5 percent of these plants employ 1,000 or more workers. Of the 1,287 plants within the region, one-third were located in Appalachian Georgia in 1980. Regional employment in the industry dropped from 280,000 in 1974 to 236,000 in 1980. Between January 1,1982 and April 1983, 1 job out of 7 in the textile industry was lost nationally (ARC 1983). Map 3-5 illustrates the change in personal income derived from textiles and apparel manufacturing from 1969 to 1989. The most substantial decline occurred in the Southern Appalachian states, although much of Appalachian Pennsylvania lost textile and apparel income as well. All of Appalachian South Carolina as well as adjoining North Carolina counties lost major textile and apparel income. Appalachian Georgia and Mississippi lost large shares as well.

The future of textiles includes more change. The industry faces increased competition from imports, including trade from the People's Republic of China. Capital expenditures in the 1980s were expected to reach a level three times that of the 1970s. These expenditures will continue to transform the industry from labor intensive to capital intensive and eliminate more jobs. Part of the pressure to modernize is coming from the Occupational Safety and Health Administration (OSHA) and its enforcement of lower cotton dust levels in the plants. This will mean fewer, larger companies and far fewer plants, an estimated 7,000 less. In addition, textile companies are expected to diversify their holdings and to acquire control of companies in other businesses. For example, Dan River, a textile company, derived 21 percent of its corporate sales from Seabrook Foods, Inc. in 1978 (Business Week 1979).

These changes in textiles and apparel manufacturing are likely to cost Appalachia heavily. Parts of Southern Appalachia gained initially by changes in these industries when firms located branch plants in the South and moving from high-wage, unionized areas, including Northern Appalachian states. Southern Appalachia now competes with other countries. It is the high-wage producer competing with lower-waged, sufficiently skilled, and equally or more productive labor in other countries. One study that followed a seat belt factory in Knoxville

Map 3-5

Change in Personal Income from Textiles and Apparel Employment, 1969 to 1989

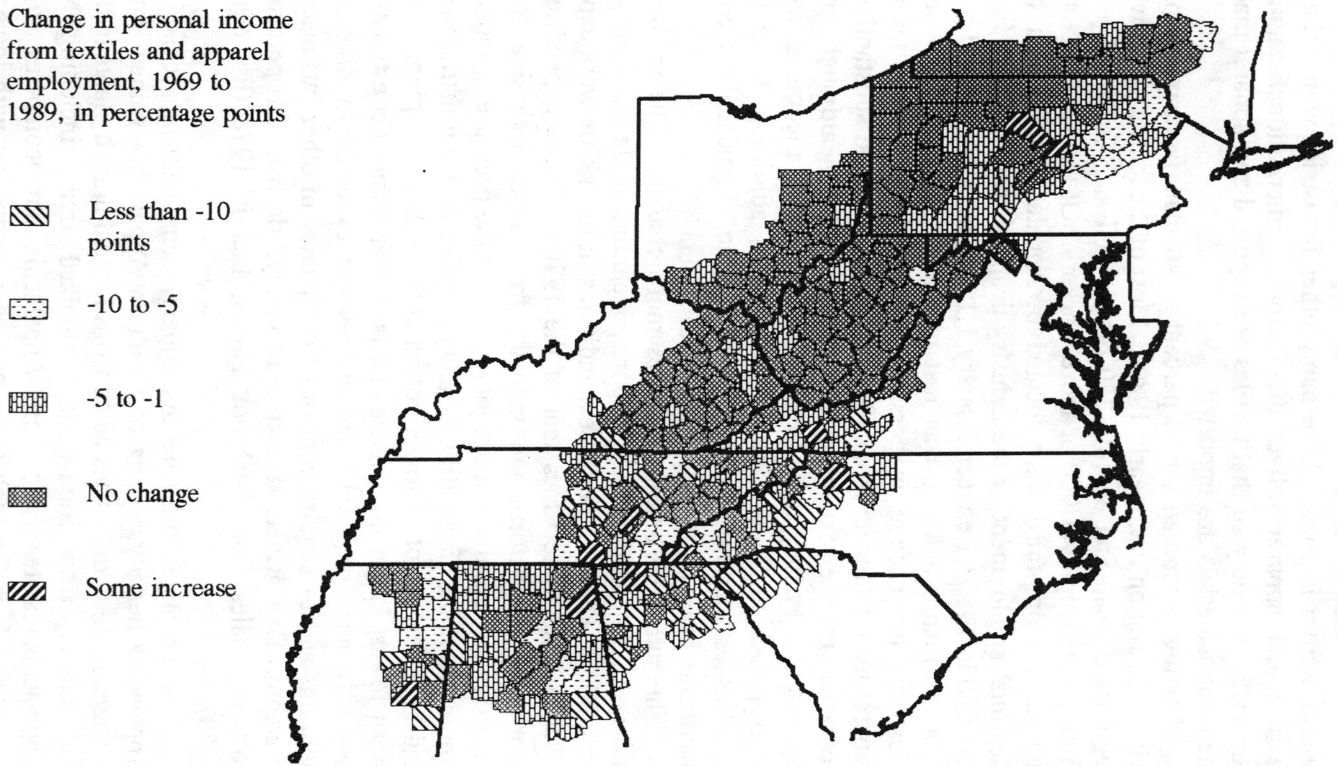

Prepared for Commission on Religion in Appalachia

illustrates how capital comes to one area from another, moves again, and then again in a continuous search for lower production costs (Gaventa 1991). Remote branch plants now find better prospects of profit in areas outside the United States from low-cost production costs of narrow profit margin, standardized products. New trade agreements only hasten the move of this segment of the industry. One comprehensive analysis traced this declining competitive position of labor-intensive and wage-sensitive industrial sectors like textiles and apparel. It suggested that "Given the new options open to corporate organizations and the impacts of heightening global competition, rural branch plants are increasingly at risk for downsizing and closure" (Glasmeier et al. 1993:8-9).

Wood Products

The Appalachian region contains 20 percent of the national supply of hardwoods. This supply and products from other forest areas support an array of jobs. Of all United States jobs in wood and wood products, 10.2 percent or about 208,000 jobs are located within the Appalachian region. Pennsylvania, Alabama, Tennessee and North Carolina have particular concentrations in this industry and together accounted for 59 percent of regional employment in wood and wood products in the early 1980s (ARC 1983A). Paper and allied products employed about 42,000 people in 1979, or 6.5 percent of the national work force in this sector. The region's furniture industry employed more than 90,000 people in 1979, or about 17.8 percent of the nation's furniture industry work force. This industry is concentrated in North Carolina, Tennessee, Mississippi, and Pennsylvania (Little 1982:II-26).

The furniture industry's future is a bright spot in the region's economy, although it, too, is subject to competition from imports and production substitution, and it reacts adversely to recessions. Likewise, projections in the industry see fewer and larger firms. But employment has remained about the same since 1970 and the industry is likely to remain as labor intense as it is. Forecasts for sales and earnings are also good, as analysts predict a surge in furniture buying as members of the baby boom generation support the market for homes and furnishings. One threat to the industry is the mismanagement of forests or the destruction of wooded areas by acid rain and other environmental degradation.

Timber and wood products provide prospects for improved economies in areas of severe poverty in the region. The abundance of hardwood trees in Eastern Kentucky, for example, has inspired frequent and recurring dreams of timber and wood product industries there. One of the earliest rural development projects of Area Redevelopment Administration, a program that preceded the Appalachian Regional Commission, established a Wood Utilization Center in Breathitt County, Kentucky in 1963. Local entrepreneurs have tested successfully the coordination of small woodwork firms in flexible business networks to produce furniture of high quality. These networks are successful and profit-making enterprises in Denmark, Italy and Spain suggesting that there is a community-based element to the global economy. Indeed, the Wood Utilization Center and the ideas of these local entrepreneurs have attracted too little attention. Requests for funds for start-up costs, for example, languished in Frankfort without response.

Without processing, the hardwoods of Eastern Kentucky and in other parts of Central Appalachia deliver only a minuscule fraction of their economic potential. In an unchanged manner, however, 75 percent of the hardwoods of Eastern Kentucky leave the state without further process exactly like they did a century before in the first "development" of the region's timber. Additional processing, from sawmills to fine-furniture making, creates between 3 to 80 jobs for each million board feet of timber. In 1993, more than 75 percent of the hardwoods of Kentucky, the fourth-largest exporter of wood in the nation, left the state without further processing. Only West Virginia lags Kentucky and its neighboring states in the number of secondary wood manufacturing firms (Bishop 1993a).

Service Sector

The growth in service sector employment is staggering. Between 1969 and 1982 this sector gained almost nine million jobs across the nation, an increase of about 60 percent. This increase was 45 percent of all new jobs nationally. Within the Appalachian region there were similar developments. Between 1970 and 1980 the service sector expanded by almost 400,000 jobs, or 59%. This equalled about one-third of all new jobs in the region. Health services not only grew substantially from 1970 to 1980 but they also provided almost 15 percent of all new employment in the Appalachian region. Other service sectors, such as eating and drinking places and business services, grew faster in that decade, but only the former came close to health services in contributing to overall employment in the region from 1970 to 1980. Increased employment in eating and drinking places contributed 11.4 percent of all the new employment in the Appalachian region from 1970 to 1980. These figures compare with 6.6 percent contribution to all new employment from coal mining, the leading industrial sector, in that decade. Thus, at a time of great boom in the coal industry, and dramatically increased employment (ARC 1983c), new employment in the service sector vastly outpaced coal mining in the generation of new employment in the Appalachian region. Map 3-6 portrays personal income from service sector employment among Appalachian counties in 1989.

The growth of employment and income in the health-related service sector has increased in Appalachia as well as the rest of the nation. Personal income from health services grew from 3.3 percent of personal income to 5.7 percent from 1969 to 1989. Most of this increase occurred in the 1980s when the portion of income almost doubled. Northern Appalachia has a higher rate than the other subregions, 6.5 percent compared to about 4.8 percent in 1989, perhaps reflecting its older population. Metropolitan counties have higher portions than rural counties, perhaps reflecting the location of larger medical care centers in metropolitan areas. Map 3-7 indicates the portion of personal income from health service employment in 1989.

The simultaneous decline in industry and increase in service is tantamount to a decrease of middle income opportunities in the region. These changes are occurring at a time when more women are entering the work force only to find declining opportunities for work and wages. These trends are likely to lead to the increased feminization of low-wage work in the region as well as the nation. This form of genderification follows from and coincides with the feminization of poverty, as we shall see in Section II.

The contribution of wages and salaries from service employment to personal income has increased over the past two decades, but not as fast as employment. The faster rate of service sector employment is good news in terms of overall employment. Service employment did not grow evenly everywhere. It tends to grow in areas of business activity where there is diversification and some elements of the economy remain dynamic, according to Daniel Saks (1983:48) in his study for the National Planning Association on distressed workers.

The inverse of this is bad news. Industry in most of the Appalachian region is not diversified but concentrated. A decline in one of these industries is more likely to mean prolonged unemployment for dislocated workers and less pay when re-employed. The real tragedy of the Homestead closing, for instance, according to Reich, is the decline in fortunes of the laid-off workers. "Most of them, after migrating West and South, got jobs in the service sector paying no more than one-half to two-thirds of what they had once earned in the mill. This is not so much the tragedy of an American steel town as it is the tragedy of

Map 3-6

Personal Income from Service Sector Employment, 1989

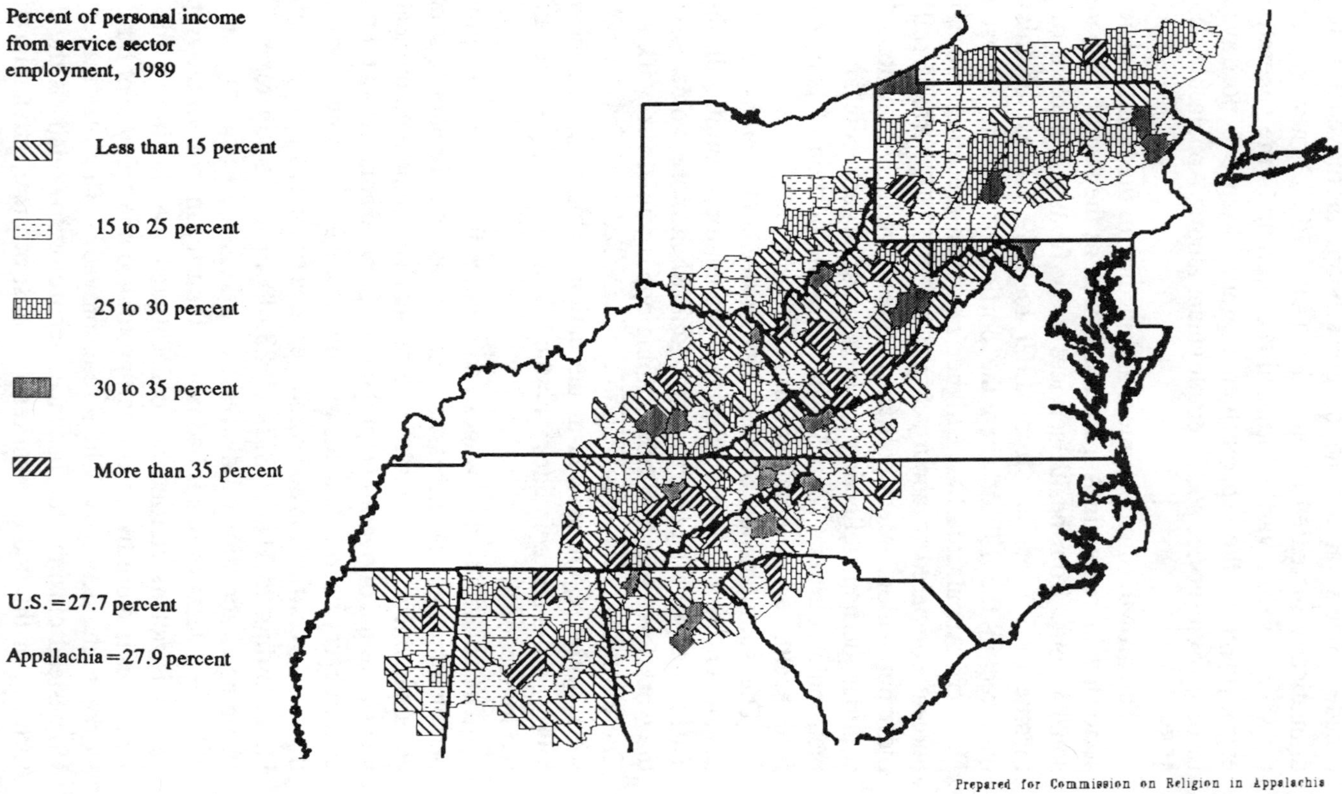

Map 3-7
Personal Income from Health Service Sector Employment, 1989

Percent of personal income from health service sector employment, 1989

- Less than 2 percent
- 2 to 5 percent
- 5 to 6 percent
- 6 to 8 percent
- More than 8 percent

U.S. = 5.0 percent

Appalachia = 5.7 percent

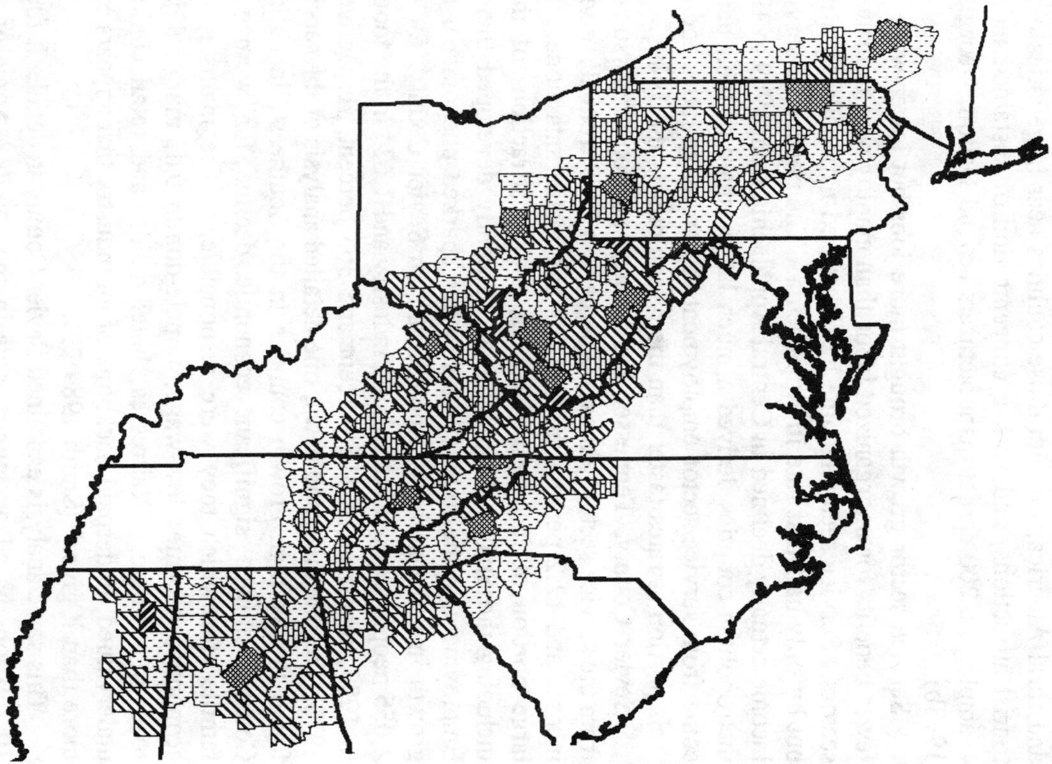

Prepared for Commission on Religion in Appalachia

modern America" (Reich 1992). Prospects for development in the region, and rural America, lie with those counties near large cities, with major tourist attractions, and with a concentration of sustained industry, for example, the 200 carpet manufacturers around Dalton, Georgia (Bishop 1993b).

Service sector growth brought more jobs but lower-wage jobs with fewer benefits for unorganized labor than employment in manufacturing sectors. Service sector income has increased nationally by almost 20% but by only half that rate in Appalachia. The portion of service sector income actually declined in Central Appalachia from 1969 to 1989. The metropolitan counties derived a much larger share of their personal income from service sector employment than rural counties and increased their portion at rates faster than the nation during the 1980s.

Sevier County, Tennessee has a large portion of personal income from the service sector, almost 40 percent in 1989 from all service sector income and 12.2 percent from hotels and restaurants alone. This very large portion of income reflects the tourist attractions of the county including the Smoky Mountains and recently developed theme parks. Employment in the tourist industry has sparked phenomenal economic growth in some areas of Appalachia. In Sevier County, for example, 2,055 people worked in the hotel industry and 1,624 in the food industry in 1989, increases of 415 percent and 363 percent, respectively, since 1970. Despite this good news, one detailed analysis of the service sector found the 84 high growth counties in the Southeast, including Sevier County, showed significant economic decline for women and the families for which they were responsible. "The mainstay of tourist economies becomes low-wage, female-dominated, marginal jobs on a road to nowhere. Waitresses, hotel maids, and retail clerks are the undervalued, underpaid backbone of an industry that appears to take far more than it gives" (Smith 1989:29).

This same analysis examined Sevier County in detail. It found some 10,760 jobs based on tourist trade in the county. Some of that trade entails the sale of local culture, often in the form of caricatured "hillbillies." Another portion of it entails physically demanding, unskilled jobs for low wages, long and unusual hours, minimal job protection, and few benefits. Women in the county doubled their labor-force participation between 1970 and 1980. Much of their work is seasonal, however. Many move from low-wage service work to AFDC assistance in the off-season. Women in the area have higher rates of unemployment, about 50 percent more than men, 14.8 percent in 1980.

The economic contribution of this service sector development and employment to local residents is ambiguous. Poverty rates in Sevier

County declined more than in other Tennessee counties and the region between 1970 and 1990. On the other hand, the population increase has meant that the same number of people as before, about 6,200 people, remain in poverty in the county (Smith 1989:31-58).

Surprisingly, even tourist attractions are part of the global economy. The example of Dolly Parton heading up the development of a theme park in her home county is atypical. More typical is the purchase of large resorts like the Homestead in Bath County Virginia by an absentee corporation or the purchase of Snowshoe Mountain Resort in Pocahontas County, West Virginia by the Japanese firm, Tokyo Tower Development Company in 1990.

High Technology

A discussion of the economic future inevitably involves a discussion of high technology industries. High tech suggests an industry that is scientifically based and that thrives on the rapid development and implementation of new techniques. Consequently, there is much more research and development and a higher percentage of technicians, scientists and engineers employed. These are the symbolic analysts of Robert Reich's analysis who were discussed in Chapter 1. Efforts were underway in the 1970s and 1980s to attract high tech industries near counties of weapons manufacturing in the region like Oak Ridge-Knoxville and Huntsville, Alabama. Cutbacks in defense spending have impeded these efforts. Other efforts to develop high speed transit systems have been discussed as successors to the steel industry in Pittsburgh.

In the production process, high tech is labor intensive rather than capital intensive. In practice, high tech is increasingly internationalized and utilizes low-cost labor in many different parts of the world for the routine, mass-production portion of the industry. If the region does acquire a greater share of high tech industry it will not be the glamour portion of high tech. It is much more likely to be the less-skilled, low-wage component manufacturing not being sent to Pacific Rim nations and economically depressed areas like Northern Ireland. An Arthur D. Little, Inc. study suggested that the region could be competitive in acquiring the low end of high tech industries.

> The (Appalachian) region...may represent one of the few areas of the country that can compete with offshore locations for lower cost component manufacturing and assembly operations in the industry. If the United States is to retain these high growth segments under such intensive international pressure, it will be

> in lower cost, labor surplus production regions such as Appalachia where development incentives and special training efforts will have to be provided to offset the aggressive programs of other nations (Little 1982:7).

The Little study concludes "Appalachia has a major stake in the private and public efforts to improve the competitiveness of U.S. industry through reindustrialization and improved productivity" (Little 1982:9). The good news is that the technology needed to keep pace with productivity increases is available. The bad news is that it does not pay some companies, such as steel companies, sufficient rates of profit to spend money to modernize. When companies do spend money on technological change it means increased productivity and a loss of jobs. In some cases there will be permanent displacement of members of the work force such as the region saw in the coal industry beginning after World War II and more recently in steel, textiles, and apparel. The Little study estimated, for example, that new technology and automated production could result in an estimated 20 to 30 percent decline in U.S. employment in the textile industry by 1995 (Little 1982:III,8-9).

One industrial transition illustrates some of the impact technology has on the Appalachian economy. The Corning ceramics plant in the New River Valley area, near Blacksburg, closed down in the face of international competition. When it re-opened in the late 1980s, it hired one-half the number of workers employed previously to produce catalytic converters for Japanese and Korean automobiles. Those hired, 150 out of 8,000, applicants earned very good salaries for the area. Starting wages averaged $28,000 and could increase to $40,000 with overtime. Those hired, and enjoying these good wages, had far more skills and education than the workers of the former plant. The new plant was computerized and its workers needed the skills to run it.

One worker, featured in coverage of the plant, represented the new manufacturing worker of the global, high-tech industry. Kevin Fleming, at age 24, had earned a business administration degree and three associate degrees. His hiring process included a three-hour orientation to the "high-performance work process"; two half-hour interviews to determine communication skills and attitudes towards work; tests on writing and math skills; and then testing in simulated work experiences for consensus building skills, ability to work without a leader, cooperation with other workers, and problem-solving skills within a group.

Fleming was not only the new worker of a portion of the changing manufacturing sector of Appalachia, he was the transitional worker as well. He left the coal fields of southwest Virginia, where there was no work. He pursued education at the urging of his mother, a coal miner and obviously another person in the transition of the Appalachian economy (Swoboda 1992).

Much of high tech is military related, and proportionately Appalachia does only modest military business, especially in weapons. The Persian Gulf War offered a grim and macabre reminder of Appalachia's military role. As the military paraded and displayed its accumulated inventory of high tech weapons, a Tennessee factory operated day and night to supply 16,099 body bags, or "human remains pouches" in Pentagon terms. The coal fields also produced more than its share of soldiers for the war as well (Jordan 1991; CORA 1991). Not to be overlooked is the impact high tech has already had on Appalachian industries. The mechanization of coal production after World War II continues with more automation that produces the same amount of coal, or more, with a fraction of the labor. Other industries, including ceramics and steel, are increasingly automated. From 1985 to 1990, Georgia textile manufacturers spent about $2.7 billion on automation and modernization. Their primary work force need is people who can install, operate, and maintain computerized machinery (Grant Thornton 1990:42)

Farming

The emphasis on service sector employment growth and the economic promise of high technology obscures farming on the economic agenda. There remain concentrations of farming in Appalachia but the portion of farming income has declined in the region as well as in the nation since 1969. The sharpest declines have been in the rural counties of Central and Southern Appalachia. Map 3-8 indicates the loss in farming income since 1969. The counties with the largest losses most likely had much higher than average regional concentration in farming.

Farming illustrates well the economic transformation of American industry. Mechanization changed the size of farms from small to large. The size of farms changed the pattern of ownership from local proprietors to absent corporations. Large farms used capital- and energy-intense methods and had less demand for labor. Employment opportunities in farming grew polarized between the high end of corporate-manager or owner-operator and the low end of seasonal and migrant laborer. The middle sector eroded. Farming families with small acreage required off-farm income to support themselves. Production centers shifted to fewer states. Food production, poultry for example, became a very integrated industry with farmers contracting with food

Map 3-8
Change in Personal Income from Farming Employment, 1969 to 1989

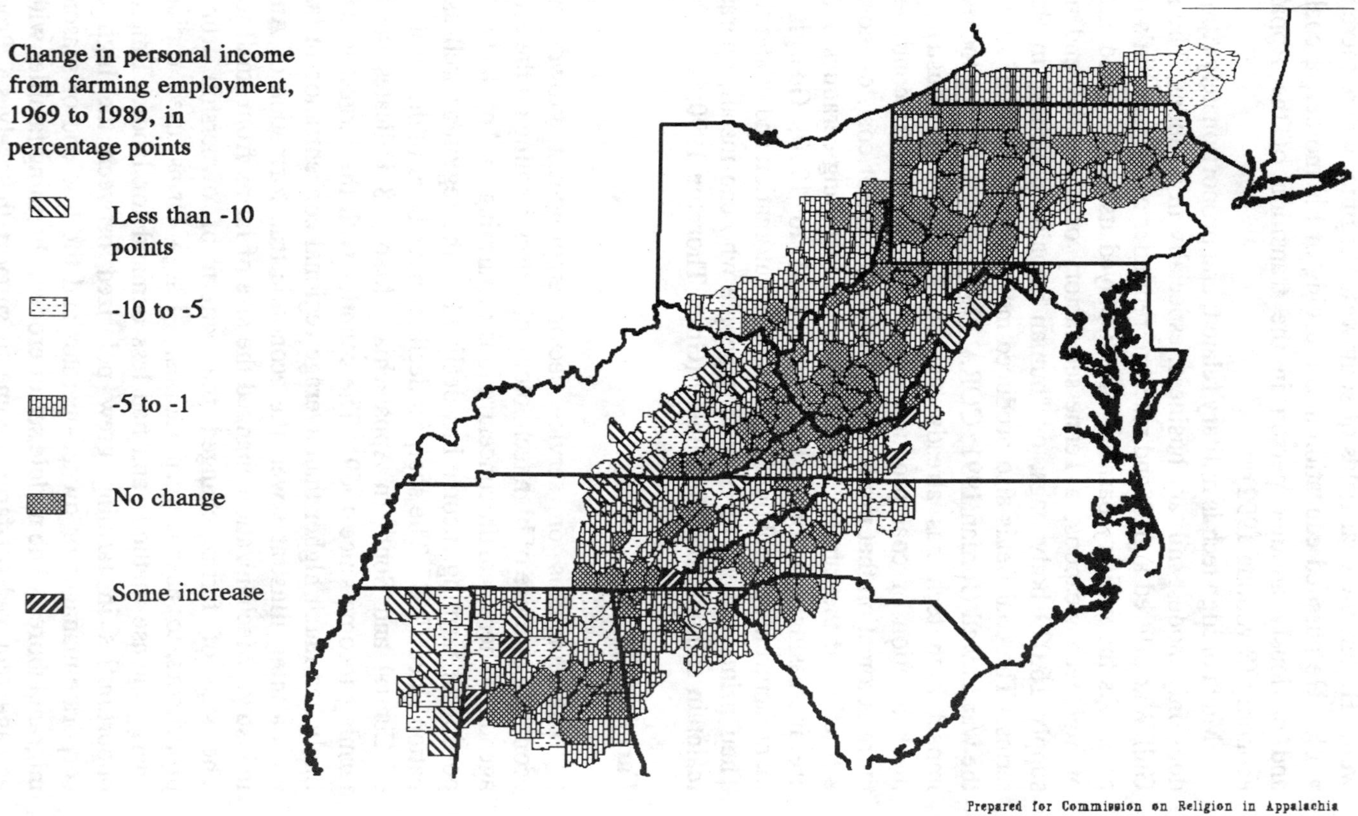

conglomerates.

Farmers in Appalachia did not fare well in face of these changes in American agriculture. Most farms in the region are small and most farm families, two-thirds of them in southwest Virginia (Virginia Tech 1987a:6), depend on "public" or off-farm income. Moreover, Appalachian farmers compete in a global market. Fruits and vegetables from around the world often have a price advantage over local and regional produce. Large buyers, chain stores, for example, also prefer produce with unblemished appearances. This puts the small, local producers at a cost disadvantage and leaves them with the dilemma of raising a crop for its quality or its appearance.

Changes in the lifestyles and diets of Americans have meant declining demand for the three staples of Appalachian agriculture: beef, dairy products, and tobacco. Fruits and vegetables are in increased demand. This offers some hope for Appalachian farmers tempered by the cost disadvantage they have with produce from other nations. To produce high quality vegetables that also look good requires land-intense and labor-intense agriculture. These factors, of course, increase costs of production. Diversification into raising sheep, horses, Christmas trees, and apples provides another alternative for Appalachian farmers (Virginia Tech 1987:13).

Tobacco, with its elaborate government regulation and support, remains a viable and important crop in the Appalachian states. Regulations on smoking may unravel the economic base of this crop. Whatever its future, tobacco's past instructs the nation about successful farming. Two pillars have kept tobacco profitable for farmers: control over the amount of production and price supports set at levels to generate fair returns to farming families for their labor.

These policies go back to the New Deal and contradict the free market approach favored by food processing and distribution corporations, such as Kellogg, RJR Nabisco, and HJ Heinz, and by agribusiness suppliers, such as Cargill. Symptomatic of the new forms of recovery in the American economy in general, these corporations enjoyed returns on equity of 20 and 30 percent during the 1980s. Food processors realized a return on equity of 14.3 percent and food chain stores had a return of 13.2 percent. At the same time, farmers "suffered the cruelest and most brutal economic depression in our nation's history" (J. Berry 1989:6).

As research director for the American Farm Bureau Federation in the 1930s, John Kenneth Galbraith depicted the problems of agriculture in an unfettered free market. Applied to the farmer in the 1930s, his analysis applies to the farmers of the 1980s as well and increasingly to workers in other sectors of the economy. It parallels John L. Lewis's criticism of the coal industry in the 1920s and his search for an industrial accord of industrywide standards for labor.

> ....Left to market forces, agriculture has a relentless, wholly normal tendency to overproduce....This has been the source of a persistent pressure of supply on price. But this is not all. Uniquely, or nearly so in the modern economy, the individual farmer has no influence or control over the supply and price of what he produces. The individual farmer is one among thousands and tens of thousands responding to a market price and situation on which not even the production decisions of the largest individual operator have any appreciable effect (J. Berry 1989:11).

In addition to these pressures, the growth of cities into surrounding areas and the search of urban residents for rural escapes have claimed farm land for development. This development has increased land values and taxes so that farms become unaffordable to the people who live there.

As with other industries, the changes in farming deplete social capital. Young people are not entering farming. Consequently, the work force is aging and the number of skilled workers is declining (MacFadyen 1984). The depletion of the social capital of farming, like the depletion of the social capital of other forms of work, undermines values and lifestyles of those who farm. In farming's case, however, the lifestyle is synonymous with rural values. In particular, work and land are valued for their productivity and not merely their price (Berry 1977; Hodges 1994).

Assessing the state of agriculture in southwest Virginia, a special study determined that much of agriculture there could not be called successful. Success had three characteristics: fair and just wages to workers; fair compensation to managers and owners; and environmental protection to preserve natural resources for future generations. Within the market system of agriculture, success in southwest Virginia would require developing improved management and skills of farmers; changes in practices and crops; strengthening marketing abilities; and applying new technologies, some of which are not yet discovered (Virginia Tech 1987:13). This slender hope for success is further frayed by the assumption of stability in the regional, national, and international economies.

In contrast, the production quotas and price supports in tobacco have demonstrated a successful policy for small farmers. Extending it to other crops would require moving from a market mentality. The regulation of tobacco use may be welcomed news in terms of health even as it undermines the production of tobacco in Appalachian states. Without applying the lessons gained from tobacco farming, however, Appalachia may lose one avenue to reach stable and attractive incomes from other crops for farmers.

Deindustrialization, Social Capital, and Appalachia

As is evident in even a cursory examination, the present economy of the Appalachian region is integrated substantially with a set of international and national developments. Technological innovation, the strength of the dollar, and international relations affecting the trade of commodities all impact upon the Appalachian region. Likewise, disinvestment in old plants and a search for lower labor costs and higher profit rates have affected the region.

The search for profit remains focused on low labor costs and low taxes. Beginning in 1979, the Chicago accounting firm of Grant Thornton polled manufacturers around the country about the factors that constitute a climate most conducive to the conduct of their business. Eight of the sixteen factors have to do with labor costs. The single most important factor, in 1990, was the average hourly wage. The lower the wage, the better the rank a state got for its manufacturers' climate. Other labor costs included the level of organized labor. The lower the level, the better the rank a state received. Four factors dealt with fiscal policies. In general, the lower the tax effort and public expenditures, the higher the rank a state received. Table 3-9 lists the sixteen measures used to determine a state's manufacturing climate; the weight of each measure; and its rank among the sixteen.

Table 3-10 reports the national and regional ranks for manufacturing climates among Appalachian states in 1990. The Southern Appalachian states ranked high nationally and held almost all of the top seven ranks within Appalachia on this index, on the factors of labor costs, and on state regulated employment costs. No other such clear difference in ranks occurred on the other factors. Northern Appalachian states did have higher ranks generally in productivity of resources. This measure included education, which ranked second to hourly wage in overall importance. Georgia ranked 49th on the education measure but rose to 39th on the productivity of resources factor. Georgia had much higher ranks on the labor cost factors. Similarly, South Carolina with low ranks on fiscal policies, 42nd, and productivity of resources, 37th, still managed a national rank of 10th overall. All seven of the Southern

Table 3-9
Factors of Manufacturing Climates

Factors	Wgt.	Rank
State & Local Grant Fiscal Policies		
Tax Effort	5.91	9
Change in Tax Effort over Five Years	5.58	13
Expenditure Growth and Personal Income	6.24	6
Debt Growth and Personal Income over Five Years	4.98	15
State Regulated Employment Costs		
Ave. Unemployment Compensation Benefits	5.76	12
Unemployment Comp. Trust Fund Net Worth	7.03	4
Statutory Avg. Workers Comp. Cost Per Case	7.03	4
Workers Compensation Insurance Levels	7.19	3
Labor Costs		
Average Hourly Wage	9.14	1
Change in Hourly Wage over Five Years	5.91	10
Percentage of Manufacturing Workers in Unions	6.61	6
Change in Unionization over Five Years	5.06	14
Productivity of Resources		
Education	8.33	2
Manhours List	4.37	16
Value Added	6.10	8
Fuel and Electric Energy Costs	5.97	9

Source: Grant Thornton, *Eleventh Annual Manufacturing Climates Study*.

Appalachian states rank in the nation's top ten heavily industrialized states with the best manufacturing climates. New York, Ohio, and Pennsylvania with older centers of production, more union labor, and higher wages cluster in the twenties in national rank. Despite the internationalization of the economy, automation of production processes, and other changes, manufacturers, in 1990, still understood low labor costs as the prime factor of a hospitable climate for profit. Southern Appalachia provided a ready labor force with manufacturing experience at some of the lowest costs in the nation.

In the 1970s, Southern Appalachia epitomized a national economic trend towards employment in lower-wage, nonunion manufacturing. By 1982, the economic gains of Southern Appalachia had slowed down as the search for lower operating costs continued. Textiles and apparel companies are going abroad or modernizing their plants to capital intense processes, just as steel and coal preceded them. Southern Appalachia has

Table 3-10
Rankings of Appalachian States on Manufacturing Climates Factors, 1990

State	State and Local Government Policies		State Regulated Employment Costs		Labor Costs		Productivity Costs		Composite of Ranks	
	Natl.	Appl.	Natl.	Appl.	Natl.	Appl.	Natl.	Appl.	Natl.	Appl.
Maryland	7	2	22	8	42	10	14	3	**	**
New York	48	13	30	10	45	12	8	1	23	9
Ohio	24	7	36	13	47	13	31	7	24	10
Pennsylvania	29	10	33	11	43	11	21	4	20	8
West Virginia	5	1	25	9	34	9	23	5	**	**
Kentucky	13	4	34	12	23	7	33	8	**	**
Alabama	14	5	12	6	10	3	40	11	5	3
Georgia	15	6	17	7	15	5	39	10	7	5
Mississippi	26	9	4	2	5	1	42	12	4	2
N. Carolina	25	8	1	1	11	4	29	6	1	1
S. Carolina	42	12	8	4	7	2	37	9	10	7
Tennessee	12	3	11	5	16	6	43	13	9	6
Virginia	31	11	7	3	32	8	13	2	6	4

** not ranked as heavily industrialized

Source: Grant Thornton, *Eleventh Annual Manufacturing Climates Study*.

underbid other regions with lower wages and fewer union members. But Southern Appalachia is now being underbid by developed and developing countries.

William Greider suggests Appalachia's precedent setting place in this new globe-hopping economy. He laments the decline of mediating mechanisms including labor in American political life and the role of the global market as the closet political dictator. The global market, for Greider, illustrates short-term, unstable capital investment which jeopardizes profitable operations and diminishes the most productive, long-term investments of capital. This global search for profit expands production capacity beyond demand and then depresses wages as a means to make profit in a market depressed by overcapacity. Lower wages for workers makes it all the more difficult for demand to catch up to supply. Greider visited the Maquiladoras factories on the Mexican-American border, a recent expression of the global search for low-wages, including low social capital costs (Greider 1991:387-400). He saw in the Maquiladoras factories an equivalent of the "sweat shops" of American industrial history. He continues:

> The Juarez slums reminded me of the squalid "coal camps" I saw years before in the mountains of Eastern Kentucky. Those still-lingering "pockets of poverty" were first created in the late nineteenth century by the coal and steel industries and they employed the very same industrial practices—low wages, neglect of public investment, dangerous working conditions, degradation of the surrounding environment [and] the use of child labor (Greider 1991:380).

The region is part of an increased internationalization of the economy. Wood from the Appalachian region is exported overseas and furniture made from the wood is imported to the United States. Department stores sell "Appalachian Trail" boots made in Romania. Pittsburgh banks invest in steel-exporting countries like Brazil and Japan. American coal companies develop the coal reserves of their multinational parent companies in Colombia and China and compete with Appalachian coal for the European steam coal market.

The global economy plays itself out in startling ironies in Appalachia. For example, Sony Corporation opened a new plant recently in the hard-hit area of New Stanton, Pennsylvania, in a former Volkswagen plant. This succession of economic activity of extranational corporations is welcomed news in this area. The succession, however, marks a net decline in manufacturing employment from 2,500 to 1,000 jobs, a shift from skilled to less skilled work, and a decrease in pay and benefits even for the one applicant in a hundred lucky to find work there.

Conclusion

Appalachia is part of the changes we described in Chapters 1 and 2. The organization of capital and its capacity for international transactions exceeds the capacity of other institutions such as unions and even government to keep up. American capital accelerates because institutional investors seek a healthy show of quarterly earnings to determine where to place their investments. As Robert Reich (1982) points out, these healthy earnings are not to be found in long term strategies of investment in plants and retraining of workers. Rather, those earnings come from phasing out outmoded processes, locating new plants in areas with lowest operating costs, or acquiring other firms whose assets can be integrated in operations or liquidated. These actions affect Appalachia's basic industries disproportionately. These economic trends have social consequences, as Section II explains.

Section II

The Social Capital of Appalachia

Chapter 4
Work and Income

The national and international changes outlined in Section I have meant new forms of work and changes in the amount and sources of income in Appalachia. The decline in industries concentrated in the Appalachian region have meant a shift from wages and salaries in manufacturing to other forms of income and a decline in income in Northern and Central Appalachia. As with so many other aspects of Appalachia, one generalization does not fit all counties, states, or subregions. Within Appalachia one can find trends and issues that illustrate the varied economic changes of America and the challenges that they pose. This chapter outlines changes in work and changes in the amounts and sources of income.

Work

Appalachia has seen a dramatic decline in its manufacturing labor force, as Figure 4-1 illustrates. From 1970 to 1990, the portion of the American labor force in the manufacturing sector declined from 25.9 percent to 20.5 percent, a rate of 20.8 percent. The steeper rate of decline in the Appalachian region, 30.8 percent, marked a shift from 33.8 percent of the Appalachian labor force in manufacturing in 1970 to 23.4 percent in 1990. The metropolitan counties of the region had larger declines than the rural counties. Some counties maintained or increased manufacturing employment. In the 1980s, Central Appalachia had an increase in manufacturing employment that supports the assertion of the 1982 Arthur D. Little study that the poorest sections of Appalachia may be competitive with off-shore locations to attract low-wage, unskilled manufacturing jobs, e.g., assembly, nondurable goods, and other work that Robert Reich called "routine producers" (1991:174-76). The rural counties of Southern Appalachia also illustrate the Little study's assertion. These counties, which were among the poorest in the region in 1970, reported the highest rates of labor force participation in the manufacturing sector and the second lowest rate of decline. Some 43.2 percent of the labor force was in manufacturing in 1970. South Carolina counties maintained a very high level of manufacturing employment. This marks perhaps the most successful transition in the region from a

Figure 4-1
Manufacturing Employment In Appalachia, 1970 to 1990

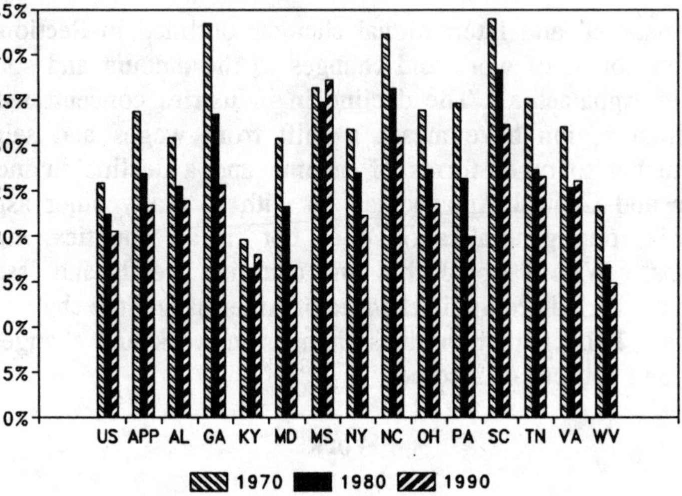

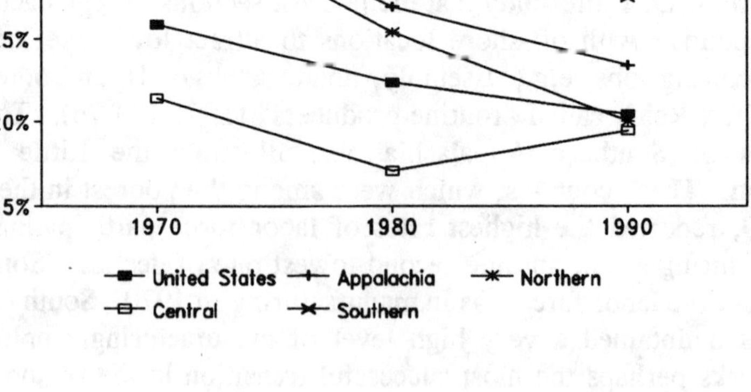

Figure 4-1 (Continued)
Manufacturing Employment In Appalachia, 1970 to 1990

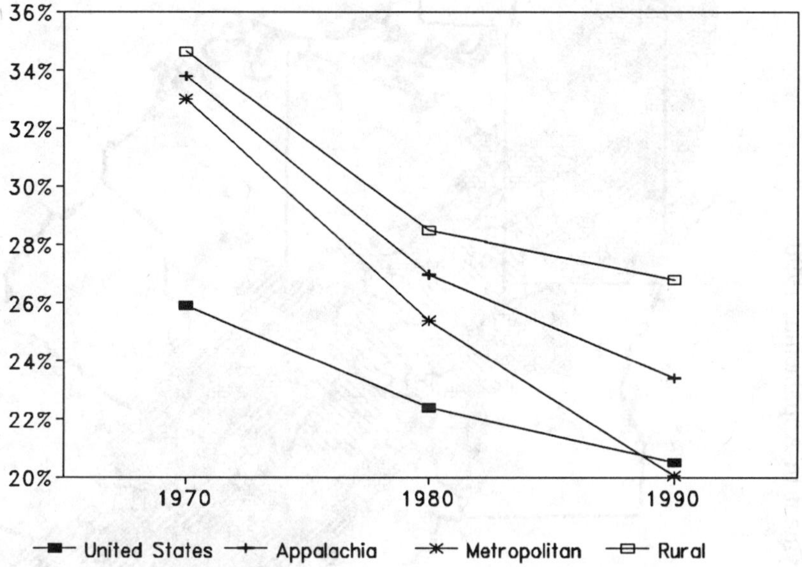

declining industry, textiles and apparel, to new manufacturing often stemming from international capital investments such as German automakers.

The Northern Appalachian counties reported the largest decline in manufacturing employment. Almost 33 percent of the labor force worked in manufacturing in these counties in 1970 but only 20 percent worked in that sector in 1990, a rate of decline of 39 percent, which exceeded the nation's rate of change, which was about 21 percent. Also, unlike any other subregion in Appalachia, the counties of Northern Appalachia had two decades of severe decline. Other subregions saw far less decline or even a gain in the portion of manufacturing employment in the 1980s. Ohio and Pennsylvania, in particular, had higher declines in manufacturing employment in the 1980s than in the 1970s. The changes in the steel industry contribute to this.

Figure 4-1 and the maps that follow present a summary and portrayal of the change in manufacturing employment and the 1990 measures. Figure 4-1 provides measures for the nation and Appalachia for 1970,

Map 4-2
Manufacturing Employment in Appalachia, 1990

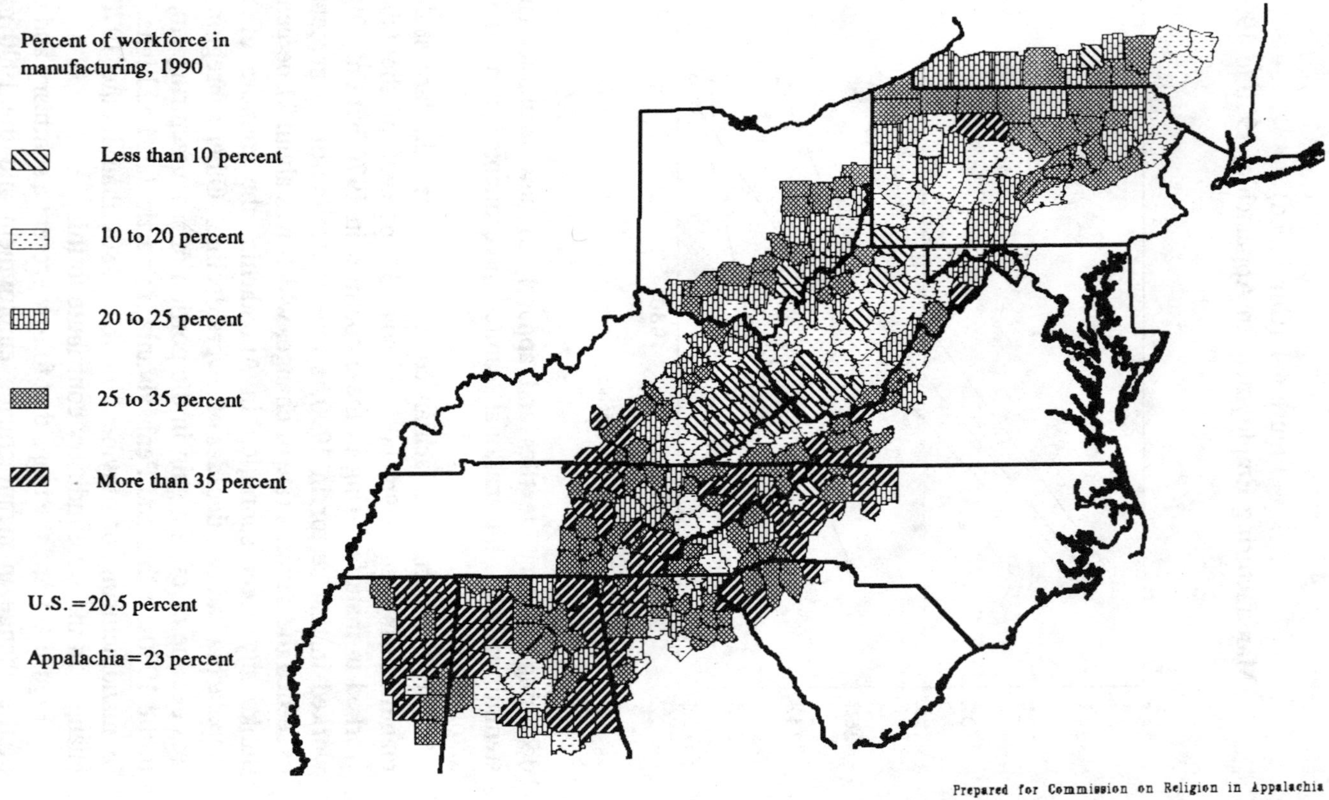

Map 4-3
Rate of Change in Manufacturing Employment, 1970 to 1990

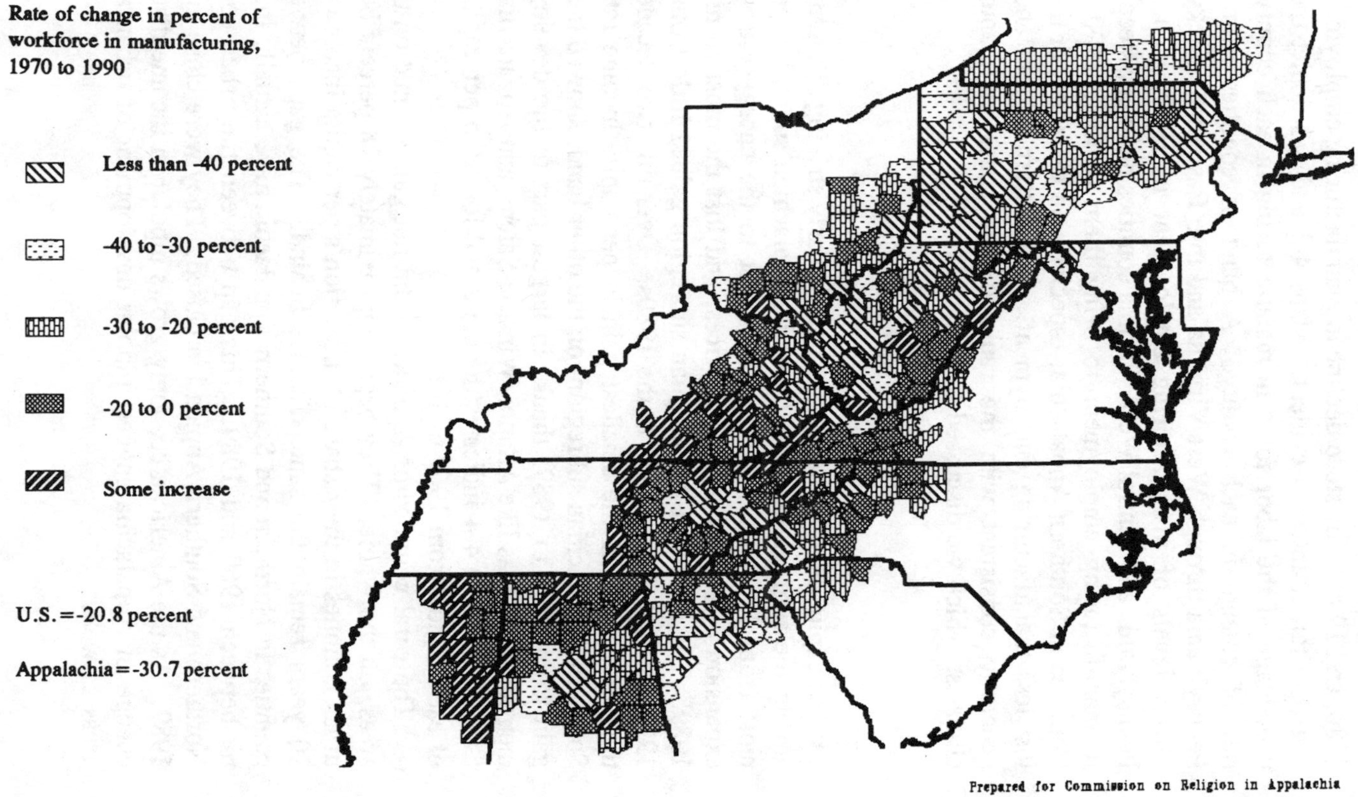

1980, and 1990. The steep decline in manufacturing employment among metropolitan counties is evident. Maps 4-2 and 4-3 depict the current percentage of the labor force in manufacturing in each county and the rate of change in each county. A band of counties from western Pennsylvania through West Virginia and into Eastern Kentucky had the lowest levels of manufacturing employment in 1990. The western Pennsylvania and central West Virginia counties had very steep declines in manufacturing employment to bring them to their 1990 position. Counties in Southern Appalachia, especially on the edges of the region, lost less manufacturing employment. The pattern of loss and gain is generally consistent with the ranks of the states on manufacturing climates, which we discussed in Chapter 3.

Income

Per capita income changed in a particularly striking different manner among the subregions. The Central Appalachian subregion gained the most from 1969 to 1979, thanks in part to the energy crisis and the expansion of coal at increased prices, and lost the most from 1979 to 1989. The Northern Appalachian subregion gained little from 1969 to 1979 and lost a great deal in the 1980s. Over this two decade period, this subregion had the smallest gain in per capita income ratio. The Southern Appalachian subregion, on the other hand, showed the greatest gain from 1969 to 1989, thanks in largest part to the development of metropolitan areas like Atlanta, Winston-Salem, and Appalachian South Carolina. Table 4-4 indicates the gains and losses in per capita income of each region from 1969 to 1989.

The rural counties of Appalachia did not gain ground on the urban areas, on the whole. They began approximately 18 percent behind the urban counties in their share of the nation's per capita income and after 20 years remain the same distance behind. The gaps between rural counties in Northern and Southern Appalachia have actually increased a bit between 1969 and 1989. This gap between the urban counties of Northern and Southern Appalachia closed. They were close to equal in 1989. As the American economy grows bipolar in income distribution, change in Appalachia suggest bipolar development of urban and rural areas as well.

Table 4-4
Appalachian Per Capita Personal Income as a Percentage of the National Average, 1969, 1979, and 1989

Region	1969	1979	1989	Percent Change 1969-1989	Percent Change 1979-1989
Appalachia	79.5%	82.7%	80.8%	1.6	-2.4
Northern	86.6%	88.4%	83.6%	-3.5	-5.4
Central	57.7%	68.3%	63.3%	9.8	-7.3
Southern	74.7%	79.2%	81.8%	9.4	3.2
Metropolitan Counties	88.4%	91.9%	90.0%	1.8	-2.0
Northern	93.2%	96.3%	91.1%	-2.2	-5.4
Central	57.7%	68.3%	63.3%	5.6	-8.6
Southern	81.7%	86.2%	89.4%	8.5	3.6
Rural Counties	70.7%	74.4%	72.3%	2.2	-2.9
Northern	78.6%	79.8%	75.8%	-3.5	-5.0
Central	55.0%	65.6%	60.9%	10.0	-7.2
Southern	67.3%	71.7%	73.1%	8.6	2.0

Source: Bureau of Economic Analysis, *Local Area Personal Income.*

Bright Spots and Shadows in the Sun Belt

Southern Appalachia presents a brighter picture of change and increased income than the other two subregions. Its per capita income figure went from 74.7 percent to 81.8 percent from 1969 to 1989. Every state portion of Southern Appalachia reported an improved share of per capita income. Georgia showed the most improvement, moving from 75.6 to 87.1 percent from 1969 to 1989. The metropolitan counties of Appalachian Georgia, which include the suburbs of Atlanta, did particularly well. They moved from 80.7 percent of the nation's per capita income to 94.3 percent. The metropolitan counties of Appalachian North Carolina, including Winston-Salem, have even higher shares of the nation's per capita income. They reached 98 percent in 1989 after having been at 87.1 percent in 1969.

It is in the South that we find nine of the ten counties that have the largest increase in their per capita income from 1979 to 1989. All ten of these counties increased their per capita income ratio by at least 11

Figure 4-5
Appalachian Per Capita Personal Income, 1969, 1979, and 1989

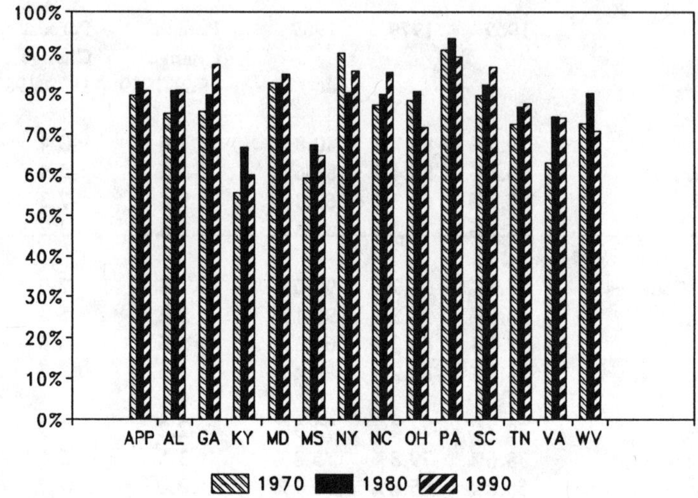

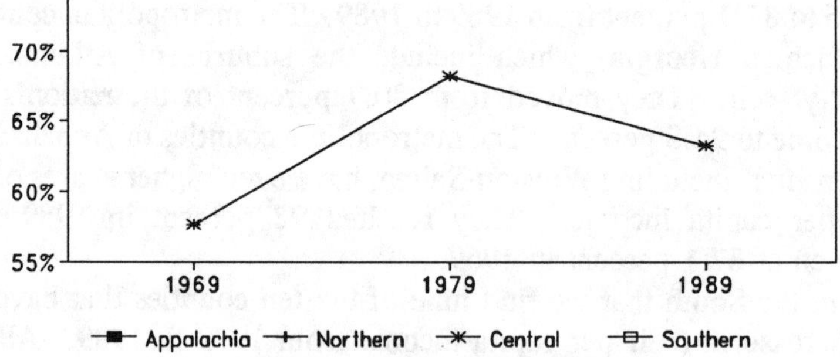

Figure 4-5 (Continued)
Appalachian Per Capita Personal Income,
1969, 1979, and 1989

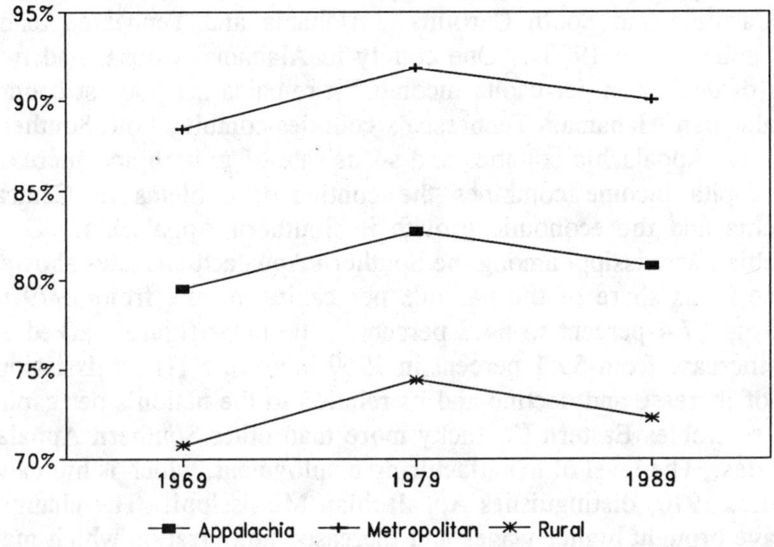

percent and up to 14.8 percent. Eight of these counties are in Georgia. The slow growth and declines of per capita incomes in Northern Appalachia and the fast and continued growth in Southern Appalachia have brought the two subregions close to parity, as Figure 4-5 indicates. The gap between Central and Southern Appalachia widened slightly from 1969 to 1989, primarily because of the serious downturn in Central Appalachia in the 1980s.

The metropolitan counties of Southern Appalachia led the gains of this subregion. With two decades of increase, they moved from a per capita income figure of 81.7 percent in 1969 to 89.4 percent in 1989. During the same time, the rural counties of Southern Appalachia made gains from 67.3 percent to 73.0 percent. Consequently, the gap between metropolitan counties and rural counties in the Southern Appalachian region is slightly greater now than it was in 1969, 16.4% instead of 14.4%. Also, despite the phenomenal growth around Atlanta, counties in the northwest corner of Georgia have had two decades of decline in their per capita income. This is due, in largest measure, to a decline in wages from textiles and apparel manufacturing employment as Map 3-5 indicated. South Carolina had increases over both decades, emulating the increased prosperity of Appalachian Georgia and North Carolina, but like those states the metropolitan counties of Appalachian South Carolina did much better than the rural counties.

Obviously, not all of Southern Appalachia fared as well as Georgia, North Carolina and South Carolina. Alabama and Tennessee made smaller gains in the 1980s. One county in Alabama, Coosa, had two decades of decline in per capita income. It remains the poorest county in Appalachian Alabama. Tennessee's counties combine both Southern and Central Appalachia counties and so its rate of growth and increase in per capita income combines the continued problems in Central Appalachia and the economic growth in Southern Appalachia. Only Appalachian Mississippi among the Southern Appalachian states showed a decline in its share of the nation's per capita income from 1979 to 1989, from 67.4 percent to 64.8 percent. The latter figure marked an overall increase from 59.1 percent in 1969 however. The Mississippi pattern of increase and decline and its relation to the nation's per capita income resembles Eastern Kentucky more than other Southern Appalachian states. The level of manufacturing employment, which is high and grew since 1970, distinguishes Appalachian Mississippi. The changes there have brought higher wages and increased unionization which may support new increases in income in the future (Thornton 1990:121).

Wearing Away in the Rust Belt

In contrast to Southern Appalachia, the counties of Northern Appalachia had modest growth or drastic decline in per capita income. Northern Appalachia's per capita income figures increased modestly on the nation's from 1969 to 1979. They then decreased greatly in the next decade, largely because of the decline in the coal and steel industries and in durable manufacturing in the 1980s. Overall, Northern Appalachia's per capita income slipped from 86.6 percent of the nation's to 83.6, a loss of 3 percent points. By 1979, the metropolitan counties' per capita income equalled 96.3 percent of the national figure. These metropolitan counties declined by 5.2 percentage points to 91.1 by 1989. The rural counties never approached parity with the nation and lost less ground than the urban counties. From 1969 to 1989, the per capita income of rural counties of Northern Appalachia went from 78.6 percent of the nation's to 75.8 percent.

The Northern Appalachian counties have a far different pattern of change in per capita personal income among themselves as well as a pattern distinct from Southern Appalachia. The Appalachian counties of New York, the southern tier of counties, had substantial declines in per capita income in the 1970s, about 10 percent. In the 1980s, all of New York's Appalachian counties had varying degrees of recovery. Two urban counties among them, Tompkins (Ithaca) and Broome (Binghamton), led the way. A population decline in that decade of about 1.5 percent went along with the recovery in Appalachian New York. After two decades of economic restructuring and change, the counties of Appalachian New York have seen their per capita income decline about 4.5 percent in comparison with the national average, despite recent recovery. Rural New York counties have had a larger decline than metropolitan counties.

The losses have been more modest in Appalachian Pennsylvania and about the same for metropolitan and rural counties. The 1980s were a decade of decline and the 1970s a decade of modest increase. Losses led declines for an overall loss of 1.7 percentage points in per capita income in Appalachian Pennsylvania.

Appalachian Ohio underwent a drastic decline in per capita income in the 1980s, about 9 percentage points. Contributing to this loss were severe drops in coal and steel producing counties, an area around Steubenville especially, where per capita income declined by 11 to 15 percent and in one case, 24 percent. These large declines were frequent in the West Virginia counties that fall into the Northern Appalachian region, as well. Every Northern Appalachian state lost ground on the nation from 1969 to 1989.

Central Appalachia

Central Appalachia had the widest swings among the subregions in gaining ground in per capita income in the 1970s. Counties there gained 10.6 percent or an incredible rate of 18.4 percent, and then slid back 5 percent by 1989. The energy crisis meant higher prices for coal, increased production and employment in the coal industry, and gains in Central Appalachia in the 1970s. Eleven coal-producing counties in the West Virginia, Kentucky, and Virginia corner had large increases in per capita income in the 1970s and equally large decreases in the 1980s. Martin County, Kentucky had the wildest boom-bust swing, moving from

Table 4-6
Ten Appalachian Counties With Largest Decline In
Per Capita Personal Income Ratio, 1979-1989

Name	Change in Ratio 1979-1989	Ratio to National Per Capita Income 1989	Pop. Change 1980-1990 (US= 9.8%)
Hancock (WVA)*	-24.8%	88.2%	-12.8%
Harrison (OH)	-24.1%	62.6%	-11.4%
Beaver (PA)*	-23.0%	79.8%	-9.0%
Jackson (WVA)	-21.4%	65.3%	0.6%
Martin (KY)	-21.1%	58.6%	-10.1%
Perry (KY)	-20.9%	61.0%	-10.3%
McDowell (WVA)	-19.6%	49.3%	-29.4%
Brooke (WVA)*	-18.4%	70.4%	-13.3%
Marshall (WVA)*	-17.6%	68.4%	-10.2%
Wyoming (WVA)	-17.6%	50.3%	-19.5%

* Indicates a metropolitan county
Source: Bureau of Economic Analysis, *Local Area Personal Income*.

34.1% of the nation's per capita personal income in 1969, to 79.6% in 1979 and to 58.6% in 1989. Other counties had double digit swings in the two decades that were not so dramatic. The rapid decline in coal industry employment in Central Appalachia and declines in public programs pulled the carpet from under this subregion. Central Appalachian counties made gains from 1969 to 1989, increasing their per capita income from 57.6 percent of the nation's figure to 63.3. Even with that gain, however, Central Appalachia lags far behind the rest of the nation in per capita income and has the lowest share of national per capita of any set of counties in Appalachia.

The Appalachian counties that incurred the greatest loss of per capita personal income were in the Central Appalachian region. Table 4-6 reports the ten counties with the greatest decline in per capita income ratio in the 1980s. They are all in Northern or Central Appalachia where manufacturing or mining declined significantly.

This table suggests the hardship that comes with a dramatic decline in income rather than chronically depressed incomes. Appalachia contains the new poor of economic restructuring and the old poor left over from the shortcomings of past forms of economic development.

Central Appalachian counties with no coal mining, in general, are worse off than coalmining counties in the region.

The following maps illustrate the changes in per capita income within Appalachia from 1969 to 1989. Table 4-4 has provided the measures for the region and subregions and the rates of change. Figure 4-5 provided a bar graph illustrating the changes within the Appalachian portion of each state. Maps 4-7, 4-8, and 4-9 portray the 1989 per capita income for each county compared with the nation's and changes from 1969 to 1989 and from 1979 to 1989.

Generally, Central Appalachian rural counties without coal are the worst off in Appalachia. Five of the ten poorest counties in Appalachia reports, are non-coal counties in Eastern Kentucky. Eastern Kentucky provides a fine point to the continued pattern. Eastern Kentucky counties started with 55.5 percent of the nation's per capita income in 1969 and ended with 60 percent in 1989. This overall progress in two decades disguises the major gains made in the 1970s. Per capita personal income reached 66.7 percent of the national figure in the 1970s. In the 1980s, it fell to 60 percent. While Eastern Kentucky counties remain ahead of where they were in 1969, they fell far behind where the coal boom of the 1970s brought them.

West Virginia provides a particularly sharp illustration of new hardship in Appalachia for the working middle class. West Virginia is the only state completely within the Appalachia region; nine of its southern counties, primarily coalmining counties, are in Central Appalachia and the remainder of the counties fall within Northern Appalachia. The state's per capita income dropped from 72.6 percent of the national figure to 70.7 percent from 1969 to 1989. The 1980s were particularly stressful on the state's economy because of its dependence on coal and steel. The per capita income fell from 80 percent of the national per capita figure in 1979 to 70.7 percent at the end of the decade. This was the largest drop of any set of Appalachian counties and a remarkable contrast to the national economic recovery.

By 1989, only eight Appalachian counties, or two percent, had per capita incomes at or above the national level. Five of them were in the Southern subregion. An examination of the ten counties with the highest per capita income reveals the complex patterns at work in the region. Table 4-10 lists the counties, the nearest large city, the change in their per capita ratio compared with the rest of the nation since 1969, and the rate of population increase in those two decades.

Map 4-7
Appalachian Per Capita Personal Income, 1989

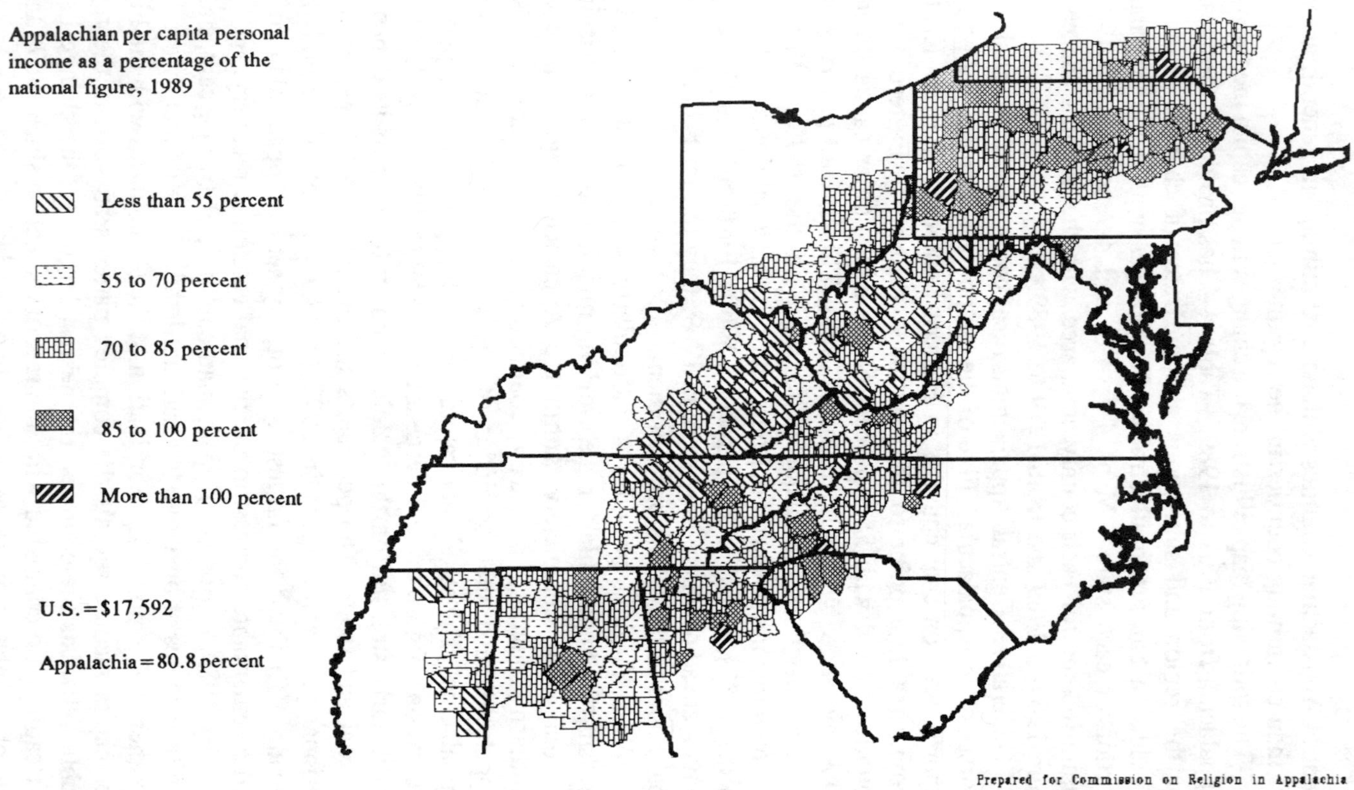

Map 4-8
Rate of Change in Appalachian Per Capita Personal Income, 1969 to 1989

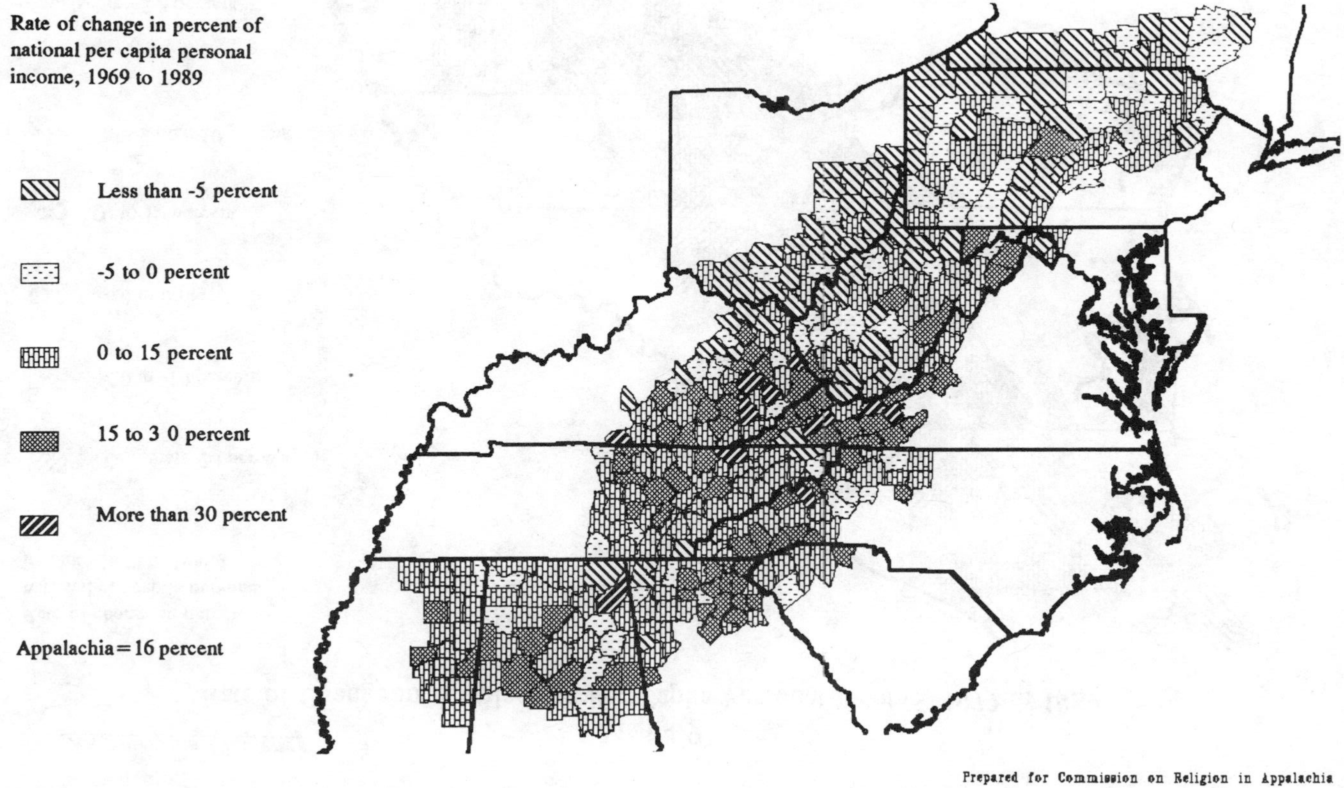

Map 4-9

Rate of Change in Appalachian Per Capita Personal Income, 1979 to 1989

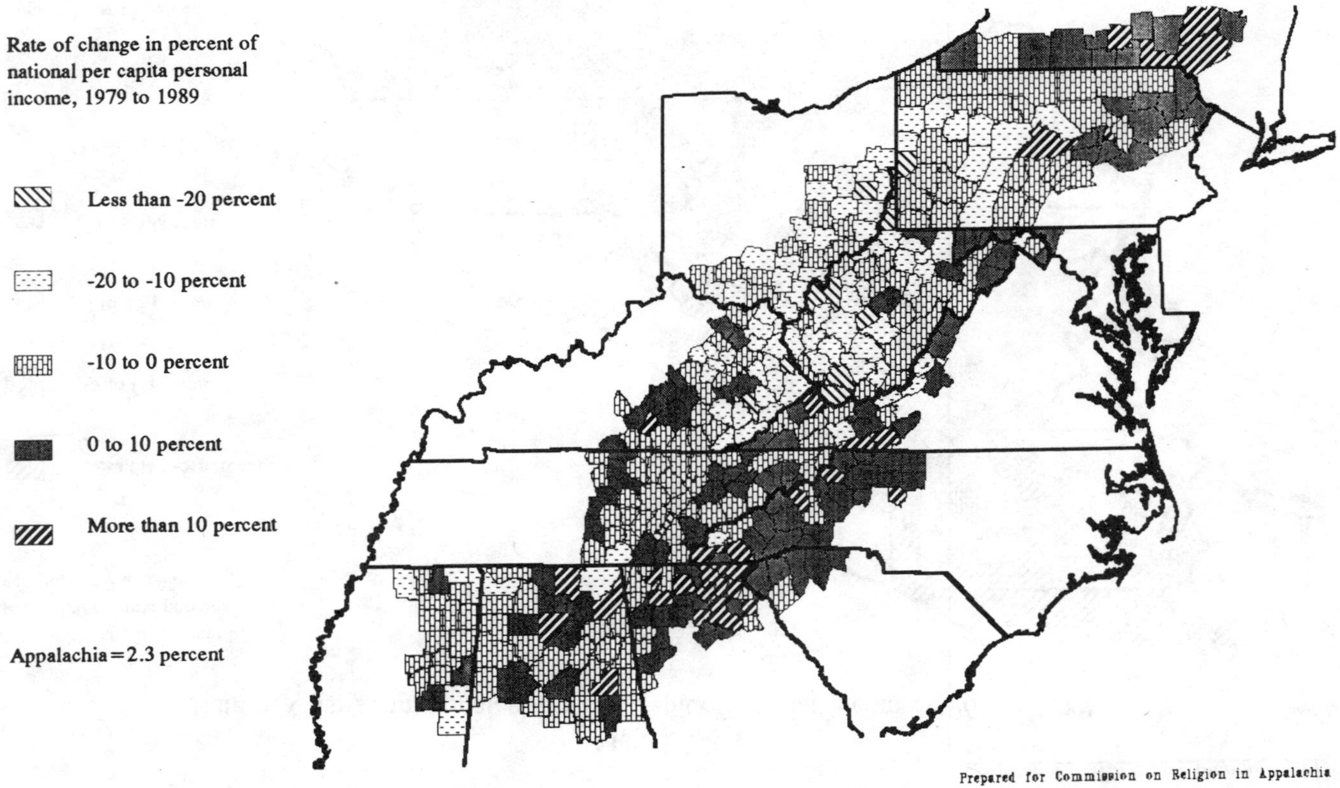

Table 4-10
Appalachia's Ten Wealthiest Counties, 1989

Name	Largest City Within 20 Miles	Ratio to National Per Capita Income	Change in Income Ratio 1969-1989	Change in Pop 1970-1990 (US= 22.1%)
Forsyth (NC)*	Winston-Salem	111.8%	12.3%	24.0%
Allegheny (PA)*	Pittsburgh	109.4%	2.3%	-16.7%
Montour (PA)	Williamsport	104.9%	22.0%	7.4%
Gwinnett (GA)*	Atlanta	104.0%	17.4%	387.8%
Broome (NY)*	Binghamton	101.9%	.8%	-4.4%
Polk (NC)	Spartanburg (SC)	100.6%	14.5%	22.9%
Forsyth (GA)*	Atlanta	100.5%	17.4%	160.4%
Madison (AL)*	Huntsville	99.9%	8.7%	28.1%
Pike (PA)	Scranton	96.1%	.3%	136.6%
Whitfield (GA)	Chattanooga (TN)	95.9%	8.8%	31.5%

* Indicates Metropolitan County
Sources: Bureau of Economic Analysis, *Local Area Personal Income*; Department of Commerce, *Census*.

Table 4-11
Appalachia's Ten Poorest Counties, 1989

Name	Ratio to National Per Capita Income	Change in Ratio 1969-1979	Change in Ratio 1979-1989	Pop. Change 1970-1990 (US=9.6%)
McCreary (KY)	38.9%	9.9%	-2.4%	-0.2%
Menifee (KY)	40.4%	.8%	-4.5%	-0.5%
Elliott (KY)	40.8%	13.7%	-8.4%	-6.6%
Owsley (KY)	41.7%	6.0%	2.9%	-11.8%
Clay (WVA)	42.2%	10.5%	-12.9%	-11.4%
Jackson (KY)	42.5%	4.0%	-2.2%	-0.3%
Maggofin (KY)	44.2%	17.4%	-7.8%	-3.2%
Summers (WVA)	44.3%	3.0%	-10.3%	-10.5%
Clay (KY)	44.7%	19.6%	-9.3%	-4.4%
Kemper (MS)	45.0%	14.1%	-8.8%	2.1%

Source: Bureau of Economic Analysis, *Local Area Personal Income*; Department of Commerce, *Census*.

Some elements of a pattern among these ten counties are apparent and significant. The two metropolitan counties in Northern Appalachia in this group had very modest gains in per capita income and significant population decline. On the other hand, the four metropolitan counties in Southern Appalachia had large gains in per capita income ratio and large population increases. The increase of both measures in the Southern counties suggests economic growth that absorbs newcomers. It may also indicate a population shift of the economically better-off from nearby urban areas. The two counties surrounding Atlanta may reflect both the growth in the size and wealth of Atlanta and a movement from the city to outlying areas. Madison County, Alabama reflects the benefit to Huntsville of increased military spending in the 1980s. Montour County, Pennsylvania is a case of a Northern Appalachian rural county that increased per capita significantly through increased service sector earnings but still lost population. The Geisinger Medical Center provides some 3,200 jobs in tiny Montour County, population 17,735. This snapshot of the "wealth" of the Appalachian region suggests the complexity of the region. There are different rates of economic growth among the better-off counties and population increases and decreases among them as well.

Another pattern is apparent among the ten poorest Appalachian counties in 1989, which Table 4-11 reports. All but one of them are in Central Appalachia, Kentucky and West Virginia. All of them have per capita incomes at or below 45% of the national average. All of them gained significantly in absolute and relative terms in per capita income in the 1970s. Most of them lost significant ground in the 1980s. With the exception of the one county in Mississippi, there was outmigration from these counties during the 1980s. The increase in that Mississippi county may measure a reverse migration stimulated by severe decline in urban areas to which residents had migrated earlier. Map 4-12 portrays the wealthiest and poorest counties in the region.

Different Sources of Income

In addition to changes in the amount of income, changed employment patterns produced changes in the sources of income. As manufacturing employment declined, manufacturing wages and salaries declined as a portion of the per capita income. As service employment increased, wages and salaries from this sector increased. Increased employment in services has not provided the amount of income lost to decreased

Map 4-12
Appalachia's Ten Wealthiest and Poorest Counties, 1990

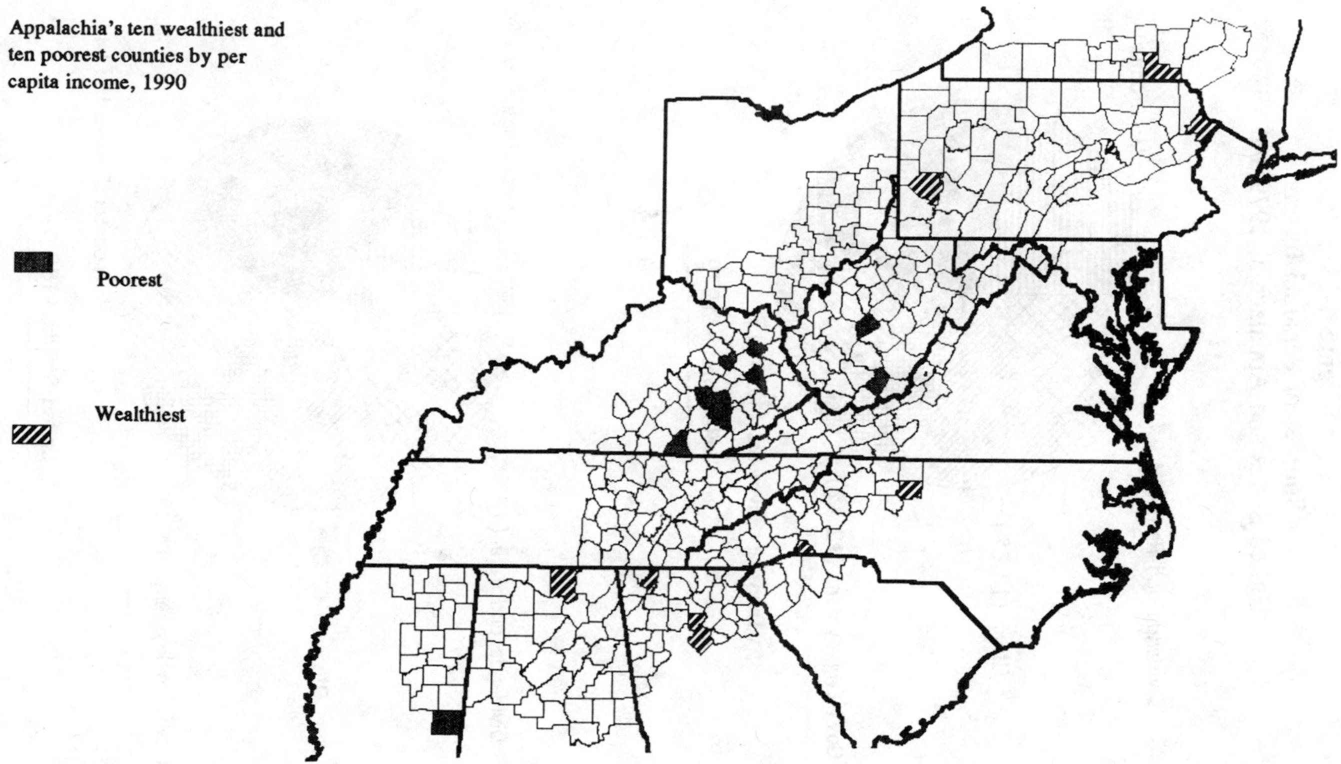

Prepared for Commission on Religion in Appalachia

Figure 4-13
Sources of Personal Income,
United States and Appalachia, 1979 and 1989

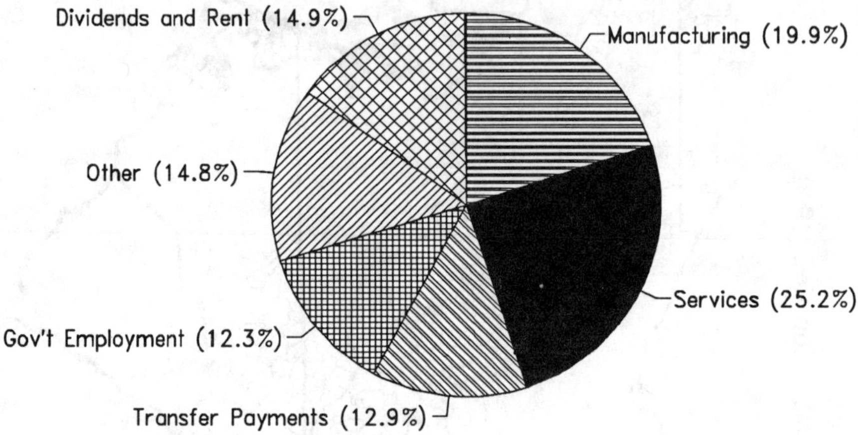

United States 1979

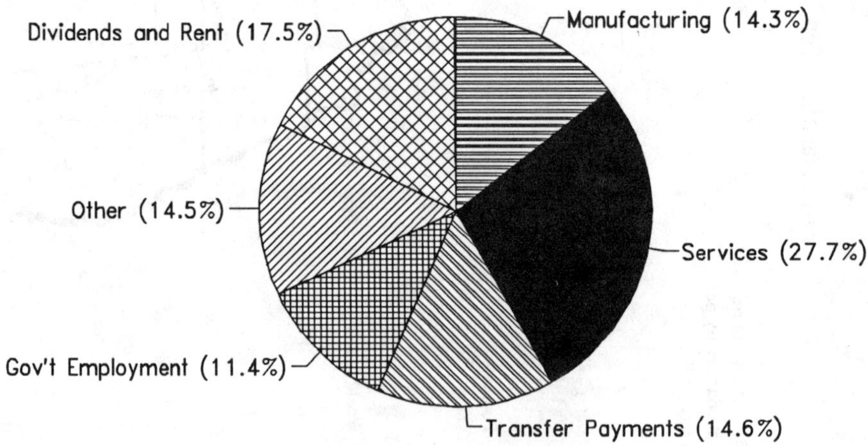

United States 1989

Figure 4-13 (Continued)
Sources of Personal Income,
United States and Appalachia, 1979 and 1989

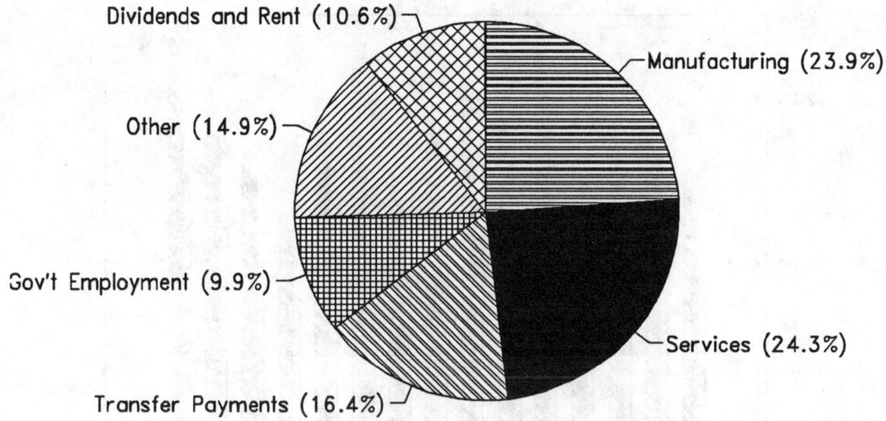

82.8% of national per capita personal income for Appalachia 1979

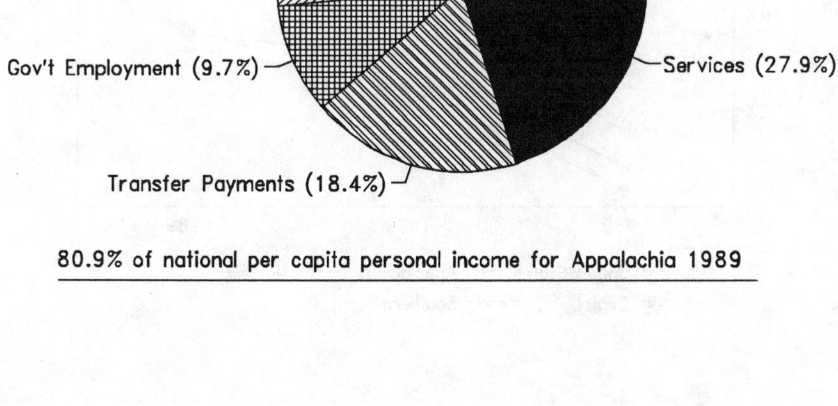

80.9% of national per capita personal income for Appalachia 1989

Figure 4-14
Transfer Payments as a Portion of Per Capita Personal Income, 1969, 1979, 1989

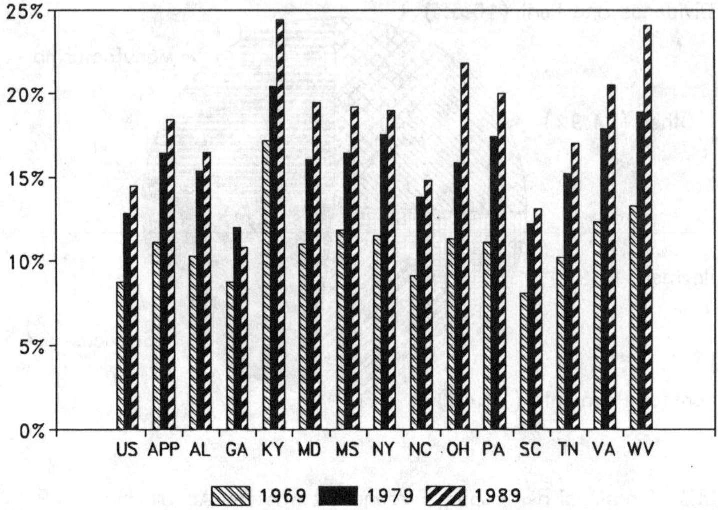

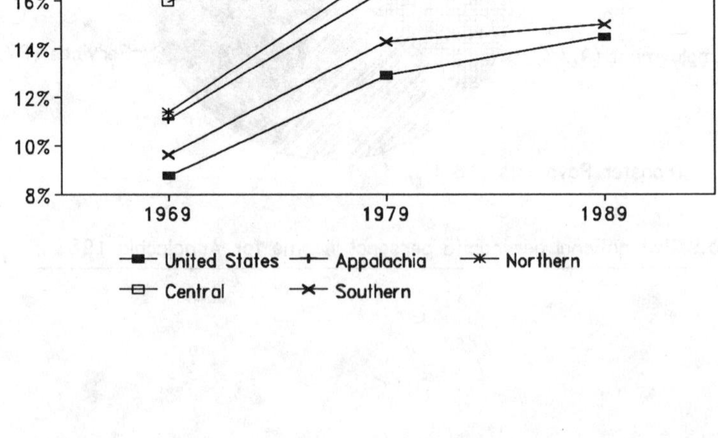

Figure 4-14 (Continued)
Transfer Payments as a Portion of Per Capita
Personal Income, 1969, 1979, 1989

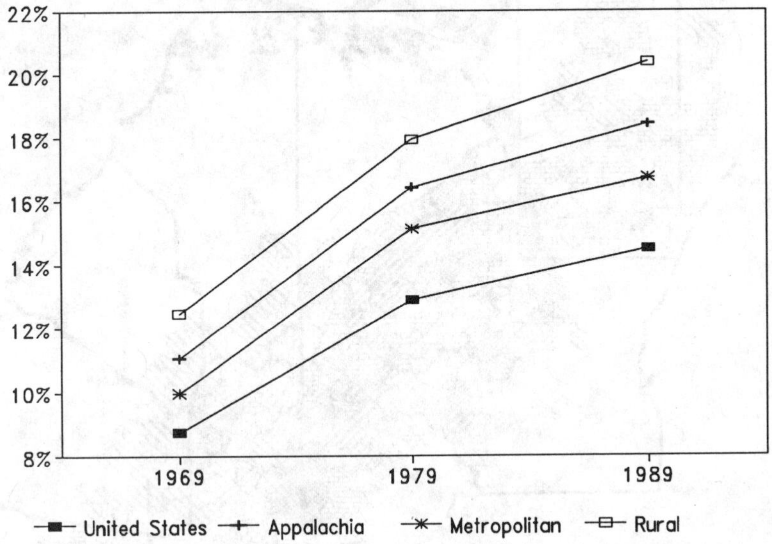

employment in manufacturing. Consequently, the amount of change in per capita income in Appalachia is explained in part by the change in the sources of income.

Figure 4-13 indicates the sources of personal income in the United States and the Appalachian region for 1979 and 1989. The category of "Other" includes wages and salaries from transportation and construction; proprietors' income, about 8.5 percent; and other smaller sources of personal income. When not reported separately in later tables, income from dividends, interest, and rents is included in the category "Other."

Appalachia differs from the nation most strikingly in two sectors of income: manufacturing, which we examined, and transfer payments. In manufacturing, Appalachian wages and salaries declined as a share of personal income more than the nation's did. On the other hand, the region has seen an increase in the portion of personal income coming from transfer payments that exceeded the national increase. Transfer payments include unemployment compensation, welfare, Medicaid, Medicare, Social Security, and income from other government programs.

Map 4-15
Transfer Payments as a Portion of Per Capita Personal Income, 1989

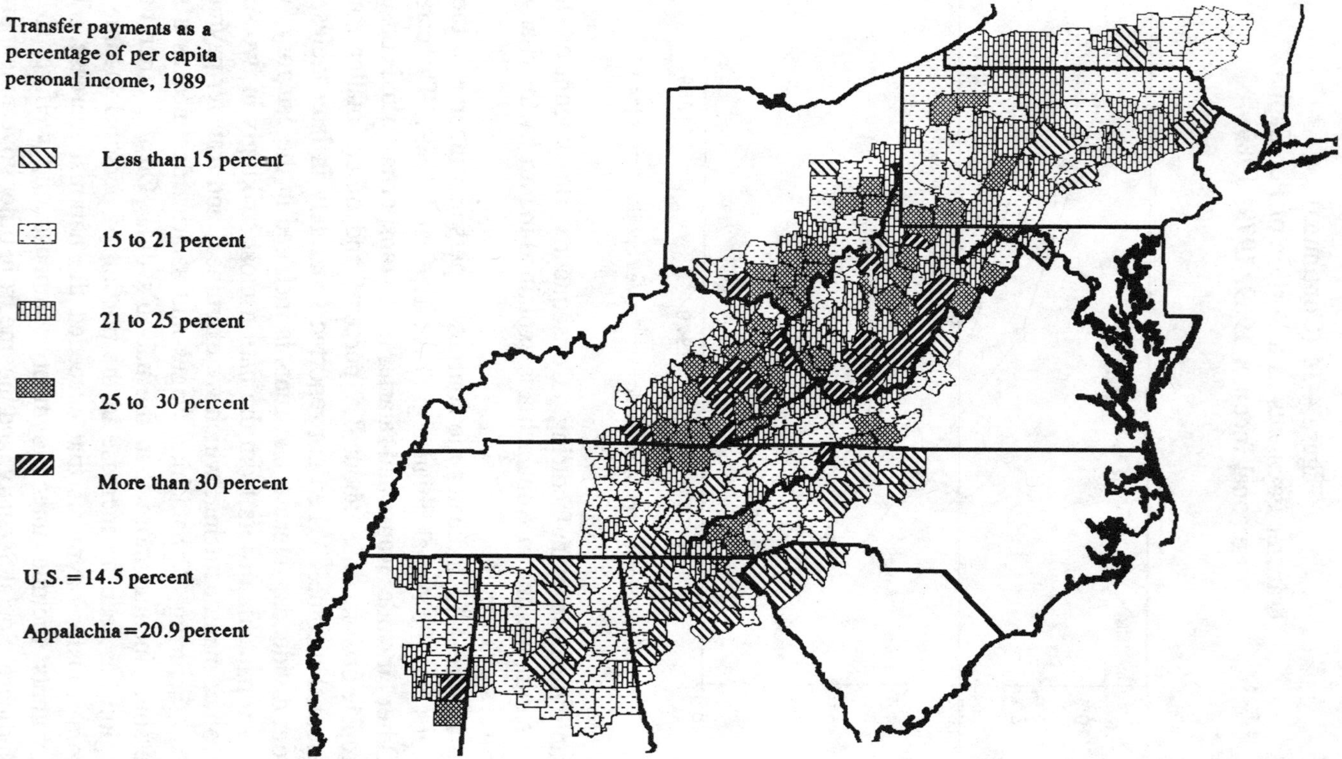

Prepared for Commission on Religion in Appalachia

Map 4-16

Rate of Change in Transfer Payments as a Portion of Per Capita Personal Income, 1979 to 1989

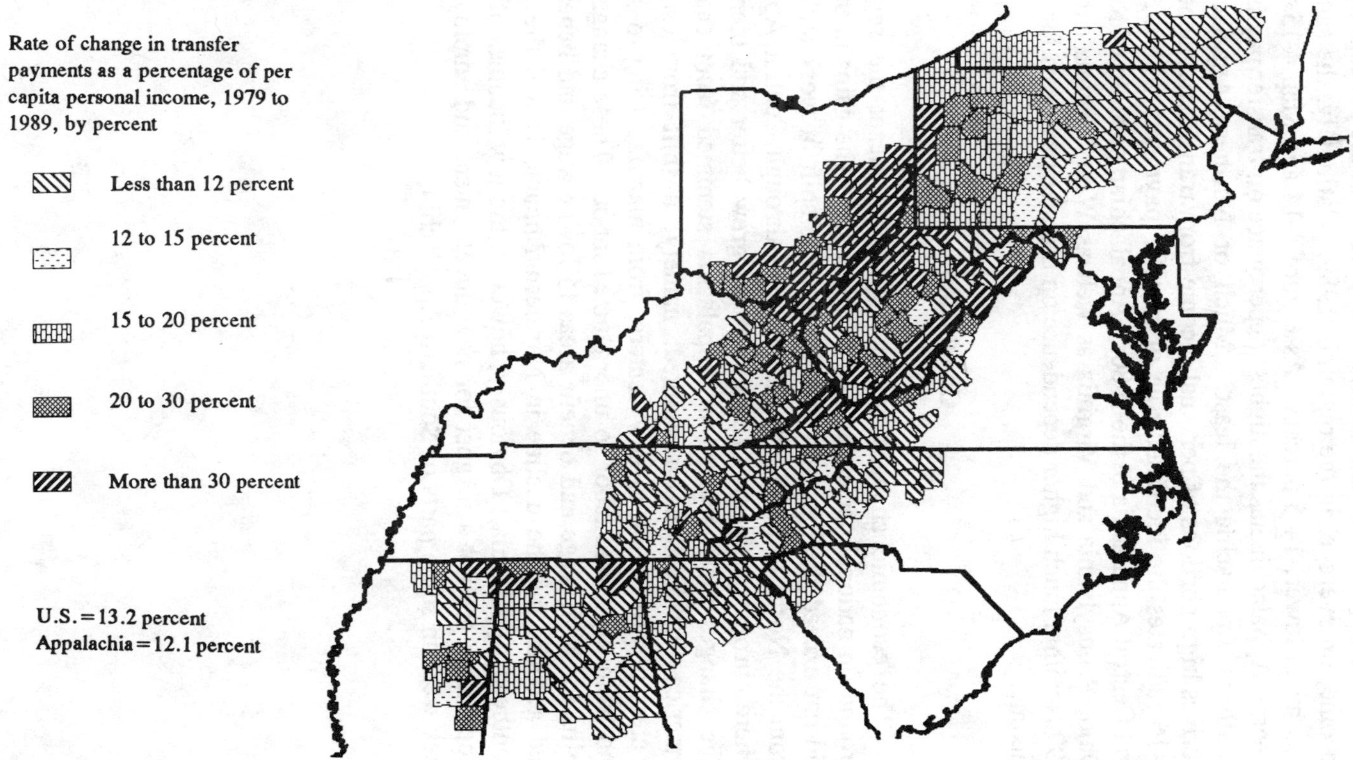

Prepared for Commission on Religion in Appalachia

Transfer payments contributed 20.9 percent of the per capita personal income, on average, in the region in 1989. Nationally, the same figure was much lower, 14.5 percent. As Figure 4-14 and Map 4-15 indicate, Central Appalachia has the highest dependence on transfer payments and Southern Appalachia the least. Much of Northern Appalachia also derives high portions of personal income from transfer payments. Map 4-16 indicates the increased role of transfer payments within Northern and Central Appalachia in the 1980s. Appalachian portions of Kentucky, Ohio, Pennsylvania and Virginia as well as West Virginia entered the 1990s with a much higher dependence on transfer payments for personal income.

Conclusion

The economic changes within Appalachia meant the region lost ground on national per capita personal income. The gains in the South did not exceed the losses in the North. The shift of work and income from the North to the South did not pass through Central Appalachia where chronic problems of low incomes grew better and then worse. The changes that occurred in Appalachia stemmed from changes in America that Section I recounted: namely, a shift from established centers of production to new centers, from manufacturing to services, and from organized labor to unorganized labor. These changes meant shifts for high wage and benefit areas to lower wage and benefit areas and account for the decline in Northern Appalachia and the gains in Southern Appalachia. Obviously, however, the low incomes of Central Appalachia are not a magnet for new development and employment as they were in some parts of Southern Appalachia.

Chapter 5

Population and Work Force

The amount of work and its compensation changed the economic and social factors that produce and sustain people in community in Appalachia. People came to areas of high employment and increasing incomes and left areas of low employment and decreasing incomes. Having already traced the changes in income and work, this chapter discusses the consequences of those changes for people. It examines the changes in population including the increased participation of women within the region. Then, the chapter examines changes in the labor force.

Population

Population growth was far slower in Appalachia than in the nation as a whole between 1970 and 1990 and especially between 1980 and 1990. Within the region people left Northern and Central Appalachia, areas of declining work and income and increasing poverty. Some of those people joined others moving to areas in Southern Appalachia where employment and income were increasing and providing alternatives to poverty. West Virginia's population declined by a staggering 8 percent in the 1980s while the nation's population increased 9.6 percent. The population of Appalachian Virginia declined in the 1980s also, by 5.8 percent. Rounding out these declines in Central Appalachia, Eastern Kentucky counties dropped 2.9 percent of their total population in the 1980s. Over the decade of the 1980s, Central Appalachia lost almost 5 percent of its population overall and slipped to approximately two million people.

Population loss occurred in Northern Appalachia as well, 3.1 percent, during the 1980s. Appalachian Pennsylvania lost 3.8 percent of its population, Appalachian New York gained a slight .5 percent, while Appalachian Ohio lost population slightly, .2 percent. Even with these changes, Northern Appalachia remains the most populous subregion, with just under half of Appalachia's total population. Likewise, despite population loss Pennsylvania still contains the largest portion of Appalachia's population, approximately 5.8 million people. The metropolitan counties of Northern Appalachia lost population at a higher rate than the rural counties, and the population is about evenly split between metropolitan and rural counties in Northern Appalachia. Table 5-1 and Figure 5-2 provide the populations of Appalachia, its subregions, and changes that have occurred since 1970.

Economic growth brought more people to Southern Appalachia but at a rate slower than the nation's growth with the singular exception of Appalachian Georgia. These counties' population increased by 36.6 percent in the 1980s. The population increase for Appalachian Georgia in the 1980s, 404,100 people, exceeded the population increase for all of Appalachia, 334,700. Gwinnett County alone accounts for more than 50 percent of the population increase of the 1980s in the entire Appalachian region. It grew by 186,100 people, or 111.6 percent. Map 5-3 portrays the population changes in the region.

Southern Appalachia's population grew 10.2 percent, led by the Atlanta area, and reached approximately 8.8 million people. Appalachian South Carolina also exceeded the nation's rate of population growth with its increase of 12 percent. All the other Southern Appalachian states saw population increases higher than the region's but less than the nation's: Alabama 4.1 percent; Mississippi 2.4 percent; North Carolina 7.3 percent; and Tennessee 3.5 percent. The population of the metropolitan counties in Southern Appalachia grew slightly faster than that of rural counties and accounts for the regional increase in metropolitan counties.

The percentage of African Americans grew in Northern Appalachia, especially in Pennsylvania and Allegheny County, and Pittsburgh where African Americans make up 11.2 percent of the population. This increase occurred, in part, because many white residents left Pittsburgh and not because African Americans came to this portion of Appalachia. Similarly, the African-American portion of Southern Appalachia's population declined because more whites than blacks moved to the region in the 1980s. Alabama, Mississippi, and South Carolina still lead the region in the African-American percentage of population but in each state the percentage has declined slightly since 1970. Table 5-4, Figure 5-5 and Maps 5-6 and 5-7 indicate the percentage of the population that is African American, and the location and concentration of African Americans.

More African Americans live in metropolitan counties than in rural counties. The number of African Americans in Central Appalachia is extremely small, hovering at 2 percent. In Southern Appalachia African Americans make up 13 percent of the population. Map 5-6 illustrates the very low percentages of African Americans in some Appalachian

Table 5-1
Changes in Population of Appalachia
1970 to 1990

	1970	1980	1990	Rate of Change 1980-90	Rate of Change 1970-90
United States	203212877	226545805	248709873	9.78%	22.39%
Appalachia	18346829	20379597	20660868	1.38%	12.61%
Northern	9841421	10236294	9917942	-3.11%	0.78%
Central	1744107	2115118	2011159	-4.92%	15.31%
Southern	6761301	8028185	8731767	8.76%	29.14%
Metro Counties	9052747	9707649	9932429	2.32%	9.72%
Northern	5405324	5393213	5134591	-4.80%	-5.01%
Central	169958	190313	185638	-2.46%	9.23%
Southern	3477465	4124123	4612200	11.83%	32.63%
Rural Counties	9294082	10671948	10728439	0.53%	15.43%
Northern	4436097	4843081	4783351	-1.23%	7.83%
Central	1574149	1924805	1825521	-5.16%	15.97%
Southern	3283836	3904062	4119567	5.52%	25.45%

Source: U.S. Bureau of the Census.

Figure 5-2
Changes in the Population of Appalachia, 1970 to 1990

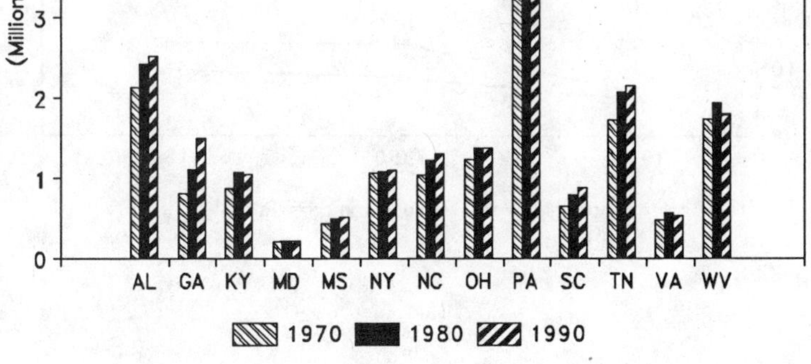

Figure 5-2 (Continued)
Changes in the Population of Appalachia, 1970 to 1990

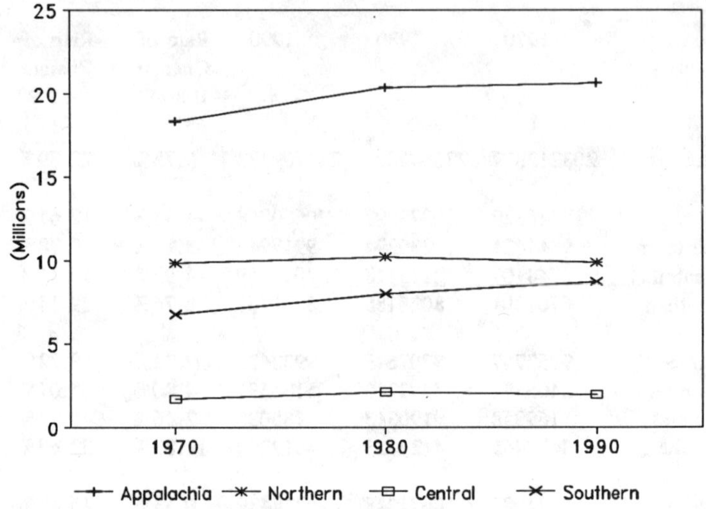

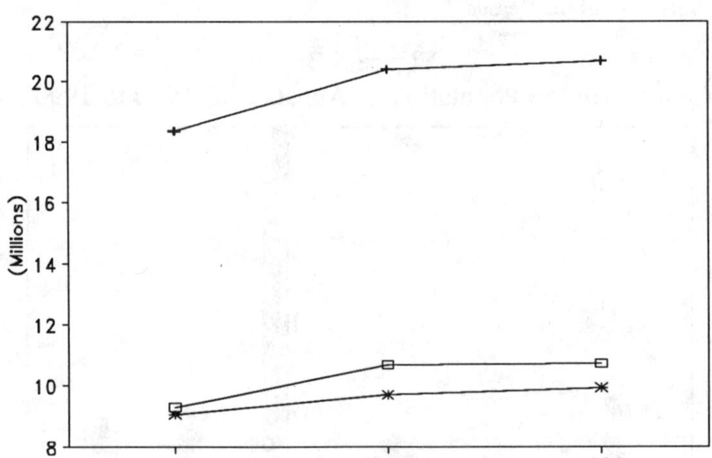

Map 5-3
Changes in the Population of Appalachian Counties, 1970 to 1990

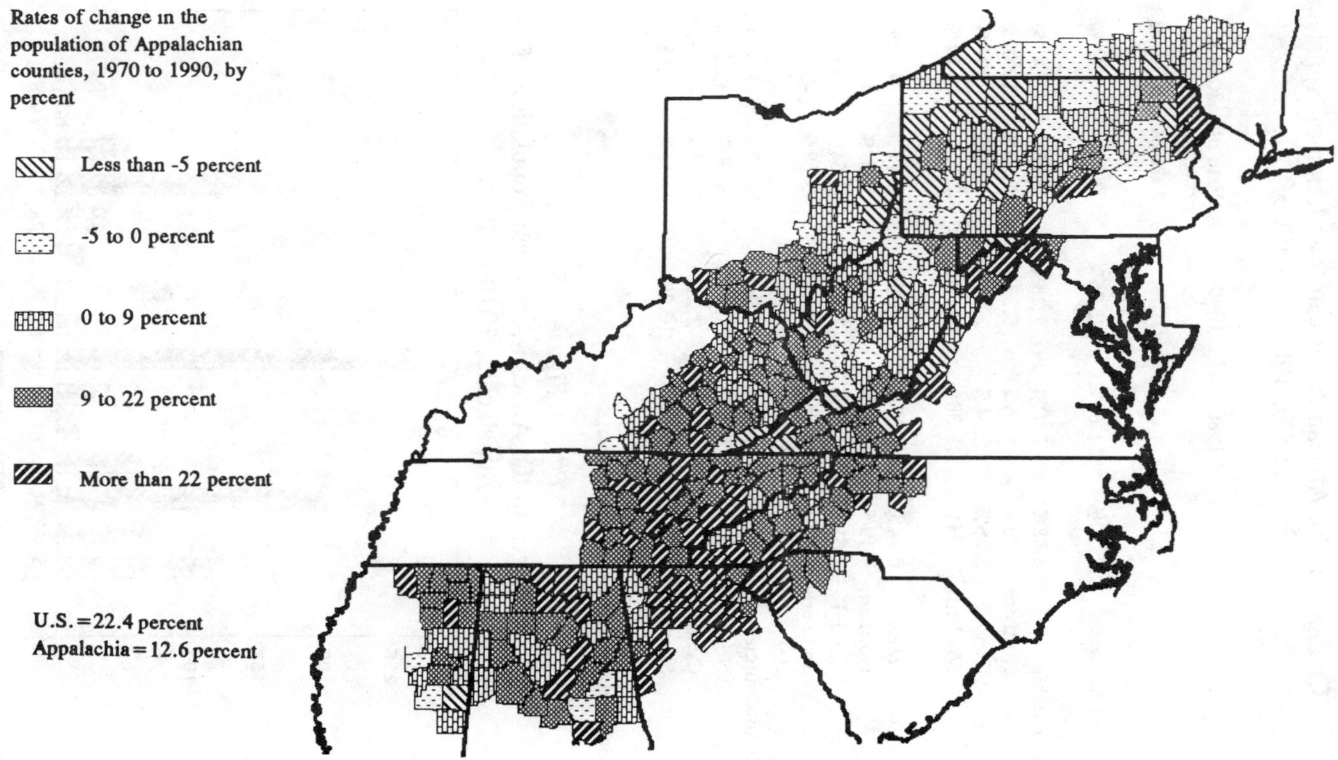

Prepared for Commission on Religion in Appalachia

Table 5-4
Changes in the African-American Population of Appalachia 1970, 1980, and 1990

	1970	1980	1990	Rate of Change 1980-90	Rate of Change 1970-90
United States	11.10%	11.69%	12.06%	3.14%	8.65%
Appalachia	6.88%	7.02%	7.25%	3.28%	5.47%
Northern	3.03%	3.16%	3.33%	5.59%	10.07%
Central	2.26%	2.34%	2.21%	-5.66%	-2.19%
Southern	13.84%	13.38%	13.00%	-2.83%	-6.04%
Metro Counties	8.84%	9.27%	9.65%	4.11%	9.22%
Northern	4.19%	4.43%	4.74%	7.07%	13.12%
Central	2.51%	2.25%	2.17%	-3.54%	-13.49%
Southern	16.27%	15.85%	15.33%	-3.28%	-5.74%
Rural Counties	4.97%	4.97%	5.04%	1.37%	1.37%
Northern	1.63%	1.76%	1.83%	4.06%	12.21%
Central	2.24%	2.35%	2.21%	-5.83%	-1.10%
Southern	11.14%	10.62%	10.28%	-3.14%	-7.68%

Source: U.S. Bureau of the Census.

Figure 5-5
Changes in the African-American Population of Appalachia, 1970 to 1990

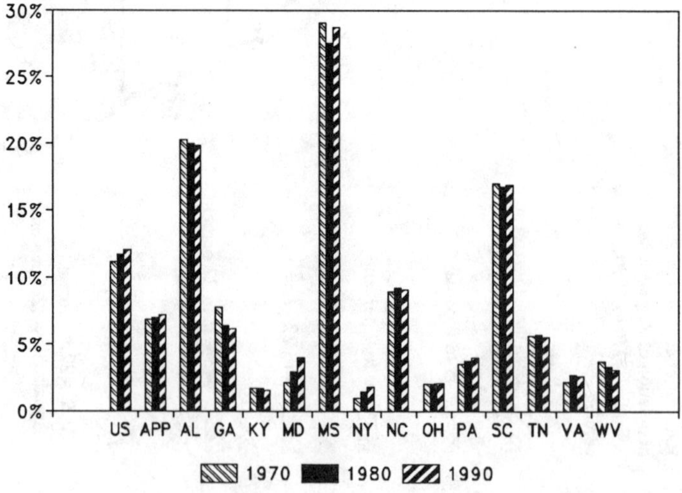

Figure 5-5 (Continued)
Changes in the African-American Population of Appalachia, 1970 to 1990

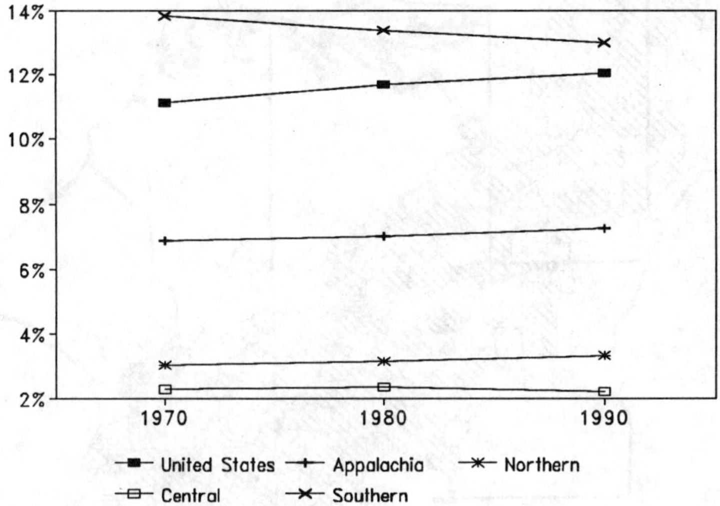

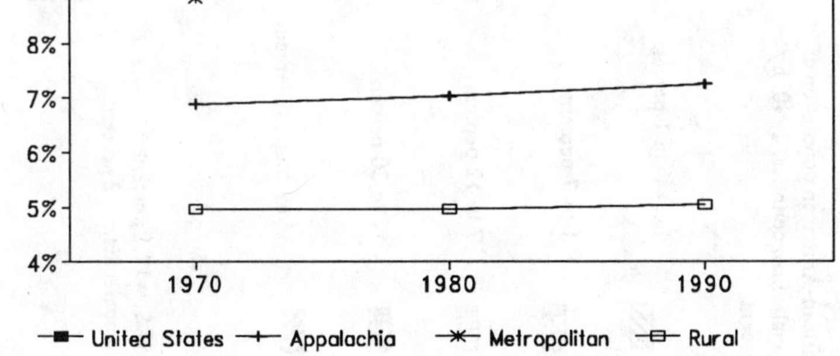

Map 5-6
African-American Population of Appalachian Counties, 1990

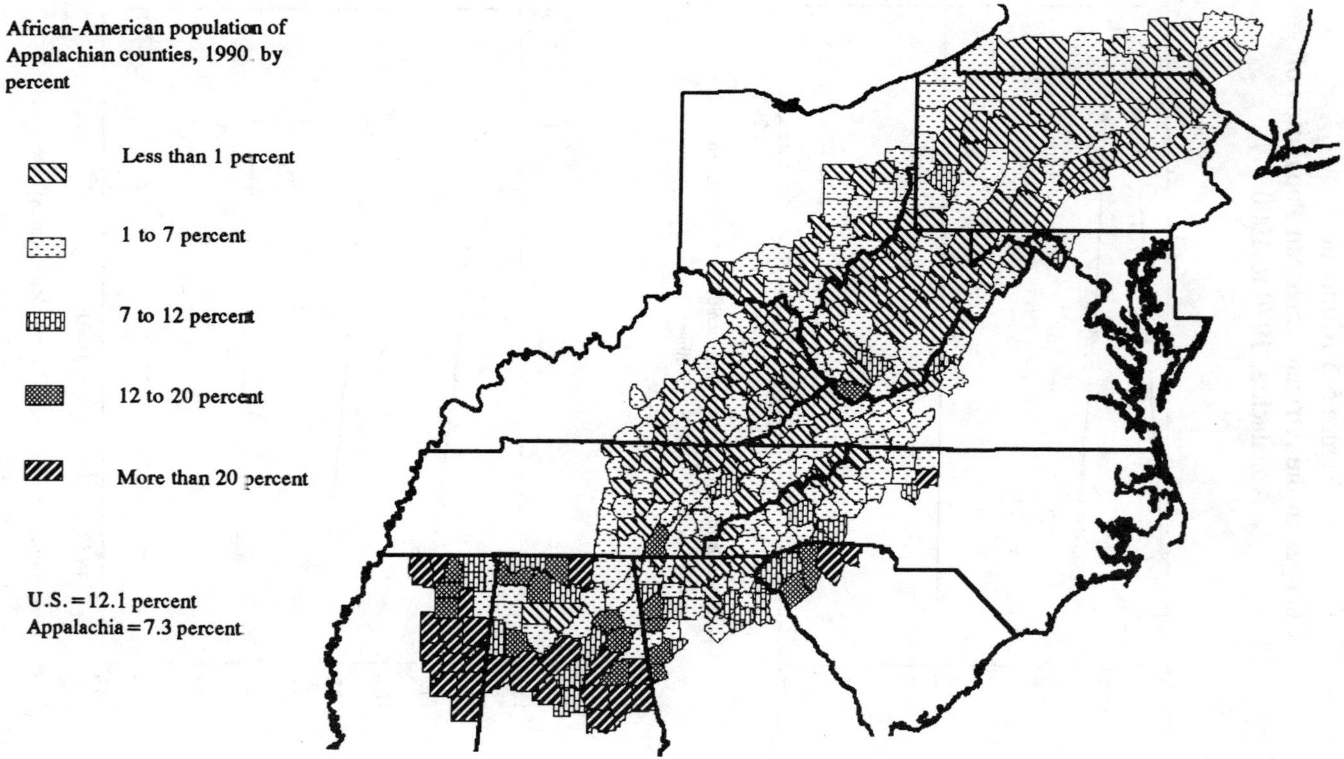

Prepared for Commission on Religion in Appalachia

Map 5-7
Changes in the African-American Population of Appalachian Counties, 1970 to 1990

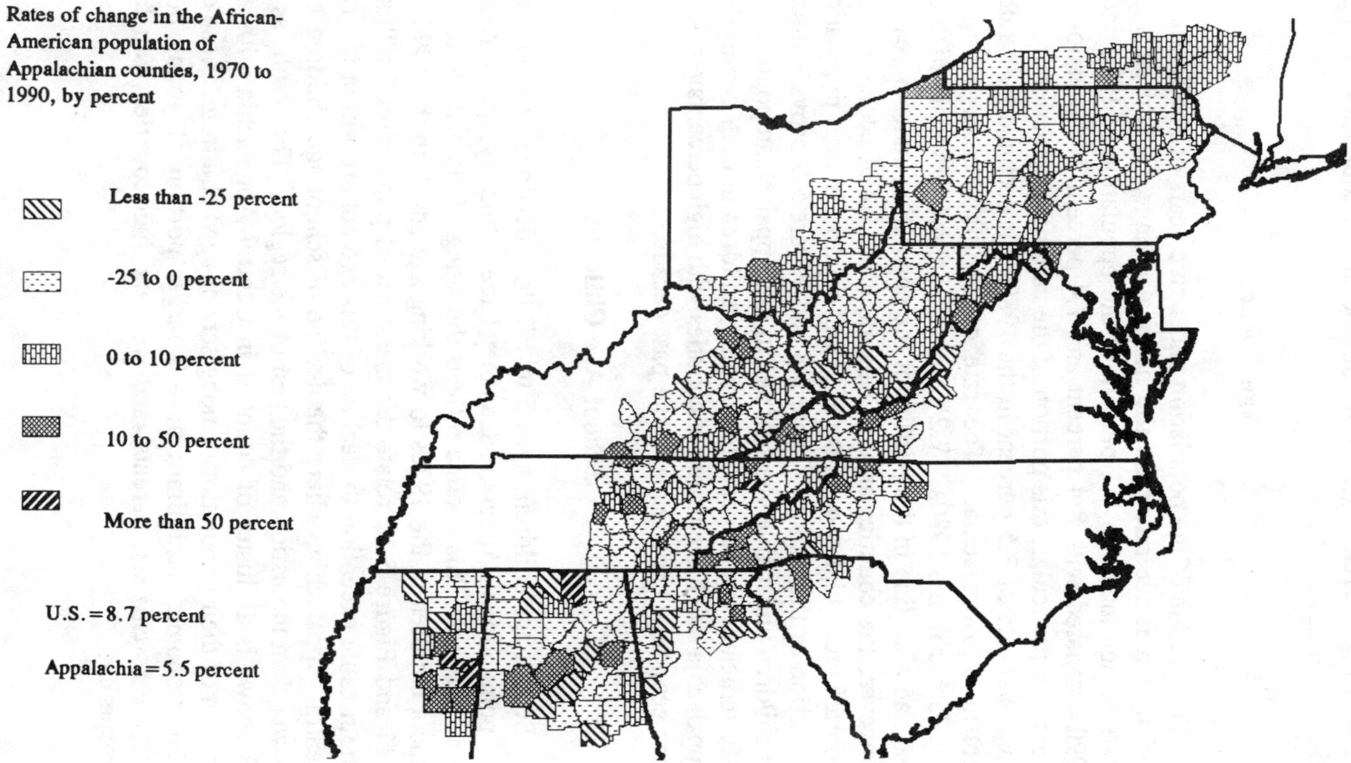

Prepared for Commission on Religion in Appalachia

subregions, counties of New York, Pennsylvania and West Virginia and the very high percentages in the Southernmost counties of Appalachian Mississippi and Alabama.

Age Cohorts

The portion of the population under five years of age declined in the region at a faster rate than the national change. Children under five years of age made up 8.1 percent of the population in 1970 and 6.5 in 1990 compared with 8.4 percent and 7.4 percent in the nation in these years. In particular, this portion of the national population increased by a national rate of 2.5 percent in the 1980s but declined by a rate of 5.9 percent in Appalachia. The rate of decline was largest in Central Appalachia in the 1980s, 17.2 percent. Southern Appalachian counties also had a decline in the portion of the population under 5 years of age. However, the counties around Atlanta, a cluster of economic strength, reported much higher portions of young children in their populations than the nation or the region. Table 5-8 and Figure 5-9 provide information on children under five years of age in the Appalachian population. Map 5-10 indicates the percentage of young children in each county. Central Appalachia still has clusters of counties with high percentages despite the poor economic experience of the past decade.

School Age Children

School age children, ages 5 to 17, have declined as a percentage of the population in Appalachia, as they have nationally, and in roughly the same portions. This decline reflects the aging of the baby boomers from school children in the 1970s to working age adults in the 1990s. Table 5-11 and Figure 5-12 relate the measures of population for this group. The notable exception to decline of this age cohort within the region is Central Appalachia, where the decline of school-age children has been slower than the nation and the rest of the region. The result, as Map 5-13 shows is a cluster of counties in Central Appalachia with a higher portion of their populations among school-aged children. Those counties with economic hard times have a larger portion of young people to prepare as citizens, parents, and workers than counties with far more prosperity.

Table 5-8
Children Under Five Years of Age as a Portion of the Population of Appalachia, 1970, 1980, and 1990

	1970	1980	1990	Rate of Change 1980-90	Rate of Change 1970-90
United States	8.40%	7.20%	7.38%	2.50%	-12.14%
Appalachia	8.14%	6.93%	6.52%	-5.86%	-19.90%
Northern	7.88%	6.68%	6.41%	-4.02%	-18.73%
Central	8.38%	7.62%	6.31%	-17.21%	-24.68%
Southern	8.46%	7.06%	6.70%	-5.09%	-20.76%
Metro Counties	7.95%	6.63%	6.59%	-0.57%	-17.06%
Northern	7.68%	6.35%	6.35%	-0.01%	-17.33%
Central	8.68%	7.32%	6.00%	-18.04%	-30.93%
Southern	8.33%	6.97%	6.88%	-1.21%	-17.40%
Rural	8.32%	7.19%	6.45%	-10.31%	-22.49%
Northern	8.13%	7.03%	6.47%	-8.03%	-20.40%
Central	8.35%	7.65%	6.34%	-17.14%	-24.13%
Southern	8.59%	7.16%	6.49%	-9.40%	-24.48%

Source: U.S. Bureau of the Census.

Figure 5-9
Children Under Five Years of Age as a Portion of the Population of Appalachia, 1970 to 1990

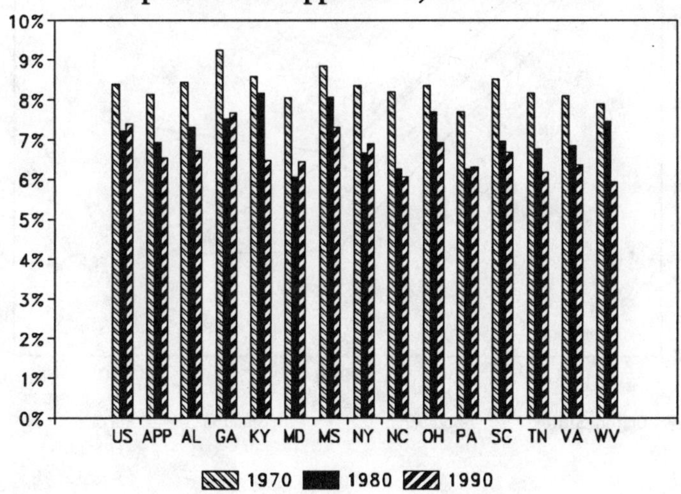

Figure 5-9 (Continued)
Children Under Five Years of Age as a Portion of the Population of Appalachia, 1970 to 1990

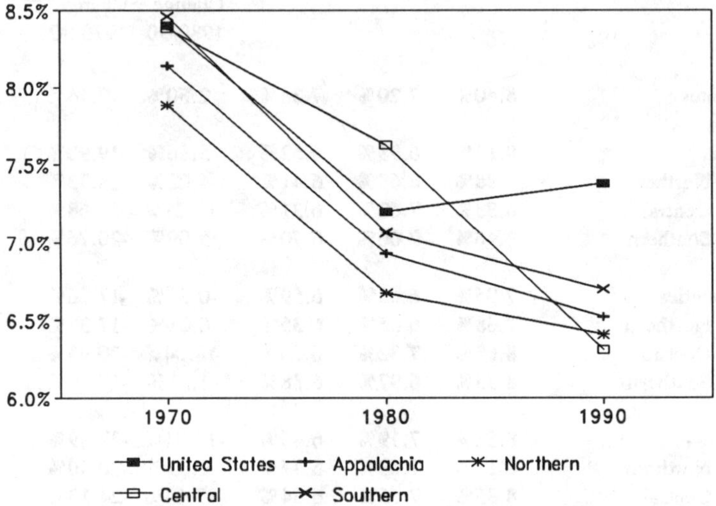

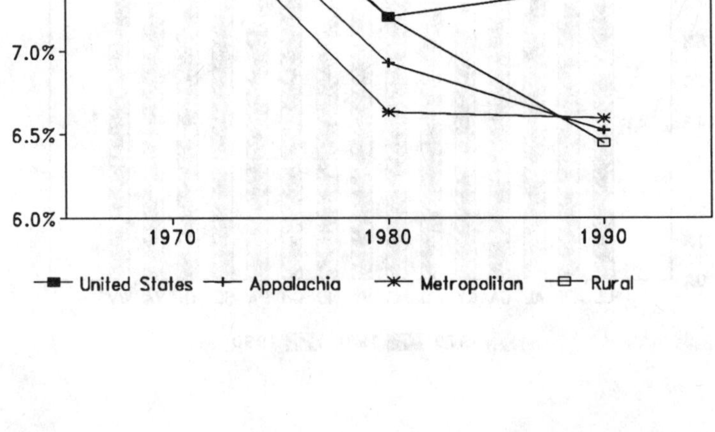

Map 5-10
Children Under Five in Appalachia, 1990

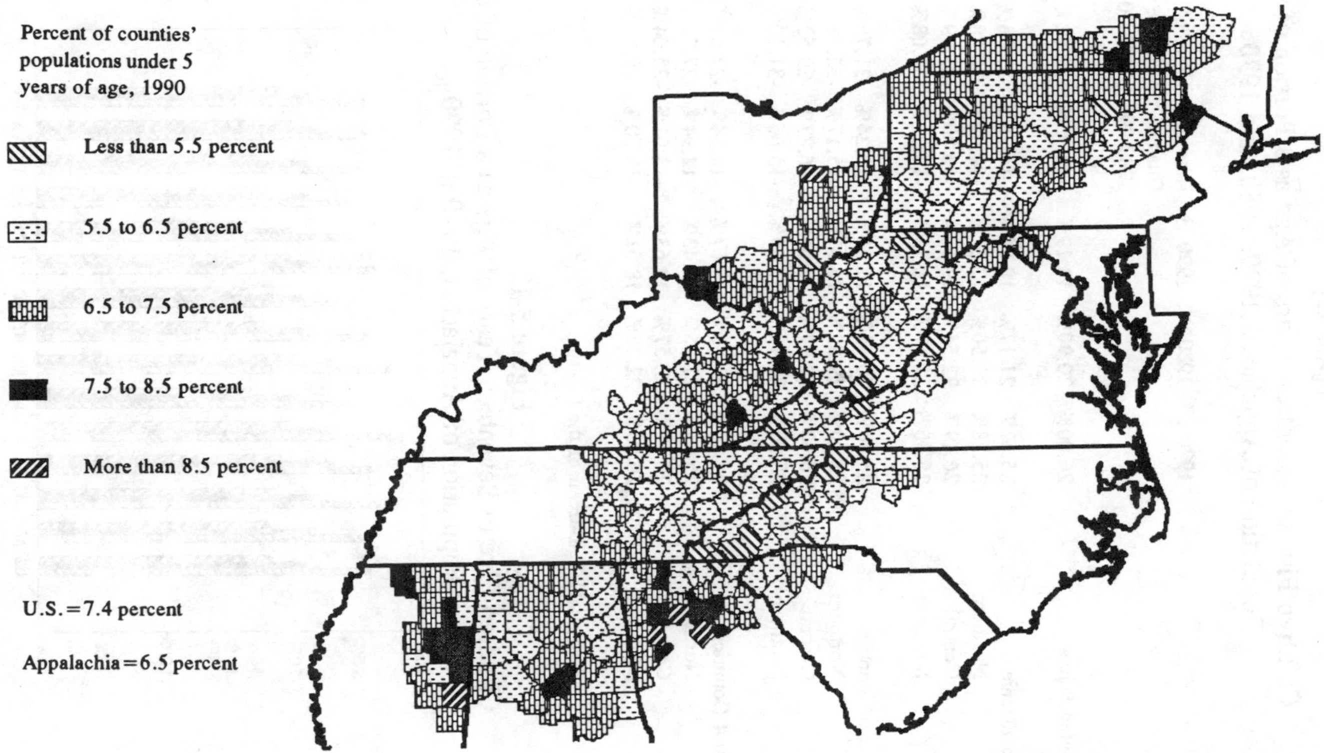

Prepared for Commission on Religion in Appalachia

Table 5-11
Children Five to Seventeen Years of Age as a Portion of the Population of Appalachia, 1970, 1980, and 1990

	1970	1980	1990	Rate of Change 1980-90	Rate of Change 1970-90
United States	26.00%	20.90%	18.19%	-12.95%	-30.02%
Appalachia	25.62%	21.17%	18.04%	-14.78%	-29.58%
Northern	25.28%	20.50%	17.62%	-14.02%	-30.28%
Central	26.19%	22.54%	19.54%	-13.30%	-25.39%
Southern	25.96%	21.67%	18.15%	-16.21%	-30.08%
Metro Counties	25.43%	20.48%	17.36%	-15.24%	-31.75%
Northern	25.10%	19.89%	16.87%	-15.17%	-32.78%
Central	26.30%	22.27%	18.54%	-16.77%	-29.52%
Southern	25.90%	21.16%	17.85%	-15.66%	-31.10%
Rural Counties	25.80%	21.80%	18.67%	-14.34%	-27.62%
Northern	25.49%	21.16%	18.43%	-12.94%	-27.72%
Central	26.19%	22.57%	19.63%	-13.01%	-25.04%
Southern	26.03%	22.22%	18.51%	-16.70%	-28.89%

Source: U.S. Bureau of the Census.

Figure 5-12
Children Five to Seventeen Years of Age as a Portion of the Population of Appalachia, 1970 to 1990

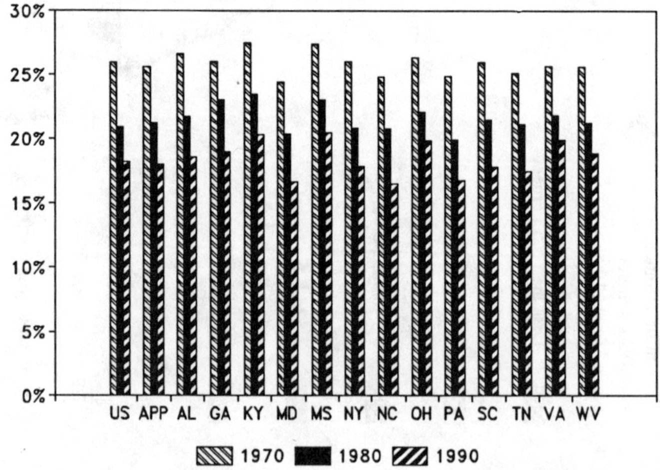

Figure 5-12 (Continued)
Children Five to Seventeen Years of Age as a Portion of the Population of Appalachia, 1970 to 1990

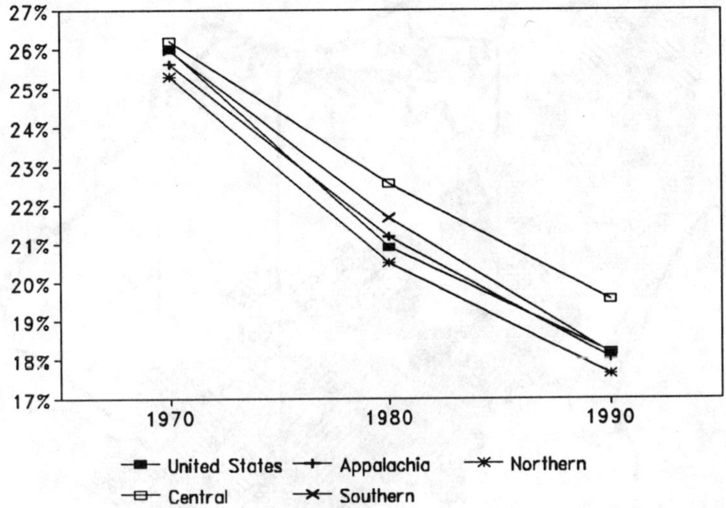

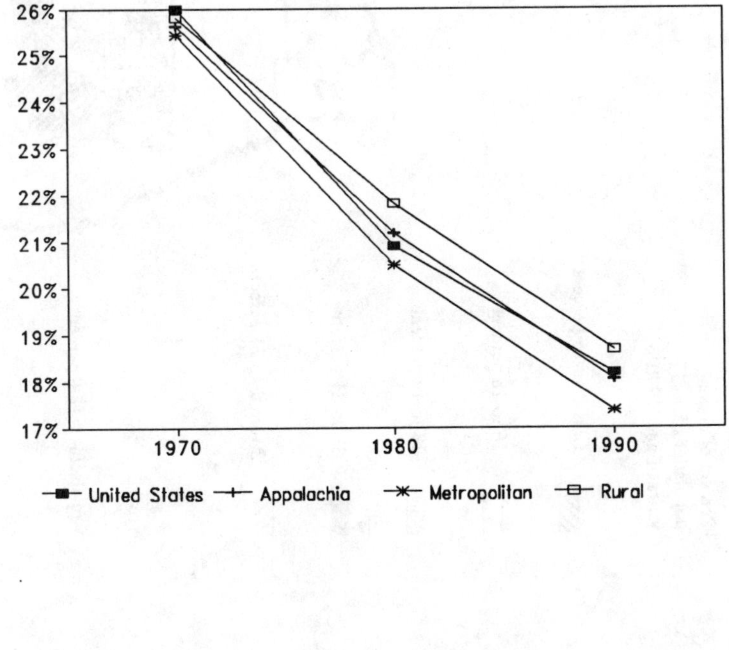

Map 5-13
Children Five to Seventeen in Appalachia, 1990

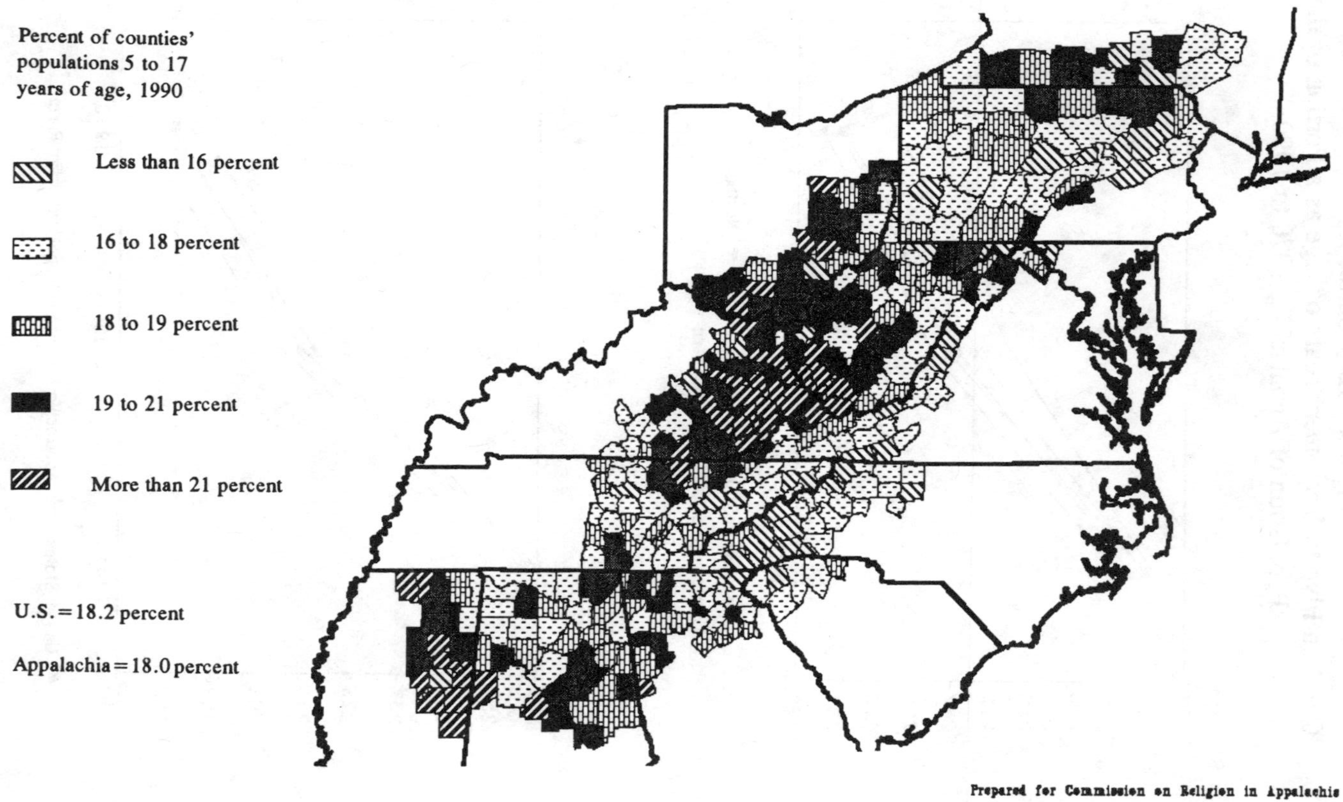

Adults Over 65 Years of Age

The portion of children in a population depends, obviously, on the portion of other age groups in the population. One reason for the significantly high portion of school-aged children in Central Appalachia is the changed portions of working age adults and adults over 65 years of age in the same counties. Population changes of the working age group may explain the changes in the population over 65 years of age that are reported in Table 5-14. Large numbers of working age people moved to Appalachian Georgia in the 1980s and reduced the portion of older adults evident in Figure 5-15. Working age adults moved from Northern Appalachia, especially Pennsylvania, during the 1980s and increased the portion of older adults also evident in Figure 5-15. Working age adults moved from Central Appalachia at earlier times, the 1940s and 1950s, and now leave a smaller portion of older population in Eastern Kentucky counties. A cluster of coal counties in Eastern Kentucky, West Virginia, and Tennessee has a dramatically smaller portion of the elderly. The earlier migration of working age people would explain both the portions of the population over 65 years of age in 1990 and the changes among other cohorts that occurred in the 1980s. The latter measures are portrayed in Map 5-16.

Northern Appalachia has a higher portion of the elderly in the population which is growing at a rate far faster than the nation's rate. This is especially true of metropolitan counties in Northern Appalachia where the rate of elderly increased by 50 percent from 1970 to 1990 and reached 16.5 percent of the total population. Appalachian Pennsylvania, Virginia, Maryland, and West Virginia have particularly high portions of the elderly. Appalachian Georgia has the lowest portion, about 10 percent.

Working Age Population

The modest differences in the distribution of working age population, 18 to 65, in Northern and Southern Appalachia in 1990 corresponds to the availability of incomes and work. As Table 5-17 and Figure 5-18 report, the percentage of working age population in Southern Appalachia, especially the metropolitan counties of Southern Appalachia, increased faster than the national increase and much faster than the entire region's increase. Conversely, the metropolitan counties of Northern Appalachia are the only counties in the region to have a decline in the percentage of

Table 5-14
Population Over 65 Years of Age in Appalachia 1970, 1980, and 1990

	1970	1980	1990	Rate of Change 1980-90	Rate of Change 1970-90
United States	9.90%	11.30%	12.56%	11.16%	26.88%
Appalachia	10.53%	12.08%	14.31%	18.47%	35.91%
Northern	11.20%	12.97%	15.72%	21.25%	40.34%
Central	10.76%	11.22%	13.40%	19.39%	24.52%
Southern	9.49%	11.18%	12.92%	15.61%	36.12%
Metro Counties	10.15%	11.95%	14.33%	19.92%	41.25%
Northern	10.92%	13.11%	16.46%	25.56%	50.63%
Central	8.99%	10.77%	14.11%	31.07%	56.96%
Southern	9.00%	10.50%	11.98%	14.10%	33.16%
Rural Counties	10.90%	12.20%	14.29%	17.19%	31.08%
Northern	11.54%	12.81%	14.94%	16.57%	29.39%
Central	10.95%	11.27%	13.33%	18.27%	21.69%
Southern	10.02%	11.89%	13.98%	17.53%	39.51%

Source: U.S. Bureau of the Census.

Figure 5-15
Population Over 65 Years of Age in Appalachia, 1970 to 1990

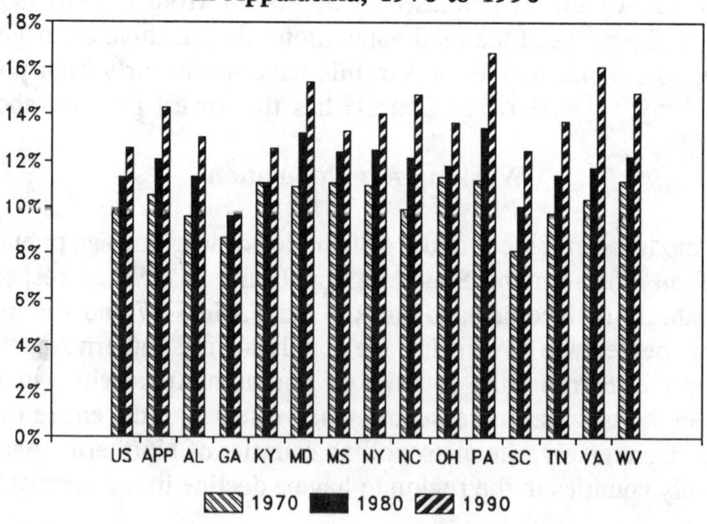

Figure 5-15 (Continued)
Population Over 65 Years of Age in Appalachia, 1970 to 1990

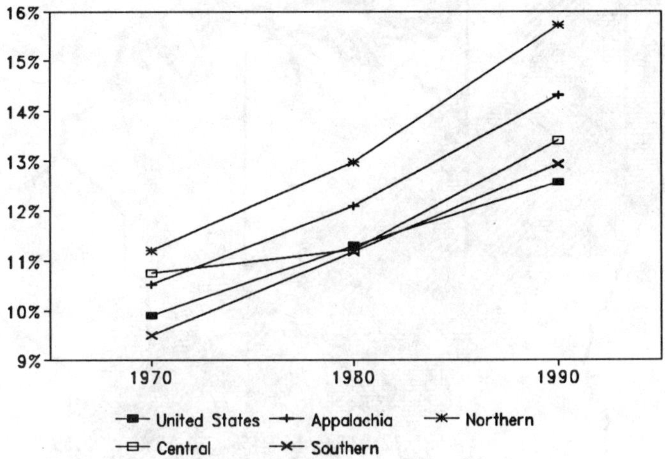

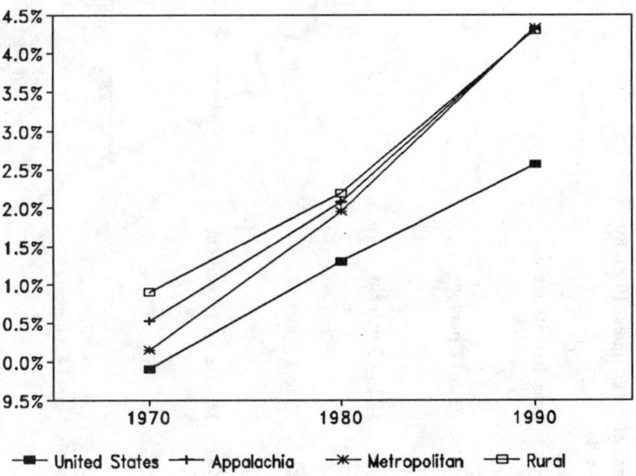

Map 5-16
Population Over Sixty-Five of Appalachian Counties, 1990

Population over sixty-five in Appalachian counties, 1990, by percent

- Less than 10 percent
- 10 to 12 percent
- 12 to 15 percent
- 15 to 17 percent
- More than 17 percent

U.S. = 12.6 percent
Appalachia = 14.3 percent

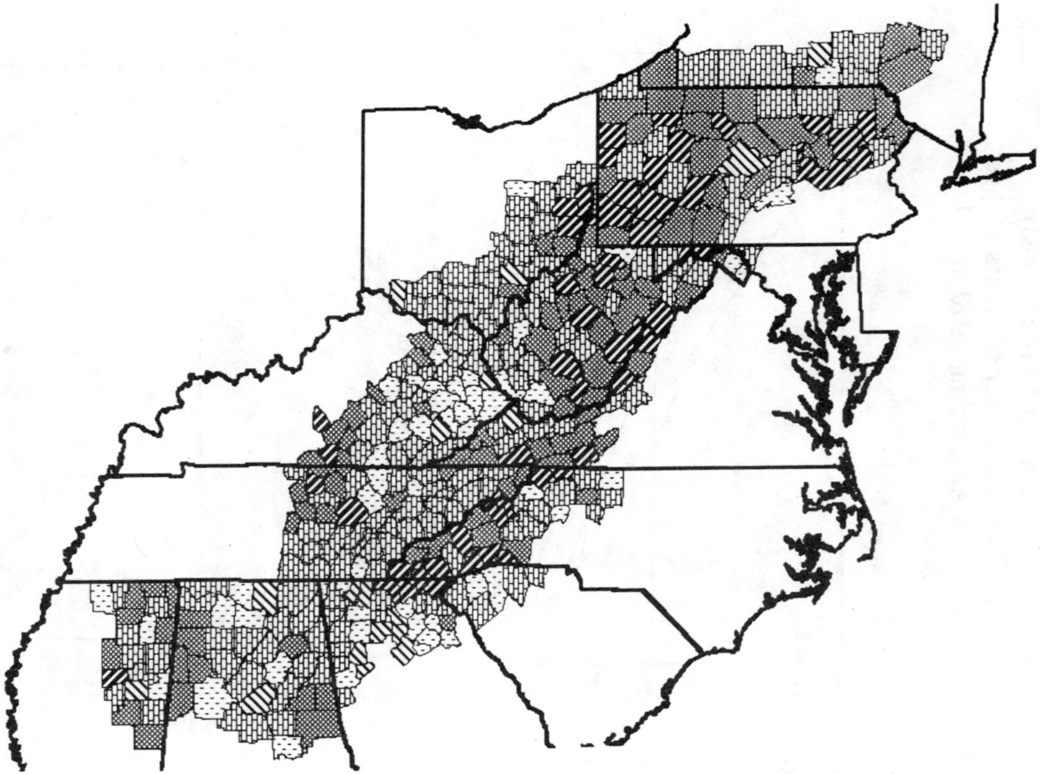

Prepared for Commission on Religion in Appalachia

Table 5-17
Working-Age Population in Appalachia
1970, 1980, and 1990

	1970	1980	1990	Rate of Change 1980-90	Rate of Change 1970-90
United States	55.70%	60.56%	61.87%	2.16%	11.08%
Appalachia	55.71%	59.82%	61.40%	2.64%	10.22%
Northern	55.67%	59.92%	60.30%	0.63%	8.31%
Central	54.51%	58.26%	61.08%	4.84%	12.05%
Southern	56.09%	60.12%	62.73%	4.34%	11.83%
Metro Counties	56.48%	60.94%	61.91%	1.59%	9.61%
Northern	56.30%	60.65%	60.34%	-0.52%	7.17%
Central	55.31%	59.78%	61.38%	2.68%	10.98%
Southern	56.79%	61.36%	63.68%	3.79%	12.14%
Rural Counties	54.97%	58.81%	60.93%	3.60%	10.84%
Northern	54.92%	59.12%	60.26%	1.93%	9.72%
Central	54.44%	58.14%	61.05%	5.00%	12.14%
Southern	55.30%	58.75%	61.66%	4.95%	11.49%

Source: U.S. Bureau of the Census, *1990 Census of Population and Housing, STF-3a.*

Figure 5-18
Working-Age Population in Appalachia, 1970 to 1990

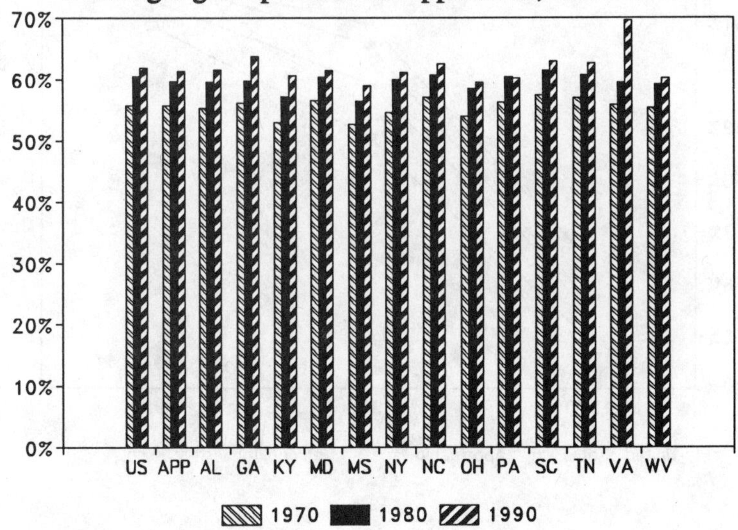

Figure 5-18 (Continued)
Working-Age Population in Appalachia, 1970 to 1990

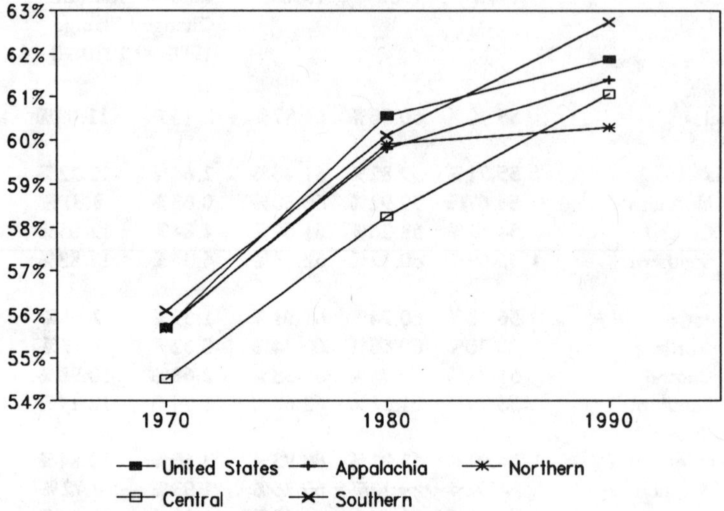

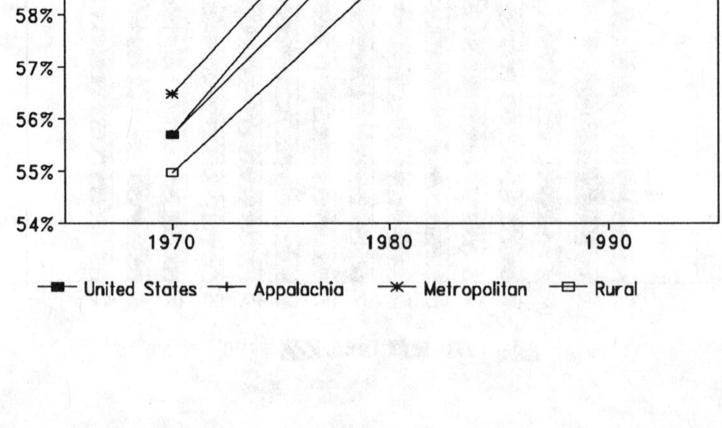

Map 5-19
Working-Age Population, 18 to 65, of Appalachian Counties, 1990

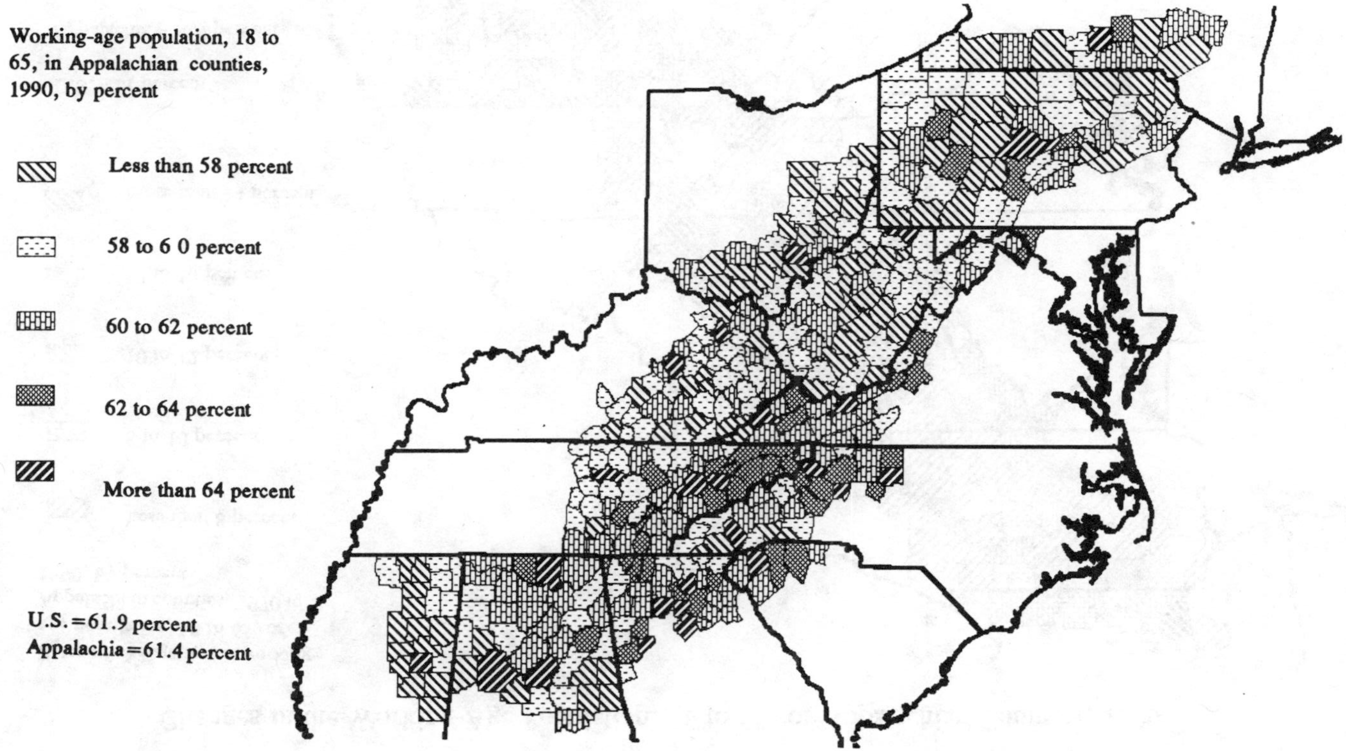

Prepared for Commission on Religion in Appalachia

Map 5-20
Changes in the Working-Age Population, 18 to 65, of Appalachian Counties, 1990

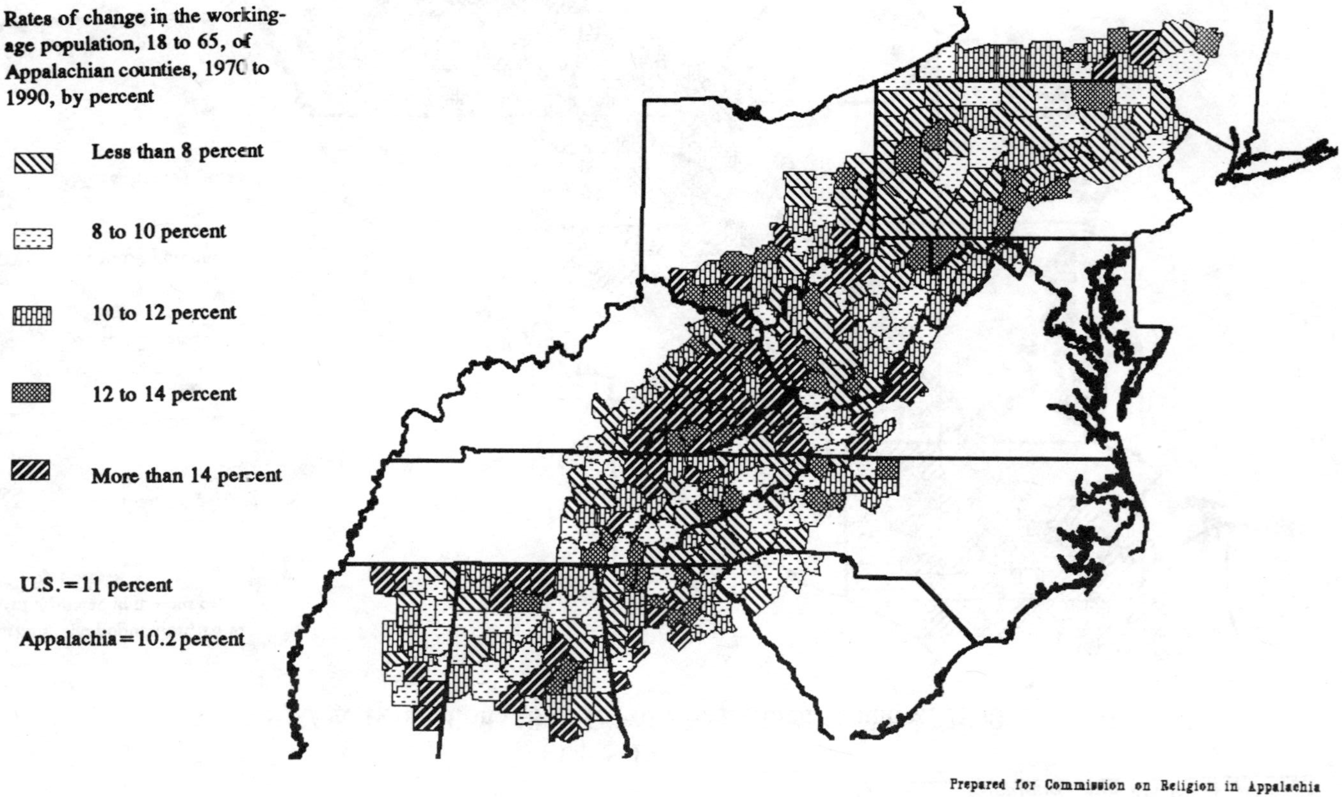

working age population in the 1980s. Central Appalachia had an increase in the portion of working age population since 1970. Although the portion of working age adults is larger, the population decline of about 5 percent meant the total of working age adults actually declined in the 1980s. Only Southern Appalachia had an absolute and relative increase in the working age population in the 1980s.

As Map 5-19 indicates, counties in Southern Appalachia report higher percentages of the working-age population than the nation as a whole. Northern and Central Appalachia report the highest number of counties with portions of working age population that are lower than the national average. We find working age adults where there is work: North and South Carolina, the Atlanta area, and the Huntsville area of Alabama. We find a smaller portion of working age adults in places where there are declining incomes and/or less work: Mississippi, portions of Eastern Kentucky, West Virginia, and much of Northern Appalachia. This is a changing picture that depends upon the availability of wage employment. Map 5-20 illustrates the changes in the working age population of Appalachia in the 1980s.

Work Force

Women have changed the labor force of Appalachia. Just as they have done nationally, women in Appalachia have increased their labor force participation in larger numbers. As Table 5-21 and Figure 5-22 report, this participation is still slightly lower in Appalachia than the nation except for Southern Appalachia. Women in both Northern and Central Appalachia increased their labor force participation at a higher rate than the nation since 1970. The rate of participation of women in the civilian labor force in Southern Appalachia was and remains highest among the subregions and slightly higher than the national rate. The rate of participation in Mississippi was and remains the highest in Appalachia. On the other hand, women increased their rate of participation fastest in Kentucky, Maryland, Ohio, Virginia, and West Virginia.

The economies which women in Appalachia have entered vary greatly. The increased participation in Southern Appalachia occurs in an economy with expanding employment and improving per capita and family income, although improvement is slower in Mississippi. In Central and Northern Appalachia women's increased participation occurs in a contracting economy with dwindling per capita and family income. The increase in Northern Appalachia may be due to fewer women than

Table 5-21
Women in the Work Force in Appalachia, 1970 to 1990

	1970	1980	1990	Rate of Change 1980-90	Rate of Change 1970-90
United States	38.10%	42.60%	45.40%	6.67%	19.16%
Appalachia	36.24%	40.63%	44.80%	10.24%	23.62%
Northern	35.20%	39.62%	44.31%	11.85%	25.88%
Central	33.76%	37.96%	43.01%	13.32%	27.39%
Southern	38.25%	42.51%	45.68%	7.46%	19.42%
Metro Counties	36.49%	41.20%	45.44%	10.31%	24.55%
Northern	35.48%	40.16%	44.98%	12.01%	26.78%
Central	30.37%	35.59%	42.13%	15.16%	38.71%
Southern	38.21%	42.65%	46.01%	7.87%	20.42%
Rural Counties	35.98%	40.08%	44.16%	10.16%	22.73%
Northern	34.84%	38.97%	43.55%	11.73%	25.00%
Central	34.08%	38.08%	43.09%	13.16%	26.43%
Southern	38.30%	42.34%	45.28%	6.93%	18.22%

Source: U.S. Bureau of the Census.

Figure 5-22
Women in the Work Force in Appalachia, 1970 to 1990

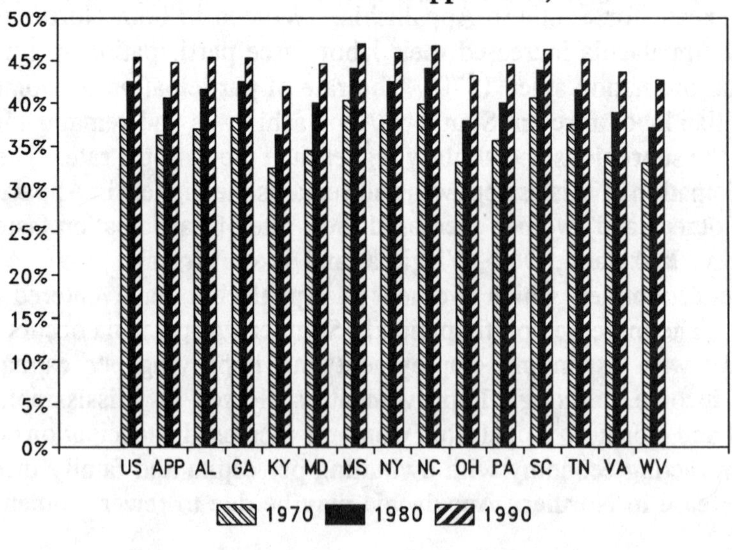

Figure 5-22 (Continued)
Women in the Work Force in Appalachia, 1970 to 1990

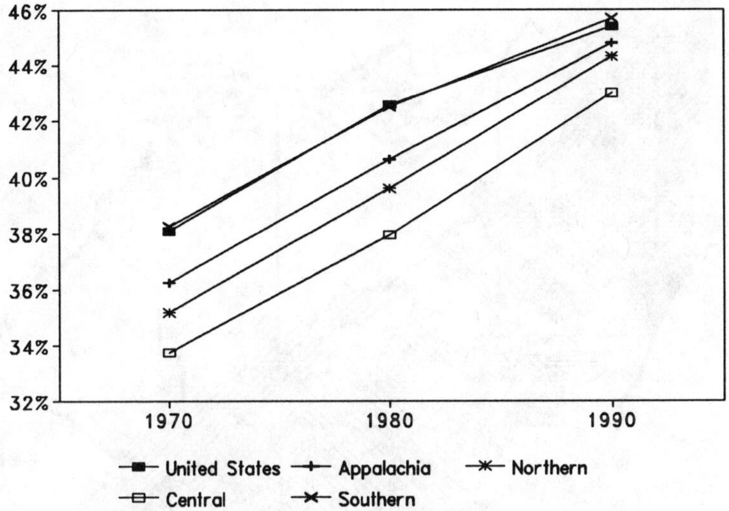

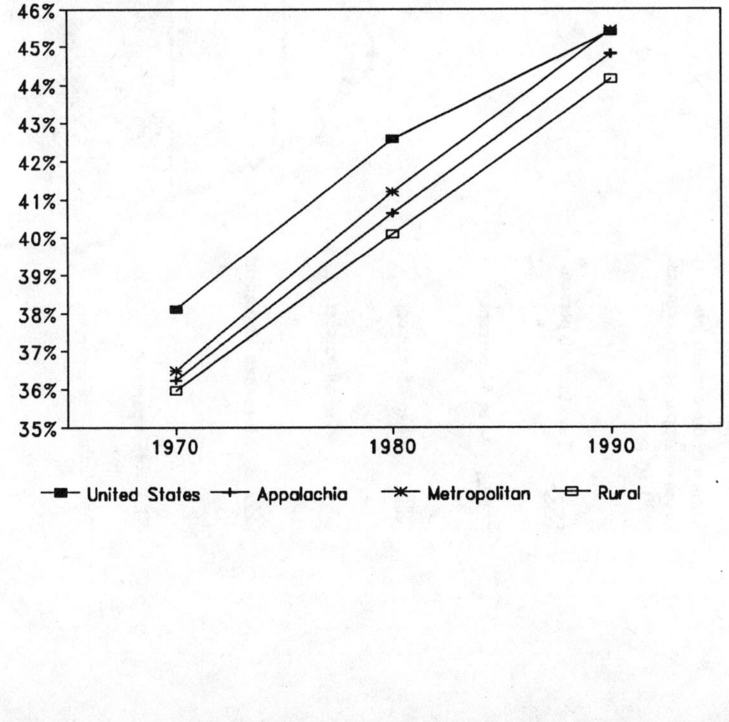

Map 5-23
Women in the Civilian Labor Forces of Appalachian Counties, 1990

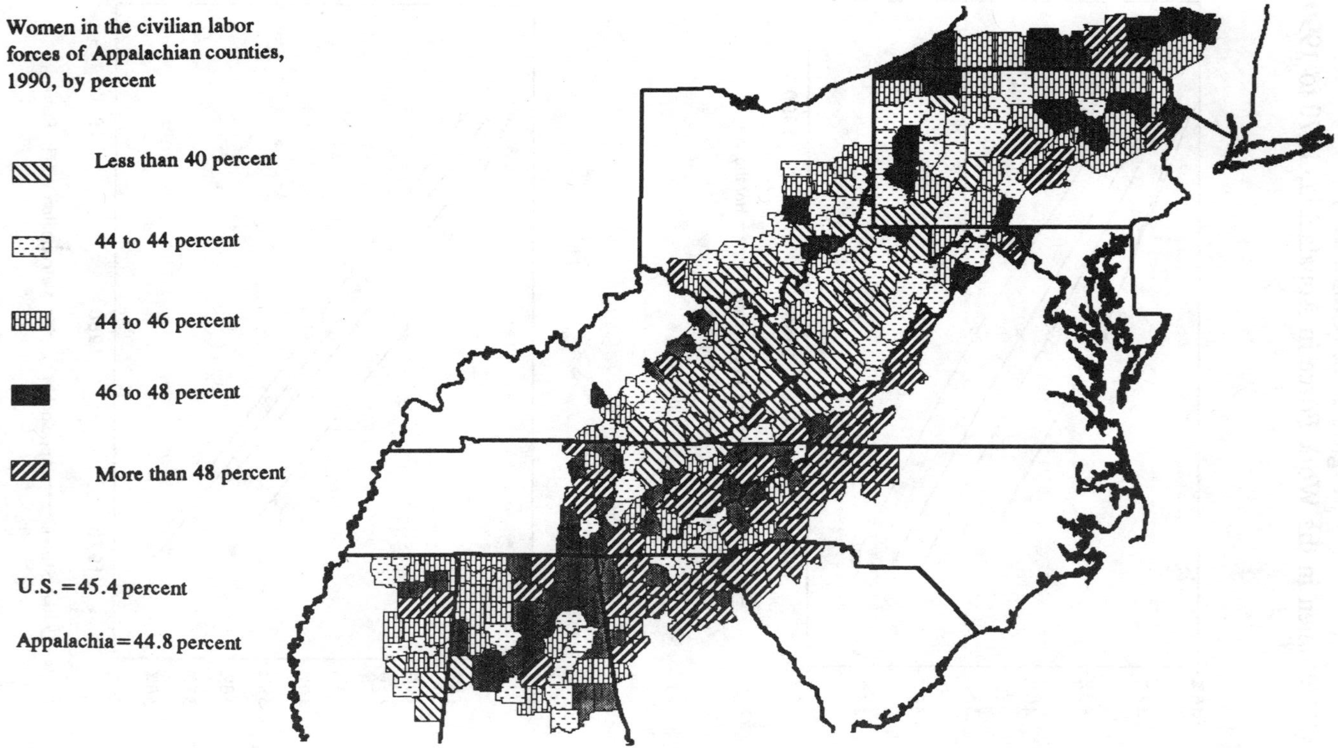

Prepared for Commission on Religion in Appalachia

Map 5-24
Changes in Women in Civilian Labor Force of Appalachian Counties, 1970 to 1990

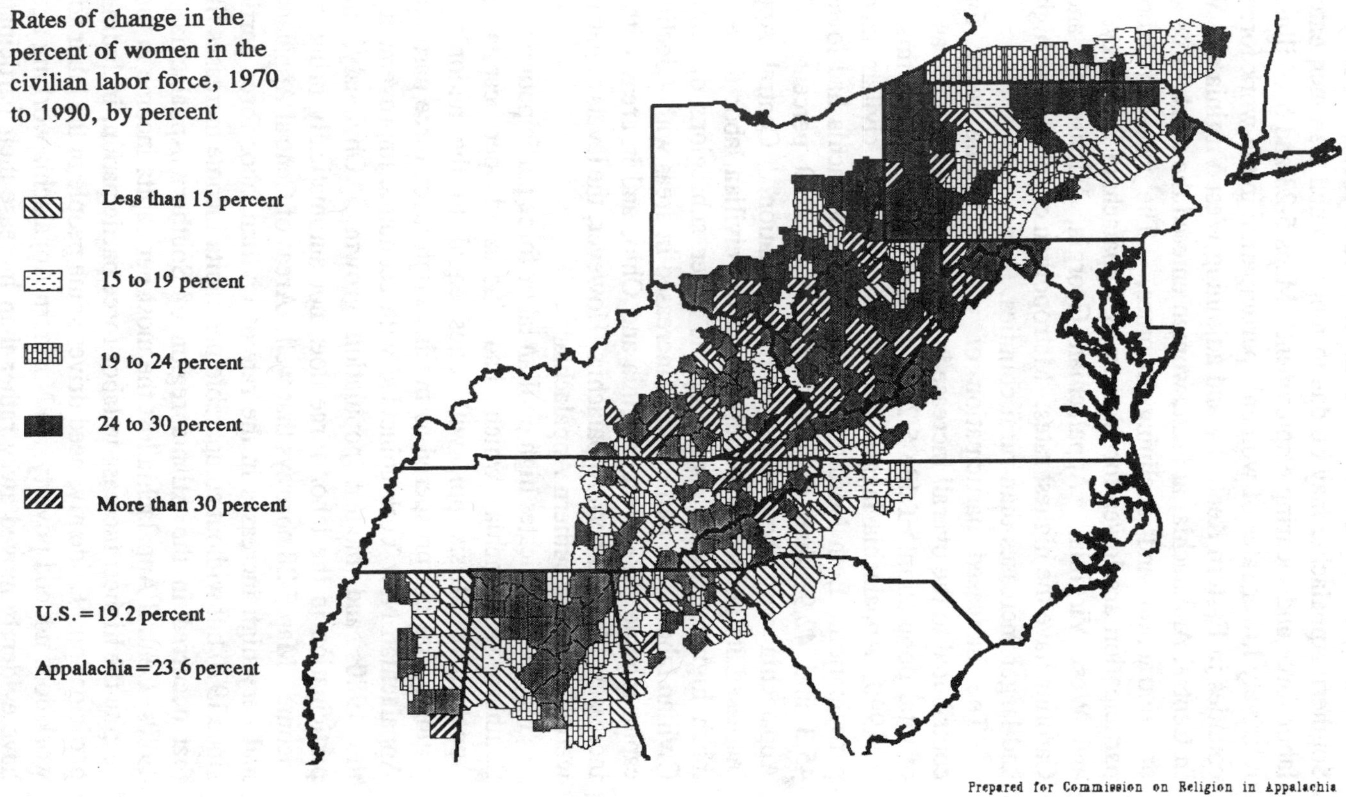

men losing their jobs in a contracting work force. The increase in Southern Appalachia may be due to more women than men entering the labor force and securing employment. Maps 5-23 and 5-24 illustrate the relatively lower rates of women's participation in the work force of coal counties in Eastern Kentucky and adjoining West Virginia and Virginia. In Central Appalachia, at least, women entered the work force at a time of contraction and declining incomes. The rates of labor force participation are lower for women in Appalachian Kentucky, Virginia and West Virginia. Appalachian Georgia, Mississippi, and South Carolina have the highest rates. Metropolitan counties have higher rates and larger increases than rural counties.

The increased participation of women in the work force has contributed to the overall increase in the civilian labor force as a percent of total population. Table 5-25 and Figure 5-26 present this measure. In 1990, Appalachia lagged behind the nation in civilian labor force participation. Both Northern and Central Appalachia had lower rates, 45.3 and 42.9, than the nation's rate of 46.9 percent. Southern Appalachia was about equal with the nation. Central Appalachia increased its portion of population in the civilian labor force at a rate much higher than the nation or the other subregions of Appalachia. Civilian labor force participation increased in areas with a decline in per capita income, like West Virginia and Ohio, and in areas with income increases, like Southern Appalachia. However, the levels of participation were higher in Southern Appalachia.

Map 5-27 indicates high civilian labor force participation in much of Southern Appalachia which had increased per capita income. Appalachian Mississippi, with rates equal to the nation's and the region's, has not prospered as much. High labor force participation in Appalachian New York coincided with economic improvement there in the 1980s and modest population growth. Obviously, increased participation in the labor force does not automatically bring increased income. Map 5-28 portrays that well. Areas of Central Appalachia have had very high increases in the rate of civilian labor force participation since 1970 but without comparable per capita income increases like those that occurred in the Atlanta region of Southern Appalachia. In the 1980s, Central Appalachia lost the most per capita income in the region despite the highest increase in labor force participation, including female participation. Evidently, need drives some people in the labor force, but work does not end poverty. In Northern Appalachia working age people have evidently moved away rather than increase their participation in a

Table 5-25
Civilian Labor Force as a Percentage of the Total Population of Appalachia, 1970 to 1990

	1970	1980	1990	Rate of Change 1980-90	Rate of Change 1970-90
United States	39.39%	46.11%	49.65%	7.68%	26.03%
Appalachia	37.35%	42.95%	46.87%	9.13%	25.47%
Northern	37.14%	42.52%	45.27%	6.46%	21.88%
Central	32.22%	37.88%	42.90%	13.23%	33.12%
Southern	39.05%	44.89%	49.67%	10.64%	27.21%
Metro Counties	38.57%	44.68%	48.51%	8.57%	25.78%
Northern	38.18%	43.96%	46.48%	5.73%	21.74%
Central	34.52%	40.67%	44.61%	9.69%	29.22%
Southern	39.33%	45.78%	50.89%	11.17%	29.39%
Rural Counties	36.17%	41.37%	45.35%	9.61%	25.36%
Northern	35.89%	40.93%	43.97%	7.43%	22.51%
Central	32.02%	37.65%	42.75%	13.55%	33.50%
Southern	38.73%	43.92%	48.25%	9.86%	24.59%

Source: U.S. Bureau of the Census.

Figure 5-26
Civilian Labor Force As A Percentage Of The Total Population In Appalachia, 1970 to 1990

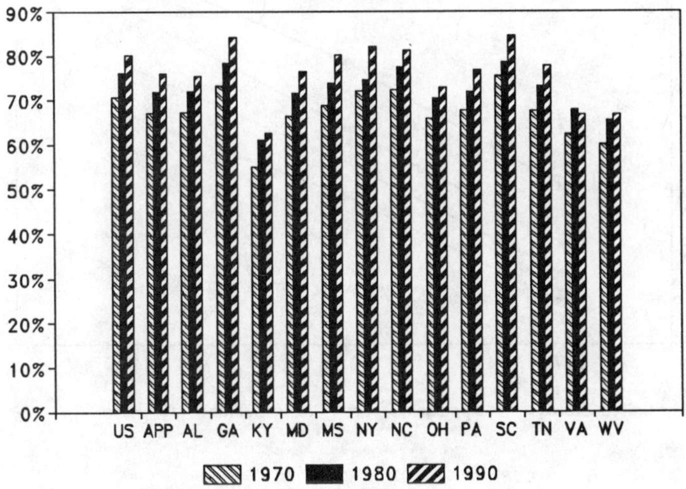

Figure 5-26 (Continued)
Civilian Labor Force as a Percentage of the Total Population in Appalachia, 1970 to 1990

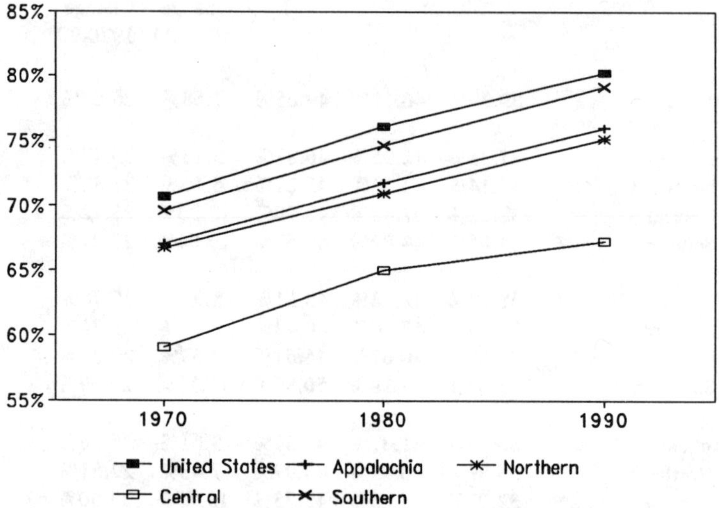

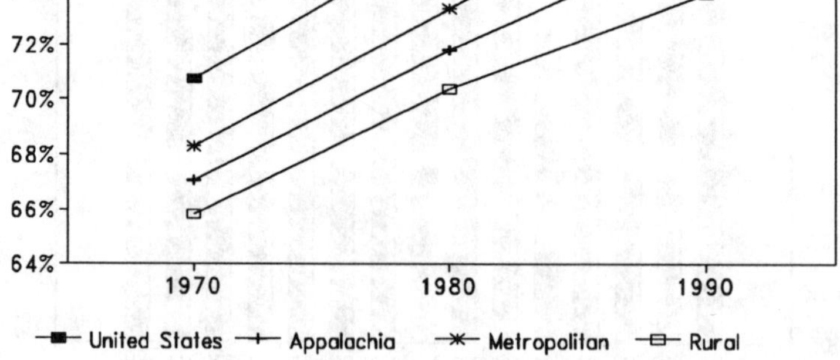

Map 5-27
Civilian Labor Force as Percentage of Appalachian Counties' Population, 1990

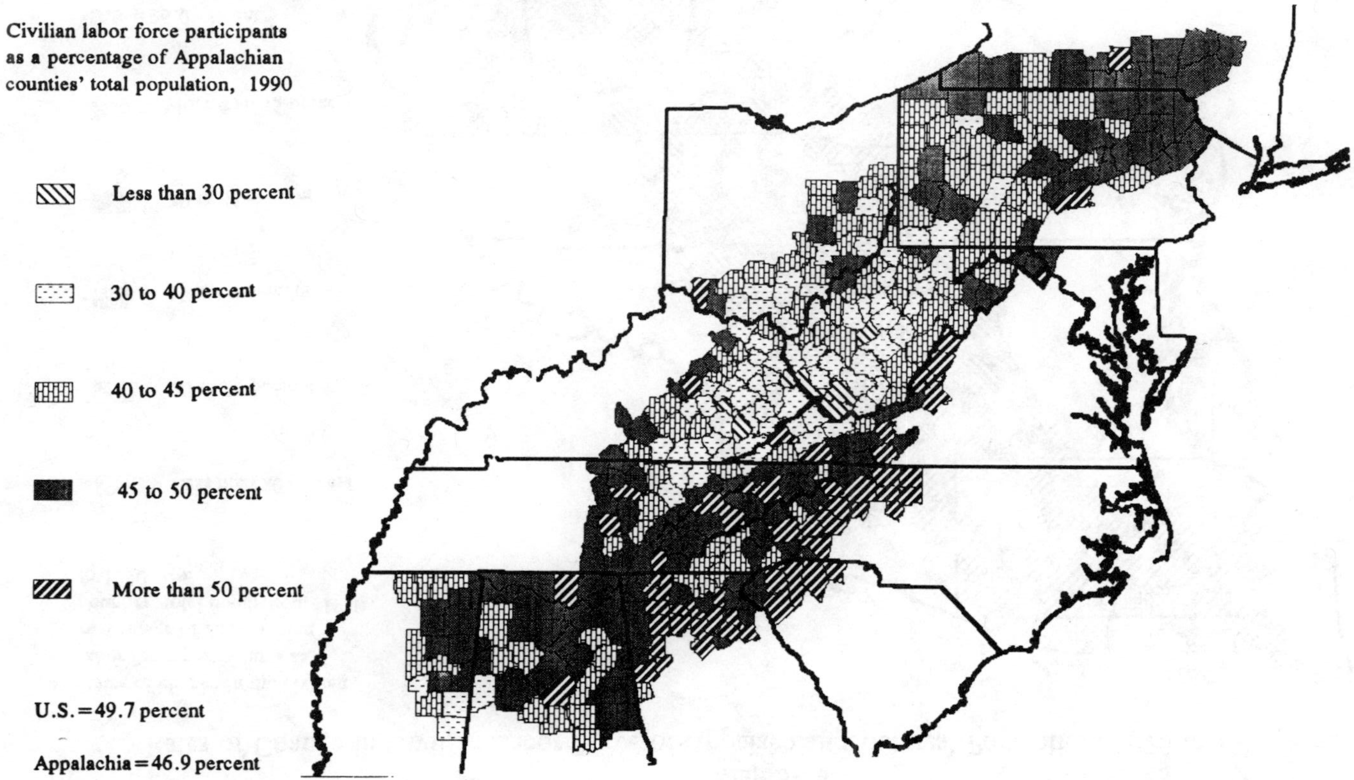

Prepared for Commission on Religion in Appalachia

Map 5-28
Rates of Change in Civilian Labor Force of Appalachian Counties' Population, 1970 to 1990

Rates of change in the civilian labor force participants as a percentage of Appalachian counties' total population, 1970 to 1990

- Less than 20 percent
- 20 to 25 percent
- 25 to 30 percent
- 30 to 35 percent
- More than 35 percent

U.S.=26.0 percent

Appalachia=25.5 percent

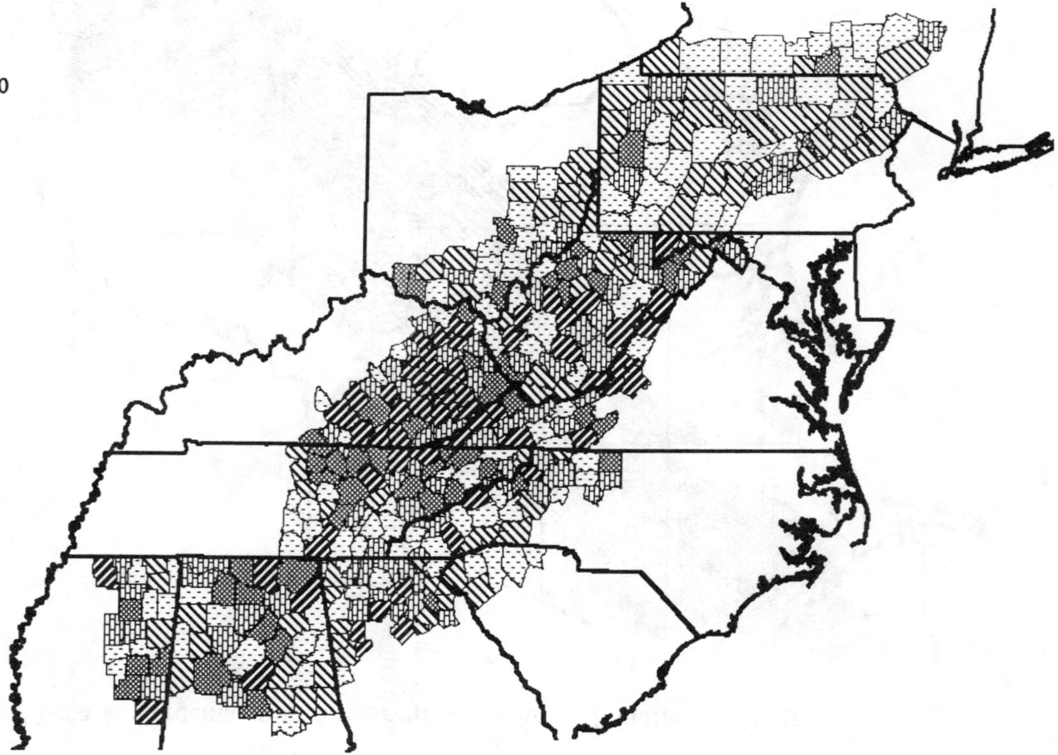

Prepared for Commission on Religion in Appalachia

declining economy.

Low levels of civilian work force participation and women's participation in the labor force are measures of hidden unemployment. Unemployment rates measure only a portion of the adult working age population who are without work. The portion of adults who do not enter the work force is another measure of the availability of work. Where these rates are lowest we have the highest rates of surplus labor and probably low amounts of social capital. This is particularly applicable to Appalachian Kentucky, Virginia, and West Virginia. On the other hand, Appalachian Mississippi illustrates the possibility of high rates of civilian labor force participation, especially by women, and low social capital, wages, and incomes.

Female-Headed Families

Changes in the make-up of families have occurred as part of changes in the population and work force. Most notably, the number of single-parent, female-headed families has increased in Appalachia. Nationally, the increase in single-parent, female-headed families from 1970 to 1990 is much higher than in Appalachia. In 1970, 10.8 percent of American families were headed by a female and in 1990 almost 16 percent of American families had a female head, an increase of almost 50 percent. At the same time, Appalachian families with female heads increased from 10.5 to 14.2, or 36 percent.

Once again, however, these broad changes vary for the subregions and for the different decades. Nationally, most of the increase in female-headed families occurred in the 1970s, a 32 percent rate of increase. The 1980s brought an increase of 11.8 percent. Increases in the Appalachian region were far smaller than the nation's in the 1970s, 20 percent, and slightly higher in the 1980s, 13.3 percent. Especially in Northern and Central Appalachia, regions with economic decline, female-headed households increased at a rate higher than the nation's in the 1980s, 14.8, 17.3, and 11.8 percent, respectively.

Southern Appalachia remains ahead of the rest of the region in the percent of female-headed families. Appalachian Alabama, Mississippi, and South Carolina, in particular, had rates near or higher than national rates. Appalachian Mississippi had the highest rate, 17.8 percent. Those areas with higher rates of female-headed households also have higher portions of African-American populations indicating, perhaps, some of the racism entailed in the inadequate distribution of social capital and the

Table 5-29
One-Parent Families With Female Heads in Appalachia, 1970 to 1990

	1970	1980	1990	Rate of Change 1980-90	Rate of Change 1970-90
United States	10.80%	14.28%	15.96%	11.75%	47.77%
Appalachia	10.45%	12.54%	14.21%	13.31%	36.03%
Northern	10.07%	12.20%	14.01%	14.78%	39.13%
Central	10.91%	11.73%	13.76%	17.29%	26.08%
Southern	10.87%	13.18%	14.55%	10.36%	33.79%
Metro Counties	10.88%	13.56%	15.18%	11.98%	39.56%
Northern	10.60%	13.17%	15.16%	15.15%	42.99%
Central	9.67%	11.55%	13.06%	13.10%	35.10%
Southern	11.36%	14.17%	15.30%	7.99%	34.61%
Rural Counties	10.03%	11.61%	13.32%	14.71%	32.87%
Northern	9.40%	11.10%	12.74%	14.82%	35.52%
Central	11.05%	11.75%	13.83%	17.72%	25.14%
Southern	10.36%	12.16%	13.73%	12.92%	32.55%

Source: U.S. Bureau of the Census.

Figure 5-30
One-Parent Families With Female Heads in Appalachia, 1970 to 1990

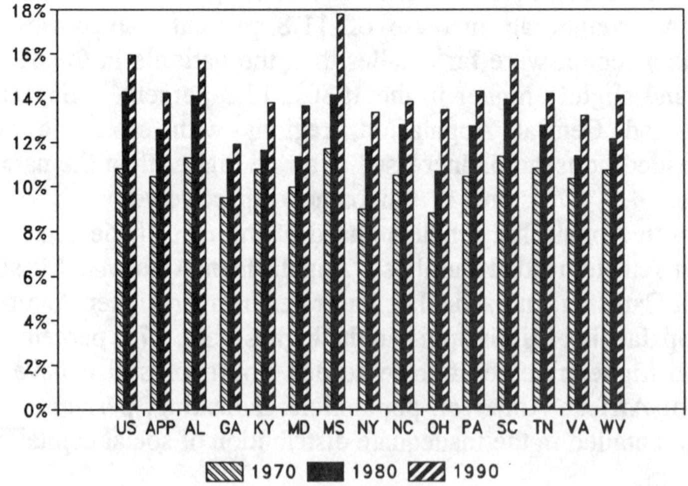

Figure 5-30 (Continued)
One-Parent Families With Female Heads in Appalachia, 1970 to 1990

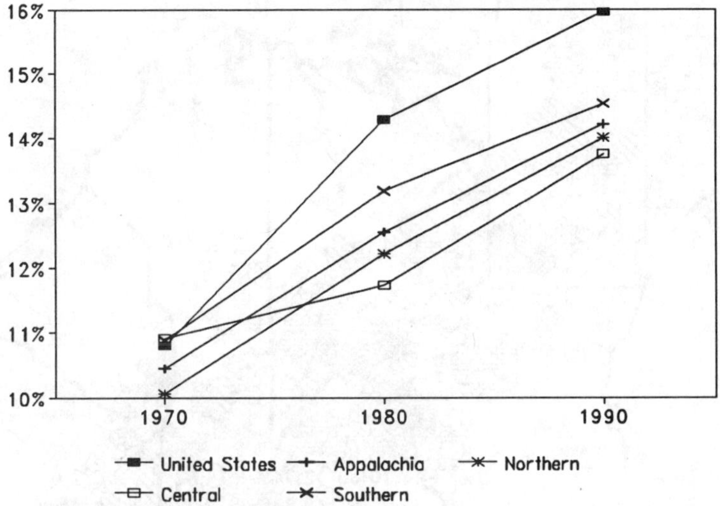

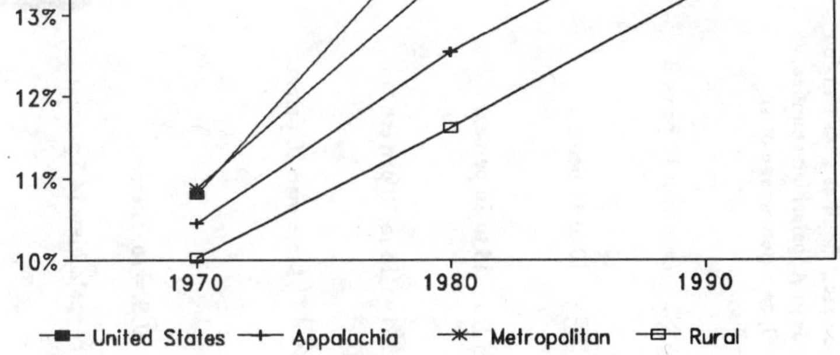

Map 5-31
One-Parent Families With Female Heads in Appalachian Counties, 1990

One-parent families with female heads in Appalachian counties, 1990, as a percentage of all families

- Less than 10 percent
- 10 to 14 percent
- 14 to 16 percent
- 16 to 20 percent
- More than 20 percent

U.S.=16.0 percent

Appalachia=14.2 percent

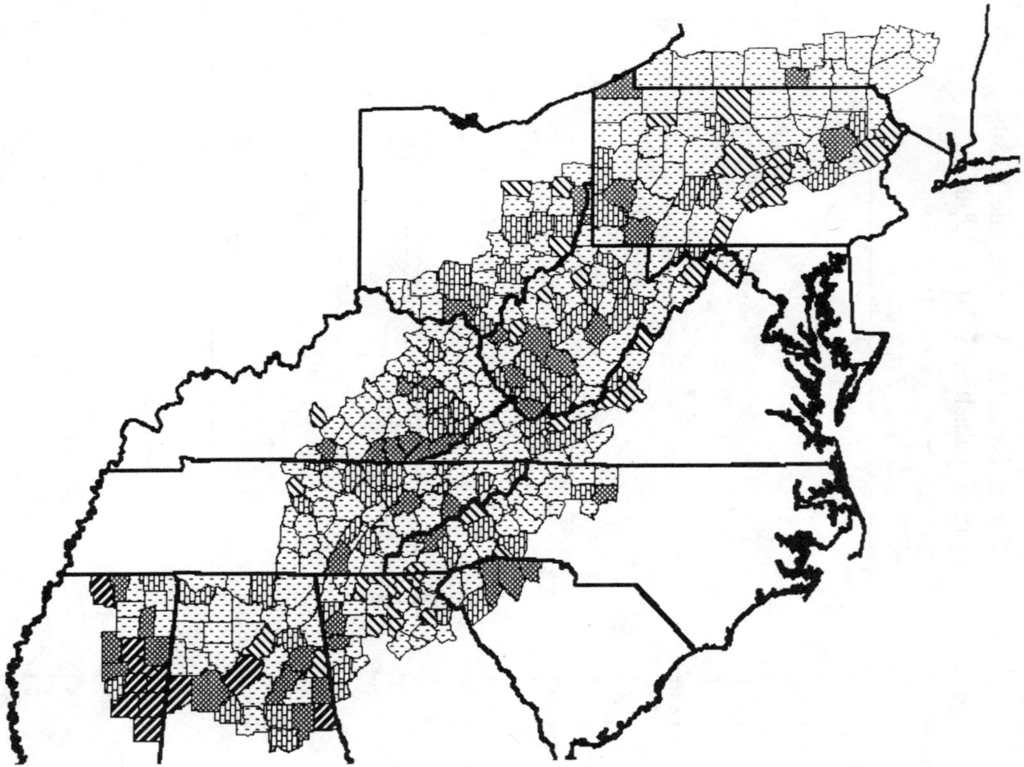

rrepared for Commission on Religion in Appalachia

Map 5-32
Rates of Change in One-Parent Families With Female Heads in Appalachian Counties, 1970 to 1990

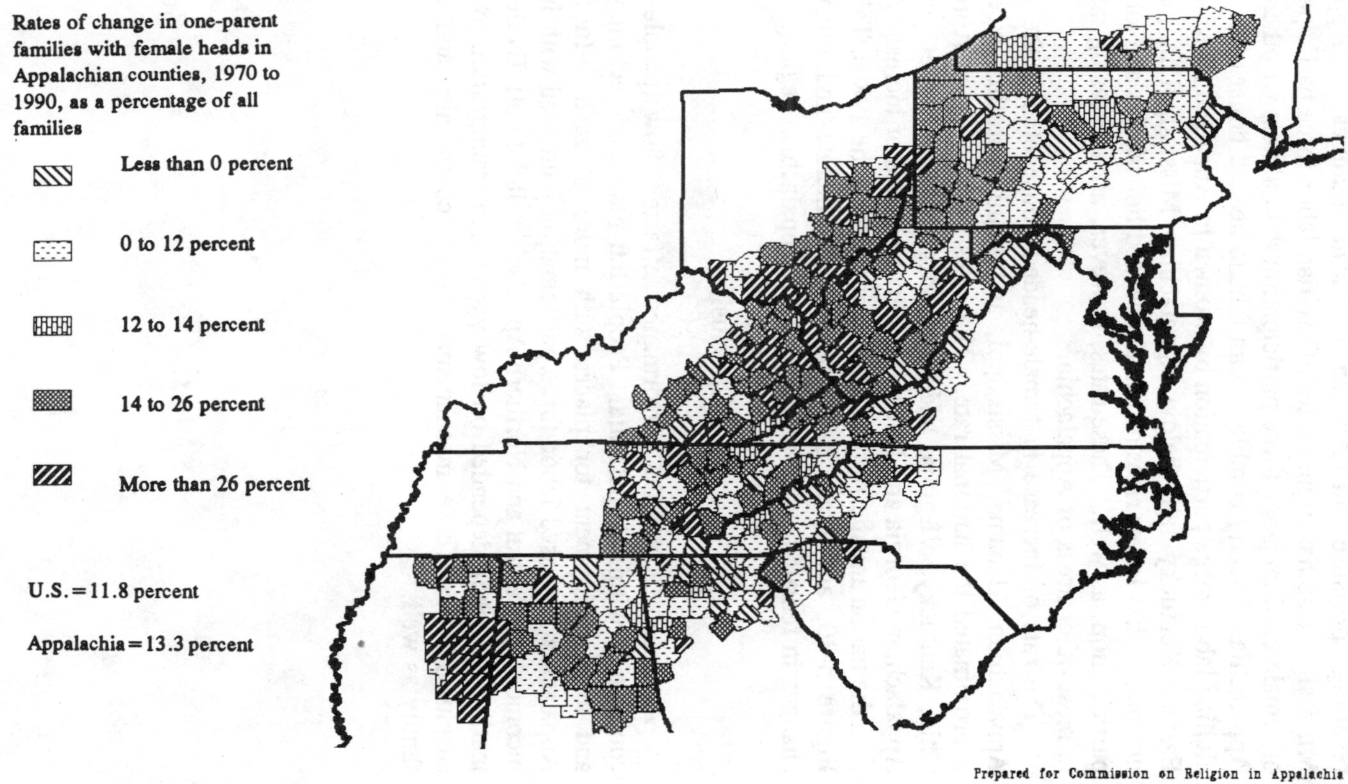

resulting pressure on African-American families. Appalachian Mississippi also has higher rates of civilian labor force participation and of female civilian labor force participation than almost all other parts of Appalachia. Poverty combines with female-headed households and high civilian labor force participation by women in Appalachian Mississippi. Eastern Kentucky falls below Appalachian Mississippi in per capita income. It has lower rates on female-headed households and labor force participation, as well. These rates, however, are increasing faster than in most other areas of Appalachia.

The rate of increase in female-headed households in the 1980s in Appalachian Alabama, Mississippi, and South Carolina exceeded or approximated the national rate. The rates of increase in Appalachian Ohio, Kentucky, Virginia, and West Virginia were higher yet. Only Appalachian Georgia and North Carolina had rates of increase far lower than the nation and the Appalachian region during the 1980s. Table 5-29, Figure 5-30, and Maps 5-31 and 5-32 enumerate and illustrate the changes in female-headed families in the Appalachian region.

Conclusion

American economic performance affected how people live in community within Appalachia. People left places of declining income and low employment for places with more of each. In Southern Appalachia increased labor force participation coincided with increased incomes. In Central and Northern Appalachia, it did not. Evidently, the market for labor depended on low wages and immigration to relocate surplus labor. These mechanisms disrupt community and probably family as well.

Chapter 6

Poverty

Changes in work and income have meant significant changes for families in Appalachia. The family, the first means of social capital, has the primary responsibility for the creation and sustenance of people in community. Yet, the changes in work and income have meant more families in poverty and families with fewer resources. These families have diminished capacity to accumulate and provide social capital. This has had a severe impact on children in many parts of Appalachia.

New and Old Poverty in Appalachia

The Appalachian region did better than the nation in reducing poverty from 1970 to 1990. During that time, the percentage of people in poverty nationally dropped modestly from 13.3 percent to 13.1 percent. Within the region, however, as Table 6-1 reports, the percentage of people in poverty declined from 17.7 percent to 14.9 percent. Despite this larger decline, the Appalachian region continues to have a higher rate of poverty than the nation. In addition, the rate of Appalachian poverty declined more sharply than poverty nationally in the 1970s but increased more sharply in the 1980s, as Figure 6-2 indicates.

As with every other measure, the rate of poverty in Appalachia requires extensive scrutiny and eludes simple generalizations. Central and Southern Appalachia had higher rates of decline in poverty than the nation, from 1970 to 1990. Of course, Central and Southern Appalachia had much higher rates of poverty in 1970. Northern Appalachia had increases in the people living in poverty. Southern Appalachia had two decades of growth in per capita personal income while Northern Appalachia had two decades of decline in per capita personal income. These income changes explain, in part, the decrease of poverty in Southern Appalachia and the increase in the North, from 1970 to 1990.

The poverty of Central Appalachia remains the highest in the region, almost twice the national rate, despite the substantial decline from 1970 to 1990. The decline in Central Appalachia marks the passing of exceedingly high rates of poverty, 40 to 60 percent in some Eastern Kentucky counties in the 1960s. The declines in those rates occurred primarily in the 1970s. The 1980s brought increased poverty in these counties. In some cases, the southern coal counties of West Virginia in particular, poverty rates are returning to pre-1970 levels. Figure 6-2

Table 6-1
Percent of Population Below Poverty Income Level in Appalachia, 1970 to 1990

	1970	1980	1990	Rate of Change 1980-90	Rate of Change 1970-90
United States	13.31%	12.40%	13.10%	2.93%	-4.14%
Appalachia	17.65%	13.68%	14.88%	8.74%	-15.69%
Northern	12.99%	10.97%	13.60%	23.97%	4.75%
Central	34.04%	22.34%	25.34%	13.43%	-25.55%
Southern	20.20%	14.85%	13.90%	-6.42%	-31.19%
Metro Counties	13.50%	11.21%	12.28%	9.54%	-9.02%
Northern	10.68%	9.36%	12.01%	28.25%	12.45%
Central	17.18%	14.04%	15.83%	12.79%	-7.83%
Southern	17.07%	13.49%	12.44%	-7.84%	-29.72%
Rural Counties	21.69%	15.93%	17.28%	8.47%	-20.34%
Northern	15.80%	12.77%	15.32%	19.97%	-3.06%
Central	35.86%	23.16%	26.30%	13.55%	-26.66%
Southern	22.85%	16.28%	15.53%	-4.62%	-32.03%

Source: U.S. Bureau of the Census.

Figure 6-2
Percent of Population Below Poverty Income Level in Appalachia, 1970 to 1990

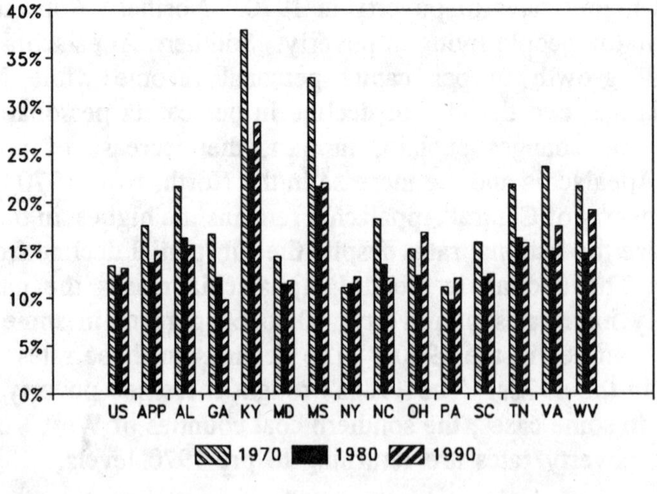

Figure 6-2 (Continued)
Percent of Population Below Poverty Income Level in Appalachia, 1970 to 1990

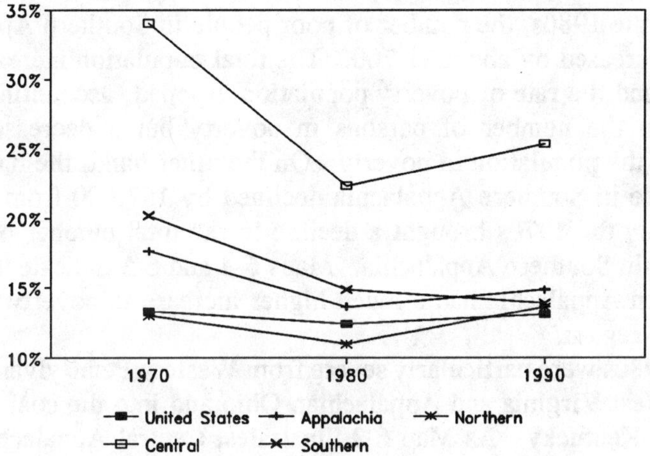

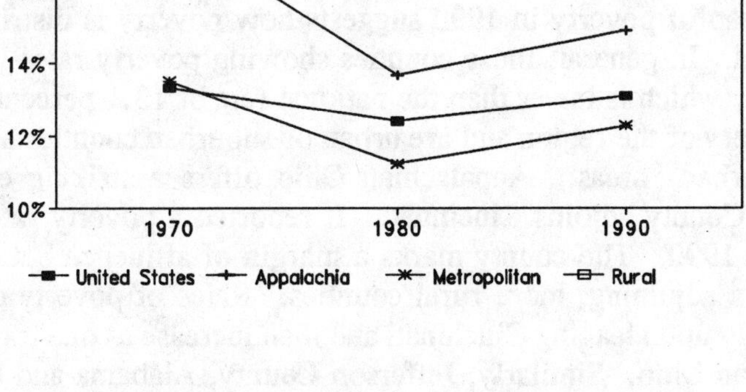

indicates the dramatic decline in poverty in the region from 1970 to 1980 and the increase in poverty from 1980 to 1990, except for a continuing modest decline in Southern Appalachia. Despite the improvements, one in four people in Central Appalachia lived in poverty in 1990.

Although the rate of poverty in Southern Appalachia continued to decline in the 1980s, the number of poor people in Southern Appalachia actually increased by about 21,700. The total population increased at a high rate and the rate of poverty population dropped, accounting for an increase in the number of persons in poverty but a decrease in the percent of the population in poverty. On the other hand, the number of poor people in Southern Appalachia declined by 152,000 from 1970 to 1980. Only the 1970s brought a decline in the total number of people in poverty in Southern Appalachia. Maps 6-4 and 6-5 indicate that most of Northern Appalachia had a much higher increase in poverty than the rest of the region.

The 1980s were particularly severe from Western Pennsylvania down through West Virginia and Appalachian Ohio and into the coal counties of Eastern Kentucky. As Map 6-3 illustrates, Central Appalachia has a concentration of counties with high levels of poverty. Mississippi has another concentration of counties with high levels of poverty and remains the Southern Appalachian state with the greatest resemblance to Central Appalachian income and poverty.

Most counties in Appalachian Pennsylvania and New York reached the range of the national and regional poverty in 1990. However, the new poverty has brought rates much higher than the nation's to already low-income counties in Appalachian Ohio and West Virginia.

Despite the improvements of two decades in Southern Appalachia, a solid core of counties in Tennessee, Alabama, Georgia, and Mississippi still have very high rates of poverty. Appalachian Mississippi had a slight increase in poverty rates from 21.7 to 22.0 percent from 1980 to 1990.

The map of poverty in 1990 suggests how poverty is distributed in Appalachia. In general, those counties showing poverty rates less than 10 percent, which is lower than the national rate of 13.1 percent, are on the periphery of the region and are urban or suburban counties and close to large urban areas. Appalachian Ohio offers a striking example. Clermont County adjoins Cincinnati. It reported a poverty rate of 8.6 percent in 1990. The county marks a margin of affluence between the city and its adjoining, more rural counties. Rates of poverty decrease immediately upon leaving Cincinnati and then increase as one travels into Appalachian Ohio. Similarly, Jefferson County, Alabama and the city

Map 6-3
Poverty Population of Appalachian Counties, 1990

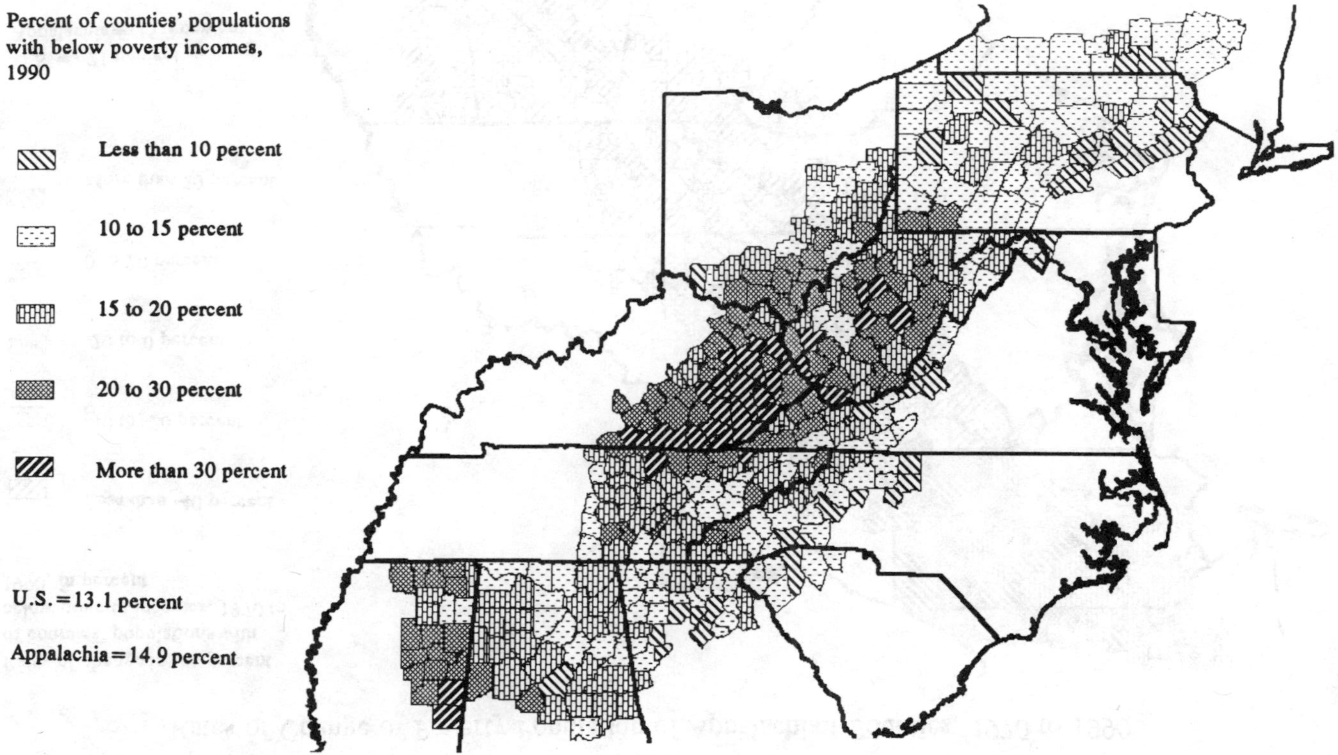

Prepared for Commission on Religion in Appalachia

Map 6-4
Rates of Change of Poverty Population of Appalachian Counties, 1970 to 1990

Rates of change in the percent of counties' populations with below poverty incomes, 1970 to 1990, in percent

- Less than -40 percent
- -40 to -20 percent
- -20 to 0 percent
- 0 to 20 percent
- More than 20 percent

U.S.=-.21 percent
Appalachia=-15.7 percent

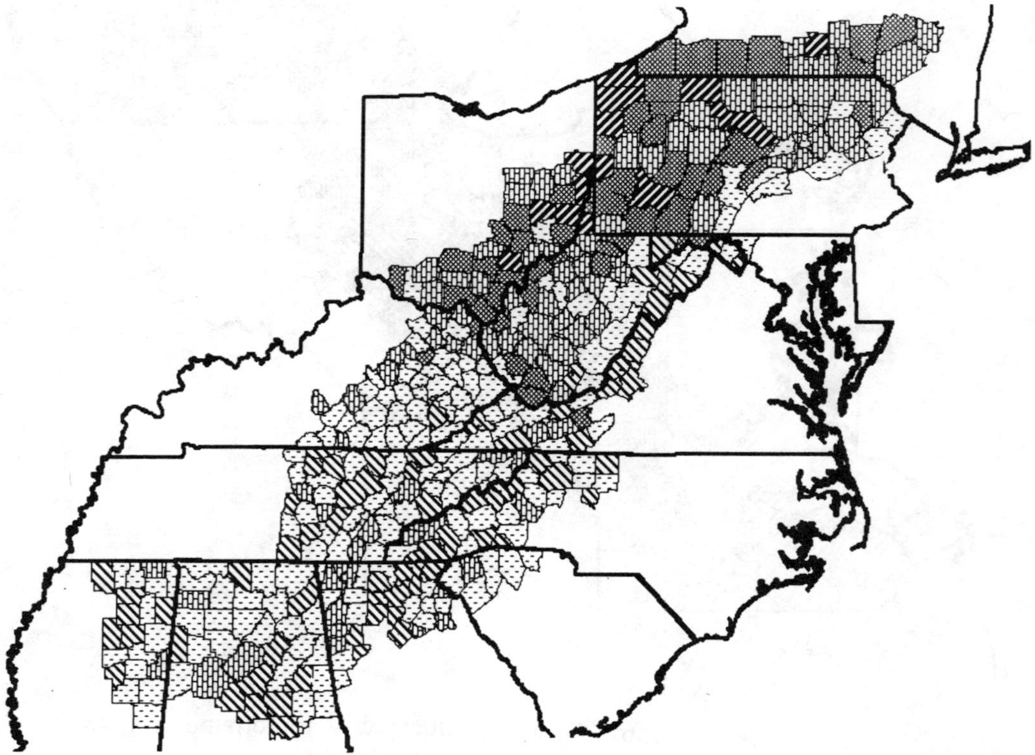

Prepared for Commission on Religion in Appalachia

Map 6-5
Rates of Change of Poverty Population of Appalachian Counties, 1980 to 1990

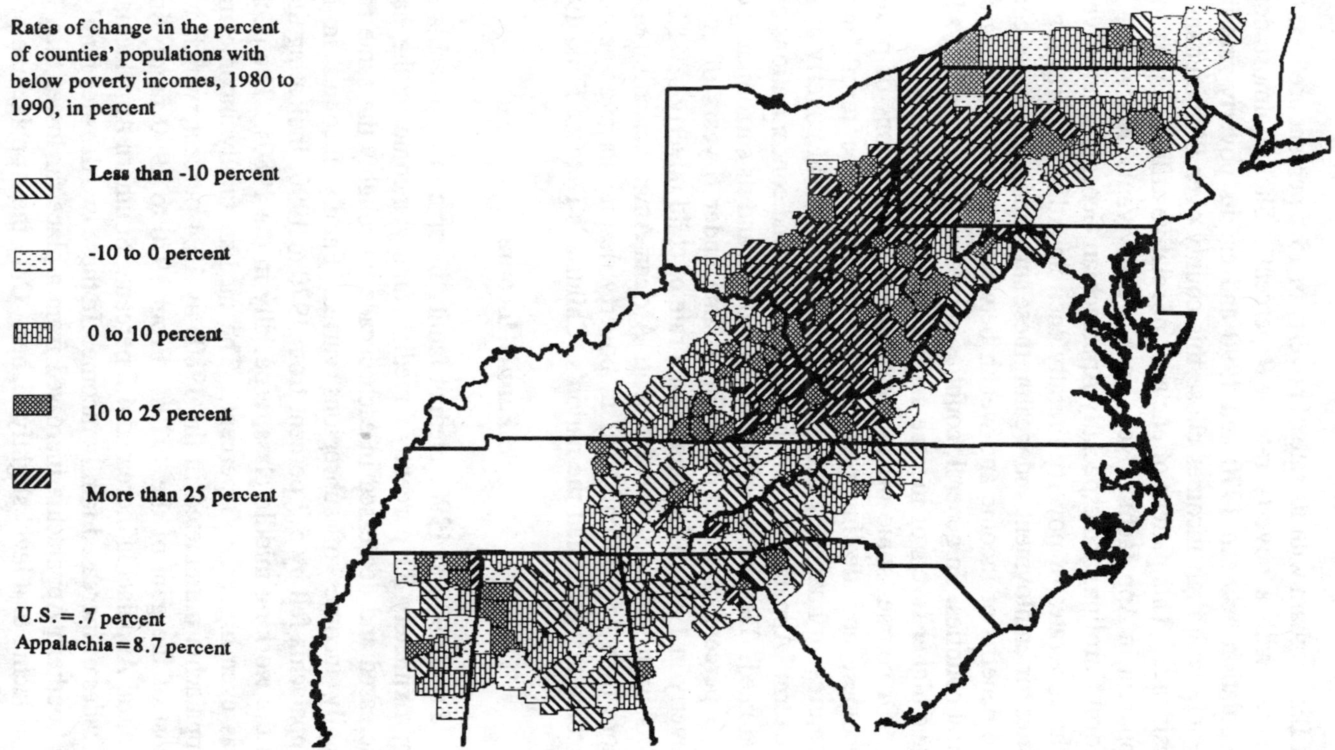

Prepared for Commission on Religion in Appalachia

of Birmingham with its rate of poverty of 15.7 percent are next to Shelby County with a poverty rate of 9 percent. Shelby almost doubled its population between 1970 and 1990 and cut its poverty rate in half as people with high incomes chose this county over Birmingham for their residence. This pattern of enclaves of relative affluence next to a city is apparent in Appalachian New York, Pennsylvania, Maryland, Virginia, North Carolina, and especially Appalachian Georgia where five counties with low rates of poverty literally encircle Atlanta. Drawing from the cities for employment and wealth, these surrounding counties concentrate the benefits of income and wealth between their neighboring cities and rural counties. In general, counties immediately surrounding a large city have higher levels of income and lower rates of poverty.

Of course, some urban areas have concentrations of poverty, low incomes, and declining economic activity. The term "inner city" conjures up images of decline, unemployment, and poverty as strong as the term "Appalachia." In these places we find concentrations of poverty and need. Despite the affluence of Atlanta and its surrounding counties, 47.3 percent of the children in Atlanta under 6 years of age were in poverty in 1990. Cincinnati had a rate of child poverty of 41.2 percent; Pittsburgh had 56.9 percent of its African-American children under 6, more than 15,000 children, in poverty despite its average per capita income that exceeded the nation's (Children's Defense Fund 1992).

Family Income

From 1970 to 1990, median family income in Appalachia stayed at approximately 83 percent of median family income in the nation. It increased and decreased in each decade by roughly the same rate. The family incomes of subregions varied. Family incomes in Northern Appalachia fell by 5.7 percent from 1970 to 1990, indicating the decline of the working middle class, especially in the 1980s. The decline then was even higher, 9.3 percent. The median family income in Central Appalachia plummeted in the 1980s by 13.4 percent, which wiped out most of the gain of the 1970s. From 1970 to 1990 family income in Central Appalachia increased 4.8 percent. Southern Appalachia had two decades of increased family income. In these two decades family income in Southern Appalachia increased from a place far lower than Northern Appalachia to a level slightly higher. Only the Appalachian portions of Georgia, North Carolina, and South Carolina had two decades of improved family income. Only Appalachian New York lost ground in the 1970s. All the other Appalachian states' portions lost ground in the

Table 6-6
Median Family Income in Appalachia as a Percentage of National Median Family Income 1970 to 1990

	1970	1980	1990	Rate of Change 1980-90	Rate of Change 1970-90
Appalachia	82.79%	87.50%	83.49%	-4.58%	0.86%
Northern	90.15%	93.75%	85.00%	-9.34%	-5.72%
Central	58.34%	70.61%	61.12%	-13.44%	4.76%
Southern	78.55%	84.18%	87.08%	3.44%	10.85%
Metro Counties	92.07%	96.32%	92.92%	-3.53%	0.92%
Northern	96.28%	100.02%	90.54%	-9.48%	-5.96%
Central	87.29%	95.44%	86.18%	-9.70%	-1.27%
Southern	85.85%	91.55%	95.80%	4.65%	11.60%
Rural Counties	73.70%	79.44%	74.85%	-5.77%	1.56%
Northern	82.55%	86.56%	78.93%	-8.82%	-4.39%
Central	55.09%	68.09%	58.53%	-14.03%	6.24%
Southern	70.94%	76.56%	77.63%	1.40%	9.43%

Source: U.S. Bureau of the Census.

Figure 6-7
Median Family Income in Appalachia as a Percentage of National Median Family Income, 1970 to 1990

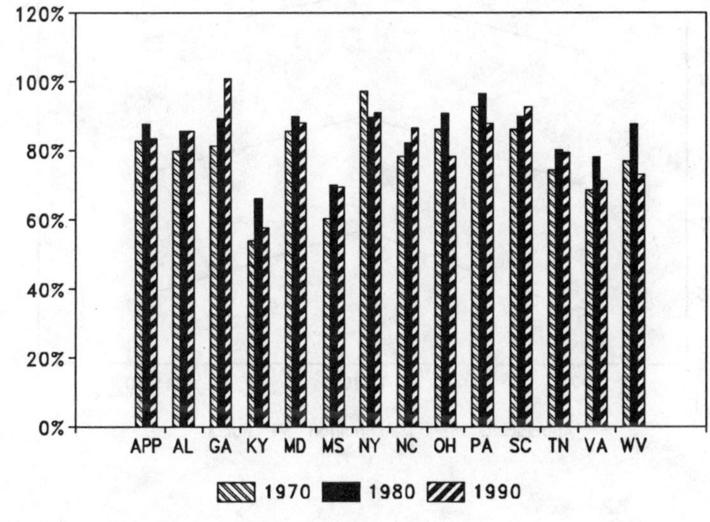

Figure 6-7 (Continued)
Median Family Income in Appalachia as a Percentage of National Median Family Income, 1970 to 1990

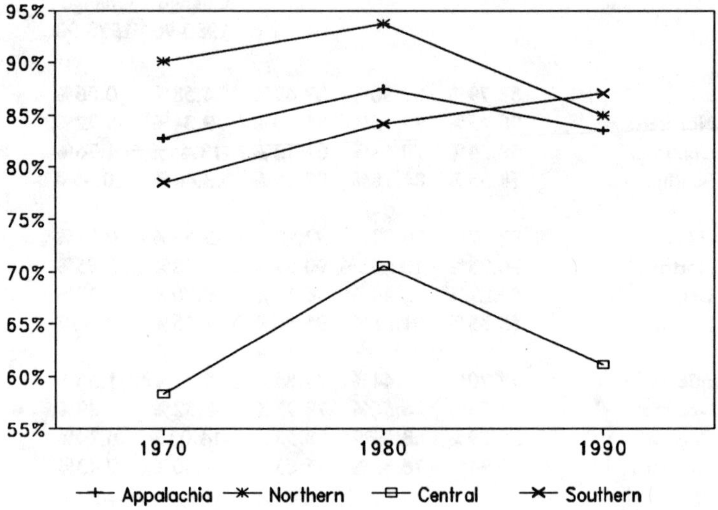

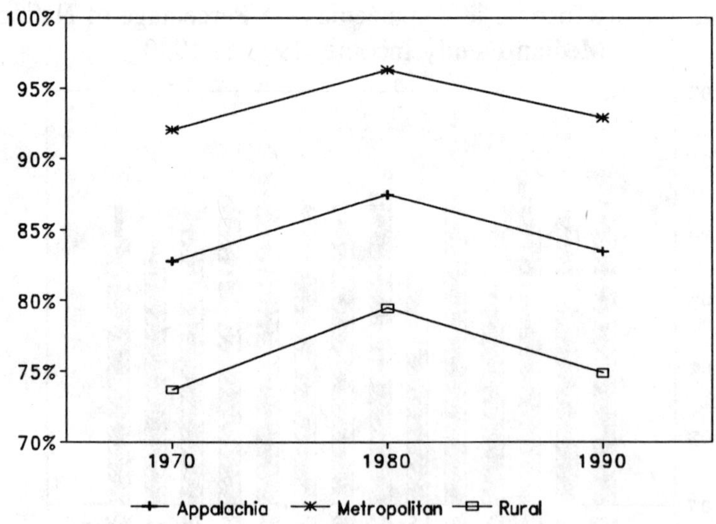

Map 6-8
Median Family Income of Appalachian Counties, 1990

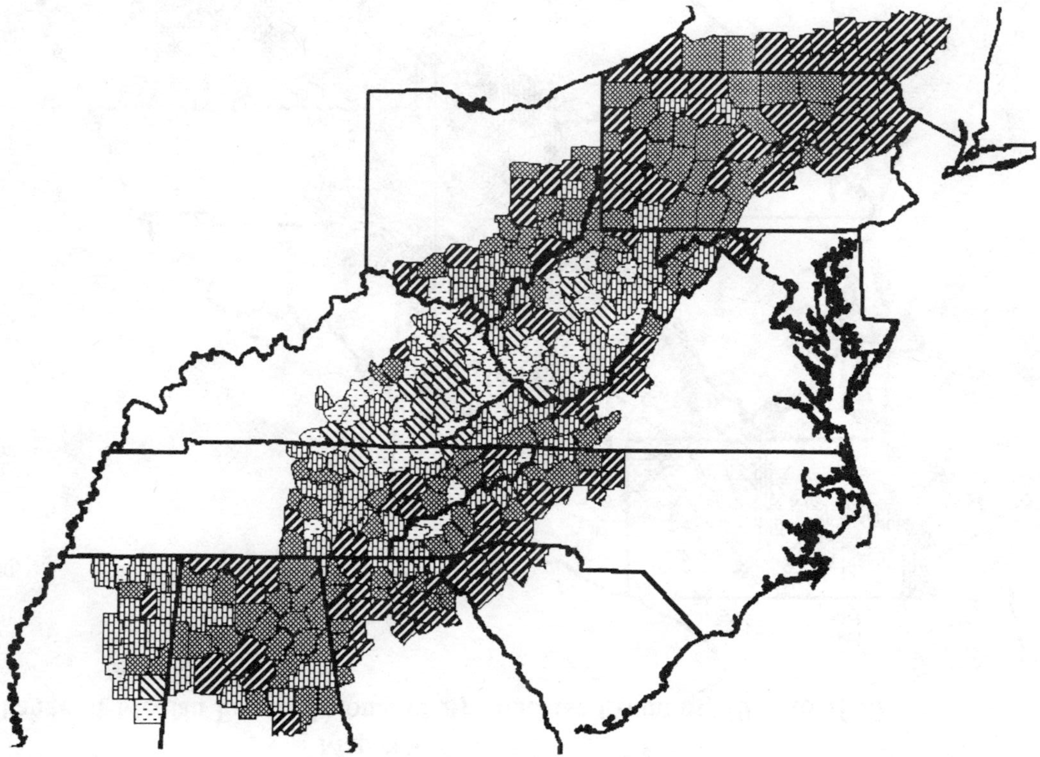

Median family income of Appalachian counties as a percent of the national median, 1990

- Less than 50 percent
- 50 to 60 percent
- 60 to 70 percent
- 70 to 80 percent
- More than 80 percent

U.S. median=$35,225

Appalachia=83.5 percent

Prepared for Commission on Religion in Appalachia

Map 6-9

Rates of Change of Median Family Income of Appalachian Counties, 1970 to 1990

Rates of change in median family income of Appalachian counties as a percent of the national median, 1970 to 1990, in percent

- Less than -20 percent
- -20 to 0 percent
- 0 to 10 percent
- 10 to 30 percent
- More than 30 percent

Appalachia = .9 percent

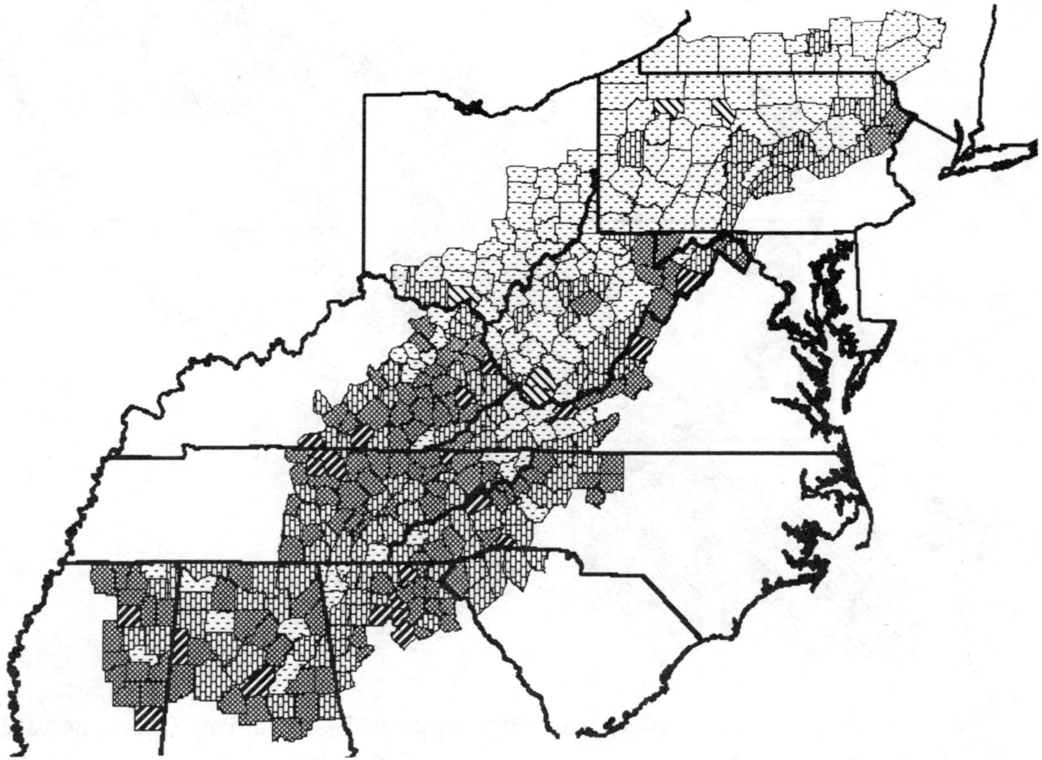

Prepared for Commission on Religion in Appalachia

1980s. Table 6-6 and Figure 6-7 provide measures for family income in Appalachia for 1970, 1980, and 1990.

As the fortunes of Northern and Southern Appalachia switched, the relation of urban and rural areas changed as well. The gap of rural and metropolitan counties in Northern Appalachia narrowed. Metropolitan and rural counties approached equality at lower levels of income for both. The gap between metropolitan and rural counties in Southern Appalachia grew. Increases in metropolitan counties were greater than those in rural counties. Urban and rural counties grew further apart at higher levels of median family income.

The high-wage and heavily unionized states of Ohio, Pennsylvania and West Virginia were worse off in family income in 1990 than they were in 1970. The drop was particularly precipitous in Appalachian Ohio, which went from a much higher than regional level to a much lower level. Maps 6-8 and 6-9 illustrate family income in 1990 and changes from 1980 to 1990. Obviously, Northern Appalachia has lost the most. Its losses, however, dropped it to a level to which Southern Appalachia rose. Central Appalachia and contiguous counties have the concentration of counties with the very lowest family incomes, especially Eastern Kentucky.

Families and Poverty

While it stands to reason that family income will change with the changes in the amount and nature of work, the extent of those changes are not apparent. The drop in family income has meant more families in poverty. In Northern Appalachia, with the most severe decline in wages and manufacturing employment in the region, we also find the largest increase in families in poverty, especially in the 1980s. By 1990, 10.7 percent of the families in Northern Appalachia were in poverty, a rate that exceeded the national rate for the first time for this set of counties. Table 6-10 reports on these changes. Other measures of family poverty appear in Figure 6-11, Map 6-12, and Map 6-13.

In Southern Appalachia, with the greatest increase in wages and retention of manufacturing employment, families in poverty declined for both decades and reached their lowest point in 1990. Despite this improvement, the urban counties of Southern Appalachia have rates of families in poverty almost equal to those of Northern Appalachia. Similarly, the large discrepancy of families in poverty between the rural counties of Northern and Southern Appalachia in 1970 had almost disappeared by 1990. Improvements in Southern Appalachia and increased family poverty in the 1980s in Northern Appalachia have

Table 6-10
Families in Poverty in Appalachia, 1970 to 1990

	1970	1980	1990	Rate of Change 1980-90	Rate of Change 1970-90
United States	10.70%	9.60%	9.97%	3.85%	-6.82%
Appalachia	14.89%	10.98%	11.94%	8.69%	-19.80%
Northern	10.38%	8.41%	10.73%	27.59%	3.40%
Central	30.19%	19.21%	22.18%	15.43%	-26.54%
Southern	17.39%	12.02%	10.87%	-9.60%	-37.51%
Metro Counties	10.97%	8.82%	9.59%	8.78%	-12.61%
Northern	8.35%	7.21%	9.49%	31.59%	13.64%
Central	14.15%	11.41%	13.35%	17.02%	-5.65%
Southern	14.85%	10.79%	9.54%	-11.51%	-35.71%
Rural Counties	18.71%	12.97%	14.09%	8.68%	-24.68%
Northern	12.90%	9.79%	12.09%	23.56%	-6.23%
Central	31.98%	20.01%	23.09%	15.40%	-27.82%
Southern	20.04%	13.30%	12.30%	-7.52%	-38.64%

Source: U.S. Bureau of the Census.

Figure 6-11
Families in Poverty in Appalachia, 1970 to 1990

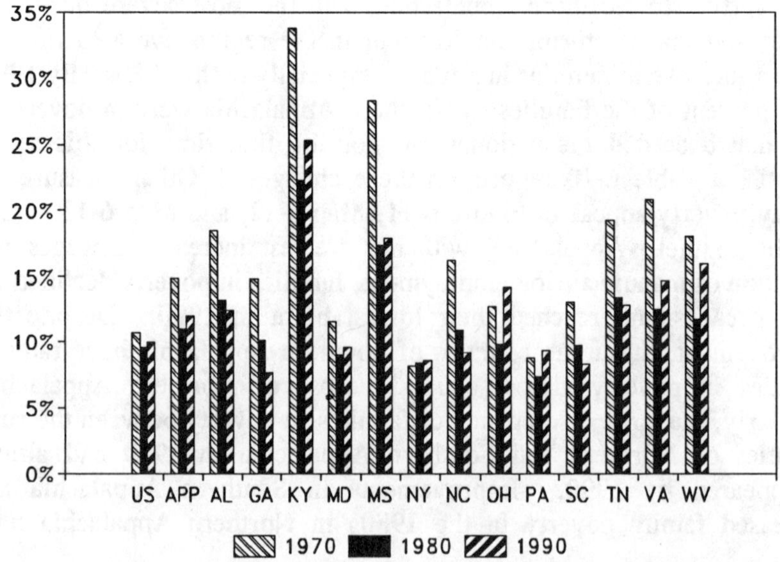

Figure 6-11 (Continued)
Families in Poverty in Appalachia, 1970 to 1990

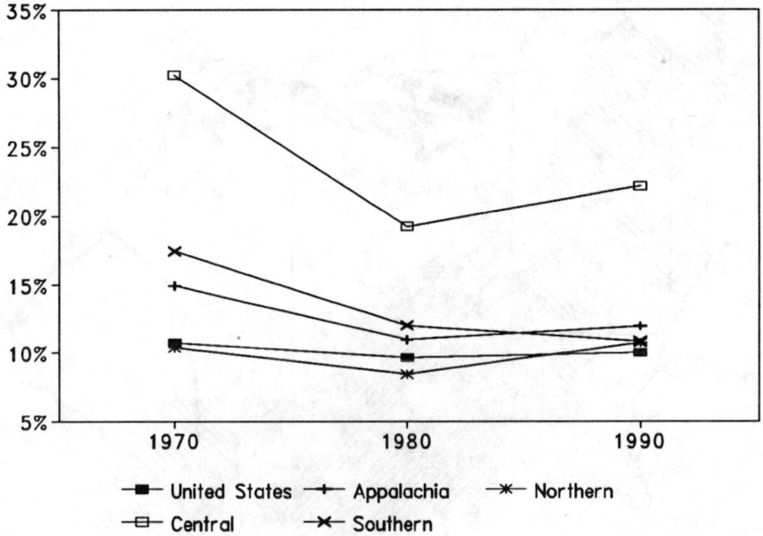

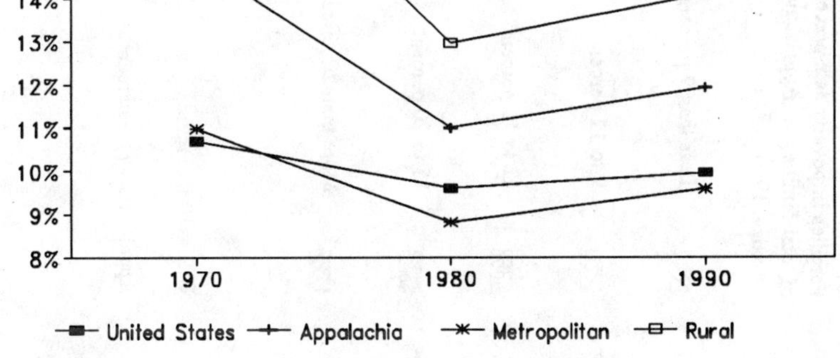

Map 6-12
Families in Poverty in Appalachian Counties, 1990

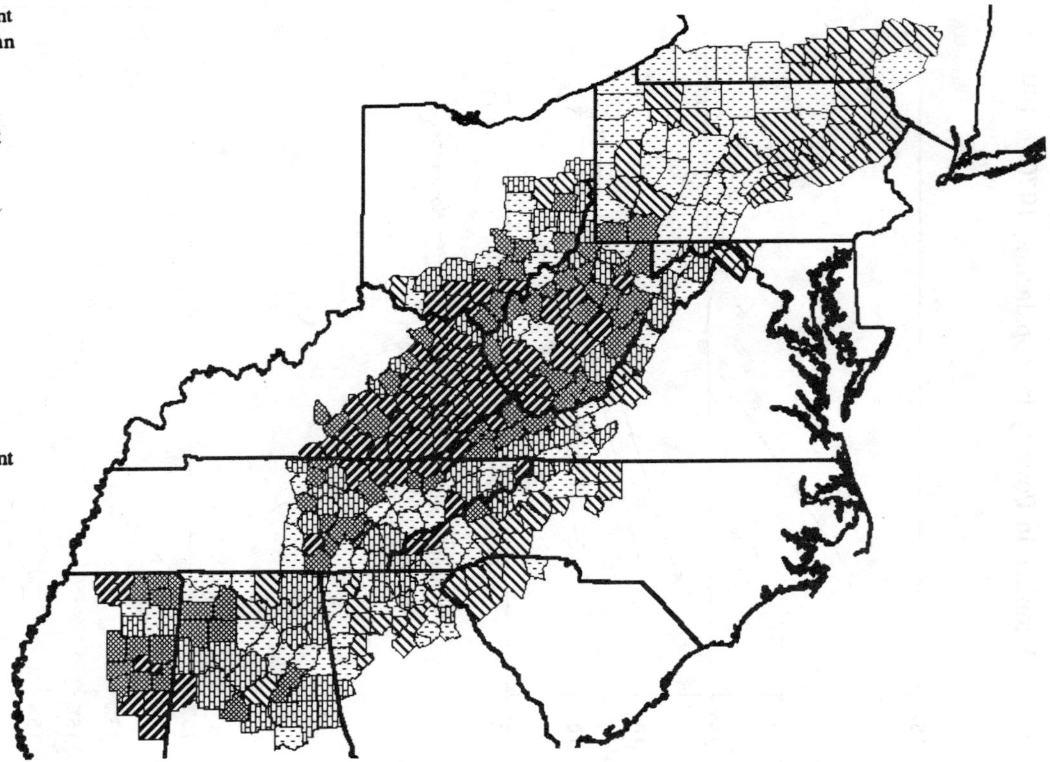

Families in poverty as a percent of total families in Appalachian counties, 1990

- Less than 9 percent
- 9 to 12 percent
- 12 to 15 percent
- 15 to 20 percent
- More than 20 percent

U.S. = 10.0 percent

Appalachia = 11.9 percent

Prepared for Commission on Religion in Appalachia

Map 6-13
Rates of Change of Families in Poverty in Appalachian Counties, 1970 to 1990

Rates of change in the families in poverty as a percent of the total families in Appalachian counties, 1970 to 1990, in percent

- Less than -15 percent
- -15 to -5 percent
- -5 to 5 percent
- 5 to 20 percent
- More than 20 percent

U.S. = -6.8
Appalachia = -19.8 percent

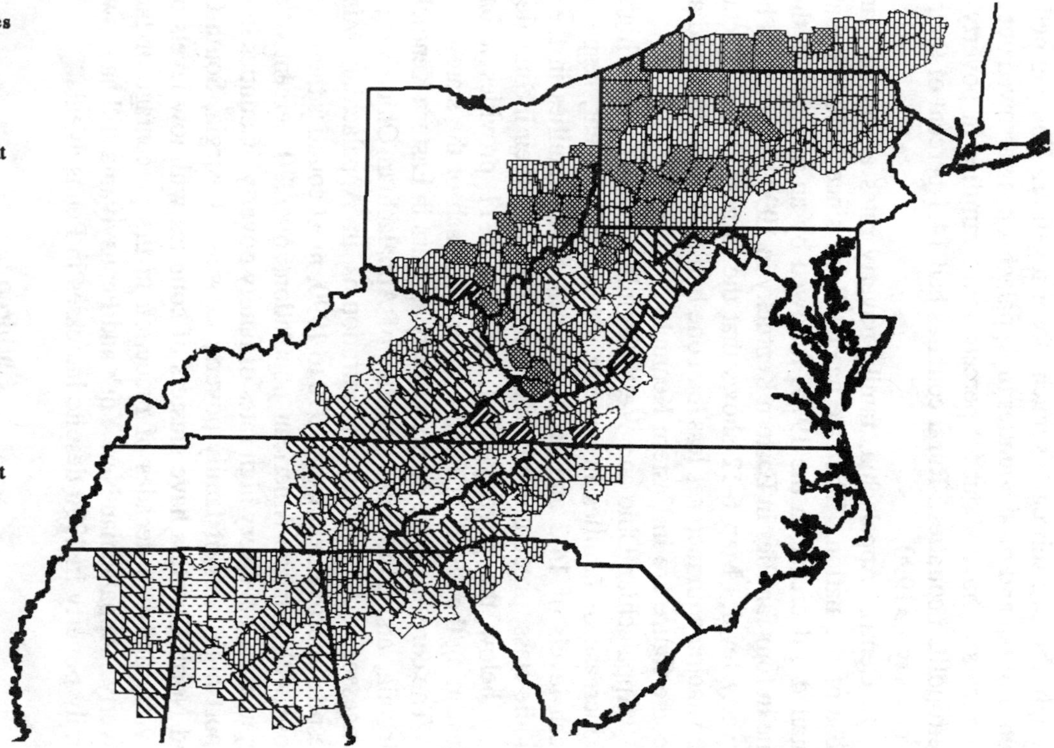

Prepared for Commission on Religion in Appalachia

brought the two subregions much closer together. The gap between the metropolitan and rural counties in Appalachia has narrowed but the rural, counties still have about 50 percent more families in poverty than the metropolitan counties. Rural counties had 14.1 percent of their families in poverty in 1990.

In Central Appalachia, family poverty rates are more than double those of the nation. The rate has declined since 1970 but that change entailed a decrease in the 1970s followed by an increase in the 1980s. One in four families in Eastern Kentucky in 1990 had incomes below the poverty level. Map 6-12 shows that the largest cluster of counties in Appalachia with incomes less than one-half of the national median family income figure are in Eastern Kentucky.

Appalachian Ohio and West Virginia had the region's highest rates of increase of families in poverty, 44 and 36 percent, respectively, to reach levels of 14.2 and 16.0 percent. Some families in the working middle class, predominantly white, not only saw their income decline but drop below the poverty level. Figure 6-11 provides a bar graph illustrating the levels of family poverty in each of the states.

The core of severe family poverty appears in Eastern Kentucky, West Virginia, and contiguous counties of Appalachian Ohio, Virginia, and Tennessee. A smaller concentration is in Appalachian Mississippi. Despite improvement from 1970 to 1990, most counties there, especially those with African-American populations over 20 percent of the total population, have very high rates of family poverty. Counties in Alabama report high rates of family poverty as well. Georgia, South Carolina, and North Carolina have clusters of counties with low levels of family poverty and two decades of reduction in the percentage of families in poverty. Appalachian New York and Pennsylvania still had low rates of family poverty in 1990 despite increases in Pennsylvania.

Children

High rates of family poverty translate into very high rates of poverty for children. In Appalachia, 33 percent of all individuals below the poverty level in 1990 were under 18 years of age. Put differently, 20.3 percent of all the children of Appalachia were in poverty in 1990 compared with 17.5 percent of all American children. The national figures represent a rate increase of 18.1 percent since 1970. Childhood poverty in Appalachia increased 7.5 percent in those twenty years. The 1970s actually saw the percentage of children in poverty decline, but the increase in the 1980s was almost 20 percent.

The measures of child poverty vary widely among states and subregions in the Appalachian region, as Table 6-14 and Figure 6-15 report. Central Appalachia's children experience more poverty than children of other subregions. This is lower than the rate of poverty among children in 1970 but much higher than the rate in 1980. Eastern Kentucky had the highest percentage of children in poverty, 37.1 percent, which was approximately midway between the rates of 1970 and 1980. As we would expect, Northern Appalachia had increased rates of childhood poverty. In 1990, for the first time, this subregion's rate, 19.7 percent, exceeded the national rate of 17.6 and Southern Appalachia's rate, 18.6 percent. Northern Appalachia had two decades of increases in childhood poverty rates. Child poverty increased by almost 50 percent in Northern Appalachia from 1970 to 1990. Northern Ohio, Pennsylvania, and West Virginia in particular had large increases in the 1980s. Appalachian New York, despite improved economic measures had an increase in the portion of children in poverty in the 1980s. Southern Appalachia had a major decline in the 1970s and a modest increase in the 1980s. Only Appalachian Georgia among the Southern Appalachian states had a decline in the rate of childhood poverty in the 1980s. Appalachian Mississippi's rate, although far lower than 1970, remains second only to Eastern Kentucky. The economic growth of North and South Carolina was not enough to push down rates of children's poverty in the 1980s. Appalachian metropolitan counties had higher rates of increases from 1970 to 1990 than the nation. Rural counties had a decrease from 1970 to 1990, but the percent of childhood poverty remains higher in rural counties of the region.

Maps 6-16 and 6-17 portray rates of childhood poverty in the 1980s and changes from 1970 to 1990. More children in Northern Appalachia are poor in 1990 than before. Central Appalachia's poverty rates for children are the worst in the region despite some improvement since 1970. Once again, improvements in the 1970s were more than offset by the losses of the 1980s. Southern Appalachia's children have lower rates of poverty than before. That progress came in the 1970s. The 1980s brought a small increase. Shockingly high rates of childhood poverty continue among some counties of Southern Appalachian states, especially Tennessee, Alabama, Mississippi, and Virginia.

In addition to concentrations of childhood poverty already described, Map 6-16 also indicates very low rates of childhood poverty in counties surrounding urban areas. The eastern tier of Appalachian Pennsylvania, counties outside of Pittsburgh, Cincinnati, Winston-Salem, Birmingham, and especially Atlanta have the region's lowest rates of childhood poverty. Further, the rates have almost all declined, especially where the

Table 6-14
Children In Poverty In Appalachia, 1970 to 1990

	1970	1980	1990	Rate of Change 1980-90	Rate of Change 1970-90
United States	14.86%	16.00%	17.55%	9.68%	18.07%
Appalachia	18.91%	17.02%	20.33%	19.44%	7.52%
Northern	13.31%	14.20%	19.65%	38.35%	47.62%
Central	34.98%	25.68%	30.10%	17.20%	-13.95%
Southern	22.60%	18.00%	18.63%	3.51%	-17.58%
Metro Counties	14.41%	14.36%	17.53%	22.13%	21.64%
Northern	10.65%	12.38%	17.69%	42.90%	66.08%
Central	20.63%	17.67%	22.87%	29.47%	10.85%
Southern	19.71%	16.61%	17.18%	3.42%	-12.82%
Rural	23.19%	19.29%	22.80%	18.21%	-1.69%
Northern	16.42%	16.06%	21.60%	34.46%	31.53%
Central	36.25%	26.33%	30.67%	16.48%	-15.38%
Southern	25.77%	19.46%	20.29%	4.27%	-21.29%

Source: U.S. Bureau of the Census.

Figure 6-15
Children in Poverty in Appalachia, 1970 to 1990

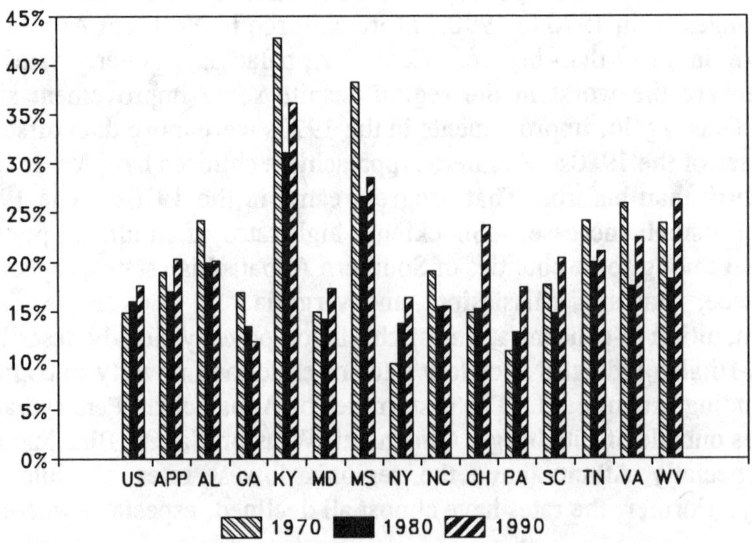

Figure 6-15 (Continued)
Children in Poverty in Appalachia, 1970 to 1990

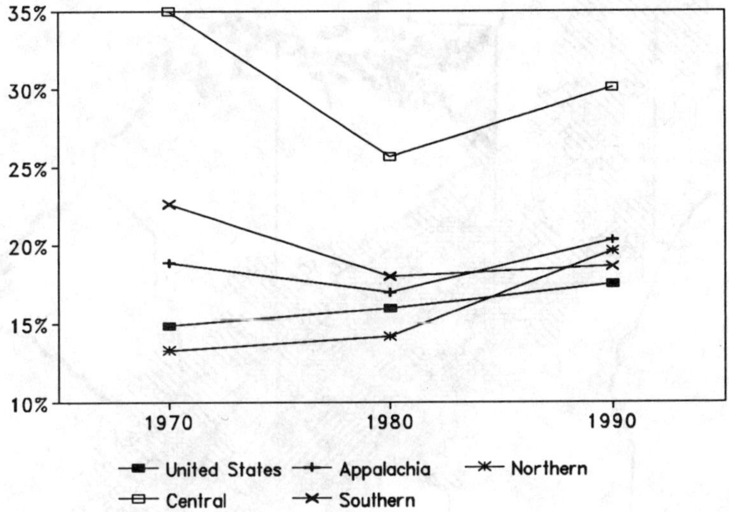

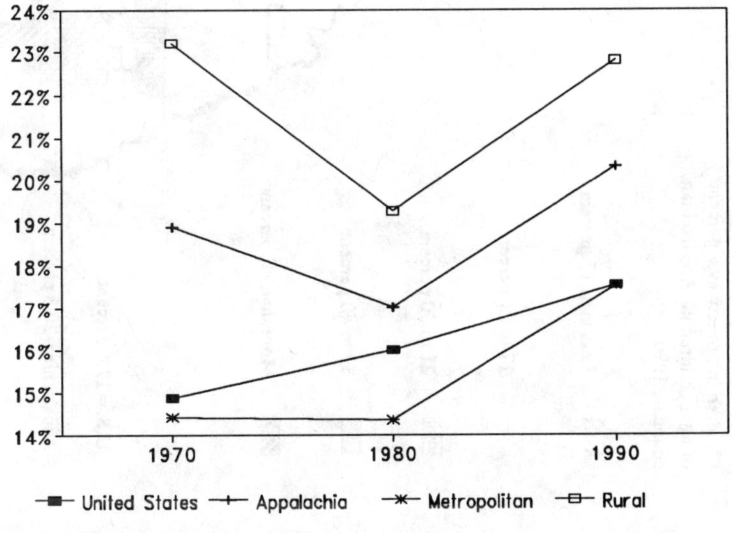

Map 6-16
Children in Poverty in Appalachian Counties, 1990

Children in poverty as a percent of total children in Appalachian counties, 1990

- Less than 17 percent
- 17 to 21 percent
- 21 to 30 percent
- 30 to 40 percent
- More than 40 percent

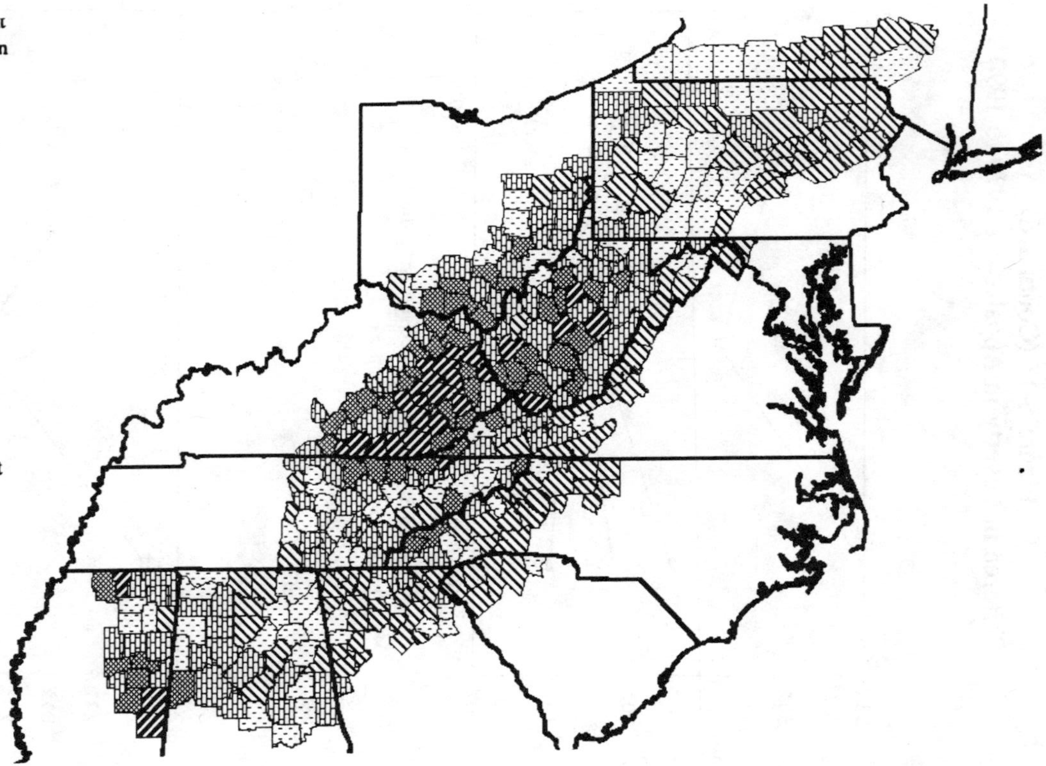

U.S. = 17.6 percent

Appalachia = 20.3 percent

Prepared for Commission on Religion in Appalachia

Map 6-17
Rates of Change of Children in Poverty in Appalachian Counties, 1970 to 1990

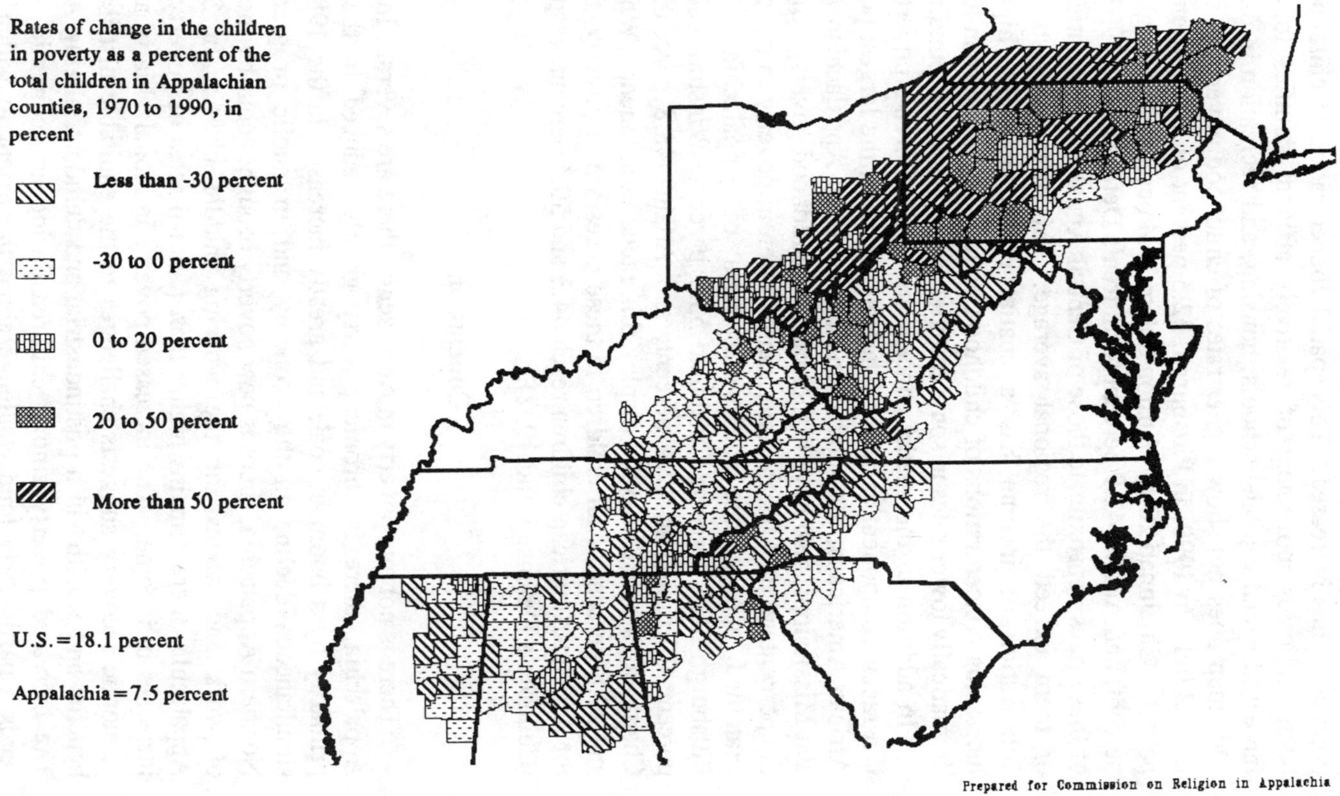

population has increased. This spatial concentration of childhood well-being indicates movement of relatively affluent families to areas of increased social capital—schools, housing, and recreation in particular. This map does not show higher rates of childhood poverty in the cities left behind. In 1990, in Pittsburgh, 32.5 percent of all children were in poverty; Cincinnati 20.6; Winston-Salem 23.4 percent; Birmingham 35.9 percent; and Atlanta 42.9 percent (Children's Defense Fund 1992). Some of these rates approximate those of Central Appalachian counties and all of them exceed the regional average. This map suggests that the polarization of income has a spatial component with higher and increasing concentrations of childhood poverty in large urban areas and dramatically lower rates in some counties immediately surrounding them.

In addition to the spatial concentration of children's poverty, there is a racial component as well. The counties with the largest portion of African Americans, the southernmost counties of Appalachian Alabama and Mississippi, also have higher rates of childhood poverty. Similarly, the percentage of African-American children in poverty in the cities we examined approximate the worst rates of Appalachian counties: Pittsburgh 56.9 percent; Cincinnati 53.9 percent; Winston-Salem 37.1 percent; Birmingham 42.4 percent; and Atlanta 48.8 percent. Even Chattanooga and Knoxville display this racial component. While 28.1 and 29.8 percent of all children in these cities are in poverty, the rates for African-American children reach 44.3 and 50.6 percent, respectively (Children's Defense Fund 1992).

Conclusion

There is not one poverty in Appalachia, there are several. In Central Appalachia, there is chronic poverty greatly reduced in the 1970s, primarily by a boom in coal, and greatly increased in the 1980s by a simultaneous decline in the economy and in public programs. In Northern Appalachia, there is new poverty brought about by the decline of work and wages for the working middle class. In Southern Appalachia, there remains higher than national rates of poverty despite increases in income. The increased poverty in Appalachia in a time of economic recovery suggests challenges to the equitable distribution of benefits and wealth in a postindustrial and deindustrializing America. The increased poverty among children during an economic recovery sends a particularly loud challenge about the extent to which we will permit American children to be impoverished by the economic misfortunes of their families.

Chapter 7

Social Capital in Appalachia

Social and economic policies and practices form the backdrop of the conditions that the chapters of this section have described. Changes in work, income, and the labor force of the region affected population, families, children, and poverty. This chapter examines the social capital conditions of Appalachia, the steps we take to produce and sustain healthy and educated citizens and community members.

Health

Several conditions suggest the disparity in resources we invest in people within the Appalachian region and the nation. Northern Appalachian and Southern Appalachian states vary greatly on measures of child health, for example. These measures are for the entire state, rather than just the Appalachian portion, however. They offer less precise measures than have been used to this point. Nonetheless, they suggest the dimensions of some measures of social capital and the rank of Appalachian states among all states. They also indicate state policies that affect conditions on the county level.

In general, Southern Appalachian states rank far lower than Northern Appalachian states and Appalachian Kentucky, which comprises most of Central Appalachia, in low-weight births, infant mortality, deaths between ages 1 to 14, and violent deaths between ages 15 to 19. Tables 7-1 to 7-4 report measures on each of these factors for the years 1985 and 1990. The low ranks of the Southern Appalachian states on these measures suggest an area of Appalachia where children have higher risk for problems at birth and at different stages of their development. This subregion of Appalachia showed the most improvement in income and employment. Part of the new global economy, apparent in Appalachia, may be that social capital investments in children are less necessary or available as they were before. Workers in postindustrial, deindustrialized economies may not have to be born healthy, sustained, and developed locally. Instead, healthy, developed workers can be expected to move to places where work is available and to compete for it at local wages with local healthy, developed workers. Rather than increasing social capital spending to develop people, we may be expecting those men and women who have benefitted most by whatever social capital was spent on them to move where they can find work. Such a step permits us to keep levels of social capital low and maintain an adequate supply of workers where they are needed.

Fortunately, the tables report improvements in all states in reduced infant mortality and, for all but two states, in reduced child death rates. Unfortunately the tables also report disturbingly high increases in low

Table 7-1
Percent Low Birth-Weight Babies in Appalachian States, 1985 and 1990

State	Indicators 1985	1990	% Change	1990 Rank
Maryland	7.6	7.8	2.63	41
New York	7.0	7.6	8.57	38
Ohio	6.6	7.1	7.58	26
Pennsylvania	6.6	7.1	7.58	26
West Virginia	6.9	7.1	2.90	26
Kentucky	**7.0**	**7.1**	**1.43**	**26**
Alabama	8.0	8.4	5.00	46
Georgia	8.1	8.7	7.41	47
Mississippi	8.8	9.5	7.95	50
North Carolina	7.9	8.0	1.27	42
South Carolina	8.6	8.7	1.16	47
Tennessee	7.9	8.2	3.80	44
Virginia	7.0	7.2	2.86	32

Source: Annie E. Casey Foundation, *Kids Count Data Book: State Profiles of Child Well-Being*, 1993.

Table 7-2
Infant Mortality Rates in Appalachian States, 1985 and 1990 (Per 1,000 Live Births)

State	Indicators 1985	1990	% Change	1990 Rank
Maryland	11.9	9.5	-20.17	31
New York	10.8	9.6	-11.11	32
Ohio	10.3	9.8	-4.85	36
Pennsylvania	11.0	9.6	-12.73	32
West Virginia	10.7	9.9	-7.48	37
Kentucky	**11.2**	**8.5**	**-24.11**	**20**
Alabama	12.6	10.8	-14.29	46
Georgia	12.7	12.4	-2.36	50
Mississippi	13.7	12.1	-11.68	49
North Carolina	11.8	10.6	-10.17	43
South Carolina	14.2	11.7	-17.61	48
Tennessee	11.4	10.3	-9.65	41
Virginia	11.5	10.2	-11.30	40

Source: Annie E. Casey Foundation, *Kids Count Data Book: State Profiles of Child Well-Being*, 1993.

Table 7-3
Child Death Rate in Appalachian States, 1985 and 1990
Ages 1-14 (Per 100,000 Children)

State	Indicators			
	1985	1990	% Change	1990 Rank
Maryland	31.7	27.2	-14.20	13
New York	30.3	29.0	-4.29	22
Ohio	29.7	29.2	-1.68	23
Pennsylvania	30.9	28.5	-7.77	19
West Virginia	29.2	25.3	-13.36	7
Kentucky	**28.9**	**29.4**	**1.73**	**24**
Alabama	36.6	38.5	5.1	48
Georgia	37.1	35.9	-3.23	39
Mississippi	47.0	44.7	-4.89	50
North Carolina	35.7	30.7	-14.01	30
South Carolina	37.9	37.5	-1.06	44
Tennessee	41.1	35.3	-14.11	37
Virginia	29.7	28.1	-5.39	17

Source: Annie E. Casey Foundation, *Kids Count Data Book: State Profiles of Child Well-Being*, 1993.

Table 7-4
Teen Violent Death Rate in Appalachian States, 1985 and 1990
Ages 15-19 (Per 100,000 Teens)

State	Indicators			
	1985	1990	% Change	1990 Rank
Maryland	56.1	76.9	37.08	36
New York	44.7	60.7	35.79	14
Ohio	50.6	54.7	8.10	8
Pennsylvania	46.3	53.5	15.55	7
West Virginia	70.1	73.2	4.42	27
Kentucky	**66.8**	**74.7**	**11.83**	**30**
Alabama	73.3	101.7	38.74	48
Georgia	71.9	74.4	3.48	29
Mississippi	74.4	99.6	33.87	47
North Carolina	70.2	71.7	2.14	22
South Carolina	71.1	75.6	6.33	34
Tennessee	67.3	75.0	11.44	31
Virginia	52.9	71.6	35.35	21

Source: Annie E. Casey Foundation, *Kids Count Data Book: State Profiles of Child Well-Being*, 1993.

Table 7-5
Public Health Report Card for Appalachian States
Reported By National Rank

States	Medical Care Access	Healthy Environ-ment	Healthy Neighbor-hoods	Health Behaviors	Community Health Services
Maryland	10	12	25	16	18
New York	14	29	27	12	7
Ohio	14	22	24	20	14
Pennsylvania	16	36	21	30	38
West Virginia	32	21	35	34	37
Kentucky	**27**	**22**	**36**	**31**	**35**
Alabama	42	22	41	30	26
Georgia	35	21	36	15	26
Mississippi	38	28	42	29	40
North Carolina	31	17	32	22	27
South Carolina	41	10	38	23	17
Tennessee	39	17	40	25	25
Virginia	27	20	24	16	14

Source: American Public Health Association, *America's Public Health Report Card.*

birth-weight babies in New York, Ohio, Pennsylvania, Alabama, Georgia, and Mississippi. Six of the Southern Appalachian states ranked among the bottom ten states nationally for the percent of low-weight babies. Similarly, violent deaths among teens increased in all Appalachian states. Maryland, New York, Alabama, Mississippi, and Virginia showed particularly high increases, 33 percent or higher. Alabama and Mississippi have the highest rates among Appalachian states and among the highest rates in the nation.

Closely related to the health of people are the policies that states undertake to protect the health of citizens. The American Public Health Association undertook in 1992 to examine these state policies. It used 25 indicators and combined them into five measures that ranged from behaviors of residents, like smoking and seat belt use, to policies for community health services, environmental quality, and medical care access. Table 7-5 provides the rank of each Appalachian state on each of the five measures of the report card.

Apart from medical care access, the subregional differences are modest. The ranks of Northern Appalachian states, with the exception of West Virginia, are higher than the other states. This indicates lower numbers of medically uninsured residents, larger Medicaid spending and less strict eligibility criteria, and more access to primary and prenatal

Table 7-6
Medically Underserved Counties and Community Health Centers In Appalachia, 1992

State	Total Appalachian Counties	Number of Designated Medically Underserved	Number With Community Health Centers	Total Percentage Designated Appalachian Counties With CHC Programs	FY '92 CHC/MHC (only) Grant Dollars	1991 CHC/MHC Users
Maryland	3	3	2	67%	410,331	4,134
New York	13	9	2	22%	533,332	5,468
Ohio	28	26	12	46%	6,053,881	34,662
Pennsylvania	51	40	19	47%	5,931,632	90,656
West Virginia	54	49	38	77%	10,231,602	111,558
Kentucky	**48**	**43**	**12**	**28%**	**4,296,529**	**37,412**
Alabama	34	34	18	53%	5,0955,778	72,249
Georgia	34	27	7	25%	1,105,416	12,681
Mississippi	19	19	8	42%	3,247,927	21,770
North Carolina	28	25	4	16%	1,630,850	6,455
South Carolina	6	6	1	17%	567,332	1,285
Tennessee	49	49	31	63%	5,477,699	47,511
Virginia	20	19	8	42%	1,563,191	21,496
TOTAL	387	349	162	46%	46,145,470	473,328

Source: Behringer, "Health Care Services in Appalachia," 1994.

care in these states. All of the Appalachian states rank below 20 on indicators of healthy neighborhoods. These indicators reflect social capital investment, such as education spending, high school graduation rates, and public assistance per family. Cigarette taxes, motor vehicle deaths, violent crime, and unemployment are other indicators in this healthy neighborhood measure. New York ranks highest on community health services—per capita government health spending, sanitation and sewage spending, and public health workers. Pennsylvania and Mississippi rank lowest among the Appalachian states, 38th and 40th, respectively. The Appalachian states cluster between 11th and 33rd on healthy behaviors, i.e., rates of seat belt use, obesity, smoking, and binge drinking. Southern Appalachian states rank slightly better than those in Northern Appalachia on the healthy environment measure. New York and Pennsylvania have the lowest average ranks, 28th and 36th, on indicators of pollution, unsafe drinking water, fluoridated water, and work related injury.

Appalachia has attracted its share of community health centers and federal funding to support them. In fiscal year 1992, for example, 13 percent of all federal grant support for community health centers came to centers within the Appalachian region. These centers served patients who had low incomes or were eligible for Medicaid and Medicare. Table 7-6 reports on the numbers of medically underserved counties in the Appalachian region and of counties with community health centers.

As Table 7-6 indicates, 46 percent of the region's medically underserved counties had community health centers serving 473,328 people in 1992. Notably, West Virginia had community health centers in 77 percent of its medically underserved counties serving 111,558 patients or almost 25 percent of all the people in the region served by community health centers. The rank of West Virginia on the American Public Health Association's report card, 32nd on access, underscores the importance of these community health centers for the health care of West Virginia. West Virginia ranked higher than the more prosperous Southern Appalachian subregion. No other state has the same reliance on community health centers. Appalachian Tennessee has almost as many centers as West Virginia, but only 47,511 users.

The federal government has another more stringent measure of medical care needs that is called Health Professionals Shortage Areas. These areas have a ratio of primary care physicians to number of population that is greater than 1 per 3,500 residents. In places with high levels of poverty and infant mortality the ratio used for designation is 1 per 3,000. Table 7-7 reports on the number of Appalachian counties in

Table 7-7
Changes in Health Professionals Shortage Areas in Appalachian Counties, 1981 to 1991

	Number of HPSA Counties					
State	**Full '81**	**Full '91**	**Part '81**	**Part '91**	**None '81**	**None '91**
Maryland	0	0	2	2	1	1
New York	2	0	9	13	3	2
Ohio	16	9	3	12	10	8
Pennsylvania	5	0	40	33	7	17
West Virginia	25	16	21	27	8	12
Kentucky	23	20	8	9	18	21
Alabama	24	17	7	9	4	9
Georgia	14	15	2	3	20	16
Mississippi	15	11	1	0	4	9
North Carolina	15	3	6	4	8	22
South Carolina	1	0	2	2	3	4
Tennessee	25	27	2	6	12	17
Virginia	8	5	2	4	9	10
TOTAL	173	123	105	124	118	148

Source: Behringer, "Health Care Services in Appalachia," 1994.

each state designated full or partial Health Professional Shortage Areas in 1981 and 1991. The number of counties with full designation has declined and the number of counties not designated has increased indicating an increase in the region in health professionals. Pennsylvania and North Carolina have made the most progress in reducing the number of full or partially designated Health Professionals Shortage Areas. Georgia, Ohio, and Tennessee have lost ground on this measure.

While far from adequate, medical services in Appalachia are better met than other needs. Medicaid and Medicare provide a source of social capital separate from work that supports community health centers in addition to direct grants from the federal and state governments that go to them. The community health centers represent the continuation of social capital policies of the 1960s and the Great Society programs. Despite the extensive criticism and reaction against these programs that came later, especially in the 1980s, the community health centers testify to the importance and lasting benefit of these programs to Appalachia. They also provide evidence that social capital policies to address human needs separate from the creation and dissolution of a labor force are possible.

Poverty Policies in Appalachia

In addition to inferring characteristics of social capital from measures of family poverty, child well-being and the like, expenditures and policies in the Appalachian states to reduce poverty provide additional characteristics. In this regard, Southern Appalachian states provide far less cash assistance to AFDC families than Northern Appalachian states. The levels of payment as well as eligibility are matters of state policies. There is no federally prescribed minimum benefit. On average across the nation, the monthly 1992 AFDC benefit for a family of three was $372 a month, roughly equal to the benefit that Maryland and Virginia provide. This benefit equalled 41 percent of the national poverty level for a family of three and when supplemented with food stamps provided a family with income equal to about 72 percent of the poverty level.

In the states of Southern Appalachia a family has to have less money to be eligible for smaller AFDC benefits (Lav et al. 1993:11). None of the Southern Appalachian states approximated the national average level of AFDC benefits. Alabama and Mississippi provide the lowest monthly benefits in the nation. Georgia, North and South Carolina, and Tennessee, states that showed prosperity in the 1980s, all have monthly maximum AFDC payments well below the national average and all but one of the Northern Appalachian states. West Virginia's monthly maximum payment of $249 was lower than Georgia's, $280, and North Carolina's, $272. Only Ohio increased its payment level from 1992 to 1993. Maryland and South Carolina reduced AFDC benefits by 4.8 percent, resulting in a decline in purchasing power of 7.5 percent. In addition to the level at which AFDC monthly benefits are set, states have options to extend other forms of assistance to low-income families. States may provide funds for special needs and emergency assistance with matching federal funds. Special needs support may go to a family on a continuing basis to prevent homelessness or loss of vital services, such as heat in winter. Emergency assistance is a short-term benefit to a family in crisis. It may assist families who are not eligible for AFDC if the averted crisis is likely to reduce a child's status to destitution. The prospect of federal matching funds for these additional forms of assistance to low-income families encouraged 37 states to provide one or both of these forms of programs. Alabama, Kentucky, Mississippi, and Tennessee were among the thirteen states with neither special needs nor emergency assistance programs within AFDC. Maryland, New York, North Carolina, Ohio, Pennsylvania, and West Virginia were among the states with both programs in 1993 (Lav et. al. 1993: 20-33).

States may, of course, devise other assistance programs for people in poverty. General assistance programs provide cash assistance programs for the poor, who for one reason or another do not meet federal eligibility requirements for AFDC Supplemental Security Income (SSI). Only Maryland, New York, Ohio, and Pennsylvania provide state-supported general assistance among the Appalachian states. Similarly, only New York and Pennsylvania provide state assistance to increase monthly federal SSI payments to the very poor elderly, blind, or disabled. These sums are very modest, $86 and $32 a month, for New York and Ohio, respectively (Lav et. al. 1993: 35-50).

Finally, states may provide additional support for the Special Supplemental Food Program for Women, Infants, and Children (WIC). WIC is widely regarded by policy analysts as an effective prevention program that increases the health of recipients and saves money in other programs. The program provides food, nutrition assessment, counselling, and health-care referrals for low-income pregnant and postpartum women, infants, and children under five years of age. Evaluations of the program associate it with reductions in late fetal deaths, and in low birth weight, prematurity, and anemia. These benefits translate into cost savings. A study of the U.S. Department of Agriculture found that every WIC dollar resulted in Medicaid savings of $1.92 to $4.21 for the postpartum mothers and their children. Similarly, a GAO study suggested an almost 3.5 to 1 ratio of averted medical care costs over 18 years with WIC dollars in one year. WIC reached only approximately 60 percent of the people eligible for the program in 1993, an increase over past years. Eighteen states in 1993 supplemented federal WIC funds with their own in order to reach more eligible women and children. Maryland, New York, North Carolina, Pennsylvania, and West Virginia are the only Appalachian states to supplement federal WIC funds. Four of the five are Northern Appalachian states. New York cut its supplement by 11.5 percent in 1993 (Lav et al. 1993:67-70).

States may provide assistance to low-income individuals and families through medical benefits. Medicaid is a state-administered program that reimburses medical providers for services to families eligible for AFDC, some pregnant women and children with higher levels of income than AFDC, and low-income elderly and disabled individuals, including most SSI recipients. In addition, states may provide general medical assistance to low-income families and individuals who are not eligible for Medicaid.

States have found themselves short of revenues in the face of the recession of the late 1980s and a slumping economy. Consequently, many of them have cut programs of general medical assistance. In the beginning of 1993, 18 states had no program of general medical

Table 7-8
Poverty Policies Among Appalachian States

State	AFDC Maximum Benefit /1993	AFDC % Change Over 1/92	AFDC Special Needs	AFDC Emergency Assistance	General Assistance	Maximum Monthly State SSI Supplements	MEDICAID Eligibility Changes	MEDICAID Service Changes	WIC Supplements % Change 1992-93
Maryland	359	-4.8	YES	YES	YES	0	NONE	-	0
New York	577	0	YES	YES	NO	86	NONE	+/-	-11.5
Ohio	341	2.1	YES	YES	YES	0	+	NONE	NA
Pennsylvania	421	0	YES	YES	YES	0	+	-	0
West Virginia	249	0	YES	YES	NO	0	NONE	+	0
Kentucky	**228**	**0**	NO	NO	NO	**0**	NONE	+	NA
Alabama	164	10.1	NO	NO	NO	0	NONE	+	NA
Georgia	280	0	YES	NO	NO	0	+	+	NA
Mississippi	120	0	NO	NO	NO	0	NONE	NONE	NA
North Carolina	272	0	YES	YES	NO	0	NONE	+	0
South Carolina	200	-4.8	NO	YES	NO	0	-	+	NA
Tennessee	185	0	NO	NO	NO	0	NONE	NONE	NA
Virginia	354	0	NO	YES	NO	0	NONE	-	NA

+ Increased - Restricted

Source: Lav, Iris J., Edward Lazere, Robert Greenstein, and Steven D. Gold, *The States and the Poor*, 1993.

assistance including, Alabama, Georgia, Kentucky, Mississippi, North Carolina, and Tennessee. Seven states decreased their general medical assistance from 1992 levels including Maryland, New York, and Pennsylvania. South Carolina in 1993 eliminated its medically needy program and thus restricted eligibility for Medicaid assistance. On the other hand, Pennsylvania and Ohio changed their eligibility requirements to include pregnant women and infants with incomes of 185 percent of the poverty level. Georgia went up to 150 percent for the same set of women and children. States also adjusted the services covered by Medicaid, most often by expanding services to pregnant women, infants, and children (Lav et al. 1993:51-66).

The expanded prenatal services, while welcomed, did not offset the cutbacks that poked holes in the "safety nets" of federal and state programs. The Reagan administration placed the safety net so near the ground that it hardly broke the economic fall of people. For example, the inflation-adjusted change in the standard of need for AFDC families had declined between 1970 and 1987 in value in every Appalachian state except North Carolina and Ohio. There the values had increased by 5.5 and 10.7 percent, respectively. In all other states, the value had declined from a minimum of about 18 percent in Pennsylvania, to a high of 68 percent in Kentucky (Shapiro, Greenstein, 1988:56). Table 7-8 provides information on the poverty policies just discussed for each of the states in Appalachia.

Education

The Appalachian region outperformed the nation in some measure of educational improvement. The portion of adults 25 years and older with four years of high school or more education increased at a faster rate in Appalachia than nationally between 1970 and 1990, 56.2 percent compared with 43.8 percent. Increased rates were even sharper in the rural counties of Appalachia. In particular, the rural counties of Central Appalachia increased the adult portion of its population with at least a high school education by 100 percent from 1970 to 1990. With this progress, the rural counties of Appalachia passed the halfway mark among its residents 25 years and older with a high school degree. This was still far behind the nation and the region as a whole, where 75.2 and 68.4 percent of adults twenty-five years of age and older had at least completed a high school education. Table 7-9, Figure 7-10, and Map 7-11 report these measures.

Appalachia saw the percentage of college graduates among its residents almost double between 1970 and 1990. The nation's college

Table 7-9
High School Graduates Among Adults
1970 to 1990

	1970	1980	1990	Rate of Change 1970-90	Rate of Change 1980-90
United States	52.30%	66.50%	75.20%	43.79%	13.08%
Appalachia	43.78%	57.40%	68.37%	56.18%	19.12%
Northern	49.94%	63.53%	73.29%	46.76%	15.36%
Central	27.99%	42.28%	53.42%	90.85%	26.36%
Southern	38.51%	53.24%	66.11%	71.64%	24.16%
Metro Counties	48.63%	62.87%	73.60%	51.35%	17.06%
Northern	51.55%	65.79%	75.50%	46.46%	14.76%
Central	47.70%	59.33%	68.79%	44.21%	15.94%
Southern	43.88%	59.04%	71.60%	63.16%	21.27%
Rural Counties	38.95%	52.25%	63.39%	62.77%	21.34%
Northern	47.91%	60.89%	70.80%	47.77%	16.26%
Central	25.80%	40.48%	51.77%	100.66%	27.89%
Southern	32.87%	47.12%	59.97%	82.45%	27.27%

Source: US Bureau of the Census

Figure 7-10
High School Graduates Among Adults, 1970 to 1990

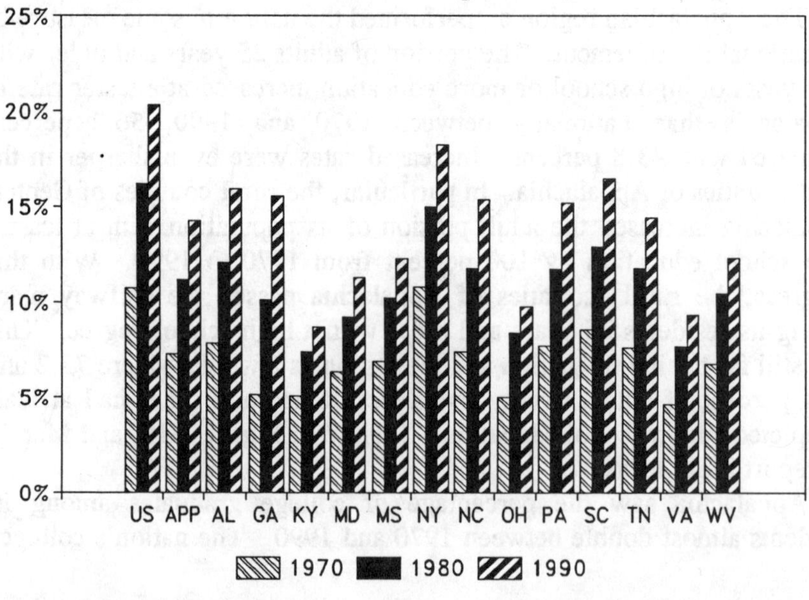

Figure 7-10 (Continued)
High School Graduates Among Adults
1970 to 1990

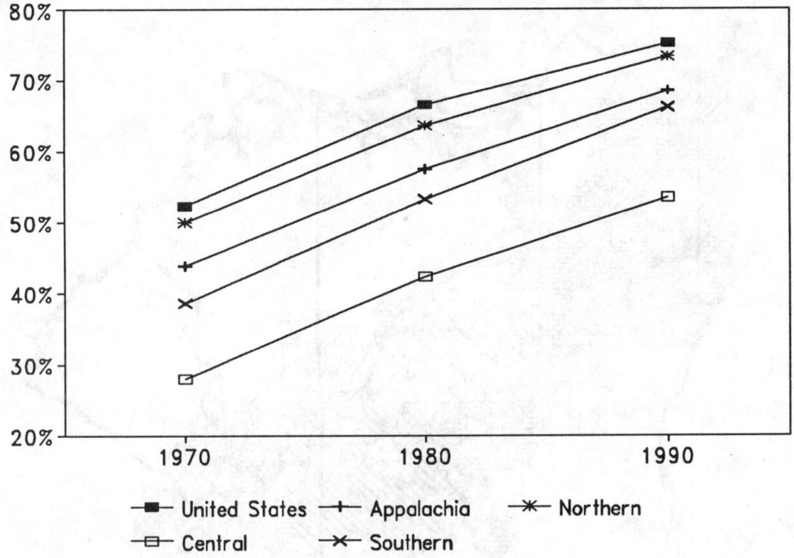

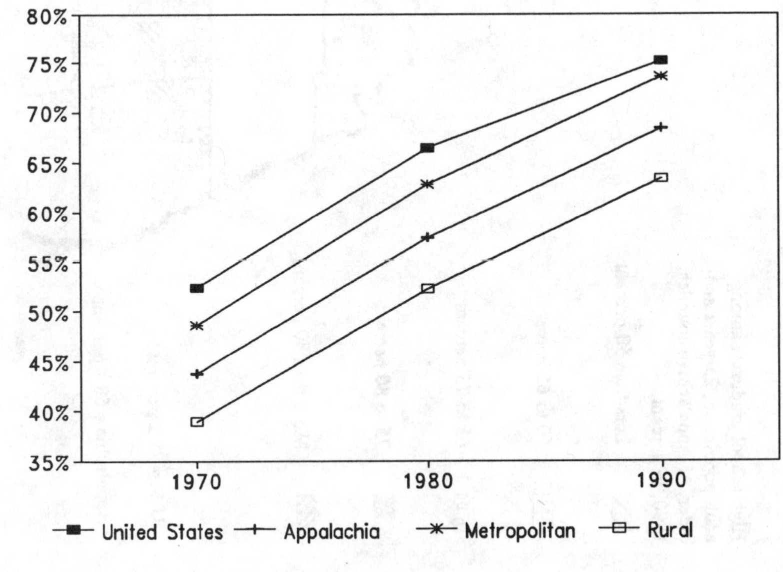

Map 7-11
High School Graduates in Appalachian Counties, 1990

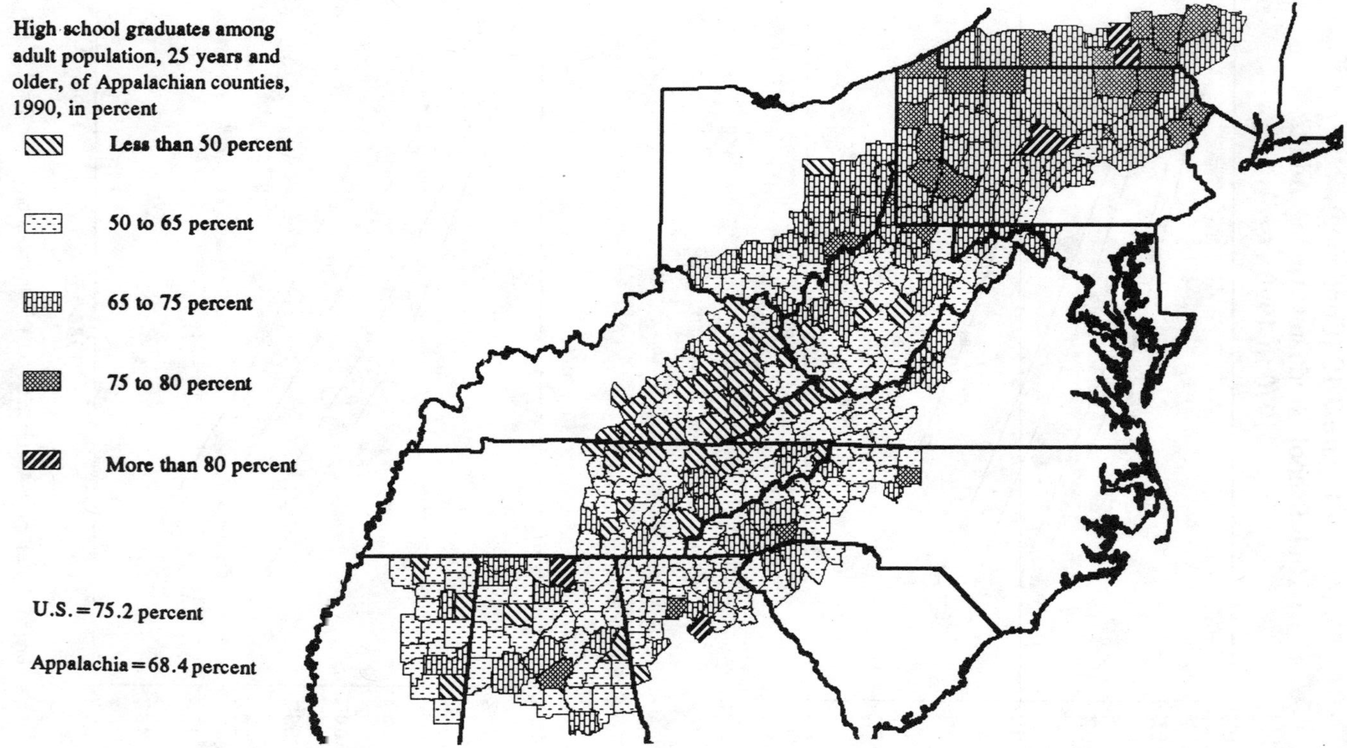

Prepared for Commission on Religion in Appalachia

graduates increased at a rate of 90 percent. By 1990, the region still lagged behind the nation considerably, 14.3 to 20.3 percent, respectively. It is apparent moreover, that the percentage of college graduates increased in highest rates in those places that enjoyed the greatest rate of income growth. Specifically, the portion of college graduates increased in the metropolitan counties of Southern Appalachia by 110 percent. The metropolitan counties of Southern Appalachia approach the 1990 national level of college graduates among their adult population over twenty-five years of age, 19.2 and 20.3 percent, respectively. Both measures exceed the regional rate of 14.3 by a wide margin. Nowhere is the association of increased education and increased prosperity more astounding than in the metropolitan counties of Georgia. There the percent of college educated adults increased by 356.5 percent. The metropolitan counties of Appalachian North and South Carolina had no similar remarkable increase.

The rates of college educated adults are higher for metropolitan counties than rural counties in every subregion of Appalachia. The gap between metropolitan and rural counties increased in Northern and Southern Appalachia from 1970 to 1990.

On the other hand, the rural counties of Kentucky, New York, Ohio, and West Virginia had the lowest rates of increase of college educated adults. These lower rates left the rural counties of Kentucky, Ohio, and West Virginia with the smallest portions of college educated adults, 8.3 percent, 9.1 percent, and 10.7 percent, respectively. Table 7-12 and Figures 7-13 and Map 7-14 provide measures, graphs, and maps for college education among adults 25 years and older in Appalachia.

The formula that education translates into higher incomes is not always applicable. Several metropolitan counties in Southern Appalachia increased the percentages of adults with high school and college educations, and had higher employment and income as well. But there have been increases in education virtually everywhere in Appalachia with economic decline in some places and economic growth in others. The combination of increased educational attainment and increased prosperity comes together primarily in the metropolitan counties on the edge of Appalachia. Improving education in rural counties, especially in Central Appalachia, may be necessary for economic improvement but so far it has not been sufficient.

Northern Appalachia provides additional insight into education and income. The former economic prosperity of Northern Appalachia was built on a work force with a high school education, not college. In 1970, almost half of Northern Appalachia's over-25 population had a high school education. In 1970, Northern Appalachia led the region on

Table 7-12
College Graduates Among Adults
1970 to 1990

	1970	1980	1990	Rate of Change 1970-90	Rate of Change 1980-90
United States	10.70%	16.20%	20.30%	89.72%	25.31%
Appalachia	7.27%	11.17%	14.26%	96.16%	27.72%
Northern	7.58%	11.49%	14.40%	89.90%	25.35%
Central	5.00%	7.60%	8.78%	75.73%	15.44%
Southern	7.38%	11.66%	15.34%	107.91%	31.65%
Metro Counties	8.54%	13.24%	17.53%	105.32%	32.44%
Northern	8.15%	12.51%	16.23%	99.20%	29.67%
Central	9.41%	12.69%	14.39%	52.95%	13.40%
Southern	9.14%	14.26%	19.17%	109.74%	34.45%
Rural Counties	6.01%	9.22%	11.14%	85.52%	20.93%
Northern	6.87%	10.28%	12.33%	79.46%	19.91%
Central	4.50%	7.07%	8.18%	81.49%	15.67%
Southern	5.53%	8.91%	11.07%	100.20%	24.26%

Source: US Bureau of the Census

Figure 7-13
College Graduates Among Adults, 1970 to 1990

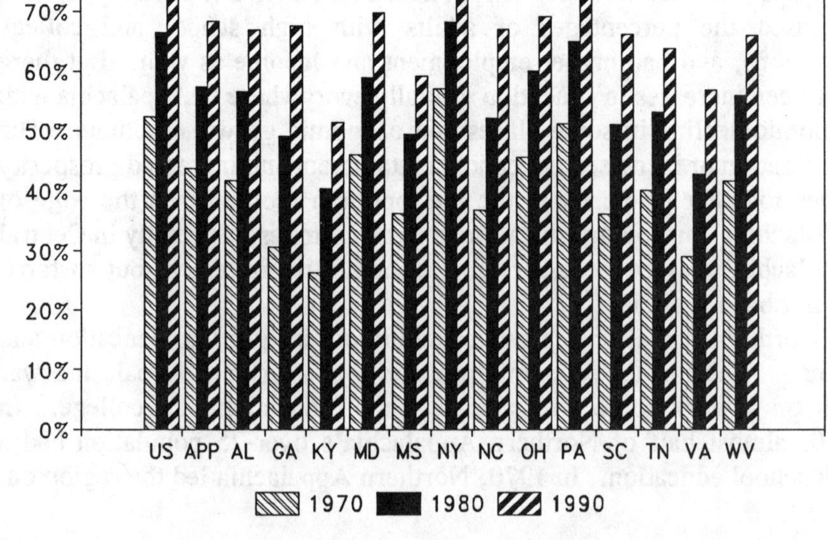

Figure 7-13 (Continued)
College Graduates Among Adults, 1970 to 1990

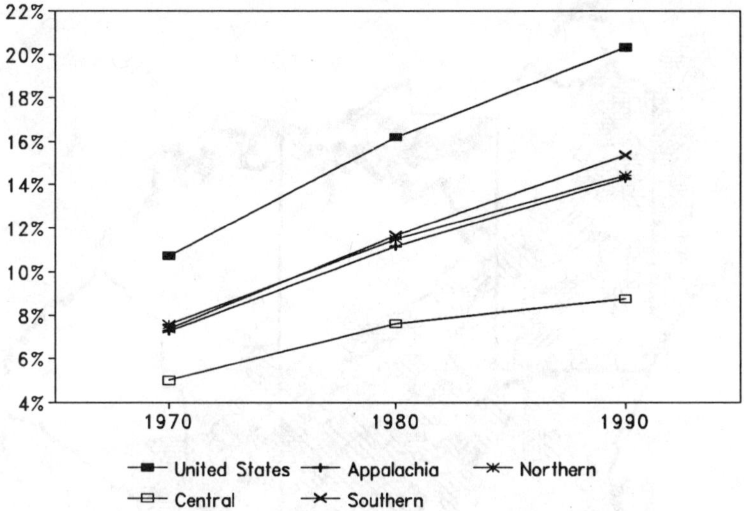

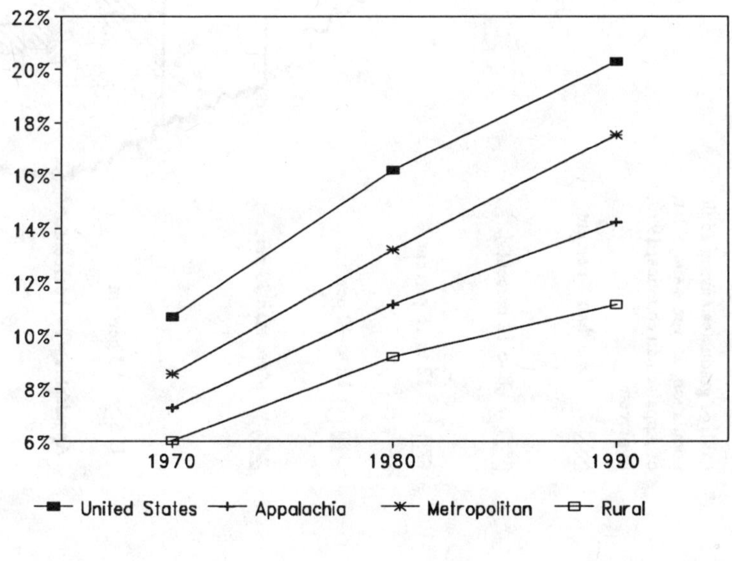

Map 7-14
College Graduates in Appalachian Counties, 1990

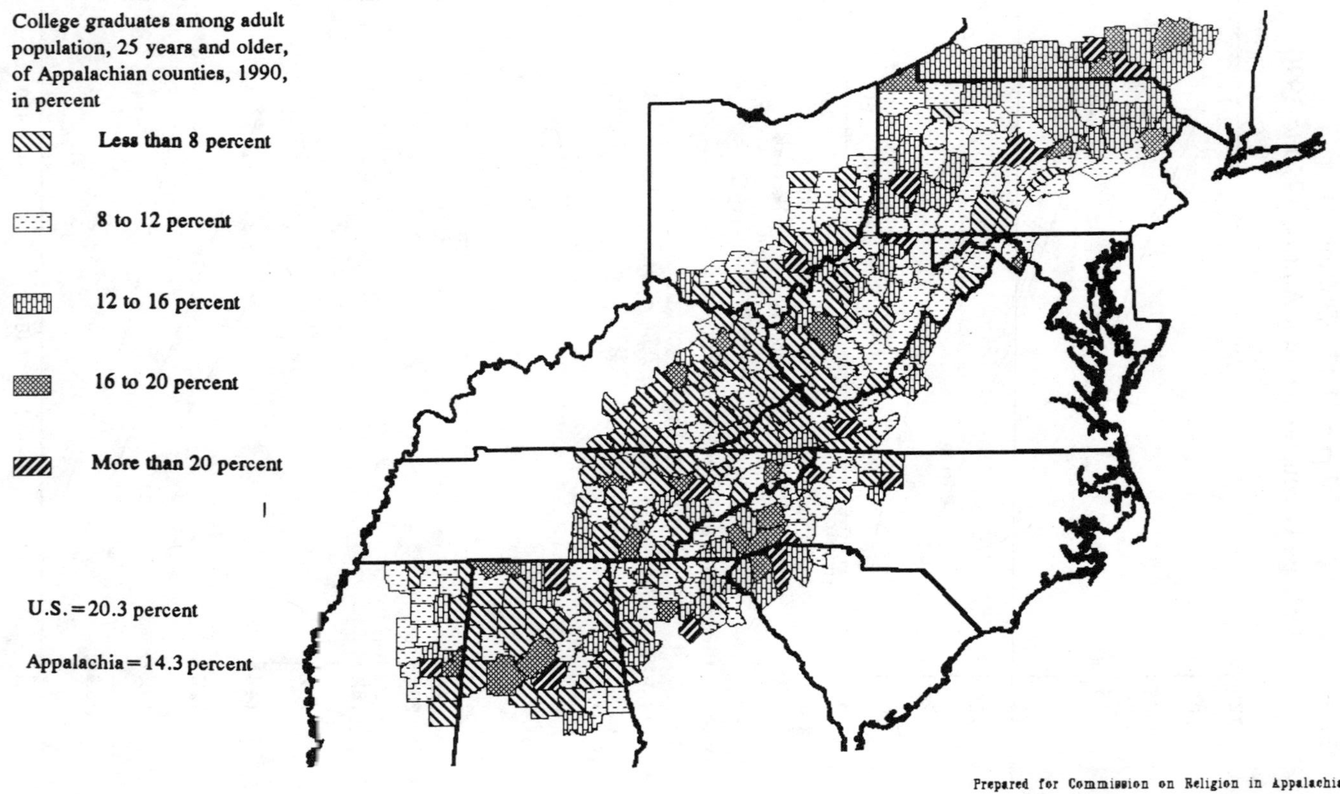

measures of school education and income. By 1990, the region had improved its high school measure but its income measure had declined. This is perhaps the single greatest change in the American economy. The decline of high wage manufacturing employment has eroded the possibility of entering or continuing in the working middle class with only a high school education. The changed employment structure has increased the educational requirement for most high wage employment. However, it does not provide improved employment opportunities in proportion to higher educational attainment.

Additional measures on education are available for the Appalachian states. Table 7-15 relates statewide measures for high school students who graduate. Only one state in Appalachia, West Virginia, ranked in the top half of states in the nation and increased between 1985 and 1990. Once again, Northern Appalachian states ranked higher on this measure than Southern Appalachian states. Pennsylvania, however, had a particularly large decline in high school graduation from 1985 to 1990 and fell behind Ohio. South Carolina's decline brought that state's 1990 measure to the lowest in the region and 48th in the nation. Once again, however, these state averages are likely to be worse than the Appalachian portions of the Southern Appalachian states and better than the Appalachian portions of Northern and Central Appalachia.

Table 7-16 indicates a similar statewide disinvestment in teenagers. Once again, Southern Appalachian states Alabama, Georgia, and Mississippi have high rates of teenagers who are neither in school nor in the labor force. New York and West Virginia, in Northern Appalachia, as well as Kentucky, have equally high rates. Pennsylvania and Virginia have the lowest statewide rates of these teenagers and thus seem to provide more social capital investment in their teenagers. Once again, these measures indicate that areas with economic growth have relatively low level of social capital. In this case, Southern Appalachia's growth and improved educational status have occurred despite relatively low investments in the education of teenagers of these states.

Environment

In 1991, the Institute for Southern Studies compiled 256 measures to construct a Green Index, a measure of environmental quality. The index had two parts: Green Conditions and Green Policies. Green Conditions compiled 179 indicators into 11 measures, e.g. water pollution, work place health, and forestry and fish, which reported on environmental quality. Green Policies had two measures. One compiled 73 indicators of state environmental policies and the other compiled four indicators of

Table 7-15
Percent of High School Students Graduating From High School in Appalachian States

State	Indicators 1985	1990	% Change	1990 Rank
Maryland	77.6	70.5	-9.15	31
New York	64.2	60.4	-5.92	46
Ohio	77.4	76.4	-1.29	19
Pennsylvania	78.7	71.7	-8.89	27
West Virginia	75.1	78.0	3.86	13
Kentucky	**69.4**	**68.5**	**-1.30**	**35**
Alabama	64.3	65.9	2.49	39
Georgia	63.1	60.8	-3.65	45
Mississippi	63.6	63.8	0.31	42
North Carolina	70.7	66.7	-5.66	38
South Carolina	63.6	58.2	-8.49	48
Tennessee	66.1	68.7	3.93	34
Virginia	73.3	69.9	-4.64	33

Source: Annie E. Casey Foundation, *Kids Count Data Book: State Profiles of Child Well-Being*, 1993.

Table 7-16
Percent of Teens Not in School and Not in Labor Force in Appalachian States, Ages 16-19

State	Indicators 1985	1990	% Change	1990 Rank
Maryland	4.9	4.3	-12.24	21
New York	5.4	6.1	12.96	42
Ohio	4.0	4.3	7.50	21
Pennsylvania	4.6	3.3	-28.26	9
West Virginia	8.4	6.6	-21.43	45
Kentucky	**7.0**	**6.2**	**-11.43**	**43**
Alabama	11.1	5.8	-47.75	41
Georgia	5.5	6.2	12.73	43
Mississippi	12.8	7.8	-39.06	49
North Carolina	4.9	4.6	-6.12	25
South Carolina	6.8	4.3	-36.76	21
Tennessee	7.2	5.2	-27.78	29
Virginia	4.5	3.3	-26.67	9

Source: Annie E. Casey Foundation, *Kids Count Data Book: State Profiles of Child Well-Being*, 1993.

Table 7-17
Rankings on Green Conditions of Appalachian States, Pollution and Water

States	Air Pollution	Water Pollution	Toxic Chemical Waste	Hazardous Solid Waste	Agri-cultural Pollution	Average Rank on Pollution and Water Measures
Maryland	24	12	18	15	15	17.3
New York	30	15	24	5	30	18.5
Ohio	49	45	49	25	18	42.0
Pennsylvania	46	37	44	38	14	41.3
West Virginia	45	48	35	45	1	43.3
Kentucky	**35**	**34**	**41**	**32**	**8**	**35.5**
Alabama	47	38	36	46	11	41.8
Georgia	42	29	32	42	28	36.3
Mississippi	27	32	34	41	36	33.5
North Carolina	44	28	42	7	30	30.3
South Carolina	29	18	33	50	21	32.5
Tennessee	48	47	48	43	6	46.5
Virginia	37	42	37	44	2	40.0

Source: Hall and Kerry, *1991-1992 Green Index*, 1991.

Table 7-17 (Continued)
Rankings on Green Conditions of Appalachian States Fun-Life Quality and Total Ranks

State	Energy Use and Production	Transportation Efficiency	Community Health	Workplace Health	Forestry and Fish	Fun and Life Quality	Green Conditions Rank
Maryland	17	4	16	5	28	35	14
New York	18	1	22	2	42	39	17
Ohio	37	15	29	14	50	48	46
Pennsylvania	31	9	19	11	32	42	34
West Virginia	40	34	47	39	4	29	41
Kentucky	**32**	**41**	**46**	**30**	**25**	**30**	**39**
Alabama	44	39	48	46	27	43	47
Georgia	21	28	39	40	28	36	38
Mississippi	39	35	50	49	22	32	44
North Carolina	27	25	40	21	20	28	37
South Carolina	29	20	43	33	18	26	35
Tennessee	24	43	38	35	31	23	45
Virginia	30	23	32	29	6	37	36

Source: Hall and Kerry, *1991-1992 Green Index*, 1991.

Table 7-18
Rankings on Green Policies Measures and Total Green Index for Appalachian States

States	State Policies	Leadership in Congress	Green Policies	Green Conditions Rank	Total Green Index
Maryland	15	10	15	14	13
New York	8	12	8	17	8
Ohio	19	24	19	46	37
Pennsylvania	20	22	21	34	26
West Virginia	47	18	45	41	44
Kentucky	**34**	**38**	**33**	**39**	**41**
Alabama	48	46	49	47	50
Georgia	30	36	29	38	39
Mississippi	45	50	46	44	47
North Carolina	16	33	18	37	23
South Carolina	31	30	32	35	36
Tennessee	41	31	40	45	45
Virginia	22	39	22	36	32

Source: Hall and Kerry, *1991-1992 Green Index*, 1991.

each state's Congressional delegation's votes on environmental issues before Congress. Each state was ranked on each of the 11 measures of the Green Conditions Index and on the two measures of the Green Policies Index. The scores on each of the 13 measures were then combined into a score and rank on the Total Green Index. Tables 7-17 and 7-18 report on the Appalachian states' ranks on all 13 measures of the Green Conditions and Green Policies Indices.

Appalachian states come off poorly in this report. Only three of the thirteen Appalachian states are among the top 25 states of the nation: New York (8th); Maryland (13th); and North Carolina (23rd). More than half of the bottom 15 states on the Total Green Index may be found in Appalachia, especially Southern Appalachia: Alabama (50th); Mississippi (47th); Tennessee (45th); West Virginia (44th); Kentucky (41st); Georgia (39th); Ohio (37th); and South Carolina (36th).

According to the Fun and Life Quality measure—some 19 indicators, most of which are related to outdoor recreation—fun has left Appalachia. Only Tennessee barely made it into the top 25 states, nationally, on this measure, primarily because of the strength of its system of state parks and the number of visitors to the Great Smoky Mountains National Park. Eight of the Appalachian states fall among the twenty states with the lowest rank for Fun and Life Quality.

The degree of pollution and waste in the environment may contribute to the low rankings on the Fun and Life Quality Index. When the four pollution indicators are examined, eight Appalachian states have average ranks below 35; eight of the Appalachian states rank among the bottom 15 states. Only Maryland (17.25) and New York (18.5) make it into the top twenty by average rank on these four measures. Among the bottom fifteen are Alabama (41.75), Georgia (36.25), Kentucky (35.5), Ohio (42), Pennsylvania (41.25), Tennessee (46.5), Virginia (40), and West Virginia (43.25).

Appalachian states rank higher on portions of these indices. For example, only four of the states are among the bottom ten on state policies: Alabama (48th); West Virginia (47th); Mississippi (45th); and Tennessee (41st). Six states are among the top states nationally on green policies; the Northern Appalachian states of New York (8th), Maryland (15th), Ohio (19th), and Pennsylvania (20th), and the Southern Appalachian states of North Carolina (16th) and Virginia (22nd).

The Green Index suggests economic changes in Appalachia represent a shift from places with more social capital in environmental factors to places with less. Northern Appalachian states of New York, Pennsylvania, and Ohio rank much higher than the Southern Appalachian states. These three Northern Appalachian states, with the heaviest losses in manufacturing employment, average a rank of 16 on the Green Policies Index compared with a rank of 33 for the Southern Appalachian states. Even on green conditions these three Northern Appalachian states come out ahead on average ranks, 32 to 40. On the Total Green Index the three Northern Appalachian states rank 24th on average compared with a rank of 39th for the Southern Appalachian states. Past environmental subsidies explain the relatively poor environmental conditions of Northern Appalachia. These subsidies seem to remain part of the calculation of economic growth and development now going on in Southern Appalachia.

Another indicator of social capital reported by the Green Conditions Index is Work Place Health. Table 7-19 extracts and reports on seven of the twelve indicators of this measure. In general, one finds higher ranks, that is more protection for workers, among the Northern Appalachian states and less among the Southern Appalachian states. West Virginia most often ranks lower than other Northern Appalachian states. Virginia and North Carolina generally rank much higher than the other Southern Appalachian states.

The rank order of the portion of manufacturing workers within unions and the composite workplace indicators suggests a complicated relationship. Where the rank of unionized manufacturing workers is much higher than the composite rank, there is generally low per capita

Table 7-19
Rankings on Green Conditions Composite of Appalachian States, Workplace

States	Workplace Deaths Per 100,000	Max. Total Disability Benefits	Max. Unemployment Benefits	Unemployed With Unempl. Insurance	Pop. With Workplace Insurance	Unions for Worker Safety	Laws for Worker Safety	Composite Workplace Indicators
Maryland	12	9	26	34	6	9	5	5
New York	3	32	13	6	26	2	5	2
Ohio	8	11	4	28	11	4	28	14
Pennsylvania	14	12	5	11	7	5	9	11
West Virginia	46	25	14	36	30	10	14	39
Kentucky	**40**	**27**	**35**	**20**	**35**	**17**	**17**	**30**
Alabama	25	26	47	37	36	27	50	46
Georgia	38	50	39	44	34	32	28	40
Mississippi	43	49	48	38	48	42	50	49
North Carolina	22	15	17	21	22	47	43	21
South Carolina	16	28	41	29	17	49	48	33
Tennessee	26	43	44	23	37	30	38	35
Virginia	32	14	38	48	19	31	46	29

Source: Hall and Kerry, *1991-1992 Green Index*, 1991.

income within the states. Alabama, Kentucky, and West Virginia illustrate this case. On the other hand, North and South Carolina rank much higher on the composite work place measure than on the percent of union labor force in manufacturing. Both states, including their Appalachian portions, have made large gains in per capita personal income. On the other hand, Alabama, Kentucky, and West Virginia lost ground on the nation during the 1980s. Ohio is one other state that fits the pattern of a high rank on unionized manufacturing workers, a lower rank on the composite score, and a declining level of per capita income. These measures seem to suggest that unions are critical to healthy and safe work places and policies of compensation for unemployment and disability. The effectiveness of unions in achieving these policies may decline in contracting economies. Expanding economies, North and South Carolina for example, may stimulate some improvement despite a low level of unionized work force.

Conclusion

The measures reported in this chapter suggest that the movement of economic activity, reported in earlier chapters, is from states with higher amounts of social capital, e.g., medical care access and educational attainment, to states with lower amounts. Environmental quality is an exception. Disregard for the environment seems part of the social capital deficit that subsidized industrial activity in the past continue to subsidize economic activity.

John Kenneth Galbraith portrays migration as a mechanism of recruitment for labor. Whites from Appalachia and blacks from the South moved to urban areas of mass-employment in manufacturing and services. That migration continues today with additional streams of workers from Mexico, Latin America, and the West Indies. Galbraith's central point is that after one round of migration from Appalachia and the South, "the modern economy—the market system—requires...an underclass and...it must reach out to other countries to sustain and refresh it" (Galbraith 1992:36-37). Population shifts indicate that the modern economy reaches into portions of Northern and Central Appalachia as well.

Migration, like immigration, subsidizes social capital deficits. America makes no social capital investment for the health, education, and development of skilled workers recruited from abroad. We also avoid having to invest more wages in low-wage work as long as we can find a supply of workers to perform that work. Poverty in America also increases the supply of low-wage laborers. American workers from one area of social capital deficit compete with workers from others, nationally and internationally. As long as the supply remains adequate the market will continue to "cream" those workers who develop best in areas of low social capital investment and move to areas of employment and higher social capital. This supply and demand process continues and thus provides alternatives to higher social capital investment in areas of need, unemployment, and low incomes like Central Appalachia and other portions of the region.

Section III

Appalachia
and
American Social Capital Policies

Chapter 8

Policies and Programs

The vagaries of recent economic change work themselves into unimagined contortions in Appalachia. While we may discuss the "garrison economy" and deplore the paucity of social capital for education, in many areas, Appalachia is one place that portrays how the garrison and the school are related. Hancock County, Tennessee financed a portion of its school budget with fees collected from the District of Columbia for incarcerating an average of 85 of its inmates for $45 a day (Anderson and Binstein 1993). The social problems of a metropolitan area became the industry of a rural, impoverished county and a source of scarce social capital. To crown the improbable with irony, Whittle Communications Corporation in Knoxville, just 70 miles from Hancock County, plans sweeping, for-profit educational reform for the nation (Passall 1994; Toch 1993). Within the Appalachian region, social capital is borrowed from the garrison economy while others plan for private profit in face of the failure to provide sufficient social capital. Challenges and contradictions like these are writ large in Appalachia but with lines borrowed from American economic trends. These trends and the social consequences that ensue have stimulated considerable thought about solutions. This chapter reviews solutions involving the federal government and suggests national policies that are especially pertinent to Appalachia.

A Policy Agenda for Work, Income, and Families

Reactions to the excesses of accumulation and redistribution of wealth of the 1980s coupled with a political change from the conservative Republican administrations of the 1980s have prodded some social analysts to suggest new policies in different issue areas. Several policy centers have outlined reforms, including the liberal, progressive Citizens Transition Project (Green 1992). Its report provides an agenda of policy reforms to achieve more equity in the distribution of wealth and a higher level of basic services to those in need. It envisions economic growth with fairness; provision of family security; increased racial harmony; and the reinvention of government or at least the restoration of public faith in public action. In summary, the report proposed

> a public-investment-led economic recovery; affordable, accessible, universal health care; bold campaign finance reform; prenatal care for all pregnant women and a fully funded Head Start program for all eligible children; a 1993 version of Food

> for Peace for the former Soviet Union to generate exports here and democracy there; scholarships for all in need, paid back over time via payroll deductions or national service; a technology extension service to help convert advanced technology into commercial uses; and the Freedom of Choice Act. One way to bundle several of these ideas together is to state the early goal will be "*health*—how to improve both the personal and economic health of all Americans by universal care and reinvestment in America" (Green 1993:11-12).

The extensive reach of this statement measures not so much a utopian approach to reform but the backlog of needs we have acquired during the time we were content to pursue the public good through the individual accumulation of wealth.

The components of the Citizens Transition Project report discuss policies in detail. Robert Kuttner (1992), for example, provides principles of reform of work that range from increased wages to improving the bargaining position of labor unions. He identifies the following policies to provide more training and security for workers and more flexibility and productivity for management:

-- a comprehensive system of lifetime learning and retraining should replace unemployment compensation as the principal public subsidy of the labor market;
-- labor law reform enacted to allow unions to contest representation elections without reprisal, to bargain collectively when they win such elections, and to prohibit the permanent replacement of striking workers;
-- government policies should establish a new social contract between labor and management that ties wage increases to productivity as part of a commitment to full employment without inflation;
-- government should encourage labor participation in corporate governance to improve the efficiency of corporations and to develop a more effective and durable form of trade unionism;
-- public policy should promote new forms of employee ownership and participation in management; and
-- participation in management should extend to work and safety on the job (Seminario 1992:578-588).

Kuttner makes three other recommendations of special relevance to

Appalachia. He urges immunity of pension funds from management raids. Pensions are an important source of income to retired workers, who are increasing in number in Northern Appalachia especially. Their pensions are particularly vulnerable because they are based on social contracts of yesterday with steel, coal, and textile firms (Drape 1991). Firms of this declining industrial sector may disappear into merger, bankruptcy, or reorganization tomorrow. Coal miners, their widows, and their dependents have seen first-hand how the razzle-dazzle of corporate reorganization can leave retired workers and their families bereft of benefits. Kuttner laments especially the use of pension funds to leverage buyouts that put workers out of jobs or the attraction a generous pool of pension assets provides to corporate raiders (1992:164-65).

Kuttner also urges efforts to convert and upgrade low-wage, dead-end and contingent jobs. Such jobs abound in the service sector. Contingent jobs, part-time and temporary work, carry with them no social capital other than the wage. They are without fringe benefits most times and provide the worker no security. They shelter employers from abrupt shifts in a company's position and require workers to subsidize this protection. Some of these jobs, especially in the human service sector such as home health care, could provide paraprofessional jobs with career ladders. Head Start provides a good example of how this can be done. This form of person-to-person service work will expand in the American economy. In addition to the employment they provide, these services add social capital in areas, such as portions of Appalachia, where it is lacking.

Finally, Kuttner urges that low wages be supplemented or subsidized to assure any full-time worker sufficient income to maintain a family above poverty. Government funds would provide a wage subsidy and a set of benefits to assure that families with full-time workers reached an income level above poverty and received supporting benefits such as child care, health insurance, and training opportunities for advancement in current or new employment.

Kuttner is one of several analysts who tie work and income together. He describes government's role as assuring enough income from work to keep a family out of poverty and providing enough income and benefits to assure that work offers more rewards than welfare does. The means to do this, within our reach, include expanding the earned income tax credit (EITC), according to Robert Greenstein (1992), executive director of the Center on Budget and Public Priorities. The EITC returns income tax paid by low-income families and provides payments to families that have earned too little to pay income tax. The EITC, unlike welfare payments, rises with earnings and is targeted to wage earners living in families with children. Child and family advocates (Edelman 1992:439; Kamarck 1992:449-50) join Greenstein in suggesting the expansion of the EITC to provide higher benefits as the number of children in a family increases. Expansion would more likely assure that working wages are living wages.

Increasing the minimum wage is another means of assuring that work eliminates poverty. Full-time work at minimum wage left a family of three above the poverty level up until the 1970s. By 1992, inflation and no minimum wage increases in the 1980s meant income that was $2,000 less than the poverty level for a family of three with one full-time worker at minimum wage. Most minimum wage workers are not poor only because there are generally other wage earners in the household. The low level of the minimum wage and only recent, modest efforts to bring it up to pre-1980 levels are a large part of the story of declining family incomes (Greenstein 1992:421).

Work and income offer direct avenues to welfare reform. The Family Support Act of 1988 provided for the Job Opportunities and Basic Skills (JOBS) program, a welfare-to-work program for AFDC recipients. Preliminary studies show that such programs eventually mean more income and less welfare payments for participants. The program requires state matching funds, which many states do not have. Consequently, in fiscal year 1991 only nine states drew full federal allotments for the JOBS program (Greenstein 1992:424). Programs like JOBS depend on the creation of new jobs for their success, especially in places of concentrated poverty, unemployment, and low levels of labor force participation, like Eastern Kentucky. Consequently, government should play the role of employer of last resort in these areas where job readiness simply means frustration because the labor force expands but employment does not.

Similarly, AFDC payments should not be terminated or reduced on the assumption that job-training means work and increased income. Under pressure to reduce spending, states take aim at AFDC, which makes an easy target because of the American disdain for welfare. Cutting already low AFDC payments will only mean increased child poverty and greater need among the poor. Ironically, budget-cutters invoke family values as partial justification for reducing AFDC payments to some women. Advocates suggest eligibility reforms that would continue some support for AFDC recipients despite work or marriage.

Poverty and family policies intersect around a set of policies for children that include:

-- providing refunds to working poor and low-income families for child care expenses in the manner of EITC;
-- increasing state and federal regulation to assure child support from absent parents;
-- establishing a federal child tax credit of $1,000, in place of personal exemption, which would assist middle class working families as well;
-- expanding Head Start to include more than the 30 percent of eligible children participating in 1992 (Greenstein 1992; Edelman 1992; and Kamarck 1992).

The Elements of Social Capital

In addition to general principles of work and income, some proposals address specific elements of social capital.

Education

Education, for example, has exemplary models for reform of school-based decision making; higher standards of academic achievement without segregation of students into tracks; school-based teacher renewal; smaller classes; more flexible and longer school days and years; links to family and children's needs for health care and social services; and performance-based assessment. Carrying out these reforms in new and broad replication efforts requires political leadership and public commitment (Littlefield 1992:457-71). College tuition and fees have increased by more than twice the cost of living between 1980 and 1992. Inflation, and states hard pressed to meet budgets in declining economic times, have pushed up college costs and restricted access to students with low and moderate incomes who stand to benefit most from their education and to contribute most to increasing the skills of the work force. While college costs increased by 110 percent, the maximum Pell grant, federal assistance with college tuition costs based on financial need, increased by about one-third. Abandoned dreams or heavy debt result. For students not going to college, including those students who do not finish high school, America needs a better system to help them acquire proficiencies for employment and to make the transition to work (Littlefield 1992:467).

Several Appalachian states, including Kentucky, Tennessee, Virginia, and West Virginia, have addressed school finance equity. Funding for schools based on property taxes has aggravated differences among sections of the region so that school districts vary widely, and in some cases unconstitutionally, in their ability to provide all students a reasonably equal education. Establishing common and higher standards for all schools compounds the problems of poorly financed school districts if their resources are adversely affected by failure to reach those standards. Minimal standards such as staying open for an entire school year and providing transportation for school students have been beyond the financial means of some of the poorest counties in Appalachian Tennessee. Obviously state and national efforts are needed to achieve a greater degree of equality among school districts that will permit them some reasonable prospects of achieving standards to which they should then be held accountable.

Health Care

The Appalachian region provides many lessons about health care for the nation. Work-related health care from company doctors to innovative union-initiated health plans have been major innovations. Community health centers, as Chapter 7 explained, continue to be a mainstay for the regions in greatest need of health services. This history instructs us about the limits of work-related health care, including recent efforts to cut back health benefits as part of the new competitiveness of American industry and companies such as Pittston. Managed competition reform efforts in health care are likely to fail in Appalachia. Trusting competition to provide more effective services in areas will not create services in areas where they cannot exist without subsidy and considerable community effort.

Principles of fundamental reform for health care include:

- -- universal insurance coverage for all Americans, with no significant deductibles or co-payment obligations on patients;
- -- comprehensive, broad coverage of all medically necessary medical care, comprehensively formulated and described;
- -- public administration and finance to promote accountability and control costs;
- -- freedom to choose providers and provider-patient autonomy in medical treatment and decision making; and
- -- portable medical insurance coverage, not tied to specific job or geographic location (Marmor and Barr 1992:399-414).

In addition to these principles, Appalachia has special health care achievements and traditions to keep in mind. First, an extensive network of community health centers came from exemplary community responses to need. Policies of reimbursement and provider training, including health providers other than physicians, need to be in tune with the cost and staffing needs of community health centers and other community-based health programs. Second, the region has exemplary prenatal and child care programs that have demonstrated the utility of employing people in paraprofessional roles that increase the well-being of residents.

These programs tie work and welfare reform together with increased investment in social capital. Health care reform needs to be flexible enough to recognize successful innovation, provide adequate support for it, and to permit new community groups and others to initiate replications.

Art and Culture

Social capital extends to the cultural expression of people in community. Some measures to provide increased support to art and culture include:

-- a box on income tax returns similar to that for presidential campaign funds that would permit taxpayers to specify up to $10 of their tax payment to state and national artistic and cultural programs;
-- increased support for international exchanges of artists and of cultural heritages;
-- increased support of artistic and cultural expression of and about women and racial and ethnic minorities; and
-- new and higher levels of support for the arts and culture to make up for the lack of real growth in spending of the past twelve years (Gund 1992:472-79).

Increased support for local artists, like support for human service paraprofessionals, could come through programs of national service and citizen participation. Efforts to encourage college students and other youth in these programs should be supplemented with efforts to support local people in local efforts.

Housing

Perhaps only health exceeds housing as a social capital dilemma.

The housing problem combines a lack of affordable housing and new levels of homeless and near homeless people. Despite the need for more affordable housing, market forces have not provided supply. Five general principles should drive specific housing policies:

- -- expand home ownership opportunities, particularly among young families;
- -- eliminate homelessness by providing direct rental assistance to Americans in poverty;
- -- restore the nation's inventory of public and subsidized housing by expanding resident participation and ownership;
- -- increase the supply of affordable housing, primarily by expanding the capacity of community-based nonprofit developers; and
- -- rebuild and stabilize the economies and social fabric of urban neighborhoods [and rural communities] by expanding job and home ownership opportunities and reinvigorating community self-help efforts (Dreier and Atlas 1992:383-98).

These last two principles have particular application in Appalachia. Numerous community-based nonprofit developers have addressed the housing needs of the region. In some cases, they have come together in state and regional organizations, such as the Federation of Appalachian Housing Enterprises, to assist one another and to affect public policy in the manner we described earlier in this chapter. Second, the concentration of poverty is related to accessibility of housing. Inner-city residents need programs, including housing, to get close to the jobs in the areas surrounding the cities. Rural residents need jobs that higher demand for home construction and improvement could supply. The context of community of which housing is a part also needs attention. Technical assistance to community-based, nonprofit organizations in planning, coalition building, research, and leadership development should be provided in housing and other programs.

Part of the costs for this and other housing reforms could come from a new graduated tax credit for homeowners. In 1991, tax deductions for mortgage interest and property taxes totalled $47 billion. Of that, 12 percent went to the wealthiest 1 percent of taxpayers with incomes in excess of $200,000 and 80 percent went to taxpayers with incomes in excess of $50,000. Permitting full deductions for the portion of mortgage interest equal to the national median and partial deductions for increments until capped at some point, such as twice the national median, would not only recover tax revenues from the wealthiest homeowners, it would also provide financial incentives for the construction and purchase of affordable housing (Dreier and Atlas 1992:397).

Part of the housing problem, especially the shortage of capital for home purchase, stems from the savings and loan debacle of the 1980s. Paying for these failures will cost taxpayers between $.5 and $1.4 trillion over 40 years. The roots of those problems extend past the 1980s, but that decade watered and nourished speculation and profit-taking with a "greed is good" nutrient. Perhaps nothing demonstrates the manner in which American public policy socializes capital risk and privatizes profits than the failures of the savings and loans. Related problems of the banking industry and some pension funds may place additional burdens on the taxpayers. Taxpayers' exposure to the liabilities of speculators should be limited. In addition, channels to encourage the flow of capital into productive economy rather than renewed speculation should be constructed. Specific, though limited, steps to accomplish this include increased public accountability, such as that provided in the Community Reinvestment Act, and the creation of community development banks (Gilbert and Goodman 1992:589-603.)

Public Revenues for Social Capital

Finding revenues for an ambitious, expanded program of social capital investment means new taxes and perhaps some increases in current ones. At the very least, tax breaks for the wealthiest Americans need to be reversed. Placing more wealth in the hands of the wealthy has not produced the economic stimulation predicted by supply-side Reaganomics. It has produced a redistribution of wealth from the lowest to the highest income brackets, increased tax burdens on middle income groups, and the most skewed distribution of wealth in America since World War II. The richest 1 percent of Americans almost doubled their income to $576,000, in constant dollars, from 1977 to 1992. Assessing higher taxes on these and other high income brackets is not a punitive soak the rich policy. It simply recognizes that a nation with an annual budget deficit, and a national debt that escalated as high income earners accumulated wealth, cannot continue to forego the $71 billion gap in tax revenues from this top 1 percent income bracket that developed between 1977 and 1992. Even Adam Smith understood that taxation should "remedy inequality of riches as much as possible by relieving the poor and burdening the rich" (McIntyre 1992:31).

Increased taxes on the most wealthy is one of three principles of progressive tax reform. The second principle protects middle and low-income families from increased taxes. The third principle would plug tax loopholes and increase the top corporate and personal tax rates. Current tax breaks for business and investment are expected to cost $291 billion in corporate taxes and $285 billion in personal taxes from fiscal 1992 to 1996 (McIntyre 1992:37). Investments related to continued or increased employment should enjoy public reward through tax laws.

These principles lead to specific policy suggestions with estimated revenues over the next five years. Some of the major provisions related to the political economic changes we have discussed include:

-- increasing tax rates to 36 percent for the wealthiest 1 percent, which would yield $53 billion dollars;
-- levying a millionaires' surtax of 10 percent on taxable income above $500,000 and another 10 percent starting at $1 million, which would yield $25 billion;
-- increasing corporate tax rates to 36 percent with a surtax of 10 percent on taxable income over $1 million, which would yield $66 billion;
-- taxing capital gains as other income rather than capping it at 28 percent, which would yield an addition $22 billion dollars;
-- scaling back depreciation write-offs to reflect the actual value of wear and tear, which would yield $24 billion;
-- ending tax breaks associated with mergers and acquisitions, which would yield $9 billion;
-- collecting taxes from multinational corporations on profits earned in the United States and overhauling the rules by which we determine what income is taxable, which would protect jobs in the United States and yield $23 billion; and
-- reforming in the Alternative Minimum Tax, designed to assure that wealthy individuals and corporations pay taxes on some minimum, which would yield $76 billion (McIntyre 1992:37-42).

This tax reform would implicitly reduce subsidies to special interest groups and the wealthiest individuals. It is part of a major change in government fiscal policy to promote economic growth. Robert J. Shapiro, executive director of the Progressive Policy Institute, provided the ground upon which the Clinton administration campaigned and took its first policy steps. He described some assumptions about government within the Clinton administration:

> In the old economy, government proliferated tax, spending, and credit subsidies for selected industries, as government's way of promoting U.S. competitiveness by helping firms to cut certain costs. In a globalized economy, most of these subsidies undermine innovation and efficiency by making many corporations too comfortable to change. National economic success in the 1990s will require that government turn away from industry subsidies and protection of almost every kind, and toward national investments in the common economic resources that help promote innovation and flexibility, principally education and training, research and development, and advanced communications and transportation systems among our markets (R. Shapiro 1992:80-81).

Based on the economic development of Appalachia, Shapiro probably overestimates how new the global economy is. He also overlooks how much the old and new global economy resemble each other. International capital developed steel and coal in Appalachia in the 19th century. Lower labor costs still attract international capital to Appalachia to manufacture automobiles or to leave the mountains for the maquiladoras, the factories on the Mexican-American border. Consequently, Shapiro's emphasis on infrastructure investment without social capital investment overstates one need and ignores another.

Shapiro (1992:81-83) also suggests reducing entitlement transfer payments, such as social security, to the wealthy. Entitlement programs make enticing targets for budget cutters. Medicaid costs have driven many state budget increases as it and Medicare have done for the federal budget. There is certainly a fiscal case for introducing some means testing to reduce entitlement programs' payments and benefits to the very rich. Politically, however, means-tested programs lend themselves to interpretation as wealth-redistributive programs. Such programs lose political support quickly. Social security has avoided stigma, criticism, and cutbacks, unlike AFDC, precisely because its universal eligibility means widespread support. The dependence of many sections of Appalachia on transfer payments increased in the 1980s. This dependence provides substantial reason for concern about any efforts to change entitlement programs. Changes might reduce political support for these programs initially and diminished political support might later encourage reduced payments and more stringent eligibility requirements.

Shapiro (1992:84) and other analysts of the Citizens Transition

Project (Steinbruner 1992; Marlin 1992; Gray 1992) agree that funds for defense spending might and should be redirected to other forms of public investment. Such a change will cause economic dislocation for workers currently employed in the defense industry. Consequently, federal funds now spent on defense might be better and more productively spent on the social issues related to current economic dislocation. However, that shift will produce its own dislocations, social issues, and need for the investment of federal funds. The peace dividend will not come without some payback provisions.

Mediating Structures and Democratic Renewal

Policies alone are not the answer. Democratically controlled interventions provide the best hope of remedy for the problems this report has discussed. Political conservatives and liberals agree on that. The conservative policy center, the American Enterprise Institute, sponsored work on mediating structures, e.g., family, church, civic and neighborhood associations, and voluntary agencies, as mechanisms of social policy. Mediating structures are those organizations that stand between individuals and large social and economic forces and have received a great deal of attention from policy analysts and advocates. Mediating structures fall within the broader spectrum of the non-profit sector and incorporate their public role that the liberal Urban Institute developed (Salamon 1982:73-78). The conservative approach actually intends to substitute local, non-governmental interventions in social problems for government programs (Berger and Neuhaus 1977). Curiously, the model of the conservative's mediating structures can be found in the community action programs of the liberals' War on Poverty (Berger and Neuhaus 1977:39-40), which conservatives otherwise disparage.

Liberals look to social movements of the 1960s for examples of mediating structures' capacity to transform social policy (Bellah et al. 1985). Federal agencies within radical reform efforts of Reconstruction, the New Deal, and the War on Poverty included the formation of mediating structures as a key component of their work (Couto 1991). Recent calls for new policy directions invoke mediating structures explicitly (Osborne and Gaebler 1992) or implicitly (Schorr 1988).

The emerging credo of mediating structures, with appropriate references to "community" and "empowerment," influenced the Progressive Policy Institute, fittingly enough a radically centrist think-tank for the moderate Democratic Leadership Council:

> Unwilling to frame every public question in terms of a choice between government provision and market competition, progressives place new emphasis on the voluntary associations and institutions of community—America's "third sector." Government's role is to empower families, voluntary organizations, and institutions to solve their own problems, not to try to replace them with public programs or institutions. Community also means taking care of citizens in need and affirming the common civic values that unite us as Americans (Marshall and Schram 1993:xvii).

Liberal and conservative proponents of mediating structures differ about their role and makeup. Some proponents suggest a minimalist role for mediating structures, the participation of voluntary organizations in the design of public policy, for example. Other proponents suggest a maximalist role for mediating structures, conducting public policy through them as service deliverers, for example (Price 1980). Within the maximalists are those who would provide public resources for the public policy role of mediating structures. Minimalists are more inclined to leave to the mediating structures, such as homeless shelters, the matter of fund raising.

Proponents also differ about the organizations that are mediating structures. At a minimum, community groups, voluntary associations, religious groups, and the family make the list of mediating structures (Berger and Neuhaus 1977). Some lists go further and include labor unions and advocacy organizations (Greider 1992). As the list expands, so does the complexity of the role of mediating structures. Maximalists generally temper their faith in mediating structures with analysis of the complexity of their role in implementing public policy (Green 1992; Salamon 1981) and in achieving social change (Social Policy 1989; Fisher 1993).

However one defines them, one can find a plethora of "mediating structures" in the Appalachian region. Whether community health centers, media centers, domestic violence shelters, or citizens' environmental groups, the response to the region's needs has been extensive and exemplary to the nation (Greider 1992). This is one field in which the region has led the nation (Fisher 1993; Horton 1989).

Labor unions have played significant roles as mediating structures in the region as well. Organizations of textile workers have improved wages and safety and health in some plants and have counterpoised the unregulated business environment of the 1980s. Steel workers have organized alternative economic development in some areas and attempted worker run plants in Weirton, West Virginia. Coal miners have addressed changed conditions at work, from job security to the provision of health and retirement benefits to former workers, earlier than other American workers. In this regard, the Massey and Pittston coalminers' strikes of the 1980s signify the potential and limits of alliances of community organizations, advocacy efforts, and labor unions as mediating structures (Couto 1993). The community support of the Pittston strike testified to the role of the UMWA as a mediating structure. The Massey strike suggested the power of companies and courts to press labor unions to their limits. The range of mediating structures within the Appalachian region indicates a vibrancy that sustains their valued place in American political traditions and the opportunity for solid partnerships in change efforts.

One finds hope as well as challenge within the Appalachian region. In the unions, the community organizations, the school reforms, the economic development efforts, the community health centers, and similar services and organizations one finds the creativity and vitality of American institutional life. It is here in "the importance of individual and social responsibility within and for institutions" that some analysts find the means to "transform the great society into the good society" (Bellah et al. 1992:17). William Greider finds hope within Appalachia to build "mediating mechanisms that enable people to connect with the higher realms of decision making" (Greider 1992:19). Among such mechanisms, Greider mentions the community-based work of the Highlander Center on the environment. Implicitly, Greider includes labor unions and community organizations, such as those in Appalachia, as the forms of mediating mechanisms that give substantive meaning to self-government and provide shared civic values for democratic process. Moving beyond rugged individualism to an American public philosophy of social responsibility requires the forms of community institutions that flourish in Appalachia and which current economic trends imperil.

Programs That Work

Moving the invisible hand for democratic renewal requires community-based efforts, many of which can be found in Appalachia. Lessons abound about providing services well in order to prevent rotten outcomes. Lisbeth Schorr surveyed a set of programs designed to break a "cycle of disadvantage" related to poverty, such as poor health, family breakdown, poor schools, and low educational attainment. Many programs, like those she examined, function in an exemplary manner in the Appalachian region. She found that interventions that work have the following characteristics:

-- a broad spectrum of services;
-- more open professional and bureaucratic boundaries;
-- flexibility;
-- a contextual understanding of the problem;
-- care and respect for those served, trust in those serving;
-- coherent and easy to use services;
-- an emphasis on needs of clients rather then traditional bureaucratic and professional roles; and,
-- new self-defined, more effective roles for professionals.

Schorr found also that ineffective interventions, which are prevalent, have common characteristics as well. Among them, she lists:

-- emphasis on efficiency and not effectiveness;
-- fragmented services; and
-- meager resources.

To move beyond models of successful interventions into full-scale programs, Schorr suggests that we need to evaluate programs for qualitative, long-term results and institute new methods of training and retaining skilled and committed personnel. Successful efforts do not come cheap and cannot be replicated with diluted resources. Likewise, flexibility is key and thus centralized, bureaucratic models need to be adapted to local circumstances. Replication can happen in a wide variety of circumstances also because of flexibility. Finally, Schorr makes a cost argument. Namely, the costs of the interventions, though expensive, save money. Prenatal care, for example, reduces risk for low birth weights and ensuing problems. Good family support reduces the need for more expensive out-of-home placement of children. In addition, there are costs of leaving social problems unattended and value, beyond dollar estimates, "of living in a fair and just society with a shared sense of civility and community" (Schorr, 1988:256-83). Citing Isabel Sawhill, Schorr concludes,

> Large deficits make it difficult to argue for new social spending [because they] lower the rate of economic growth and threaten future standards of living. Unfortunately, a failure to invest in the next generation has precisely these same effects (Sawhill in Schorr 1988:294).

Schorr's work offers an inventory of successful interventions. It also offers hope that our social problems are manageable given care, compassion, and public commitment to economic justice and social equality.

Conclusion

Joblessness and poverty are increasingly concentrated in places like the inner city, portions of the rural South, and portions of Appalachia; among groups of minorities; and members of female-headed households. Reducing poverty where we find it means increasing incomes of poor people. This should be done primarily by providing employment. But employment is scarce where social capital is low, i.e., areas of concentrated poverty. Human capital investment, education, job training, and health care, are necessary increases of social capital but they fall short of jobs in terms of reducing poverty. This investment can, however, create jobs in places like Central Appalachia where both the services and the jobs are needed. Community organizations are crucial elements of addressing poverty and providing employment through increased social capital investment such as housing, environmental quality, and health care. To raise incomes without providing employment requires income transfer, a redistribution of wealth, the most unpopular form of public policy in America. Yet we know that it works in some instances. The poverty of Americans over 65 years of age has dropped dramatically thanks to increases in social security and the inception of Medicare.

Chapter 9

Reforms for the Long Haul

Policy and program recommendations, such as those of the previous chapter, depend on a set of specific circumstances that change on short notice. Proposals to reverse economic trends and to address social issues depend on the analysis of the historical causes of those trends and issues. Such proposals take long-run trends and issues into account. They provide the basis for policy and program recommendations. This chapter suggests that America's fundamental challenge entails establishing new patterns of economic development. It means adapting capitalism to meet the promise and responsibilities of a democratic society.

Turning Things Around

Charles Murray and other conservative social analysts of the 1980s attributed economic stagnation to the excesses of the 1960s' programs and their consequence of removing incentives to work from low-income groups. Such an analysis leads inevitably to a solution of reduced social programs and the creation of excessive hardship as an incentive for the poor and unemployed to improve their behavior.

Economic advisors in the Reagan and Bush administration attributed strong economic performance to private investment. Consequently, they worked to place more income into private, wealthy hands by deregulation and tax reform. Even in its last gasps, capital gains tax cuts were on the lips of the Bush administration.

George Gilder expressed the unbounded confidence of the 1980s in the "high adventure and redemptive morality of capitalism" and the "altruistic creativity" at the foundation of capitalism. The task of reducing poverty, according to Gilder, entailed changing the poor by extending them values of family and faith as well as freedom and opportunities (Gilder 1981:x).

Other economic analysts differ sharply from these economic assumptions of the 1980s and their prescriptions of deregulation, unregulated markets, the privatization of matters of wealth and its distribution, and the altruistic creativity of unfettered capitalism. In contrast to the policies of the 1980s, another set of analysts assert a social relationship among Americans that extends beyond the marketplace to incorporate common responsibility for the hardships of some, the increasing difficult transitions common to many workers, and the equitable distribution of income and other resources among members of society. Robert Reich, for example, emphasizes the global nature of the economy of which America is a region. To turn the trends of the last two decades around, Reich offers a "positive economic nationalism, in which each nation's citizens take primary responsibility for enhancing the capacities of their countrymen for full and productive lives." One part of this positive economic nationalism addresses the central economic need in the Appalachian region "the transition of a work force out of older industries and technologies in which there was worldwide overcapacity."

> This [policy] might take the form of severance payments, relocation assistance, extra training grants, extra unemployment insurance, regional economic aid, and funds for retooling or upgrading machinery toward higher-value-added production (Reich 1991:311-15).

Reich might find Appalachia instructive. Appalachia has been a region in a national economy with characteristics that Reich extends to America as a region in a global economy. America has been "Appalachianized." Reich's solutions would go far to "Americanize" Appalachia's problems by bringing them under national policy.

Robert Kuttner's sharper analysis of recent economic trends leads him to more complete recommendations than Reich's. Kuttner's recommendations range over a variety of specific policies to improve the American work force through improved education, including apprenticeship programs; to increase investment in productive and not merely profitable enterprise; to increase investment in public goods including transportation, infrastructure, and technology; to increase government regulation to correct or prevent free market excesses; to create an equitable and universal health insurance system; and to reform taxes to route savings into productive investment (Kuttner 1992). Kuttner proposes, like Reich and other economic analysts, "a functioning social contract, anchored in a coherent set of public policies, and a competent public sector" (Kuttner 1992:285).

Samuel Bowles, David M. Gordon, and Thomas E. Weisskopf (1992), work from their "garrison economy" analysis to propose a worker-led productivity growth. The principles of this long range strategy include fostering the growth of labor unions and the rights of workers; promoting full employment and higher wages through government job creation—including public infrastructure investment—and increased levels for the minimum wage; and creating incentives for productive capital formation and investment.

These proposals share three assumptions central to long term reform. First, they presume that "an economy consists fundamentally of people and that its basic relationships are therefore social relationships" (Bowles et al. 1990:7). This differs sharply from the dominant, mechanistic view of the economy as a self-regulating and balanced machine to which human relations should be entrusted. Secondly, these proposals assume that it is possible to reach a greater degree of equity and to provide low-income workers and the poor a higher standard of well-being. To achieve these new standards, these proposals assume, finally, that government has to play a major role and that it may conduct its role competently.

Alternative Development Approaches

Alternative approaches to economic development incorporate all three assumptions of these analysts. Within traditional approaches to economic development, as Chapter 3 discussed, manufacturers ranked Southern Appalachian states very high in terms of a climate of low labor costs and less restrictive state regulations. These preferences have had a hand in attracting large amounts of capital investment in auto manufacturing, in particular, into Southern Appalachian states. There are benefits to this investment, without a doubt, including increased wages and increased unionization among workers. The success of these states, however, comes in a bidding war over infrastructure and social capital, a race to the bottom line. States promise to invest in roads and land, to train workers, and to forego tax revenues from the corporation (Bishop 1993c, 1993d; Garber 1990). Such development underbids and undermines the wages and social capital of established productions centers. Evidence abounds that the gains of new production areas are temporary because other areas are preparing to underbid them. The losses of the former production areas seem to be lasting however. Bringing new jobs to areas of low wages, low employment, and low income obviously benefits people in those areas. Preserving old jobs of high wages, high employment, and working middle class income areas is also important.

In contrast to the traditional development schemes of manufacturers' preferences, which choose among states that compete with labor costs and social capital for branch manufacturing plants, alternative development schemes emphasize support for existing business and entrepreneurs. They emphasize investment in education and training for workers and quality of life factors rather than lower labor costs. They also emphasize government's role in building the foundations of an economy, especially the social capital of an economy, rather than an intrusive element to be minimized (Ansley 1993; Keesler 1991; Corporation for Enterprise Development [CfDE] 1987). Alternative development approaches point out the costs to home-grown producers of the traditional development incentives, such as tax holidays (CfDE 1987:7).

A specific alternative scheme that the Corporation for Enterprise Development offered used very different elements for its development index and an intentional specific rebuttal of the manufacturers' climate approach. The Performance Index, for example, included levels of employment, income, job quality, equity—including levels of AFDC payments and quality of life—and measures of health and mortality. The Business Vitality Index included competitiveness and entrepreneurial energy, which included women and minority-owned enterprises. The Capacity Index included capital, such as physical infrastructure, and social capital, including educational measures and funding for health and art. Finally, the Policy Index included improved governance and regulation, the effectiveness and equity of the tax code, the mobilization of capital, the enhancement of technology and business development, the construction and maintenance of public works, investment in human resources, and aid to distressed counties (CfDE 1987). Elements of each index combined for a letter grade, like school, for each state on each of the indices.

Table 9-1

Ranks of Appalachian States on Enterprise Development

State	Indices			
	Performance	Business Vitality	Capacity	Policies
Maryland	B	B	B	B
New York	B	B	A	A
Ohio	C	C	C	A
Pennsylvania	B	F	B	A
West Virginia	F	D	F	A
Kentucky	F	D	F	C
Alabama	F	F	F	F
Georgia	D	D	D	D
Mississippi	F	F	F	D
North Carolina	D	F	D	D
South Carolina	F	F	F	C
Tennessee	F	F	F	F
Virginia	B	C	C	D

Source: CfED, *Making the Grade: The Development Report Card for the States*.

The measures of these indices led to very different ranks among the Appalachian states. The manufacturers' preference ranked Southern Appalachian states much higher than Northern Appalachian states. The enterprise development measures ranked the Northern Appalachian states much higher than those in the South, as Table 9-1 reports.

The indices of this alternative development give high ranks to states with a high-wage, well-developed industrial base, such as Michigan and Massachusetts. In contrast, South Carolina, an Appalachian success story by traditional measures, appears as "a monument to the crippling long-term economic effects of following the traditional 'business climate' prescription for economic health." The study acknowledges some shift in South Carolina from "a low wage, low skill, low cost business climate" to new, and better, state policies in the mid-1980s of investment in children's health and education and the development of in-state businesses.

Massachusetts is the "valedictorian" of the development measures. The state, according to the report, pioneered policies, such as those suggested in the Policy Index, that helped refocus private energies in the 1980s on the development of new products, services, production processes, and markets (CfED 1987:67-79). By 1990, Massachusetts was a mired miracle, however. In retrospect, the miracle had very ordinary origins in deficit spending on the military during the Reagan years.

South Carolina, on the other hand, by 1992, had attracted yet more international capital investment to the Appalachian portion of the state. This mountain miracle had its own tarnish. The head of BMW assured local leaders that the firm was not locating a production center in the United States to pay the wages that German workers received. Nor did he mention the social capital investments that South Carolina had made in children for any role they may have played in attracting this international capital investment. Tennessee also, with the lowest possible grades on the alternative development index, had snagged two major automobile manufacturing plants, Nissan and Saturn. Without a doubt, large scale manufacturing investment continues to go to low-wage, less regulated areas with low social capital stock.

Alternative development priorities are helpful to imagine more equitable approaches. They stop short of explaining other important factors that determine the location of capital investment, however. Likewise, they fall short of explaining the fit of Appalachian conditions and capital investment. Proximity to markets, to supplies, and to resources, for example, influence economic development and capital investment. Areas without these factors necessarily fall back on low-wages. Areas with natural resources will always be attractive to extractive industries, timber and coal, for example. Similarly, a "must" of economic development is whether a location is an "attractive place for engineers and managers to live" (CfED 1987:7). The relatively low cost of some forms of social capital that come from personal income, like housing, is among those attractions.

Those parts of Appalachia are especially attractive that have little "run down" factor. This is a term that E.F. Schumacher (Couto 1990), who believed that "small is beautiful," used to describe the costs of doing business in an established setting rather than a pristine one. For example, a coal mine that has been worked for decades will have more water and roof problems than a new mining site. Coal will be more expensive to extract than it had been initially. Similarly, the mine's production costs will be higher than new mines with new technology, more accessible seams of coal, and fewer costs related to past production. Obviously, the older industrial areas of Appalachia have higher run down factors including environmental degradation, higher costs of pensions and benefits for former workers, dislocation of current workers, and new degrees of poverty. Areas without a run down factor have a comparative advantage. An economy based on seizing the comparative advantage in every instance, however, leaves people in communities to meet the costs of the run down factor and social capital deficits without adequate resources. This is true of the communities left behind by relocation and those where capital is headed.

Moving the Invisible Hand

The run down of one area and the benefit to another is an enduring characteristic of capitalism if we are to believe Adam Smith. Smith foresaw development bringing a general increase in well-being initially but that after a time, "[the] full complement of riches" based on an area's resources and geographic location would be reached. At that point, accumulation of capital stops and so does growth. The working class of an area where growth has stopped enters a decline in living standards that can drop below subsistence. Smith is often invoked by those who see "progress" in economic transitions and dislocations. Smith himself was deeply pessimistic about a market economy left on its own. The working class was subject to social decay and economic decline. "All the nobler parts of the human character may be in great measure obliterated and extinguished in the great body of the people" (Heilbroner 1993:124).

The economist Robert Heilbroner incorporates much of Adam Smith's work in his own attempt to look into the twenty-first century to discern likely paths for the American economy. Heilbroner's prognosis is not bright. He foresees a variety of capitalist economies rooted in national cultures and traditions that will influence each nation's ability to adapt its form of capitalism to new economic and social needs. "Unadaptive capitalisms, with restive and ideologically charged political traditions, weak structures of public administration, and unorganized union and corporate sectors would almost certainly not fare as well" as adaptive capitalisms will (Heilbroner 1993:141). In some ways, the differences between the manufacturers' preferred climate measures and the measures of alternative enterprise development indicate the distinction of unadaptive and adaptive capitalism. Heilbroner makes clear that the United States has all the characteristics of an unadaptive capitalism. In fact, in some portions of the Appalachian South, there is still short term, local benefit to the characteristics of unadaptive capitalism. These benefits are calculated in terms of jobs and wages without calculating the public costs to social capital.

Heilbroner offers additional insight into the political economy of Appalachia and the fundamental economic and political challenges to America. He first establishes economics as a series of dynamic waves of social interventions that alter productive capabilities of society, its social composition, and even the relationship of society to nature. He identifies five economic waves of innovation: industrialization; transportation; electricity; automobile transportation; and electronification. Next he explains that capital is wealth whose value inheres in its use to create a larger amount of capital. Capitalism is dynamic because the greatest accumulation of capital occurs when one process or product is displaced by another. To be among the few, earlier suppliers of a new market of high demand offers the avenue to greatest wealth. It also provides an incentive to look for existing products and processes to displace.

Thus, employment in Appalachia's dominant industries declines because more capital may be accumulated by substituting other products for theirs or new processes to produce the same product. One set of production processes and products gives way quickly to new products and producers. Deindustrialization and postindustrialization are, at root cause, new forms of capital accumulation that are taking place in new regions of the country and the world. Appalachia is one region of a global pattern of capital accumulation. It was one in the nineteenth century as well as the twentieth. At one time, one or more portions of the region attracted capital because of the profits to be made there. This is occurring still in parts of Southern Appalachia. At other times, one or more portions of the region lost capital because of the profits to be made elsewhere. This is occurring now in Central and Northern Appalachia. The divestment of capital must inevitably happen in the parts of Southern Appalachia that are enjoying good times now. The dynamic nature of economics and the particular pattern of accumulation of capital generate "persistent and powerful tendencies to change," according to Heilbroner (1993:35-54).

Described as progress, most often within "the restive and ideologically charged traditions" of the United States, the accumulation process of capitalism produces wealth and social loss simultaneously. How to produce wealth and to minimize social and environmental loss is the task of adaptive capitalism. This report indicates how both wealth and social loss in the Appalachian region occur precisely because of the displacement of one accumulation process or product by another. The ideological commitment to the salutatory effects of unadaptive, market capitalism inclines Americans to minimize the social consequences of such economic displacements. Poverty and the declining incomes of some workers are treated as externalities, that is, unintended costs of doing business. As little as possible of the social costs is included in the price of doing business. Instead, as much as possible of the social costs is passed on to those who incur them in the form of unemployment, declining incomes, and poverty. The extent to which such externalities should become part of the cost of doing business is the central question for adaptive capitalism. Heilbronner warns it is also "border warfare between the public and private realms" (Heilbroner 1993:110-14).

The outcome of this border warfare is key to the social consequences of America's economic trends in this decade and the next century. The central political issue, or challenge, is how to relate the state and the economy to fashion the social structure within which capitalist accumulation takes place and social costs are met. America fashioned the welfare state from the political-economic relationship during the New Deal and the Great Society programs. Most recently, public policy fashioned the political-economic relationship based on a mechanistic model of markets (Heilbroner 1993:61-62). To some extent, Appalachia saw the consequences of different public/private, political-economic formulations in the economic border wars. Gains in income and declines in poverty occurred in the 1970s and losses and increases happened in the 1980s, despite economic growth in some areas.

Heilbroner emphasizes the markedly different relationships of the state and the economy that four major economic theorists describe. Adam Smith, Karl Marx, John Maynard Keynes, and Joseph Schumpeter all foresaw problems with the internal workings of capitalism. Heilbroner recounts Keynes' discussion of the practical tasks of the public realm to correct the problems of the economic realm. Heilbroner calls this economic problem solving by the state, adaptive capitalism. Minimally, Keynes felt, the state should prevent massive unemployment by transfer payments and the purchase of public goods and services. Maximally, the state should promote full employment (Heilbroner 1993:86). Heilbroner concludes that investment in infrastructure, including social capital such as education, is key to adaptive capitalism.

> Utilized as a deliberate agency for sustaining growth, investment in infrastructure might become the twenty-first century's solution to the problem of achieving and sustaining adequate growth, especially in the United States which has fallen so far behind in this regard (Heilbroner, 1993:135).

This investment, for Heilbroner, expresses the mutual dependence of capital and the state. The realm of capital cannot accumulate without the support of the state. The state needs healthy businesses to acquire the revenues for its own goals (Heilbroner 1993:76-77). However, the greatest single issue in the future, according to Heilbroner, will be the mix of political and economic realms. These will vary from country to country. In the United States, our mix is likely to be a contest between the view of the state as a "wasteful drag" on the economy and the view, that Heilbroner grounds in the work of Adam Smith, of the state as "an indispensable source of strength for a private economy" (Heilbroner 1993:91). This contest has a bias towards a limited role of the state to prepare people as workers and places as locations for business. Reich's works display this bias of reform.

Conditions within Appalachia in the 1980s challenge us to go beyond that role. Kevin Phillips' analysis of the 1980s, discussed in Chapter 1, offers a more political, and limited, analysis than Heilbroner but reaches a similar conclusion. The accumulation of wealth in the 1980s brought a new degree of inequity in income that created "a rising imperative for a new political and economic outlook" that evidently entailed a new relation of the economy and the state and "a very different chapter in the annals of the wealth and power of the United States." Phillips offers far more diagnosis than prescription. But having offered historical comparisons to previous eras of gross income disparities, he draws from them for approaches to our own disparity. He cites Herbert Croly's influential work of the Progressive Era, the early twentieth century, *The Promise of American Life*, for ideas for our own time:

> The remedy, he [Croly] said, was a "new nationalism"—a

> renewal of national spirit through democratically controlled (as opposed to oligarchic) government activism. Higher taxes, additional economic regulation, a greater commitment to easing inequality and belief in the usefulness of the central government all had a role to play, as did a redefinition of purpose going beyond moneymaking and the marketplace. (Phillips 1990:220).

Almost a century after Croly wrote these words, the principles remain applicable. The conditions have changed and the stakes are higher, however.

Alternative economic development, the adaptation of capitalism, attempts to humanize a system and require it to redress its adverse social consequences. People who have been shut out or dislocated by patterns of development are beneficiaries of adaptive capitalism. Their rights as human beings and citizens, people with loving and creative powers, are more prominent in adaptive capitalism. The mechanistic market that creates redundant people in winner-take-all competitions is left behind for economic patterns of inclusion of benefits (Friedmann 1992:13). The underlying tasks of adaptive capitalism are to balance the structure of powers in society by making state and corporate action more accountable to people whom they adversely affect (Friedmann 1992:31). Elements of that accountability should include: the spatial distribution of income, which Chapter 6 illustrated; the inclusion of high unemployment, poverty, and environmental degradation as direct costs of doing business (Friedmann 1991:44); and the poverty of children, which Chapter 6 discussed as well. Finally, adaptive capitalism supports the creation and support of human beings in community that provides people personal meaning and collective identity. Within community, including the family, human beings form bonds with the generations that precede and succeed them. Adaptive capitalism requires accountability for the destruction of community (Friedmann 1992:124).

Some find hope in current conditions of unadaptive, mechanistic, and market capitalism. David Brody, a labor historian, for example, sees in the current economic conditions the prospect of a new social contract between labor and capital:

> Basic structural forces are in contradiction: postindustrial technology demands involvement and commitment from employees, but the competitive market and corporate restructuring now deny to all but the most sheltered firms the means for assuring the job security and predictable treatment on which employee commitment depends (1992:40).

When those contradictions become severe enough workers will once again look to labor unions as their best means to acquire job-related justice. Whatever the role of labor, Brody and others emphasize that political and not merely economic change is required for adaptive capitalism.

Similarly, those analysts concerned with rural development advocate a broad range of reform and collaborative effort. Leaders in rural areas that have managed to keep abreast economically attribute their success to the cooperation of local industries in technology, worker training, and marketing; strong communities with deliberate programs of leadership training and development; and education and training programs for the region's work force (Bishop 1993e). Analysts who study and assist rural development have a similar list of principles of sound development. It extends to the development of civic activities for the action participation of community members; ethical politics and honest government; educated, skilled workers; an holistic approach in which communities attempt to do everything well; and local leaders who manage to have hope in their communities' futures and inspire confidence in that hope in others (Bishop 1993f). The most extensive set of principles of rural development comes from the Heartland Center for Leadership Development (Bishop 1993g). These principles include:

-- evidence of community pride;
-- emphasis on quality in business and community life;
-- willingness to invest in the future;
-- participatory approach to community decision-making;
-- cooperative community spirit;
-- realistic appraisal of future opportunities;
-- awareness of competitive position;
-- knowledge of the physical environment;
-- active economic development program;
-- deliberate transition of power to a younger generation of leaders;
-- acceptance of women in leadership roles;
-- strong belief in and support for education;
-- problem-solving approach to providing health care;
-- strong multigenerational family orientation;
-- strong presence of traditional institutions that are integral to community life;
-- attention to sound and well-maintained infrastructure;
-- careful use of fiscal resources;
-- sophisticated use of information resources;
-- willingness to seek help from the outside; and

-- conviction that, in the long run, you have to do it yourself.

Culture, Contentment and Political Reform

Alternative economic development requires political change and both of them require changes in American cultural values that hinder the pursuit of social, political, and economic equity. John Kenneth Galbraith pointed to the "culture of contentment" as a primary obstacle to the political solution of the new American inequality, in a profoundly pessimistic assessment of the 1980s. In this culture, a semipermanent underclass conducts the tedious and unskilled work for low wages that makes urban life pleasant and possible. As the poor of the inner city became the underclass, minority communities changed from "benign and culturally engaging" groups into "centers of terror and despair." Galbraith traces the economics and the politics of contentment in terms similar to those we have examined. He sees a culture in which "the fortunate and the favored...do not contemplate and respond to their own longer-run well-being. Rather, they respond, and powerfully, to immediate comfort and contentment."

This culture has four characteristics, according to Galbraith. The contented assert that wealth and power are rewards for merit. The contented prefer short-run public inaction on social problems rather than public action for long-run solutions. They look upon government as a burden and ineffective except for financial rescue of failed businesses, military rescue of real or alleged American economic interests and self-esteem abroad, social expenditures on the well-to-do, and interest payments on the national debt. The latter served as a substitute for policies of equity during the 1980s. Finally, the contented accept vast degrees of inequality rather than redistributive measures (Galbraith 1992:13-29).

Galbraith uses Appalachia as a lens on American economics and society. The region presents advanced stages of trends, including a functional underclass, and the challenge to reverse those trends and to address their attendant social issues by long-range planning and commitments to equity and social welfare policies. Experience within the region tempers optimism for easy solutions to reverse a national culture of contentment through social, political, and economic change. That same experience suggests the wisdom and necessity for reforms.

In an analysis of American politics since 1960, E. J. Dionne (1992) attributes the inability to undertake political reform to address American problems to "cultural wars" rather than a culture of contentment. The cultural wars divide Americans between liberals and conservatives and within each group. The broadest division separates those who believe that the public good can be achieved through political action to establish and expand government programs from those who believe that the public good can be achieved through political action to abolish and limit government programs. Fissures that run through these two large divisions are the primacy of the individual and the primacy of traditional values; race; and America's international role. The frequency and nature of American elections provide politicians the incentive to merely arrange electoral pluralities among these divisions and fissures. This means the increased symbolic use of issues to scare voters and discredit opponents. Rather than focusing on issues, our political campaigns become enmeshed in discussions of personal character, drug use, Vietnam, and veiled references to race and ethnicity. Dionne concludes that far from being content, as Galbraith supposes, Americans have lost hope of addressing social problems and concerns through politics. They "hate" politics, at least at the national level, because it seems to work so poorly in addressing important matters.

Others agree, for different reasons, that the capacity of Americans for political change falls short of their need. Lester Thurow (1981:212-14) faults the American political system for its failure to nourish political parties that can propose, secure and implement policies in the direction of more, not less, equity. Kuttner similarly faults American political leaders for supporting an illusion that equity and economic growth are in conflict. Clearly, other nations prove that the economics of equality work better than America demonstrates (Kuttner 1992:278). Both Japan and Germany, for example, have a far more equitable distribution of income than America's. Kevin Phillips (1990) pointed this out. Phillips faults the Republican Party for excesses of the 1980s. He suggests that however difficult the politics of equity may be, the politics of inequality are readily within the abilities of American political leaders.

For Bennett Harrison and Barry Bluestone, the politics of inequality express a "two-thirds society." Conservative governments, in Europe as well as America, have mobilized the support of the "middle third" of insecure workers into alliance with the social upper third with wealth and power. This alliance supports conservative, laissez-faire political economic arrangements and blocks social programs for the "lower third"— marginalized workers, the physically and mentally handicapped, and the young and the elderly of the lower classes.

Reich raises the specter of the upper fifth of American society seceding from the rest. He suggests that moral persuasion might move the upper fifth of society to take on the social issues that the economy creates. Reich calls for compassion within "positive economic nationalism" and not a political solution (Reich 1991:282-315).

Harrison and Bluestone (1988:194-96), on the other hand, place little faith in the voluntary response of the well-to-do. They conclude that the end of mechanistic economics, expressed most recently through laissez-faire politics and a corresponding tolerance for new levels of poverty and inequality, "will not occur without a major political alignment and a renewed commitment, especially within the Democratic Party, to the principles of social security and economic justice."

Robert N. Bellah and his colleagues join the chorus of support for political change but go beyond political parties. They call for a revitalization of institutions, including the church, that entails an examination of the premises of human relations embedded in social valuations of institutions:

> We believe that the modern ideal of a democracy governed by intelligent public opinion and participation not only is worth redeeming in our own society but requires, as far as possible, extension to the human community as a whole. In making this argument we shall attempt to renew earlier efforts to create an American public philosophy less trapped in the cliches of rugged individualism and more open to an invigorating, fulfilling sense of social responsibility. But responsible social participation, with an enlightened citizenry that can deal with moral and intellectual complexity, does not come about just from exhortation. It is certainly not enough simply to implore our fellow citizens to "get involved." We must create institutions that will enable such participation to occur, encourage it, and make it fulfilling as well as demanding (Bellah et al. 1992:15).

William Greider puts the task of revitalization in terms of redefining American democracy. He sees action on behalf of the American ideal in some places, including Appalachia. That ideal simply states that people will participate in the processes by which their lives are organized. The economic trends and social issues outlined here suggest an urgency for new forms of participation and re-organization of the political economy that now affects the lives of Americans adversely. Greider's hope in the promise of democratic renewal lies in the democratic process itself. "At the most creative moments in the American past, the nation found its true source of political energy and ideas among those citizens in unexpected quarters who took it upon themselves to renew the search [for the American democracy]." At those creative moments Americans once again "aspire to self-realization and rebel against powerlessness." Greider expects the American moment to occur again "when Americans find the courage to speak honestly again in the language of democracy" (Greider 1992:405-15).

Conclusion

In their function as service providers, community organizations, like churches, health centers, housing groups, women's groups, and nonprofit development corporations, serve the first of two primary social intervention needs. The second need is to engage in that "border war" Heilbroner described that establishes where the state and the economy meet. This means dealing with the systemic aspects of a social problem; tracing it back to economic trends and social issues. In practice, this means domestic violence shelters explaining the context of domestic violence, including declining incomes, changed male-female employment patterns, increases in female-headed households, and the public response needed. Adapting capitalism to the needs of the twenty-first century also means emulating community environmental groups and replicating their efforts across a wide variety of issue areas. In particular, local efforts need to enter into state organizations and into collaboration with related federal advocacy organizations. A federal system of change efforts that parallel government structures and collaborate among themselves at every level have the best prospect to redress public policy issues at the bottom of local problems. This means also provides the hope for institutional renewal of American life and democracy. Perhaps that is the challenge to America: to find its own voice and to express again its best sense of self. In Appalachia, the nation can find the language of its best self as well as the absolute necessity to regain its voice.

Conclusion

In his classic study of American race relations, Gunnar Myrdal found an American "dilemma" in the ideals of American society and its everyday world. Fifty years after that study, that gap still exists in race relations. It is apparent in the conditions of Appalachia as well. Appalachia has long been the scene of economic changes that shaped America. It currently embodies the changes of deindustrialization and postindustrialization. Along with those changes comes the challenge of maintaining the American Creed.

An American Creed

The dilemma that Myrdal found and the challenge that this book outlines is the painful but plain contrast of the conditions of some Americans and our principles of democratic equality. Appalachia, like race, presents the dilemma Myrdal observed: "America believes in and aspires to something much higher than its plane of actual life (1962:21). Having examined some elements of the plane of actual life, let us now examine American aspirations.

Americans have a "Creed," according to Myrdal, with a few profound tenets fashioned around "the essential dignity of the individual human being...the fundamental equality of all [people] and...certain inalienable rights to freedom, justice, and a fair opportunity" (Myrdal 1962:5). This creed holds that there is nothing wrong with economic inequality by itself. It also holds, however, that no American group should be allowed to fall under a certain minimum of living and should have equal opportunity. Homelessness, the underclass of the inner city, and the new and intense forms of poverty of portions of Appalachia violate that creed.

The strong ethos of individualism and the premise of abundant and adequate opportunity for economic success, summarized in our faith in an invisible hand, discounts the public nature of poverty, inequality, and decline in the position of the working middle class. In terms of redress to these problems, we look to individual solutions, migration or increased effort, and not public, collective action, such as social guarantees of health, housing, educational standards, income, and employment. Approaching a public problem primarily through individual action obfuscates the moral nature of public problems. It treats public problems like individual decisions rather than social relations. If our public problems are individual decisions, they are not made primarily among the poor and the working middle class but in corporate board rooms and government forums. The poor and powerless do not ordinarily decide the social and economic relations of a nation. Those decisions come intentionally and unintentionally from choices people make, and choice increases with power and wealth.

This leads to a set of premises about social problems, such as the political economy of Appalachia, that may be adapted from those that Myrdal used:

- -- the problems of the poor and working middle class are an integral part of, or a special phase of, the whole complex of problems in the larger American society;
- -- the affluent and powerful determine the place of the poor and the working middle class;
- -- the moral struggle for greater equality and opportunity goes on within people of both groups and not merely between them;
- -- the poor and working middle class eagerly ascribe to the American Creed. The task for the affluent and powerful is to achieve the creed in the plane of the actual life of the poor and working middle class not to defend it against them;
- -- the starting point for change in policies of work and social capital is the ordinary person's own ideas, doctrines, theories, and mental constructs;
- -- the interrelations between the conditions of the poor and the working middle class and people's valuations of and beliefs about these conditions are precisely what make poverty, political economy, and social capital a social problem (Myrdal 1962:lxix-lxiii).

An American Challenge

Myrdal suggests, as does this report, that social problems have dual natures. They are what they are and they are what we say about them. The Appalachia this report describes is a two-fold social problem. First, there is the social problem of our valuations and interpretations of poverty and other conditions of human need in the Appalachian region. "Poverty" and even the term "Appalachia" are laden with conceptual meanings. These defend those who are not poor or not within the region *from* the American Creed. If the plane of actual life, as Myrdal called it, contradicts the values to which we aspire, then we defend ourselves from those values by offering a defense *of* facts of actual life that contradict our values. If conditions in parts of Appalachia do not conform to the expectations created by the American Creed, then we explain those conditions in terms of the people there, their culture, or their geography. We may also use the facts of concentrations of poverty in parts of Appalachia to substantiate our valuations about the people, culture, and geography of the region. Our first social problem is how we understand our social problems.

Much of the recent work on Appalachia has made clear that interpretations of Appalachian conditions serve to justify the interventions of political and economic interests outside the region. The poorer those interests portray Appalachia and the more they emphasize the lack of economic opportunity in the region, the more likely they are to interpret economic exploitation as development. The global economy has made this problem with social problems international. The creation of a low-wage labor pool with minimal social capital occurs now at the edges of America, like the maquiladoras, as it once occurred in the heartland of industrial America. The same promises of development and progress made in Appalachia before can be heard now in several different languages. Missing in those promises are descriptions of the roles of government to adapt capitalism to the needs of working people and of mediating structures to permit workers and community residents some say in the economic and political processes that organize and affect their lives.

This report has dealt less with the valuations and pejorative cultural interpretations of Appalachia and more with the second of the social problems of Appalachia, its political economy. It places the trends and issues of the Appalachian region within the changes occurring nationally. These trends and issues include declining employment opportunities, declining wages, increased poverty, concentrations of poverty, and inadequate public investments in people within their families and communities.

Appalachia's geography entails the political economy of the nation including its place in a global economy. The exchanges of European settlers with the native tribes of the region announced the arrival of a global economy. French and British colonial powers fought over a lucrative trading site on the Ohio River within the world's mercantile economy in the 18th century. Fort Duquesne became Fort Pitt and finally Pittsburgh. In the south of Appalachia, British capital replicated the industrial revolution of coal and steel development and named the place of this transformation for a city in England, Birmingham.

By the 20th century American capital transformed the places between and around Pittsburgh and Birmingham. Coal towns throughout the region bear the names of company presidents, board members, their wives, and family members. Industrial relations of owners and workers were stubbornly controverted throughout the region. The unions of miners and workers in the region wrote a chapter of American labor history. It said that economic transformation meant social transformation and that meant a contest over the meaning of justice, fairness, decent living conditions, and other valuations of American society.

The current voices of a global economy and economic transition join a chorus that has been heard and felt in the Appalachian region for more than two centuries. Conflict envelops the current economic transition like every other one before it. This time the conflict is not merely about the work place and the terms of labor. It is about living space and the terms of creating and sustaining people in community. The transition that is occurring marks the passing not only of industries and forms of work but the communities that they sustained.

That message is not yet clear. There are some who still hope for an economy without community. An economy without public social capital. Robert Reich, for example, did not find tragedy in marking the passage of the steel mill and town of Homestead, Pennsylvania:

> Why should we care about Homestead, or for that matter, about any town or city in decline? ...Americans are always leaving some place behind; departures are in our ancestral genes ...Homestead and its people...are separable.

Reich's concern falls on the people. He finds the most important question to be, How did the people of Homestead fare once they left? How did they make out in the transition from steel to other work? The answer is probably not very well. Most of them probably got jobs farther west or south in the service industry making one-third to one-half the income they had in the steel mill. This Reich finds is "not so much the tragedy of an American steel town as it is the tragedy of modern America" (Reich 1993:16).

Declining incomes bring on difficulty and tragedy, certainly, but if we separate work from the place where people live we invite further and worse tragedies. Tragedies for families and communities. If work is not tied to the maintenance and sustenance of community, work may eventually and literally erode the ground, poison the air, and contaminate the water that supports community. But not all communities, only those where working people and poor people live. The maquiladoras suggest that the global market of today can construct social relations of a pillage and not a village. The declining coal towns and steel towns of Appalachia suggest the same, an economy of wealth that cannot sustain large numbers of people in the place they live and prefer to work. An economy where wealth requires the literal destruction of community produces many areas that are "written off."

William Serrin, reflecting on Homestead, Pennsylvania, came to a conclusion far different from Reich. He contrasted the development of Pittsburgh and its white, upper-class northern suburbs at the same time that

> unattractive areas, be they old industrial areas, working class communities, or inner-city black and Hispanic areas, were being written off ...Money was following money—the American way. It was the mentality of the frontier—extract and leave. It was an unethical way for the country to live, but no one seemed to care...(Serrin 1993:420).

This "American way" conflicts with the American Creed. Myrdal asserted that Americans were changing their "Creed" to "include a decent living standard and a measure of economic security among the liberties and rights which are given...highest moral sanction" (Myrdal 1962:212). Shortly following this assertion, Appalachia witnessed the destruction of community in the 1950s when changes in the production and use of coal eroded the social capital of the coal fields. That produced a vast outmigration from Central Appalachia, especially. In the 1980s, another migration marked another round of decline of community and erosion of social capital. Some fifty years after that assertion, Homestead, Pennsylvania and hundreds of towns like it in Appalachia testify that the American way needs more of the American Creed: a new social contract about work, income, mutual responsibility, higher levels of social capital, and community.

The change Myrdal envisioned, or perhaps only hoped for, entails the hard and expensive work of developing resources to solve problems of work, income, and poverty where we find them. It entails confronting the valuations that permit us to concentrate wealth and poverty in geographic areas and then to ascribe characteristics to the people who live there as if those characteristics explain wealth and poverty. Those valuations permit us to entrust to the invisible hand the tangible problems of poverty, income, family change, and work. We entrust little else but human need to the invisible hand. We would certainly not trust it with the next quarter's earnings of any American corporation or the re-election of a political leader. The change that Myrdal envisioned entails using the facts of our "plane of actual life" to measure our distance from the values of the American Creed. That change entails accepting the challenge of the American Creed to provide a decent living standard and a measure of economic security for everyone rather than building defenses from our ideals because of the obvious poverty of some.

Theology for the American Creed

It is fitting that a creed have a theology. The Commission on Religion in Appalachia (CORA) has fashioned a theology of economic development (1993) that serves also as a theological start for the economic justice embedded in Myrdal's American Creed. This theology shares some of Myrdal's assumptions, tenets of belief, about the nature of social problems like economic inequality, namely,

-- The United States' economy should reflect the careful stewardship of the resources of land and people...Economic activity has a three-fold moral significance: First, it embodies the distinctive human capacity for self-realization and self-expression. Second, work is one of the chief ways that human beings seek self-fulfillment, both the fulfillment of their basic material needs and the spiritual need to express initiative and creativity. Finally, work should enable everyone to make a contribution to the human community to the extent each is able.

-- Human beings as participants in, and as the benefactors of the economy, have basic rights by virtue of their creation by God, regardless of class, sex, race or place in the economy.

-- The purpose of a nation's economy is the well-being of its people. The success of an economy should be judged by how those fare who are the poor and oppressed; "the least among us..."

-- The purpose of a nation's economy is to give every person an equal opportunity for appropriate education of high quality, creative work and a meaningful life.

-- We believe in a wholistic economy which emphasizes cooperation and the building up of community as opposed to practices which divide and destroy community and family life.

-- Human creativity is to be valued over technology. Technology should enhance creativity rather than diminish it.

-- Economic activity must contribute to the development and well-being of human community.

-- We are called to work as co-creators in the building of a just future aimed at meeting human needs and caring for the earth and its resources.

-- We believe in the right for all to be involved in the economic as well as political decisions which affect their individual and common life. We believe in the right to be trained and empowered to enforce the laws and regulations concerning economic behavior, health care, and community health and safety.
-- We share a sense of responsibility with our sisters and brothers around the world for the economic well-being of all (CORA 1992).

These assumptions or tenets of belief produce a theology of economics and work that emphasizes stewardship. Meeting human needs and caring for the earth and its resources are fundamental to stewardship. So is work, "meaningful, useful, celebrative, and productive work aimed at gathering and building community, meeting the basic needs of community, and sharing in the care of the land and its resources" (CORA 1992:6)

These tenets of belief lead to theologies of involvement and of risk as well. This theology affirms the need for churches and community organizations to build a new solidarity among those whose basic rights are under attack. But the theology of involvement needs to extend from these groups, especially the poor and near-poor, to those who are well-off and privileged. The bedrock of this theology is a shared understanding of the need for radical, systemic change and action to achieve it. Such action requires institutions, including churches, to identify with, and act in solidarity with, the oppressed throughout the world. In these actions, hopefully, the human family can find inspiration to begin or sustain movements for economic justice.

Finally, a theology of hope is expressed in the tenets of belief. This hope springs from the prophetic vision of new creation and resurrection and of transformation of the social, economic, and political system. Obviously, this theology assumes that new creation is a social and not merely a personal task. So, it calls upon each of us to work with each other to probe for signs of an entirely different, better and more human order of social, economic, and political affairs. That vision foresees a true commonwealth of land, natural resources, and the means of production within which it is possible for everyone to work to gather and build communities which struggle for the common good. This theology of hope looks beyond the valuations of individual gain or loss for the social bonds that economic and political life entail. The theology of hope, as the prophet Amos expressed it, also makes demands: "Take away from me the noise of your songs; to the melody of your harps I will not listen. But let justice roll down like waters, and righteousness like an everflowing stream."

Appendices

Appendix A

Beyond Distress
Measures of New Economic Need In Appalachia

Reports of the Appalachian Regional Commission (ARC) in 1992 suggested new levels of economic problems in the Appalachian region. Economic trends and the recession of the late 1980s had evidently brought new levels of poverty to Appalachia that, in some counties, eluded previous measures.

The ARC ranked each of the 399 counties of Appalachia as severely distressed; distressed; middle; strong; and very strong. ARC constructs its ranks from three measures: a three year average unemployment rate; per capita market income, personal income minus transfer payments; and the rate of poverty. Each county measure is compared with the national rate. For example, the average of three year unemployment rates of each county are classified at 150 percent or more of the national figure, 125 percent to 149 percent, 101 to 124 percent, 76 to 100 percent, or less than 75 percent. The 1990 poverty rate of the county are classified in the same manner. Per capita market income is classified as below 2/3 of the national level, 2/3 to 4/5 of the national level, and more than 4/5 of the national level. To be labelled severely distressed an Appalachian county needs to have a three year unemployment rate of at least 150 percent of the official national figure, 5.8 percent; a poverty rate of 150 percent or more of the 1990 national rate, 13.1 percent; and per capita market income less than 67 percent of the 1990 national amount, $15,895. Very strong counties, on the other end of the economic spectrum, have measures of 75 percent of unemployment, 80 percent of income, and 75 percent of the national rate of poverty. According to the ARC listings, there are 90 counties severely distressed; 54 distressed; 223 middle; 25 strong; and 7 very strong.

Eleven counties in Eastern Kentucky, perennially the poorest region of Appalachia, and four counties in Tennessee were ranked as improved from severely distressed in 1988. Rather than improved, however, they had moved beyond distress. In Owsley County, Kentucky, for example, one out of two people was poor and the average income in the county was only 28 percent of the nation's average, according to 1990 census figures. The 1990 census reported also that 64 percent of the children in the county lived in poor families. Yet Owsley County's economic status initially "improved" from severely distressed to distressed in the rankings of the ARC. On the other hand, four counties in Ohio ranked severely distressed in 1992 but ranked either middle or distressed in 1988 and, for the first time, a county in Pennsylvania declined two notches to the rank of severely distressed.

The core of poverty counties in Central Appalachia moved beyond distress while areas of Appalachian Ohio and Pennsylvania, especially declining industrial areas, moved down to replace them. The economic ladder now has a lower rung where no Appalachian county stood before. The fifteen "beyond distress" counties failed to meet the criteria of 150 percent of the national unemployment figure. Hancock County in East Tennessee, for example, has a rate of poverty 3 times the national average and income of 38 percent of the national amount. Fifty percent of the children in Hancock County are in poverty, according to the 1990 census figures. Yet it too is no longer severely distressed because its *official* unemployment rate is 5.2 percent. Hancock County, along with three other counties that are beyond distress, "improved" their economic classification from severely distressed to middle.

Anyone familiar with Hancock County would pause in amazement at the suggestion that unemployment is only 5.2 percent. Critics have alleged for a long time that the official unemployment rate is a seriously flawed underestimation of the people who want work and cannot find it. The official rate does not include the long-term unemployed, the discouraged workers who give up trying to find work, and men and especially women who do not enter the work force because of the futility of trying to find work. In counties of great poverty and low income, these "unofficially" unemployed reach staggering proportions. The Appalachian Center of the University of Kentucky reported "real" or "unofficial" unemployment rates of the 52.5 to 10.5 percent for the 11 Eastern Kentucky counties which are no longer categorized severely distressed. By these measures, Owsley County had an "unofficial" unemployment rate of 46.8 percent (Keesler 1991). The Appalachian Center of the University of Kentucky also estimated surplus labor for each county of the state. This takes into account labor force participation of adults over 16 years of age and attempts to measure the discouraged workers in a county. On this measure, Owsley County had 63.3 percent potential labor surplus and ranked last among the 120 counties of Kentucky (Goetz, Ilvento, and Eller 1992).

The inadequacy of unemployment measures simply underscores that some areas of Appalachia are moving beyond distress. The prospects of employment in the poorest portion of Appalachia are so bad that official unemployment rates fall as an expression of chronic depression and individual discouragement rather than economic improvement or new hope. The recession of 1989 has exacerbated trends apparent throughout the 1980s and have brought new degrees of poverty and need to the Appalachian region. Literally, some parts of Appalachia have moved so low that what was down is beginning to look like up according to the measures for poverty and economic needs that we have used.

Table A-1
Profile of Beyond Distress Counties

Name	1990 Pop.	1989-90 Ave. % Unempl.	Univ. of KY Unempl. Est.	1990 Per Capita Mkt. Income	Poverty Rate %	1992 Rank*
Kentucky Counties						
Casey	14,211	8.5	36.7	$7,649	29.4	2
Floyd	43,586	8.4	40.2	9,178	31.2	2
Johnson	23,248	8.5	38.9	9,155	28.7	2
Lee	7,422	8.5	25.6	5,399	37.4	2
Leslie	13,642	7.7	52.5	7,119	35.6	2
Owsley	5,036	8.5	46.8	4,513	52.1	2
Pulaski	49,498	8.4	17.5	9,990	22.7	2
Rockcastle	14,803	7.3	10.5	7,790	30.7	2
Russell	14,716	7.2	4.7	9,632	25.6	3
Wayne	17,468	8.6	23.4	6,723	37.3	2
Whitley	33,326	8.2	40.7	8,659	33.0	2
Tennessee Counties						
Grainger	17,095	7.5	n.a.	8,190	20.5	2
Hancock	6,739	5.2	n.a.	6,115	40.0	3
Jackson	9,297	7.2	n.a.	7,482	20.0	3
Pickett	4,548	7.1	n.a.	6,140	24.9	3
Average	18,308	7.8	n.a.	7,582	31.3	2.27
Appalachia	—	6.5	n.a.	12,432	15.2	—
United States	—	5.8	n.a.	15,895	13.1	—

* 2=Distressed 3=Middle
Sources: Appalachian Regional Commission; Keesler 1991.

An examination of these 15 beyond distress counties suggests a profile of high rates of poverty and low per capita income together with misleading figures on "official" unemployment. The rates of poverty in these counties average, twice the regional rate and 2.4 times the national poverty rate. The per capita market income of these counties is less than half the national average. Table A-1 provides a summary of average measures for these counties and the University of Kentucky's Appalachian Center's estimate of unofficial poverty. The increased severity of poverty in Appalachia provides one of the two challenges to the American economy. The decline in economic status of the working middle class provides the other.

Map A-2 portrays the counties of the region by their economic status as reported originally by ARC in 1992. The map reports some counties as "beyond distress" rather than by their improved ranks according to the ARC's measures. Appendix B lists all the counties and their measures that combine to provide their economic rank.

Map A-3 portrays changes in the ARC economic ranking of Appalachian counties from 1988 to 1992. Thirty-eight counties improved their economic status according to the measures of the ARC. This total does not include the "beyond distress" counties. Fifty-eight counties, including the "beyond distress" counties declined in economic status. Improvement occurred largely in Southern Appalachia, Alabama, North Carolina, and Tennessee especially. Counties including and around Pittsburgh also reported improvement. West Virginia and Ohio had the largest share of counties with a decline in their economic ranks from 1988 to 1992.

Map A-2
Economic Ranks of Appalachian Counties, 1992

ARC designation of the economic strength of Appalachian counties, 1992

- Beyond Distress*
- Severely Distressed
- Distressed
- Middle
- Strong
- Very Strong

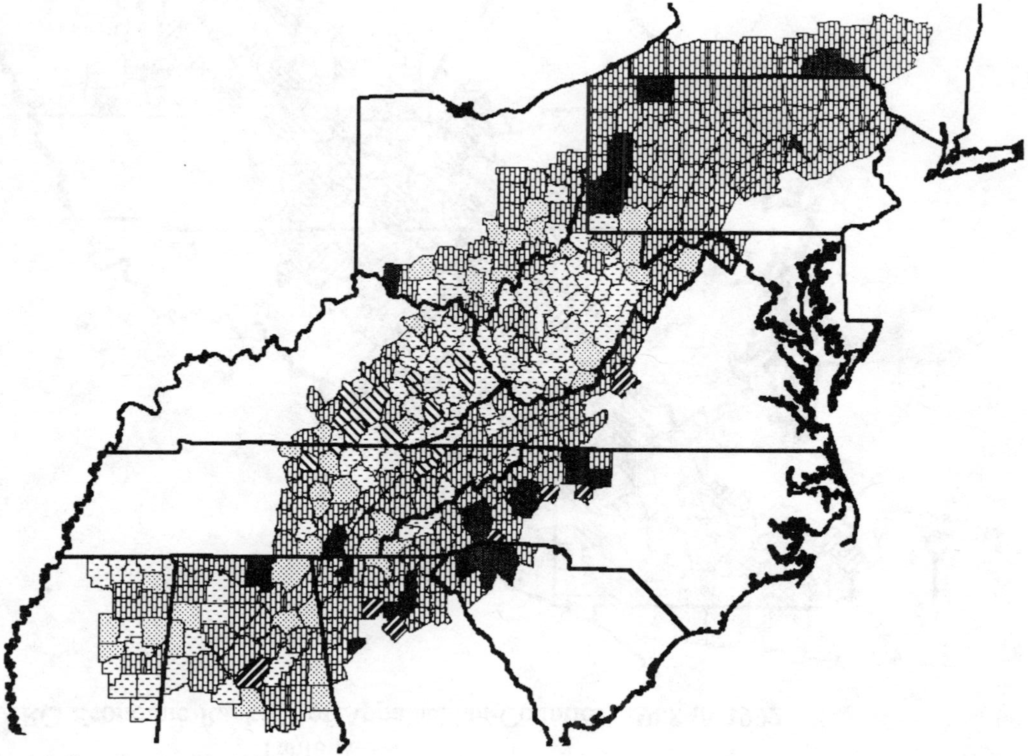

*This category added.

Source: Appalachian Regional Commission, August 25, 1992

Table A-3
Changes in ARC Economic Ranking of Appalachian Counties, 1988 to 1992

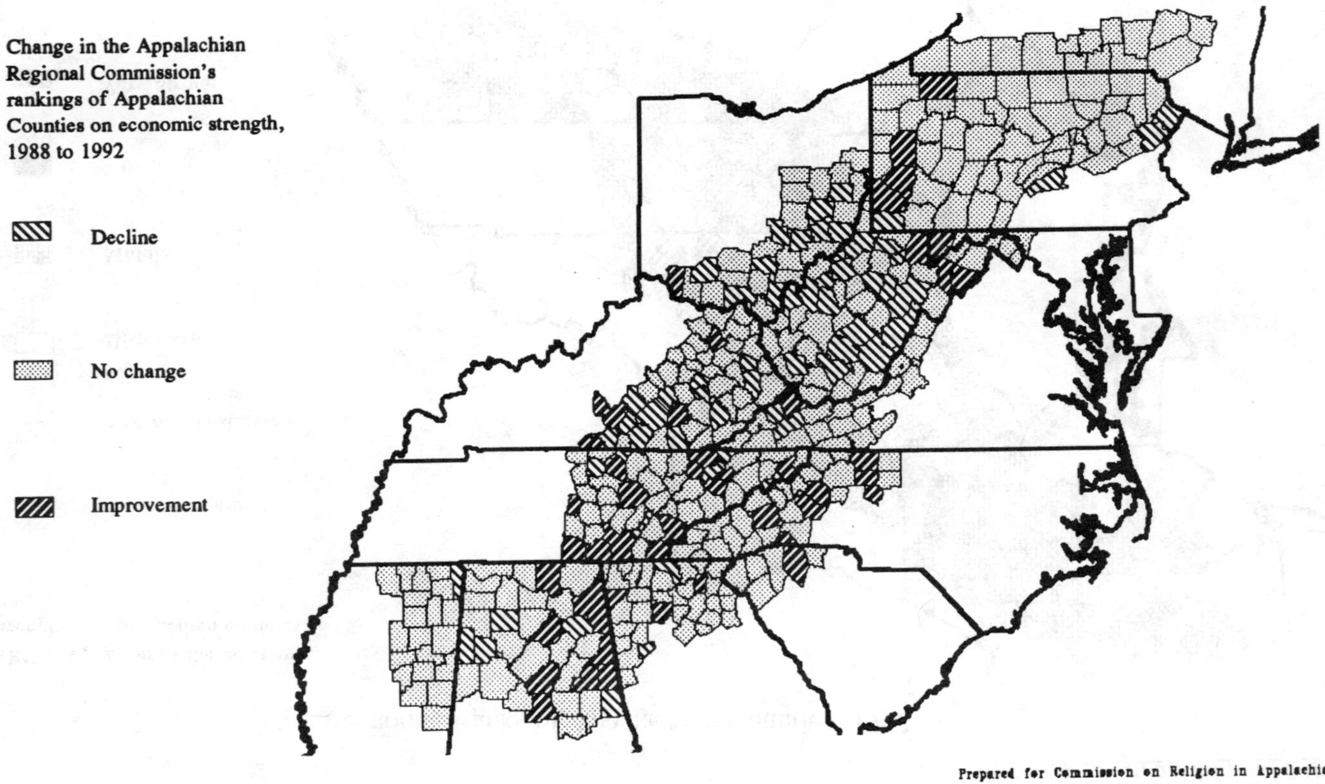

Appendix B

Selected Characteristics of Appalachia and Appalachian Counties

Summary Level	1990 Census Population	% Change Pop. 1970-80	% Change Pop. 1980-90	1990 % Pop. 65 and Over	1980 Per Capita Income	1990 Per Capita Income	1990 % Workforce Unemp.	1989 % Pop. Below Poverty	1990 % Pop. 25 and Over With H.S. Diploma	5-Year Infant Mortality Rate 1984-88	1990 Pop. per Patient-Care Doctor	ARC* 1988 Distressed Counties
Total U.S.	248,799,500	11.5	9.8	12.6	9,526	18,746	5.5	12.8	75.2	10.4	516.4	
Total Appalachia	20,701,400	11.1	1.6	14.3	7,790	15,331	6.2	14.8	68.4	10.4	680.8	
Northern	9,917,800	4.1	-3.1	15.7	8,343	15,722	6.4	13.6	73.3	9.6	626.2	
Central	2,015,200	21.4	-4.7	13.3	6,438	12,315	7.9	25.3	53.3	10.8	1,046.3	
Southern	8,768,400	18.8	9.4	12.9	7,441	15,582	5.7	13.8	66.1	11.2	693.5	
AL Total	4,040,500	13.1	3.8	12.9	7,482	15,018	6.8	17.9	66.9	12.6	673.5	
AL Part	2,529,600	13.8	4.1	13.0	7,696	15,636	6.5	15.5	67.1	12.2	625.5	
AL Bibb	16,600	13.8	5.7	12.7	6,037	12,114	8.6	21.2	51.8	13.2	1,844.4	1
AL Blount	39,200	35.7	7.4	13.1	5,245	13,135	7.4	15.3	60.5	7.5	3,266.7	2
AL Calhoun	116,000	16.3	-3.2	12.4	7,122	13,776	7.0	15.7	67.4	12.8	899.2	3
AL Chambers	36,900	7.7	-5.9	16.9	6,678	12,968	7.3	18.8	54.3	18.3	1,366.7	3
AL Cherokee	19,500	20.5	3.7	14.8	5,642	12,642	10.4	17.6	53.5	13.9	2,785.7	1
AL Chilton	32,500	21.4	6.2	13.9	6,043	12,043	8.8	17.1	56.6	14.1	2,954.5	1
AL Clay	13,300	8.7	-2.9	16.8	6,061	12,948	6.2	17.4	53.8	27.5	2,660.0	1
AL Cleburne	12,700	14.5	0.8	13.4	5,509	12,287	7.2	15.3	49.8	9.9	3,175.0	2

Summary Level	1990 Census Population	% Change Pop. 1970-80	% Change Pop. 1980-90	1990 % Pop. 65 and Over	1980 Per Capita Income	1990 Per Capita Income	1990 % Workforce Unemp.	1989 % Pop. Below Poverty	1990 % Pop. 25 and Over With H.S. Diploma	5-Year Infant Mortality Rate 1984-88	1990 Pop. per Patient-Care Doctor	ARC* 1988 Distressed Counties
AL Colbert	51,700	10.1	-5.1	14.7	7,689	13,380	7.9	14.6	65.2	11.4	907.0	3
AL Coosa	11,100	7.5	-2.6	14.4	5,886	10,664	6.2	18.2	53.9	12.8	5,550.0	3
AL Cullman	67,600	17.6	9.7	14.5	6,638	13,794	7.1	15.3	58.8	13.5	1,229.1	3
AL DeKalb	54,700	28.2	1.9	14.6	5,733	14,374	7.0	17.4	53.0	11.8	2,025.9	2
AL Elmore	49,200	29.6	13.4	11.7	7,060	14,870	6.0	14.5	66.5	11.7	2,236.4	3
AL Etowah	99,800	9.6	-3.2	15.9	7,425	13,394	10.7	16.5	64.1	12.2	702.8	3
AL Fayette	18,000	16.0	-4.3	16.3	6,648	12,352	9.4	20.3	56.6	12.2	1,800.0	3
AL Franklin	27,800	18.8	-2.1	15.5	6,692	13,736	10.5	20.7	55.1	11.5	1,463.2	3
AL Jackson	47,800	31.1	-7.0	12.6	7,046	12,767	9.8	16.6	58.1	8.5	1,770.4	2
AL Jefferson	651,500	4.1	-2.9	14.0	9,375	18,624	5.1	16.0	73.8	13.7	288.0	3
AL Lamar	15,700	14.6	-4.8	15.7	6,786	12,636	7.5	18.0	52.9	10.2	3,140.0	3
AL Lauderdale	79,700	18.4	-1.0	14.3	7,920	14,403	6.6	14.9	67.9	10.4	705.3	3
AL Lawrence	31,500	11.0	4.3	11.9	5,562	11,763	9.7	19.8	55.6	12.0	2,423.1	1
AL Limestone	54,100	10.3	17.6	11.3	6,488	14,617	5.9	14.0	63.1	9.8	2,352.2	3
AL Madison	238,900	5.6	21.3	9.0	8,896	18,990	4.7	10.9	80.2	9.8	620.5	3
AL Marion	29,800	26.6	-0.7	15.2	6,008	11,001	12.3	19.1	50.0	10.0	1,655.6	2
AL Marshall	70,800	21.0	7.9	14.1	7,224	15,204	7.7	17.2	61.5	11.2	1,609.1	3
AL Morgan	100,000	16.7	10.9	11.7	7,521	16,458	6.6	12.0	69.4	9.4	833.3	3

*Distressed county ranks: 1 = severely distressed, 2 = distressed, 3 = middle, 4 = strong, and 5 = very strong.

Summary Level	1990 Census Population	% Change Pop. 1970-80	% Change Pop. 1980-90	1990 % Pop. 65 and Over	1980 Per Capita Income	1990 Per Capita Income	1990 % Workforce Unemp.	1989 % Pop. Below Poverty	1990 % Pop. 25 and Over With H.S. Diploma	5-Year Infant Mortality Rate 1984-88	1990 Pop. per Patient-Care Doctor	ARC* 1988 Distressed Counties
AL Pickens	20,700	5.9	-3.7	16.4	6,044	11,418	10.3	28.9	56.2	16.3	2,070.0	1
AL Randolph	19,900	9.8	-1.0	16.5	5,643	12,069	8.3	18.9	50.3	12.9	2,487.5	1
AL Shelby	99,400	74.9	49.9	7.6	6,892	15,935	3.9	9.2	78.2	9.6	1,875.5	3
AL St. Clair	50,000	47.7	21.4	11.6	6,050	13,056	6.0	14.8	61.0	10.4	2,777.8	3
AL Talladega	74,100	13.2	0.4	12.9	6,291	12,212	9.6	20.2	60.7	11.1	1,576.6	1
AL Tallapoosa	38,800	14.5	0.3	16.1	6,641	14,235	6.1	16.0	57.8	15.4	1,437.0	3
AL Tuscaloosa	150,500	18.5	9.5	11.3	7,032	15,113	5.1	20.1	69.6	13.8	543.3	3
AL Walker	67,700	22.2	-1.5	14.4	7,855	14,556	9.3	17.3	56.0	10.4	1,440.4	3
AL Winston	22,100	32.5	0.5	14.1	6,274	12,023	11.2	19.8	48.8	13.9	2,455.6	3
GA Total	6,477,700	19.1	18.6	10.1	8,087	17,114	5.4	14.3	70.9	12.7	626.7	
GA Part	1,508,000	35.8	36.6	9.7	7,127	16,420	5.6	9.8	67.5	10.2	1,242.2	
GA Banks	10,300	26.1	18.4	11.5	5,225	13,906	5.5	15.1	56.6	8.6	1,716.7	3
GA Barrow	29,700	27.4	38.8	10.9	7,264	14,322	8.1	14.7	58.8	9.6	2,475.0	3
GA Bartow	55,900	24.8	37.0	10.0	7,285	14,007	8.5	10.7	58.7	10.4	1,644.1	3
GA Carroll	71,400	24.3	26.8	10.2	6,975	14,463	6.2	14.4	60.5	11.4	952.0	3
GA Catoosa	42,500	30.7	14.9	10.9	5,548	12,860	4.2	12.0	63.8	7.6	1,465.5	3

*Distressed county ranks: 1 = severely distressed, 2 = distressed, 3 = middle, 4 = strong, and 5 = very strong.

Summary Level	1990 Census Population	% Change Pop. 1970-80	% Change Pop. 1980-90	1990 % Pop. 65 and Over	1980 Per Capita Income	1990 Per Capita Income	1990 % Workforce Unemp.	1989 % Pop. Below Poverty	1990 % Pop. 25 and Over With H.S. Diploma	5-Year Infant Mortality Rate 1984-88	1990 Pop. per Patient-Care Doctor	ARC* 1988 Distressed Counties
GA Chattooga	22,200	6.3	1.4	14.9	6,102	11,867	7.7	14.6	50.1	11.4	5,550.0	2
GA Cherokee	90,200	66.8	74.5	7.0	5,935	18,035	4.4	6.1	75.2	9.0	2,652.9	4
GA Dade	13,100	24.2	6.5	10.9	5,556	10,728	6.2	14.6	55.3	9.8	2,183.3	3
GA Dawson	9,400	33.3	95.8	8.9	6,962	13,313	8.5	12.8	60.1	16.8	4,700.0	3
GA Douglas	71,100	90.2	30.2	7.0	7,418	17,217	4.8	6.6	72.3	8.7	1,269.6	5
GA Fannin	16,000	10.5	8.8	17.9	5,671	12,313	7.4	17.2	55.8	10.8	2,666.7	3
GA Floyd	81,300	8.3	1.9	14.6	8,079	16,062	7.1	13.6	63.9	13.6	414.8	3
GA Forsyth	44,100	64.7	57.5	8.9	6,494	20,455	4.8	6.8	67.6	7.2	2,205.0	4
GA Franklin	16,700	18.8	9.9	15.5	6,197	14,760	6.4	16.5	54.1	12.5	1,284.6	3
GA Gilmer	13,400	24.7	20.7	13.6	6,401	15,236	6.8	16.6	52.3	20.9	1,675.0	3
GA Gordon	35,100	27.5	16.6	10.7	6,888	14,885	6.2	11.1	58.4	10.5	1,350.0	3
GA Gwinnett	352,900	130.8	111.4	4.8	8,088	19,861	4.3	4.0	86.7	8.1	1,341.8	5
GA Habersham	27,600	20.8	10.4	13.2	6,407	15,125	4.3	11.6	59.0	12.6	2,123.1	3
GA Hall	95,400	27.5	26.2	10.8	8,276	16,943	5.6	10.6	65.1	8.3	636.0	4
GA Haralson	22,000	15.7	19.6	13.3	7,216	13,336	7.8	14.4	56.0	13.9	1,466.7	3
GA Heard	8,600	20.4	32.3	12.0	6,910	11,132	6.0	19.1	49.1	21.6	4,300.0	3
GA Jackson	30,000	19.9	18.6	12.0	6,561	15,328	5.6	14.1	54.5	12.5	2,500.0	3
GA Lumpkin	14,600	24.1	35.2	10.1	5,427	14,351	3.9	15.3	60.2	10.9	1,123.1	3

*Distressed county ranks: 1 = severely distressed, 2 = distressed, 3 = middle, 4 = strong, and 5 = very strong.

Summary Level	1990 Census Population	% Change Pop. 1970-80	% Change Pop. 1980-90	1990 % Pop. 65 and Over	1980 Per Capita Income	1990 Per Capita Income	1990 % Workforce Unemp.	1989 % Pop. Below Poverty	1990 % Pop. 25 and Over With H.S. Diploma	5-Year Infant Mortality Rate 1984-88	1990 Pop. per Patient-Care Doctor	ARC* 1988 Distressed Counties
GA Madison	21,100	31.1	19.2	11.0	5,970	13,057	6.1	15.7	59.7	9.4	4,220.0	3
GA Murray	26,100	51.5	32.5	8.2	6,413	12,399	7.2	11.3	52.1	11.7	3,728.6	3
GA Paulding	41,600	49.1	59.4	7.3	6,321	13,613	6.1	8.8	64.1	9.9	5,200.0	3
GA Pickens	14,400	21.9	23.1	13.5	6,672	15,770	10.0	12.8	56.8	21.2	2,057.1	3
GA Polk	33,800	9.5	4.3	14.2	6,858	12,767	11.6	16.3	51.8	10.7	1,988.2	3
GA Rabun	11,600	26.5	10.5	18.2	5,538	12,657	4.9	13.6	62.7	11.1	1,160.0	3
GA Stephens	23,300	7.4	6.9	15.0	6,882	13,487	6.9	17.0	60.1	13.6	776.7	3
GA Towns	6,800	21.7	21.4	23.8	5,170	12,368	3.7	14.0	58.2	13.6	1,700.0	3
GA Union	12,000	38.2	27.7	18.4	4,305	11,595	4.7	18.3	58.7	13.2	1,500.0	3
GA Walker	58,300	11.7	3.2	13.3	7,073	13,149	6.3	12.8	58.3	13.8	3,886.7	3
GA White	13,000	29.5	28.7	14.9	5,525	15,078	4.5	12.5	62.9	15.8	1,625.0	3
GA Whitfield	72,500	19.6	10.2	9.9	8,078	17,860	4.9	11.1	59.8	10.1	725.0	4
KY Total	3,685,100	13.8	0.7	12.7	7,645	15,012	5.8	18.5	64.6	10.6	633.7	
KY Part	1,045,300	23.1	-2.9	12.5	6,086	11,759	7.7	28.4	51.5	11.2	1,183.8	
KY Adair	15,400	16.9	1.3	15.6	5,053	11,803	6.4	25.1	46.3	7.9	1,400.0	2
KY Bath	39,700	8.7	-3.0	15.2	5,669	11,223	9.9	27.3	46.3	11.1	1,616.7	1

*Distressed county ranks: 1 = severely distressed, 2 = distressed, 3 = middle, 4 = strong, and 5 = very strong.

Summary Level	1990 Census Population	% Change Pop. 1970-80	% Change Pop. 1980-90	1990 % Pop. 65 and Over	1980 Per Capita Income	1990 Per Capita Income	1990 % Workforce Unemp.	1989 % Pop. Below Poverty	1990 % Pop. 25 and Over With H.S. Diploma	5-Year Infant Mortality Rate 1984-88	1990 Pop. per Patient-Care Doctor	ARC* 1988 Distressed Counties
KY Bell	31,500	10.3	-8.2	13.3	6,508	10,728	9.1	36.2	46.7	8.7	670.2	1
KY Boyd	51,200	6.1	-7.7	14.8	9,473	16,824	5.8	16.5	68.9	10.7	487.6	3
KY Breathitt	15,700	19.7	-7.6	10.9	5,254	10,531	9.1	39.5	47.8	10.2	3,140.0	1
KY Carter	24,300	26.8	-3.2	12.8	4,766	10,370	13.5	26.8	51.3	13.4	4,860.0	1
KY Casey	14,200	13.8	-4.1	15.1	4,295	10,241	7.7	29.4	43.1	16.1	3,550.0	1
KY Clark	29,500	17.4	4.2	12.5	8,090	14,739	6.7	17.7	65.1	9.0	1,053.6	3
KY Clay	21,700	23.9	-4.8	10.7	5,134	8,693	8.2	40.2	38.9	13.3	2,411.1	1
KY Clinton	9,100	13.4	-2.2	15.3	3,956	8,875	10.0	38.1	44.4	5.0	3,033.3	1
KY Cumberland	6,800	7.4	-6.8	18.0	4,960	9,900	7.4	31.6	39.5	19.6	3,400.0	3
KY Elliott	6,500	16.9	-5.8	12.4	4,499	7,880	17.3	38.0	44.0	5.6	3,250.0	1
KY Estill	14,600	13.3	0.7	13.8	5,972	10,053	12.2	29.0	46.5	11.1	2,920.0	1
KY Fleming	12,300	8.8	0.0	15.5	5,387	11,511	7.6	25.4	53.8	17.8	2,460.0	2
KY Floyd	43,600	35.9	-10.7	11.5	6,162	12,571	6.9	31.2	50.8	10.4	927.7	1
KY Garrard	11,600	16.0	6.4	15.4	6,894	13,328	7.3	18.1	54.3	7.8	2,320.0	3
KY Green	10,400	6.8	-5.5	17.9	5,866	12,137	6.1	21.6	49.0	11.7	1,155.6	2
KY Greenup	36,700	18.1	-6.1	12.2	7,332	14,002	6.0	17.6	64.7	10.5	2,446.7	3
KY Harlan	36,600	12.6	-12.6	13.0	6,738	11,610	7.6	33.1	49.5	12.7	1,045.7	1
KY Jackson	12,000	21.2	0.0	13.2	4,131	8,391	10.4	38.2	38.3	7.3	6,000.0	1

*Distressed county ranks: 1 = severely distressed, 2 = distressed, 3 = middle, 4 = strong, and 5 = very strong.

Summary Level	1990 Census Population	% Change Pop. 1970-80	% Change Pop. 1980-90	1990 % Pop. 65 and Over	1980 Per Capita Income	1990 Per Capita Income	1990 % Workforce Unemp.	1989 % Pop. Below Poverty	1990 % Pop. 25 and Over With H.S. Diploma	5-Year Infant Mortality Rate 1984-88	1990 Pop. per Patient-Care Doctor	ARC* 1988 Distressed Counties
KY Johnson	23,200	39.4	-4.9	11.8	6,589	12,273	7.1	28.7	54.7	5.8	966.7	1
KY Knott	17,900	21.8	0.0	10.5	5,353	9,185	8.6	40.4	45.1	9.9	3,580.0	1
KY Knox	29,700	27.4	-1.7	13.0	4,956	9,941	7.0	38.9	46.6	13.9	2,970.0	2
KY Laurel	43,400	42.3	11.3	11.4	5,758	12,069	6.3	24.8	52.7	12.8	2,170.0	2
KY Lawrence	14,000	31.8	-0.7	13.0	5,788	9,755	9.7	36.0	46.4	21.8	1,166.7	1
KY Lee	7,400	18.2	-5.1	14.4	4,484	8,788	8.3	37.4	43.4	9.3	1,850.0	1
KY Leslie	13,600	28.4	-8.7	9.3	4,707	9,929	5.7	35.6	40.4	14.4	1,511.1	1
KY Letcher	27,000	32.9	-12.1	11.7	6,030	10,892	7.7	31.8	45.6	13.3	1,080.0	1
KY Lewis	13,000	17.9	-10.3	13.5	4,607	10,513	9.9	30.7	45.4	7.7	6,500.0	1
KY Lincoln	20,000	14.4	4.7	14.2	5,380	10,316	8.5	27.2	50.4	14.4	2,857.1	1
KY Madison	57,500	25.1	7.7	10.3	6,248	12,672	5.1	21.2	64.8	8.8	809.9	3
KY Magoffin	13,100	28.6	-3.0	10.1	4,868	8,843	14.9	42.5	38.2	10.8	3,275.0	1
KY Martin	12,500	49.5	-10.1	8.7	7,043	12,062	7.8	35.4	44.4	13.8	2,083.3	1
KY McCreary	15,600	24.8	0.0	11.2	4,058	7,663	14.1	45.5	40.2	8.6	1,950.0	1
KY Menifee	5,100	27.5	0.0	12.1	3,872	8,206	10.9	35.0	46.0	20.3	5,100.0	1
KY Monroe	11,400	6.9	-8.1	16.1	5,212	12,208	6.3	26.9	47.1	11.7	1,900.0	2
KY Montgomery	19,600	30.7	-2.0	13.0	6,488	13,215	11.6	21.0	56.1	7.0	980.0	1

*Distressed county ranks: 1 = severely distressed, 2 = distressed, 3 = middle, 4 = strong, and 5 = very strong.

Summary Level	1990 Census Population	% Change Pop. 1970-80	% Change Pop. 1980-90	1990 % Pop. 65 and Over	1980 Per Capita Income	1990 Per Capita Income	1990 % Workforce Unemp.	1989 % Pop. Below Poverty	1990 % Pop. 25 and Over With H.S. Diploma	5-Year Infant Mortality Rate 1984-88	1990 Pop. per Patient-Care Doctor	ARC* 1988 Distressed Counties
KY Morgan	11,600	19.8	-4.1	12.5	4,550	9,497	9.9	38.8	44.1	18.4	1,450.0	1
KY Owsley	5,000	11.8	-12.3	15.6	3,779	8,551	8.5	52.1	35.5	15.7	*	1
KY Perry	30,300	31.5	-10.4	10.5	6,477	13,563	7.2	32.1	47.6	11.0	704.7	1
KY Pike	72,600	33.0	-10.5	10.7	7,298	13,109	7.2	25.4	50.2	10.8	1,052.2	1
KY Powell	11,700	44.2	5.4	10.5	4,984	9,883	9.1	26.2	50.1	14.5	3,900.0	1
KY Pulaski	49,500	30.1	8.1	14.2	6,168	12,942	8.2	22.7	56.2	11.5	900.0	1
KY Rockcastle	14,800	13.8	5.7	13.3	4,451	10,600	7.0	30.7	44.9	5.2	1,850.0	1
KY Rowan	20,400	12.4	7.4	10.0	5,493	10,397	5.9	28.9	57.9	16.0	510.0	2
KY Russell	14,700	30.5	7.3	16.1	4,810	12,726	5.9	25.6	50.2	3.5	1,837.5	1
KY Wayne	17,500	19.7	2.9	13.9	4,657	9,527	8.3	37.3	44.6	7.5	1,590.9	1
KY Whitley	33,300	38.6	-0.3	12.9	6,506	12,390	7.2	33.0	53.0	11.6	640.4	1
KY Wolfe	6,500	19.6	-3.0	11.8	4,460	8,991	15.3	44.3	42.8	14.7	3,250.0	1
MD Total	4,781,100	7.5	13.4	10.8	10,405	21,952	4.7	8.1	78.4	11.6	371.1	
MD Part	224,400	5.2	2.0	15.4	7,824	15,405	7.6	11.8	69.7	9.8	688.3	
MD Allegany	74,900	-4.2	-7.0	18.5	7,627	14,786	8.8	16.5	71.0	9.1	499.3	3

*No patient care doctor in county.

*Distressed county ranks: 1 = severely distressed, 2 = distressed, 3 = middle, 4 = strong, and 5 = very strong.

Summary Level	1990 Census Population	% Change Pop. 1970-80	% Change Pop. 1980-90	1990 % Pop. 65 and Over	1980 Per Capita Income	1990 Per Capita Income	1990 % Workforce Unemp.	1989 % Pop. Below Poverty	1990 % Pop. 25 and Over With H.S. Diploma	5-Year Infant Mortality Rate 1984-88	1990 Pop. per Patient-Care Doctor	ARC* 1988 Distressed Counties
MD Garrett	28,100	23.8	6.0	13.8	6,330	13,172	8.9	14.7	68.4	14.4	1,277.3	2
MD Washington	121,400	9.0	7.3	13.8	8,276	16,238	6.7	9.3	69.3	9.1	788.3	3
MS Total	2,573,500	13.7	2.1	12.5	6,684	12,834	7.4	24.5	64.3	13.3	783.9	
MS Part	510,600	15.0	2.5	13.3	6,241	12,241	8.2	22.0	59.3	12.8	1,179.2	
MS Alcorn	31,700	21.3	-3.9	15.4	6,842	12,691	10.1	20.8	56.3	7.6	1,093.1	2
MS Benton	8,000	9.3	-2.4	14.9	4,740	10,183	11.2	29.7	46.4	6.3	*	1
MS Calhoun	14,900	7.5	-5.1	16.9	5,381	10,991	9.1	21.5	52.8	6.6	2,980.0	2
MS Chickasaw	18,100	6.5	1.1	13.8	6,028	11,672	14.1	21.3	52.9	20.6	2,262.5	1
MS Choctaw	9,100	5.9	1.1	14.6	5,379	9,735	10.9	25.0	57.6	10.8	4,550.0	1
MS Clay	21,100	12.2	0.0	13.3	6,467	12,291	9.9	25.9	60.4	14.9	1,623.1	1
MS Itawamba	20,000	21.3	-2.4	15.4	5,661	11,497	6.8	15.6	49.0	12.3	5,000.0	3
MS Kemper	10,400	-1.0	3.0	15.7	4,598	8,984	10.7	35.1	56.3	12.2	3,466.7	1
MS Lee	65,600	23.9	14.9	11.6	7,899	14,627	6.5	15.4	67.8	15.5	475.4	3
MS Lowndes	59,300	15.5	3.5	10.2	7,213	14,000	6.3	22.1	69.0	10.2	801.4	3

***No patient care doctor in county.**

*Distressed county ranks: 1 = severely distressed, 2 = distressed, 3 = middle, 4 = strong, and 5 = very strong.

Summary Level	1990 Census Population	% Change Pop. 1970-80	% Change Pop. 1980-90	1990 % Pop. 65 and Over	1980 Per Capita Income	1990 Per Capita Income	1990 % Workforce Unemp.	1989 % Pop. Below Poverty	1990 % Pop. 25 and Over With H.S. Diploma	5-Year Infant Mortality Rate 1984-88	1990 Pop. per Patient-Care Doctor	ARC* 1988 Distressed Counties
MS Marshall	30,400	22.1	3.8	11.5	4,408	11,434	11.9	30.0	51.7	15.2	3,377.8	1
MS Monroe	36,600	6.7	0.5	14.3	6,321	12,312	8.1	21.2	55.6	12.5	1,307.1	2
MS Noxubee	12,600	-7.0	-4.5	13.3	4,635	8,942	12.8	41.4	49.6	15.0	3,150.0	1
MS Oktibbeha	38,400	25.0	6.7	8.9	6,089	11,234	4.8	30.1	73.0	11.9	1,066.7	3
MS Pontotoc	22,200	20.1	6.2	14.3	5,682	12,763	5.5	17.2	57.4	9.0	1,850.0	3
MS Prentiss	23,300	18.8	-2.9	14.2	5,614	11,449	7.7	21.5	52.9	9.5	1,941.7	2
MS Tippah	19,500	17.6	4.3	15.4	5,984	11,818	8.0	22.6	54.4	21.4	1,772.7	1
MS Tishomingo	17,700	22.7	-3.8	16.8	6,477	11,231	14.9	20.3	55.0	14.9	1,361.5	3
MS Union	22,100	14.2	1.8	15.4	6,414	11,957	6.7	16.4	57.3	11.2	1,300.0	3
MS Webster	10,200	2.0	-1.0	17.6	6,144	11,372	7.6	24.4	58.6	11.1	2,040.0	2
MS Winston	19,400	6.0	-0.5	15.4	5,694	11,489	8.1	26.6	59.1	13.2	1,940.0	1
NC Total	6,628,900	15.8	12.7	12.1	7,761	16,325	4.1	12.5	70.0	12.0	596.9	
NC Part	1,306,700	17.4	7.3	14.9	7,596	16,165	4.3	12.1	67.1	10.8	557.9	
NC Alexander	27,500	28.2	10.0	11.0	6,484	14,995	3.8	9.8	59.0	11.3	3,055.6	5
NC Alleghany	9,600	18.5	0.0	18.6	6,120	12,950	3.9	20.1	52.6	13.4	1,600.0	3
NC Ashe	22,200	13.8	-0.4	17.1	5,691	12,468	5.8	18.4	55.6	12.4	1,585.7	3
NC Avery	14,900	13.4	3.5	14.6	5,072	12,517	4.1	14.6	62.2	3.1	620.8	3

*Distressed county ranks: 1 = severely distressed, 2 = distressed, 3 = middle, 4 = strong, and 5 = very strong.

Summary Level	1990 Census Population	% Change Pop. 1970-80	% Change Pop. 1980-90	1990 % Pop. 65 and Over	1980 Per Capita Income	1990 Per Capita Income	1990 % Workforce Unemp.	1989 % Pop. Below Poverty	1990 % Pop. 25 and Over With H.S. Diploma	5-Year Infant Mortality Rate 1984-88	1990 Pop. per Patient-Care Doctor	ARC* 1988 Distressed Counties
NC Buncombe	174,800	11.0	8.6	16.1	7,984	16,934	3.3	11.4	74.5	9.8	405.6	3
NC Burke	75,700	20.2	4.4	13.0	7,138	15,096	3.9	10.1	60.1	8.4	707.5	4
NC Caldwell	70,700	19.4	4.4	12.1	6,768	14,945	4.3	10.8	56.8	11.4	1,159.0	3
NC Cherokee	20,200	16.0	6.9	18.9	5,239	12,271	8.8	20.4	59.9	7.3	1,262.5	2
NC Clay	7,200	29.4	9.1	20.2	5,047	11,992	5.7	17.9	62.9	8.1	1,440.0	3
NC Davie	27,900	30.9	13.4	13.8	7,222	18,339	4.6	8.4	69.6	9.1	1,550.0	4
NC Forsyth	265,900	13.7	9.1	12.2	9,787	20,645	3.9	10.5	77.6	13.0	249.2	4
NC Graham	7,200	9.1	0.0	16.1	6,107	9,223	19.1	24.9	56.9	4.4	1,800.0	1
NC Haywood	46,900	11.2	0.9	18.2	7,238	14,235	5.2	12.7	68.0	8.0	732.8	3
NC Henderson	69,300	37.2	18.3	21.8	8,300	18,175	3.1	10.5	76.2	10.3	630.0	4
NC Jackson	26,800	19.4	3.9	13.8	6,004	12,870	4.2	16.7	68.7	11.7	515.4	3
NC Macon	23,500	27.8	16.3	22.5	6,608	14,093	3.7	16.5	66.7	11.0	783.3	3
NC Madison	17,000	5.0	1.2	16.7	5,396	12,190	4.4	20.4	56.4	7.7	2,125.0	3
NC McDowell	35,700	14.7	1.7	14.4	7,200	12,466	6.5	11.4	58.5	14.9	1,373.1	3
NC Mitchell	14,400	7.5	0.0	17.7	6,243	12,188	6.4	16.0	55.3	5.5	900.0	3
NC Polk	14,400	11.1	10.8	24.7	8,589	20,106	3.1	9.6	69.6	19.9	720.0	3
NC Rutherford	56,900	13.7	5.8	15.6	6,894	14,198	5.3	12.3	59.4	8.8	1,293.2	3

*Distressed county ranks: 1 = severely distressed, 2 = distressed, 3 = middle, 4 = strong, and 5 = very strong.

Summary Level	1990 Census Population	% Change Pop. 1970-80	% Change Pop. 1980-90	1990 % Pop. 65 and Over	1980 Per Capita Income	1990 Per Capita Income	1990 % Workforce Unemp.	1989 % Pop. Below Poverty	1990 % Pop. 25 and Over With H.S. Diploma	5-Year Infant Mortality Rate 1984-88	1990 Pop. per Patient-Care Doctor	ARC* 1988 Distressed Counties
NC Stokes	37,200	39.1	12.4	11.5	6,262	14,257	4.4	9.8	62.8	7.4	4,650.0	3
NC Surry	61,700	15.8	3.9	14.8	7,195	15,460	4.7	11.4	57.3	14.7	1,312.8	3
NC Swain	11,300	30.4	9.7	15.3	5,781	9,930	10.3	27.6	59.0	11.7	941.7	1
NC Transylvania	25,500	18.8	9.0	18.5	7,412	15,435	3.1	13.5	72.1	11.1	910.7	3
NC Watauga	37,000	35.5	16.7	10.6	6,040	12,734	2.8	21.5	72.0	9.5	649.1	3
NC Wilkes	59,400	18.6	1.2	13.2	7,171	14,699	3.9	13.3	54.1	11.5	1,563.2	3
NC Yadkin	30,500	15.4	7.4	14.8	7,650	15,261	4.5	12.0	58.9	9.3	1,906.3	3
NC Yancey	15,400	18.3	3.4	17.2	5,152	12,068	4.7	18.7	60.7	8.0	3,850.0	3
NY Total	17,990,700	-3.7	2.5	13.1	10,293	22,143	5.2	12.7	74.8	10.8	363.7	
NY Part	1,088,600	2.5	0.5	14.0	7,921	15,383	4.7	12.2	77.3	9.3	697.4	
NY Allegany	50,500	11.4	-2.3	13.4	6,466	12,590	5.9	14.8	76.9	8.2	1,402.8	3
NY Broome	212,200	-3.7	-0.7	15.0	9,146	18,058	4.1	10.5	78.9	11.0	499.3	4
NY Cattaraugus	84,200	5.0	-1.8	14.0	7,064	13,698	6.2	14.0	74.5	7.2	859.2	3
NY Chautauqua	141,900	-0.3	-3.4	15.7	8,150	15,197	5.4	13.8	74.4	9.1	865.2	3
NY Chemung	95,200	-3.8	-2.6	15.1	8,420	15,885	4.4	11.4	77.2	8.7	503.7	3
NY Chenango	51,800	6.5	5.1	14.0	7,286	14,604	6.1	11.7	75.5	9.2	1,328.2	3
NY Cortland	49,000	6.6	0.4	12.1	7,243	14,164	5.5	12.7	76.8	6.0	1,042.6	3
NY Delaware	47,200	4.7	0.9	16.4	7,118	14,232	5.3	12.8	74.0	11.2	1,151.2	3

*Distressed county ranks: 1 = severely distressed, 2 = distressed, 3 = middle, 4 = strong, and 5 = very strong.

Summary Level	1990 Census Population	% Change Pop. 1970-80	% Change Pop. 1980-90	1990 % Pop. 65 and Over	1980 Per Capita Income	1990 Per Capita Income	1990 % Workforce Unemp.	1989 % Pop. Below Poverty	1990 % Pop. 25 and Over With H.S. Diploma	5-Year Infant Mortality Rate 1984-88	1990 Pop. per Patient-Care Doctor	ARC* 1988 Distressed Counties
NY Otsego	60,500	5.2	2.4	15.1	7,188	15,503	4.0	13.9	77.7	7.8	305.6	3
NY Schoharie	31,900	20.2	7.4	14.2	6,119	14,273	5.0	11.5	73.7	9.6	1,519.0	3
NY Schuyler	18,700	6.0	5.6	14.2	7,103	12,797	5.7	11.2	74.2	7.3	984.2	3
NY Steuben	99,100	-0.5	-0.1	14.6	8,250	14,768	5.5	13.5	75.0	10.2	962.1	3
NY Tioga	52,300	7.1	5.0	10.9	7,975	15,272	4.4	9.3	80.6	7.6	1,584.8	4
NY Tompkins	94,100	13.1	8.0	9.0	7,632	15,271	2.2	18.9	87.2	11.7	635.8	3
OH Total	10,847,100	1.4	0.5	13.0	9,434	17,586	5.7	12.2	75.7	10.1	553.8	
OH Part	1,372,800	11.3	-0.2	13.7	7,542	13,442	7.0	16.9	69.2	9.4	1,357.9	
OH Adams	25,400	28.6	4.5	13.5	5,351	10,063	12.0	28.5	58.4	8.3	1,953.8	1
OH Athens	59,500	2.7	5.5	9.8	5,785	11,586	5.9	28.7	74.6	8.4	2,203.7	3
OH Belmont	71,100	2.2	-13.9	18.7	8,862	14,166	5.7	17.4	72.3	9.7	1,110.9	3
OH Brown	35,000	19.9	9.7	12.8	7,059	13,011	7.9	14.2	64.9	10.2	2,187.5	3
OH Carroll	26,500	19.1	3.5	13.7	7,099	13,033	6.2	11.7	71.5	11.7	5,300.0	3
OH Clermont	150,200	34.1	16.9	8.7	8,484	16,231	5.0	8.7	72.8	7.4	1,877.5	3
OH Columbiana	108,300	4.9	-4.7	14.9	7,866	12,597	5.9	15.9	71.8	9.9	1,370.9	3
OH Coshocton	35,400	7.8	-1.7	14.4	8,275	13,726	6.5	13.2	71.3	9.6	1,770.0	3

*Distressed county ranks: 1 = severely distressed, 2 = distressed, 3 = middle, 4 = strong, and 5 = very strong.

Summary Level	1990 Census Population	% Change Pop. 1970-80	% Change Pop. 1980-90	1990 % Pop. 65 and Over	1980 Per Capita Income	1990 Per Capita Income	1990 % Workforce Unemp.	1989 % Pop. Below Poverty	1990 % Pop. 25 and Over With H.S. Diploma	5-Year Infant Mortality Rate 1984-88	1990 Pop. per Patient-Care Doctor	ARC* 1988 Distressed Counties
OH Gallia	31,000	19.4	3.0	12.8	7,347	12,832	7.7	22.5	64.2	7.4	484.4	3
OH Guernsey	39,000	11.7	-7.1	14.9	7,168	12,841	8.7	17.5	71.4	9.4	886.4	3
OH Harrison	16,100	7.1	-11.5	17.3	7,390	10,851	11.1	19.7	69.8	8.6	1,341.7	3
OH Highland	35,700	15.9	6.6	15.0	6,947	13,255	8.0	16.5	66.5	6.5	1,983.3	3
OH Hocking	25,500	19.7	4.9	13.3	6,621	12,334	9.4	15.7	67.8	12.6	2,550.0	3
OH Holmes	32,800	27.8	11.6	10.8	5,771	11,016	4.7	17.2	46.9	8.2	1,640.0	3
OH Jackson	30,200	12.9	-1.3	14.0	6,202	11,492	8.5	24.2	60.9	8.5	4,314.3	2
OH Jefferson	80,300	-4.8	-12.3	17.2	9,225	14,583	6.1	17.1	71.9	10.5	912.5	3
OH Lawrence	61,800	12.3	-3.1	13.3	7,102	11,841	6.2	23.5	65.9	10.9	2,131.0	3
OH Meigs	23,000	19.8	-2.5	15.0	6,797	11,562	7.5	26.0	64.0	11.2	2,875.0	2
OH Monroe	15,500	10.8	-10.9	15.6	6,887	13,192	10.8	21.5	69.4	5.0	7,750.0	3
OH Morgan	14,200	15.4	0.0	15.0	7,500	12,978	8.7	21.2	71.6	12.4	4,733.3	3
OH Muskingum	82,100	7.2	-1.4	13.8	7,963	14,963	8.5	14.7	71.1	9.3	695.8	3
OH Noble	11,300	8.7	0.0	15.1	6,246	12,407	8.5	16.4	69.9	10.1	11,300.0	3
OH Perry	31,600	13.1	1.9	12.9	6,424	11,688	11.9	19.1	68.6	9.4	6,320.0	3
OH Pike	24,200	19.4	6.1	13.6	5,939	12,013	9.7	26.6	60.8	14.4	1,423.5	1
OH Ross	69,300	6.2	6.6	12.4	7,674	13,476	8.1	17.7	67.6	11.8	1,066.2	3
OH Scioto	80,300	10.0	-5.0	14.9	6,630	12,674	8.7	25.8	63.8	9.5	1,131.0	2

*Distressed county ranks: 1 = severely distressed, 2 = distressed, 3 = middle, 4 = strong, and 5 = very strong.

Summary Level	1990 Census Population	% Change Pop. 1970-80	% Change Pop. 1980-90	1990 % Pop. 65 and Over	1980 Per Capita Income	1990 Per Capita Income	1990 % Workforce Unemp.	1989 % Pop. Below Poverty	1990 % Pop. 25 and Over With H.S. Diploma	5-Year Infant Mortality Rate 1984-88	1990 Pop. per Patient-Care Doctor	ARC* 1988 Distressed Counties
OH Tuscarawas	84,100	9.7	-0.6	14.9	7,982	14,958	6.4	11.1	71.9	9.0	1,201.4	3
OH Vinton	11,100	23.4	-4.3	13.7	5,633	11,048	9.1	23.6	58.7	12.2	*	2
OH Washington	62,300	12.4	-3.1	13.6	7,946	14,645	6.0	13.7	77.5	8.2	1,132.7	3
PA Total	11,881,700	0.6	0.2	15.4	9,401	18,696	5.4	10.8	74.7	10.4	463.9	
PA Part	5,769,400	1.1	-3.8	16.7	8,759	16,775	6.2	12.1	75.0	9.6	548.6	
PA Allegheny	1,336,400	-9.7	-7.8	17.4	10,938	20,681	4.2	11.5	79.0	11.2	281.7	3
PA Armstrong	73,500	2.9	-5.5	17.5	7,753	16,738	8.1	12.8	71.1	9.7	1,289.5	3
PA Beaver	186,100	-2.0	-9.0	16.9	9,126	15,162	7.8	13.1	74.9	10.2	989.9	3
PA Bedford	47,900	10.6	2.4	15.3	6,373	12,924	9.2	13.6	68.5	9.5	1,842.3	3
PA Blair	130,500	0.9	-4.5	17.0	7,563	14,779	7.2	14.1	75.0	10.2	633.5	3
PA Bradford	61,000	8.4	-3.0	14.7	7,224	15,246	5.5	13.3	75.7	7.3	352.6	3
PA Butler	152,000	15.5	2.8	13.5	8,289	17,251	5.5	9.7	78.6	9.5	1,288.1	3
PA Cambria	163,000	-1.9	-11.1	18.8	8,221	14,473	7.7	14.0	71.2	8.8	576.0	3
PA Cameron	5,900	-5.6	-11.9	18.6	8,347	14,900	7.7	11.3	73.1	4.2	1,180.0	3

*No patient care doctor in county.

*Distressed county ranks: 1 = severely distressed, 2 = distressed, 3 = middle, 4 = strong, and 5 = very strong.

Summary Level	1990 Census Population	% Change Pop. 1970-80	% Change Pop. 1980-90	1990 % Pop. 65 and Over	1980 Per Capita Income	1990 Per Capita Income	1990 % Workforce Unemp.	1989 % Pop. Below Poverty	1990 % Pop. 25 and Over With H.S. Diploma	5-Year Infant Mortality Rate 1984-88	1990 Pop. per Patient-Care Doctor	ARC* 1988 Distressed Counties
PA Carbon	56,800	5.5	5.6	18.5	8,373	15,177	7.8	9.4	69.4	7.2	1,420.0	3
PA Centre	123,800	13.7	9.8	9.0	7,104	15,476	5.3	18.2	83.6	8.6	732.5	3
PA Clarion	41,700	13.3	-3.9	13.9	7,766	13,989	8.9	18.1	73.1	6.5	4,170.0	3
PA Clearfield	78,100	12.2	-6.6	16.6	7,803	14,415	9.9	13.9	70.2	11.1	964.2	3
PA Clinton	37,200	3.7	-4.6	16.0	7,339	13,115	9.8	15.4	72.5	10.5	1,062.9	3
PA Columbia	63,200	12.5	1.9	15.8	7,242	14,406	6.7	10.6	73.1	8.0	877.8	3
PA Crawford	86,200	9.3	-3.0	15.4	7,499	14,417	7.1	15.5	74.1	12.1	990.8	3
PA Elk	34,900	1.6	-8.9	16.0	8,388	16,872	6.3	9.5	74.9	8.1	943.2	3
PA Erie	275,600	6.1	-1.5	13.8	8,750	16,331	5.5	12.9	77.5	10.8	613.8	3
PA Fayette	145,400	3.0	-8.8	17.9	7,299	14,051	7.9	20.9	67.8	10.0	1,182.1	2
PA Forest	4,800	4.1	-5.9	20.2	7,265	13,115	9.1	11.8	70.5	7.7	4,800.0	3
PA Fulton	13,800	18.5	7.8	13.0	6,329	14,393	7.5	12.2	64.0	8.6	4,600.0	3
PA Greene	39,600	12.5	-2.2	16.4	6,909	12,645	9.1	21.4	68.0	12.2	1,237.5	3
PA Huntingdon	44,200	8.2	4.5	13.5	6,498	12,158	10.0	13.4	71.2	5.2	1,133.3	3
PA Indiana	90,000	16.1	-2.5	13.8	7,771	13,841	8.8	18.7	74.0	11.2	1,058.8	3
PA Jefferson	46,100	10.8	-4.6	17.2	7,752	14,809	7.5	13.6	72.6	7.9	1,152.5	3
PA Juniata	20,600	15.0	7.3	14.5	7,677	14,626	10.4	9.8	65.2	10.9	4,120.0	3
PA Lackawanna	219,000	-2.6	-3.9	19.7	8,217	16,963	6.7	10.7	73.3	8.7	530.3	3

*Distressed county ranks: 1 = severely distressed, 2 = distressed, 3 = middle, 4 = strong, and 5 = very strong.

Summary Level	1990 Census Population	% Change Pop. 1970-80	% Change Pop. 1980-90	1990 % Pop. 65 and Over	1980 Per Capita Income	1990 Per Capita Income	1990 % Workforce Unemp.	1989 % Pop. Below Poverty	1990 % Pop. 25 and Over With H.S. Diploma	5-Year Infant Mortality Rate 1984-88	1990 Pop. per Patient-Care Doctor	ARC* 1988 Distressed Counties
PA Lawrence	96,200	-0.3	-10.3	18.5	7,821	14,774	5.7	13.9	73.0	9.3	1,249.4	3
PA Luzerne	328,100	0.2	-4.4	19.7	8,218	16,405	7.2	11.2	72.0	8.2	586.9	3
PA Lycoming	118,700	4.6	0.3	15.1	8,049	15,778	7.2	11.5	74.5	8.0	527.6	3
PA McKean	47,100	-2.5	-6.9	16.7	8,418	14,408	6.9	14.9	75.4	8.8	1,121.4	3
PA Mercer	121,000	0.9	-5.7	17.2	8,497	15,177	5.3	12.8	75.1	7.7	834.5	3
PA Mifflin	46,200	3.8	-1.5	16.0	7,115	13,509	8.2	13.4	68.2	7.8	783.1	3
PA Monroe	95,700	52.9	37.9	13.1	8,220	17,592	6.8	7.3	78.0	7.9	817.9	4
PA Montour	17,700	1.8	6.0	16.5	7,725	18,116	5.3	8.5	75.2	12.8	51.6	4
PA Northumberland	96,800	1.3	-3.6	18.9	7,862	14,570	8.6	11.6	68.5	5.7	1,257.1	3
PA Perry	41,200	25.3	15.4	11.1	7,156	14,941	5.8	7.5	72.3	6.6	4,120.0	4
PA Pike	28,000	55.1	53.0	15.6	6,946	19,145	5.8	7.1	79.2	7.5	2,800.0	4
PA Potter	16,700	8.6	-5.6	16.5	6,399	13,897	7.2	14.9	73.8	12.0	878.9	3
PA Schuylkill	152,600	0.4	-5.0	20.0	7,750	15,853	7.8	10.7	68.4	9.1	1,082.3	3
PA Snyder	36,700	14.7	9.2	12.6	7,133	17,610	7.5	11.0	64.4	7.1	1,595.7	3
PA Somerset	78,200	7.0	-3.7	16.9	7,857	14,270	7.5	14.3	68.9	10.0	965.4	3
PA Sullivan	6,100	6.8	-3.2	20.9	6,099	14,335	5.5	18.0	70.2	3.3	6,100.0	3
PA Susquehanna	40,400	10.5	6.6	15.3	6,296	13,987	7.8	12.1	76.0	8.4	1,442.9	3

*Distressed county ranks: 1 = severely distressed, 2 = distressed, 3 = middle, 4 = strong, and 5 = very strong.

Summary Level	1990 Census Population	% Change Pop. 1970-80	% Change Pop. 1980-90	1990 % Pop. 65 and Over	1980 Per Capita Income	1990 Per Capita Income	1990 % Workforce Unemp.	1989 % Pop. Below Poverty	1990 % Pop. 25 and Over With H.S. Diploma	5-Year Infant Mortality Rate 1984-88	1990 Pop. per Patient-Care Doctor	ARC* 1988 Distressed Counties
PA Tioga	41,100	3.3	0.2	15.0	6,967	12,993	7.2	14.6	72.9	7.0	1,141.7	3
PA Union	36,200	15.4	10.0	12.6	7,477	15,297	5.5	10.3	73.1	9.1	635.1	3
PA Venango	59,400	3.4	-7.8	15.0	8,764	16,267	5.9	15.1	74.2	10.9	667.4	3
PA Warren	45,100	-0.4	-4.9	15.6	8,602	16,918	4.9	9.6	76.6	11.5	850.9	3
PA Washington	204,600	2.9	-5.8	17.5	8,872	16,625	5.5	12.8	73.2	10.0	905.3	3
PA Wayne	39,900	19.3	13.4	17.0	6,942	16,246	6.9	11.3	74.2	9.8	752.8	3
PA Westmoreland	370,300	4.1	-5.6	17.1	8,991	17,069	5.7	10.7	77.7	7.7	743.6	3
PA Wyoming	28,100	38.9	6.4	12.6	6,580	15,503	6.6	11.1	77.6	9.0	1,040.7	3
SC Total	3,487,000	20.6	11.7	11.4	7,310	15,191	4.7	14.8	68.3	13.4	674.5	
SC Part	888,100	20.7	12.1	12.5	7,916	16,179	4.3	11.2	66.3	12.7	666.2	
SC Anderson	145,200	26.5	9.0	13.6	7,285	14,205	5.4	12.0	64.0	12.7	748.5	3
SC Cherokee	44,500	11.4	8.5	13.0	7,332	14,683	5.7	14.9	57.2	12.3	1,390.6	3
SC Greenville	320,200	19.7	11.2	11.9	8,654	17,874	3.6	10.5	71.6	13.3	517.3	4
SC Oconee	57,500	19.4	18.3	13.7	6,927	15,682	5.2	11.4	63.4	12.5	871.2	3
SC Pickens	93,900	34.6	18.4	11.2	6,721	14,903	4.1	12.5	65.4	9.8	1,467.2	4
SC Spartanburg	226,800	16.2	12.3	12.7	8,012	15,776	4.4	11.8	63.0	13.1	633.5	3
TN Total	4,876,900	17.1	6.2	12.7	7,667	15,901	5.2	15.3	67.1	11.3	547.5	

*Distressed county ranks: 1 = severely distressed, 2 = distressed, 3 = middle, 4 = strong, and 5 = very strong.

Summary Level	1990 Census Population	% Change Pop. 1970-80	% Change Pop. 1980-90	1990 % Pop. 65 and Over	1980 Per Capita Income	1990 Per Capita Income	1990 % Workforce Unemp.	1989 % Pop. Below Poverty	1990 % Pop. 25 and Over With H.S. Diploma	5-Year Infant Mortality Rate 1984-88	1990 Pop. per Patient-Care Doctor	ARC* 1988 Distressed Counties
TN Part	2,146,800	19.7	3.5	13.7	7,215	14,757	5.6	15.7	63.9	9.8	638.2	
TN Anderson	68,300	11.6	1.5	15.4	9,671	16,402	4.5	14.3	72.4	7.8	529.5	3
TN Bledsoe	9,700	23.4	2.1	12.0	4,546	10,367	4.7	19.2	52.1	11.3	3,233.3	3
TN Blount	86,000	22.3	10.5	14.7	7,690	15,304	5.3	12.4	68.5	11.1	728.8	3
TN Bradley	73,700	33.1	9.2	11.1	7,096	14,665	4.7	13.8	64.4	10.2	809.9	3
TN Campbell	35,100	34.2	0.6	14.7	5,496	10,912	10.8	26.8	47.5	11.4	1,671.4	1
TN Cannon	10,500	21.4	2.9	15.2	6,217	13,587	7.7	14.5	54.6	5.0	1,500.0	2
TN Carter	51,500	17.8	2.6	15.2	5,599	11,390	4.9	18.0	57.5	9.2	1,661.3	2
TN Claiborne	26,100	26.8	6.1	13.0	5,362	12,766	6.3	25.7	50.8	12.1	2,175.0	2
TN Clay	7,200	16.7	-6.5	16.3	4,756	12,031	4.0	23.0	48.5	2.6	1,440.0	3
TN Cocke	29,100	13.8	1.0	12.9	5,296	10,794	11.0	25.3	50.4	10.1	1,940.0	1
TN Coffee	40,300	17.8	5.2	14.0	7,701	15,518	5.3	15.2	65.1	10.8	857.4	3
TN Cumberland	34,700	38.6	20.9	17.6	5,407	12,420	7.7	18.1	59.8	9.8	867.5	1
TN DeKalb	14,400	22.5	5.9	15.8	6,484	13,018	6.1	20.3	50.3	6.8	1,600.0	3
TN Fentress	14,700	17.5	-0.7	13.4	4,141	9,617	9.3	32.3	44.9	8.4	1,633.3	1
TN Franklin	34,700	17.6	8.4	14.4	6,143	11,797	4.9	14.4	63.5	8.4	1,388.0	2
TN Grainger	17,100	20.0	1.8	12.9	5,022	10,504	6.5	20.5	46.3	5.9	4,275.0	1

*Distressed county ranks: 1 = severely distressed, 2 = distressed, 3 = middle, 4 = strong, and 5 = very strong.

Summary Level	1990 Census Population	% Change Pop. 1970-80	% Change Pop. 1980-90	1990 % Pop. 65 and Over	1980 Per Capita Income	1990 Per Capita Income	1990 % Workforce Unemp.	1989 % Pop. Below Poverty	1990 % Pop. 25 and Over With H.S. Diploma	5-Year Infant Mortality Rate 1984-88	1990 Pop. per Patient-Care Doctor	ARC* 1988 Distressed Counties
TN Greene	55,900	14.5	2.8	13.8	6,246	13,017	8.7	16.9	58.1	9.4	947.5	3
TN Grundy	13,400	30.2	-2.9	14.3	4,681	11,020	9.1	23.9	44.7	8.1	4,466.7	1
TN Hamblen	50,500	27.4	2.4	12.0	6,352	13,779	6.0	13.9	61.6	8.4	952.8	2
TN Hamilton	285,500	13.1	-0.8	13.4	8,880	18,242	4.2	13.1	72.5	11.1	400.4	3
TN Hancock	6,700	3.0	-2.9	15.8	4,046	8,996	4.8	40.0	42.4	13.1	2,233.3	1
TN Hawkins	44,600	30.4	1.8	13.2	5,574	12,061	4.8	17.9	58.0	7.0	2,347.4	3
TN Jackson	9,300	16.0	-1.1	17.2	4,333	9,846	6.8	20.0	45.2	6.6	1,860.0	1
TN Jefferson	33,000	25.7	5.4	13.3	6,399	13,309	6.8	15.1	60.5	3.5	1,833.3	2
TN Johnson	13,800	18.1	0.7	16.4	5,793	9,901	7.3	28.5	47.2	8.6	2,760.0	1
TN Knox	335,700	15.7	5.0	12.7	8,446	17,382	4.0	14.1	74.6	10.5	357.5	3
TN Loudon	31,300	17.7	9.4	14.5	7,079	13,832	5.1	13.6	63.8	5.8	1,360.9	3
TN Macon	15,900	27.6	1.3	14.5	6,296	11,601	7.3	19.3	49.2	12.7	2,650.0	2
TN Marion	24,900	19.0	2.0	12.2	6,493	12,024	7.0	19.3	51.9	9.6	1,778.6	1
TN McMinn	42,400	18.4	1.2	14.3	6,463	13,455	8.1	17.2	57.1	9.1	1,115.8	3
TN Meigs	8,000	42.3	8.1	12.3	6,077	11,666	9.4	22.3	52.7	14.5	8,000.0	3
TN Monroe	30,500	22.1	6.3	13.7	5,014	11,772	8.1	17.8	49.9	11.5	2,541.7	1
TN Morgan	17,300	22.1	4.2	11.8	4,344	10,639	8.9	20.2	56.7	7.1	8,650.0	1
TN Overton	17,600	18.1	0.0	15.4	4,918	9,642	9.2	17.9	44.1	8.9	2,514.3	1

*Distressed county ranks: 1 = severely distressed, 2 = distressed, 3 = middle, 4 = strong, and 5 = very strong.

Summary Level	1990 Census Population	% Change Pop. 1970-80	% Change Pop. 1980-90	1990 % Pop. 65 and Over	1980 Per Capita Income	1990 Per Capita Income	1990 % Workforce Unemp.	1989 % Pop. Below Poverty	1990 % Pop. 25 and Over With H.S. Diploma	5-Year Infant Mortality Rate 1984-88	1990 Pop. per Patient-Care Doctor	ARC* 1988 Distressed Counties
TN Pickett	4,500	18.9	2.3	17.2	3,970	8,645	7.5	24.9	45.8	0.0	*	1
TN Polk	13,600	17.2	0.0	14.4	6,137	10,979	11.8	18.3	51.3	13.2	1,360.0	1
TN Putnam	51,400	34.7	7.8	13.0	6,220	14,550	5.4	16.6	63.2	8.7	815.9	3
TN Rhea	24,300	41.5	0.4	14.3	7,455	13,841	7.3	19.0	56.0	13.8	2,700.0	3
TN Roane	47,200	24.4	-2.5	14.9	5,706	15,411	6.8	16.0	66.7	6.7	1,815.4	3
TN Scott	18,400	30.4	-4.7	12.0	5,054	11,119	8.9	27.8	51.2	16.5	2,628.6	1
TN Sequatchie	8,900	36.5	3.5	12.2	5,246	11,197	5.4	22.9	51.4	0.0	2,966.7	2
TN Sevier	51,000	46.8	23.2	12.6	6,574	13,577	9.4	13.2	63.0	8.8	2,040.0	3
TN Smith	14,100	19.2	-5.4	15.9	5,828	14,726	6.7	14.5	54.2	6.8	1,566.7	3
TN Sullivan	143,600	13.0	-0.3	14.3	8,474	15,747	3.6	13.6	66.8	9.3	403.4	3
TN Unicoi	16,500	7.9	0.6	17.2	6,771	12,683	7.4	17.1	59.6	10.3	2,062.5	3
TN Union	13,700	28.6	17.1	11.0	5,066	9,843	5.6	21.3	45.6	10.6	13,700.0	2
TN VanBuren	4,800	27.0	2.1	12.3	3,919	9,753	9.3	19.2	48.0	10.2	4,800.0	2
TN Warren	33,000	21.1	0.9	14.5	7,847	13,222	8.1	16.8	57.0	11.1	1,064.5	3

*No patient care doctor in county.

*Distressed county ranks: 1 = severely distressed, 2 = distressed, 3 = middle, 4 = strong, and 5 = very strong.

Summary Level	1990 Census Population	% Change Pop. 1970-80	% Change Pop. 1980-90	1990 % Pop. 65 and Over	1980 Per Capita Income	1990 Per Capita Income	1990 % Workforce Unemp.	1989 % Pop. Below Poverty	1990 % Pop. 25 and Over With H.S. Diploma	5-Year Infant Mortality Rate 1984-88	1990 Pop. per Patient-Care Doctor	ARC* 1988 Distressed Counties
TN Washington	92,300	20.2	3.9	14.0	7,515	15,982	4.2	15.5	68.4	10.2	290.3	3
TN White	20,100	15.3	2.6	16.1	5,339	12,777	9.7	17.0	53.2	8.0	1,827.3	2
VA Total	6,186,800	15.1	15.7	10.7	9,331	19,784	4.3	9.9	75.2	11.0	534.5	
VA Part	517,800	17.2	-5.8	14.6	6,905	14,098	7.4	17.3	56.4	9.5	988.2	
VA Alleghany	24,800	1.8	-12.7	18.1	7,783	14,521	7.6	11.9	66.9	8.0	576.7	3
VA Bath	4,800	13.5	-18.6	15.5	7,119	18,408	12.5	14.2	67.3	0.0	600.0	3
VA Bland	6,500	16.7	3.2	13.7	5,167	12,674	5.7	10.0	62.6	3.0	6,500.0	3
VA Botetourt	25,000	28.0	7.3	12.2	7,999	17,462	3.3	6.2	72.9	8.4	1,315.8	5
VA Buchanan	31,300	18.8	-17.6	8.7	7,650	13,944	8.5	21.9	42.5	12.6	1,841.2	1
VA Carroll	26,600	18.2	-2.6	16.0	5,290	12,664	6.5	14.1	49.7	10.0	633.3	3
VA Craig	4,400	11.4	12.8	14.0	6,682	13,297	5.8	9.8	68.4	0.0	4,400.0	3
VA Dickenson	17,600	23.8	-11.1	12.2	6,510	13,530	13.7	25.9	47.1	12.2	2,933.3	2
VA Floyd	12,000	18.4	3.4	16.6	5,545	14,618	7.0	14.0	60.2	6.7	3,000.0	3
VA Giles	16,400	6.6	-7.9	16.7	6,914	14,503	9.4	12.2	64.5	5.2	1,261.5	3
VA Grayson	22,900	6.9	-0.9	17.7	6,530	12,533	8.2	16.3	52.5	11.0	4,580.0	3
VA Highland	2,600	16.0	-10.3	19.6	6,456	12,883	6.2	13.6	61.8	6.3	1,300.0	3
VA Lee	24,500	28.1	-5.8	15.6	5,879	11,457	8.3	28.7	48.0	10.2	1,531.3	1

*Distressed county ranks: 1 = severely distressed, 2 = distressed, 3 = middle, 4 = strong, and 5 = very strong.

Summary Level	1990 Census Population	% Change Pop. 1970-80	% Change Pop. 1980-90	1990 % Pop. 65 and Over	1980 Per Capita Income	1990 Per Capita Income	1990 % Workforce Unemp.	1989 % Pop. Below Poverty	1990 % Pop. 25 and Over With H.S. Diploma	5-Year Infant Mortality Rate 1984-88	1990 Pop. per Patient-Care Doctor	ARC* 1988 Distressed Counties
VA Pulaski	34,500	19.3	-2.0	14.7	6,636	13,386	9.7	13.4	59.6	9.7	1,277.8	3
VA Russell	28,700	29.8	-9.7	12.2	6,471	12,975	9.1	22.5	50.6	10.9	2,207.7	3
VA Scott	23,200	2.9	-7.6	16.7	5,841	12,024	5.5	20.9	51.2	9.2	4,640.0	3
VA Smyth	32,400	6.7	-3.0	15.1	5,975	14,316	7.7	16.7	53.3	8.7	736.4	3
VA Tazewell	46,000	27.2	-8.9	13.6	8,001	14,606	6.9	19.0	57.3	9.4	474.2	3
VA Washington	64,300	17.8	-1.8	15.5	6,840	15,265	5.8	16.7	60.5	9.0	1,108.6	3
VA Wise	43,800	21.8	-9.9	13.2	8,246	15,505	7.8	22.1	52.4	12.0	547.5	3
VA Wythe	25,500	15.4	0.0	15.4	6,637	13,770	7.7	17.5	61.8	7.3	1,108.7	3
WV Total	1,793,300	11.8	-8.0	15.0	7,669	13,719	8.3	19.2	66.0	10.2	628.1	
WV Part	1,793,300	11.8	-8.0	15.0	7,669	13,719	8.3	19.2	66.0	10.2	628.1	
WV Barbour	15,700	19.4	-5.4	16.0	6,727	9,735	15.7	28.5	59.8	8.0	1,308.3	1
WV Berkeley	59,300	28.9	26.7	11.8	7,565	13,345	7.2	12.0	68.4	8.6	1,022.4	3
WV Boone	25,900	21.1	-14.8	12.6	7,392	14,420	9.0	27.0	54.1	9.3	2,590.0	3
WV Braxton	13,000	9.4	-6.5	17.1	5,368	12,452	11.9	25.8	56.8	7.5	2,166.7	1
WV Brooke	27,000	5.1	-13.2	16.4	8,401	13,424	7.2	12.1	71.6	13.4	2,700.0	3
WV Cabell	96,800	-0.2	-9.4	16.4	8,806	15,781	6.2	19.1	71.9	10.5	296.9	3
WV Calhoun	7,900	16.9	-4.8	15.7	5,254	8,952	17.5	32.0	56.3	11.6	1,128.6	1

*Distressed county ranks: 1 = severely distressed, 2 = distressed, 3 = middle, 4 = strong, and 5 = very strong.

Summary Level	1990 Census Population	% Change Pop. 1970-80	% Change Pop. 1980-90	1990 % Pop. 65 and Over	1980 Per Capita Income	1990 Per Capita Income	1990 % Workforce Unemp.	1989 % Pop. Below Poverty	1990 % Pop. 25 and Over With H.S. Diploma	5-Year Infant Mortality Rate 1984-88	1990 Pop. per Patient-Care Doctor	ARC* 1988 Distressed Counties
WV Clay	10,000	21.5	-11.5	12.8	4,995	8,754	14.5	39.2	49.4	7.4	5,000.0	1
WV Doddridge	7,000	15.6	-5.4	16.2	5,166	9,948	8.6	23.0	64.6	8.0	2,333.3	1
WV Fayette	48,000	17.4	-17.1	17.1	6,715	11,334	10.7	24.4	57.1	8.0	1,090.9	2
WV Gilmer	7,700	7.8	-7.2	16.2	5,583	10,141	8.7	33.5	56.6	17.7	7,700.0	1
WV Grant	10,400	18.6	2.0	14.9	6,192	13,401	8.8	15.5	60.2	8.0	800.0	1
WV Greenbrier	34,700	17.4	-8.0	16.9	6,540	13,088	11.0	17.9	63.0	6.4	680.4	3
WV Hampshire	16,500	27.4	10.7	13.7	5,544	12,345	11.4	18.2	61.8	6.0	2,750.0	2
WV Hancock	35,200	1.5	-12.9	16.0	10,065	16,718	6.4	11.9	72.5	6.7	748.9	3
WV Hardy	11,000	13.6	10.0	15.3	5,686	13,483	6.1	14.6	55.3	6.5	5,500.0	2
WV Harrison	69,400	6.4	-10.7	17.7	7,989	14,463	8.8	17.4	70.6	13.7	568.9	3
WV Jackson	25,900	23.4	0.4	13.4	8,002	11,602	10.9	20.0	65.4	8.0	1,850.0	3
WV Jefferson	35,900	42.3	18.5	11.4	7,191	14,293	5.4	10.6	68.2	12.7	1,495.8	3
WV Kanawha	207,600	0.9	-10.3	15.7	9,858	17,192	6.0	15.3	72.4	8.6	386.6	3
WV Lewis	17,200	5.6	-8.5	16.5	6,544	11,644	10.7	23.7	62.1	14.4	1,146.7	2
WV Lincoln	21,400	25.4	-9.7	12.5	5,211	9,509	12.7	33.8	49.1	12.0	5,350.0	1
WV Logan	43,000	9.7	-15.2	12.6	7,479	13,245	11.1	27.7	53.4	7.6	754.4	2
WV Marion	57,200	7.2	-13.1	18.3	8,201	14,242	8.6	19.0	71.4	11.7	969.5	3

*Distressed county ranks: 1 = severely distressed, 2 = distressed, 3 = middle, 4 = strong, and 5 = very strong.

Summary Level	1990 Census Population	% Change Pop. 1970-80	% Change Pop. 1980-90	1990 % Pop. 65 and Over	1980 Per Capita Income	1990 Per Capita Income	1990 % Workforce Unemp.	1989 % Pop. Below Poverty	1990 % Pop. 25 and Over With H.S. Diploma	5-Year Infant Mortality Rate 1984-88	1990 Pop. per Patient-Care Doctor	ARC* 1988 Distressed Counties
WV Marshall	37,400	10.9	-10.1	15.2	7,364	13,184	7.9	16.0	70.9	6.4	1,335.7	3
WV Mason	25,200	11.6	-6.7	14.1	6,890	12,166	9.6	22.1	61.1	12.4	1,008.0	3
WV McDowell	35,200	-1.4	-29.5	14.8	7,221	10,062	15.7	37.7	42.3	13.5	1,760.0	1
WV Mercer	65,000	16.9	-12.0	16.6	7,553	15,067	8.0	20.4	63.1	13.3	503.9	3
WV Mineral	26,700	17.7	-1.8	14.7	6,295	12,839	5.5	14.8	72.8	10.0	2,053.8	3
WV Mingo	33,700	13.7	-9.7	10.4	6,880	12,874	9.3	30.9	50.4	13.6	962.9	1
WV Monongalia	75,500	17.7	0.7	10.9	7,416	15,178	3.7	20.6	75.4	9.1	170.0	3
WV Monroe	12,400	15.2	-3.9	16.9	5,745	11,862	7.1	21.0	62.1	15.3	1,771.4	2
WV Morgan	12,100	25.9	13.1	16.9	6,031	13,180	6.6	11.0	64.8	9.4	2,016.7	3
WV Nicholas	26,800	24.9	-4.6	13.9	7,215	11,856	13.8	24.4	61.2	10.5	1,488.9	2
WV Ohio	50,900	-4.2	-17.1	18.9	9,233	18,181	5.2	15.0	75.1	12.4	217.5	3
WV Pendleton	8,100	12.9	2.5	17.2	4,770	10,762	5.2	17.0	60.6	12.5	2,025.0	3
WV Pleasants	7,500	12.3	-8.5	14.6	7,674	13,081	13.1	19.4	68.7	16.1	1,071.4	3
WV Pocahontas	9,000	12.5	-9.1	18.9	5,537	12,849	12.3	21.2	60.6	8.7	4,500.0	3
WV Preston	29,000	19.6	-4.9	14.0	6,448	10,234	8.1	18.9	62.7	14.3	1,526.3	1
WV Putnam	42,800	38.4	12.0	11.0	7,610	13,831	7.9	12.0	73.8	9.2	1,945.5	3
WV Raleigh	76,800	23.8	-11.5	15.3	7,763	13,267	9.1	19.9	63.2	8.1	486.1	3

*Distressed county ranks: 1 = severely distressed, 2 = distressed, 3 = middle, 4 = strong, and 5 = very strong.

Summary Level	1990 Census Population	% Change Pop. 1970-80	% Change Pop. 1980-90	1990 % Pop. 65 and Over	1980 Per Capita Income	1990 Per Capita Income	1990 % Workforce Unemp.	1989 % Pop. Below Poverty	1990 % Pop. 25 and Over With H.S. Diploma	5-Year Infant Mortality Rate 1984-88	1990 Pop. per Patient-Care Doctor	ARC* 1988 Distressed Counties
WV Randolph	27,800	16.7	-3.1	15.8	6,677	12,302	14.2	21.9	65.9	13.7	695.0	2
WV Ritchie	10,200	11.8	-10.5	17.4	5,987	11,218	12.4	26.0	61.5	11.4	10,200.0	2
WV Roane	15,100	13.5	-5.6	15.5	5,823	9,944	16.1	28.1	57.2	9.3	1,372.7	2
WV Summers	14,200	20.5	-10.7	17.5	5,670	9,091	11.0	24.5	58.0	6.6	1,290.9	1
WV Taylor	15,100	19.4	-9.0	16.2	6,020	10,182	10.4	22.9	66.0	5.9	3,020.0	3
WV Tucker	7,700	17.6	-11.5	16.8	5,623	12,036	11.4	17.0	64.0	11.4	1,100.0	2
WV Tyler	9,800	14.1	-13.3	15.4	6,601	12,749	8.7	18.3	68.7	6.3	4,900.0	3
WV Upshur	22,900	23.2	-2.1	14.7	6,835	10,743	11.4	21.2	64.3	8.2	954.2	2
WV Wayne	41,600	22.3	-9.6	13.7	6,560	11,840	8.4	21.8	63.1	8.9	6,933.3	1
WV Webster	10,700	24.5	-12.3	15.5	4,919	9,608	19.2	34.8	46.5	13.4	2,675.0	1
WV Wetzel	19,300	7.9	-11.9	14.8	7,789	13,494	9.1	20.5	70.1	9.5	1,484.6	3
WV Wirt	5,200	19.5	6.1	14.3	6,419	8,421	15.4	22.0	66.2	10.8	*	2
WV Wood	86,900	8.0	-7.2	14.8	8,673	15,618	7.4	14.1	73.2	10.9	730.3	3
WV Wyoming	29,000	19.6	-19.4	10.9	6,460	10,159	12.9	27.9	53.0	10.9	2,636.4	1

*No patient care doctor in county.

*Distressed county ranks: 1 = severely distressed, 2 = distressed, 3 = middle, 4 = strong, and 5 = very strong.

SOURCE: Rural Health Research Program, Cecil G. Sheps Center for Health Service Research, University of North Carolina at Chapel Hill, NC. Prepared originally for *Sowing Seeds in the Mountains*, Appalachia Leadership in Cancer, National Cancer Institute, NIH Publication No. 94-3779.

DATA SOURCE: Health Resources and Services Administration, September 1993 Area Resource File, with additional information on the economic status of Appalachian counties from the Appalachian Regional Commission, "Distressed County Data for Appalachian Counties," August 25, 1992.

Appendix C

Methods

Analysis of the Appalachian region presents difficult problems of data collection and analysis. Because the region is spread over 399 counties in 13 states, measures for the region must be collected from county level data and then calculated. Although some of this data is available from federal sources, it is not aggregated for the Appalachian region as standard practice. If one wants to find measures for the Appalachian region or the Appalachian portion of any state, one must aggregate the measures of the counties of the region or the appropriate counties of any state. Maryland and West Virginia offer easy targets for this task. Maryland has only three Appalachian counties and all of West Virginia is in Appalachia. The eleven remaining states offer various degrees of difficulty. Similarly, calculating subregional measures and offering more precise measures of trends in the region compound the problems of analysis because the Appalachian counties of some states, Virginia, West Virginia, and Tennessee, fall into two subregions. Finally, the independent cities of Virginia, six of which are in the Appalachian portion of the state, increase the difficulty of aggregating data for the Appalachian portion of that state. Unless otherwise indicated, the measures of the independent cities of Virginia have been combined with the counties where they are located.

These problems mean that few researchers deal with the entire region. Studies of Appalachian conditions conducted by university centers often included only portions of the state in which the university is located. ARC compiles data on census and income data for the entire region but does so for only a fraction of the measures that are available from various government agencies. Consequently, this report constructed a set of measures for this analysis that were not already available for the entire region.

In addition to the problems of constructing measures, there are the problems of constructing significant measures. What do we know when we learn the per capita income of an Appalachian county, of a subregion, or the entire region? This information becomes more instructive when we know if it represents an increase or decrease over preceding years and how it compares to national measures and changes. For this reason, this report deals with trends, measures and their changes over time, and compares regional and national trends. Assessing trends creates new problems. The number of counties in Appalachia changes from one period of time to another, as counties are added. Since beginning this work in 1989, two counties were added to the Appalachian region bringing the total of counties up from 397 to 399. Data for Appalachian counties in 1980 will not have counties added since then.

A second problem is finding comparable measures over time. Two sources provide county data for intervals shorter than a decade or annually: the County and City Data Book and the Local Area Personal Income (LAPI) reports of the Bureau of Economic Analysis. The first source has the advantage of being the only source of computer accessible county level census data from 1970 to the present. The second source offers the best annual information for each county on the nature and amount of personal income. This provides information into the amount of income and employment, the nature of work, and their relationship in a county. Census data for 1990 came from summary tape file 3A.

Each source has its limits. The population census offers many more measures of the population and social and economic characteristics of each Appalachian county than the County and City Data Book. The LAPI does not provide information on employment by economic sector, only income. Shifts in the number and nature of jobs are discernible primarily through census data which do not provide a sufficient breakdown for our purposes. On the other hand, the LAPI offers detail about the contribution of each economic sector to the personal income of the population of a county. This measures the significance of employment in a sector. For example, a particular county may see an increase in service sector employment and a decrease in manufacturing employment. The LAPI information, as used here, permits us to determine how that change in employment pattern has affected the amount and sources of personal income.

This study summarizes some of the 60 tables prepared for this analysis. These source tables report data for 1970 and 1980 from the County and City Data Books of 1973 and 1983 and from the 1990 census for the nation, each Appalachian state, and each Appalachian county of each state. The measures were aggregated and reported for the Appalachian portion of each state, for each subregion, for metropolitan and rural counties of the region and for each subregion. In addition, they report changes over a ten-year period. Some summary measures of these tables are reported, graphed and mapped in this report.

The measures on personal income presented a more formidable challenge. Figures used in this analysis come from the Bureau of Economic Analysis of the U.S. Department of Commerce. They report on each county of the Appalachian region for 11 categories of industries and many more breakdowns. The report created per capita amounts of total personal income, and then divided the per capita income from a particular source, e.g. durable manufacturing, by the total per capita income of the county. The result is the portion that any one source of income contributes to the per capita personal income. For every measure, comparable figures for the United States and the state are given. Each measure was reported for the entire Appalachian region; the three subregions, Northern, Central, and Southern; and for metropolitan and rural counties in the region and in each subregion. In all cases, measures for 1969, 1979, and 1989 were used because these correspond to annual incomes reported in the next year's census.

These methods may be easily replicated in local churches, civic organizations, and classrooms. The measures are readily available. Working with a smaller set of counties, or only one county, permits more attention to a larger number of measures than the space here provided. In addition to providing a limited measure of economic trends and social issues, this report's purpose is to encourages people to develop their own measures for similar analysis. I hope also to stimulate new interest in the political economy of Appalachia, other efforts to replicate these methods, and more analysis of the political economy of smaller portions of the region. The tables constructed for this report are available in complete form, with maps and graphs, from CORA.

Consistent with one of the objectives of CORA for this study, we used a variety of reports that put Appalachia in a national economic and social context. We also used recent studies of the Appalachian region. The severe recessions beginning in 1979, the general sluggish economic performance of the 1970s, and the robust and then anemic economic growth of the 1980s have stimulated numerous studies of present and future national economic trends. These have also been summarized. Relatedly, a 1982 Arthur D. Little, Inc. report gave an overview of the Appalachian economy and its changing structure that contributed a useful framework of analysis for this report. The retrenchment of social policies and the retreat of the federal government to deregulation stimulated several other studies of state and federal policies, eligibility and terms of public assistance, and changes in measures of well-being. In particular, the Center on Budget and Public Priorities, the Children's Defense Fund, and the Institute of Southern Studies have conducted studies and released reports that inform this report and set standards of accuracy and clarity for it. The Citizens Transition Project (Green 1992) provided substantial material for the specific policy recommendations of Chapter 8. These sources provide invaluable companion policy pieces to this report. As mentioned in the Introduction, this report's emphasis on regional trends and issues mutes the importance of innumerable local efforts at change and alternative economic development. Highlander Research and Education Center, the newsletters of numerous local and regional organizations—including CORA—the Appalachian centers of the University of Kentucky, Berea College, and other colleges and universities discuss these local developments. These accounts are also valuable companion pieces to this report.

References

American Public Health Association. 1992. *America's Public Health Report Card: A State-by-State Report on the Health of the Public.* Washington, D.C.: American Public Health Association.

Anderson, Jack and Michael Binstein. 1993. Prisoners and Poverty in Appalachia. *The Washington Post* (May 6):B23.

Ansley, Fran. 1993. Standing Rusty and Rolling Empty: Law, Poverty, and America's Eroding Industrial Base. *The Georgetown Law Journal* 81(5):1757-1896.

Appalachian Regional Commission (ARC). 1977. *Appalachia - A Reference Book, 1st Edition.* Washington, D.C.: Appalachian Regional Commission.

———. 1977a. *Appalachia - An Economic Report.* Washington, D.C.: Appalachian Regional Commission.

———. 1979. *Appalachia - A Reference Book, 2nd Edition.* Washington, D.C.: Appalachian Regional Commission.

———. 1979a. *Appalachia Into the 80s.* Conference Proceedings, Binghamton, N.Y. Washington, D.C.: Appalachian Regional Commission.

———. 1979b. ARC Sponsors Conference on Raising a New Generation in Appalachia. *Appalachia.* (Jan.-Feb.): 1-56.

———. 1983. The 1983 Unemployment Situation in Appalachia (mimeo). Washington, D.C.: Appalachian Regional Commission.

———. 1983a. Report on the State of the Region's Economy, No. 001. Washington, D.C.: Appalachian Regional Commission.

———. 1983b. Report on the State of the Region's Economy, No. 002. Washington, D.C.: Appalachian Regional Commission.

———. 1983c. Job Skills for the Future. Conference Proceedings, Jackson, Mississippi. Washington, D.C.: Appalachian Regional Commission.

Barancik, Scott. 1990. *The Rural Disadvantage: Growing Income Disparities Between Rural and Urban Areas.* Washington, D.C.: Center on Budget and Policy Priorities.

———. 1990. *Falling Through the Gap: Hispanics and the Growing Income Disparity Between Rich and Poor.* Washington, D.C.: Center on Budget and Policy Priorities.

Batteau, Allen W. 1990. *The Invention of Appalachia.* Tucson: The University Press of Arizona.

Behringer, Bruce. 1994. Health Care Services in Appalachia, in *Sowing Seeds in the Mountains*, eds. Richard Couto, Nancy Simpson and Gale Harris. Washington, D.C.: National Institutes of Health, 60-78.

Bellah, Robert N., Richard Madsen, William M. Sullivan, Ann Swidler and Steven M. Tipton. 1985. *Habits of the Heart: Individualism and Commitment in American Life*. Berkeley: University of California Press.

———. 1992. *The Good Society*. New York: Vintage Books.

Berger, Peter and Richard J. Neuhaus. 1977. *To Empower People: The Role of Mediating Structures in Public Policy*. Washington, D.C.: American Enterprise Institute for Public Policy Research.

Berry, John Jr. 1989. When We Awake...Will There Still be a Tobacco Program? Berea: Community Farm Alliance.

Berry, Wendell. 1977. *The Unsettling of America: Culture and Agriculture*. New York: Sierra Club Books.

Billings, Dwight B., Jr. 1979. *Planters and the Making of the "New South:" Class, Politics and Development in North Carolina 1865-1900*. Chapel Hill: University of North Carolina Press.

Bishop, Bill. 1993. Unfinished Business: The Search for Prosperity in Kentucky and Rural America. *Lexington (Ky.) Herald Leader* (March 28-December 26).

———. 1993a. One Small Group Charts the Way for New Economy. *Lexington (Ky.) Herald Leader* (August 1):E1.

———. 1993b. Rural America Strangles in Grip of Lasting Poverty. *Lexington (Ky.) Herald Leader* (June 6):D1.

———. 1993c. Alabama Raises Stakes in States' Tax-Break Poker Game. *Lexington (Ky.) Herald Leader* (October 6):A11.

———. 1993d. South Continues to Give Away Its Future for Today's Gain. *Lexington (Ky.) Herald Leader* (November 24):A13.

———. 1993e. Choosing Prosperity: New Policies and Attitudes are Keys to Development. *Lexington (Ky.) Herald Leader* (December 26):D1.

———. 1993f. Real Development Means More Than Just Creating Jobs. *Lexington (Ky.) Herald Leader* (October 13):A15.

———. 1993g. In Oregon, the Future Lies in Rebuilding Communities. *Lexington (Ky.) Herald Leader* (September 22):A13.

Bluestone, Barry and Bennett Harrison. 1982. *The Deindustrializing of America: Plant Closings, Community Abandonment and the Dismantling of Basic Industries*. New York: Basic Books.

Bok, Derek. 1993. *The Cost of Talent: How Executives and Professionals Are Paid and How It Affects America*. New York:

The Free Press.
Booz-Allen and Hamilton, Inc. 1982. *Transporting Export Coal from Appalachia*. Washington, D. C.: Appalachian Regional Commission.
Bowles, Samuel, David M. Gordon, and Thomas E. Weisskopf. 1990. *After the Waste Land: A Democratic Economics for the Year 2000* Armonk, NY: M.E. Sharpe, Inc.
———. 1992. An Economic Strategy for Progressives. *The Nation* 254:5 (February 10): 146, 163-65.
Brody, David. 1992. The Breakdown of Labor's Social Contract. *Dissent* 39:1 (Winter): 32-41.
Brown, J. Larry. 1992. Thirty Million Hungry Americans. Analysis Prepared for the House Select Committee on Hunger. Medford, MA: Tufts University Center on Hunger, Poverty & Nutrition Policy.
Business Week. 1979. More Gloom for U.S. Textiles. (April 9): 68-9.
Carey, Max L. Occupational Growth Through 1990. *Monthly Labor Review* (August 1981): 48.
Carlson, Peter. 1992. The Magic and the Misery. *The Washington Post Magazine* (November 22): 9-13, 20-27.
Caudill, Harry M. 1962. *Night Comes to the Cumberlands: A Biography of a Depressed Area*. Boston: Little, Brown & Company.
Center for Community Change. 1992. *25 Years of Community Change*. Washington, D.C.: Center for Community Change.
Center on Budget and Policy Priorities. 1989. Poverty Rates and Household Income Stagnate as Rich-Poor Gap Hits Post-War High. Washington, D.C.: Center on Budget and Policy Priorities (Oct. 20).
Chang, Clara and Constance Sorrentino. 1991. Union Membership Statistics in 12 Countries. *Monthly Labor Review* 114:12 (December): 45-53.
Checchi and Company. 1969. *Capital Resources in the Central Appalachian Region*. Washington, D.C.: Appalachian Regional Commission.
Children's Defense Fund. 1992. City Child Poverty Data from 1990 Census. Washington, D.C.: Children's Defense Fund (August 11).
Choate, Pat. 1983. Training Implications of the Changing Economy. Paper presented at ARC Conference, Job Skills for the Future. Jackson, Mississippi.
Cimini, Michael H. and Susan L. Behrmann. 1992. Lengthy Dispute Ends at Ravenswood. *Monthly Labor Review* 115:9 (Sept.):44-45.
CORA. Comission on Religion in Appalachia. 1982. Assessment and Planning for the 80s (mimeo). Knoxville: Commission on Religion in Appalachia.

———. Appalachian Development Projects Committee. 1991. Statement on the Mideast War (mimeo). Knoxville: Commission on Religion in Appalachia.

———. 1992. *Economic Transformation: The Appalachian Challenge*, compact edition. Knoxville: Commission on Religion in Appalachia.

Corn, David. 1992. Workers United, A Town Divided, Part I. *The Nation* (February 17):181ff.

———. 1992. The Union & the Billionaire, Part II. *The Nation* (February 24):228-32.

The Corporation for Enterprise Development (CfED). 1987. *Making the Grade: The Development Report Card for the States*. Washington, D.C.: The Corporation for Enterprise Development.

Couto, Richard A. 1975. *Poverty, Politics, and Health Care: An Appalachian Experience*. New York: Praeger Publishers.

———. 1987. Changing Technologies and Consequences for Labor in Coal Mining. In *Workers, Managers and Technological Change* ed. Daniel B. Cornfield. New York: Plenum Press, 175-202.

———. 1990. Regional Development Within National Industrial Policies: An Analysis of the British Coal Industry. *Growth and Change* 21(4): 51-68.

———. 1990a. Towards a Human Service Economy. In *Communities in Economic Crisis: Appalachia and the South*, eds. John Gaventa, Barbara Ellen Smith, and Alex Willingham. Philadelphia: Temple University Press, 251-62.

———. 1991. Heroic Bureaucracies. *Administration & Society* 23(1):28-43.

———. 1991a. *Ain't Gonna Let Nobody Turn Me Round: The Pursuit of Racial Justice in the Rural South*. Philadelphia: Temple University Press.

———. 1992. The Memory of Miners and the Conscience of Capital. In *Fighting Back in Appalachia: Traditions of Resistance and Change* ed. Steve Fisher. Philadelphia: Temple University Press, 264-94.

———. 1994. Appalachia, in *Sowing Seeds in the Mountains*, eds. Richard Couto, Nancy Simpson and Gale Harris. Washington, D.C.: National Cancer Institute, 17-28.

———. forthcoming. *Which Side Are You On? Mediating Structures and American Democratic Promise*.

Drape, Joe. 1991. Through the Mill. *Southern Exposure*. (Fall):8-12.

Dreier, Peter and John Atlas. 1992. Housing. In *Changing America: Blueprints for the New Administration*, ed. Mark Green. New York: Newmarket Press: 383-398.

Dreiser, Theodore. 1970rpt. *Harlan Miners Speak*. New York: Da

Capo Press.

DuBois, Tom. 1983. Steel: Past the Crossroads. *Labor Research Review*. Chicago: Midwest Center for Labor Research (Winter): 5-25.

Edelman, Marian Wright. 1992. In *Changing America: Blueprints for the New Administration*, ed. Mark Green. New York: Newmarket Press, 431-442.

Eller, Ronald D. 1982. *Miners, Millhands, and Mountaineers: Industrialization of the Appalachian South, 1880-1930*. Knoxville: The University of Tennessee Press.

Fisher, Steve. 1990. National Economic Renewal Programs and Their Implications for Appalachia and the South. In *Communities in Economic Crisis: Appalachia and the South* eds. John Gaventa, Barbara Ellen Smith and Alex Willingham. Philadelphia: Temple University Press, 263-78.

———. ed. 1993. *Fighting Back in Appalachia: Traditions of Resistance and Change*. Philadelphia: Temple University Press.

Fleishman, Jeffrey. 1994. Appalachia's Anguish: A Way of Life Unravels. *The Philadelphia Inquirer*. (January 9-12).

Ford, Thomas R. 1962. *The Southern Appalachian Region: A Survey*. Lexington: University of Kentucky Press.

Freidmann, John. 1992. *Empowerment: The Politics of Alternative Development*. Cambridge, MA: Blackwell.

Galbraith, John Kenneth. 1992. *The Culture of Contentment*. Boston: Houghton Mifflin Company.

Garber, Carter. 1991. Saturn: Tomorrow's Jobs, Yesterday's Myths. In *Communities in Economic Crisis: Appalachia and the South,* eds. John Gaventa, Barbara Ellen Smith, and Alex Willingham, Philadelphia: Temple University Press, 175-89.

Gaventa, John. 1980. *Power and Powerlessness: Quiescence and Rebellion in an Appalachian Valley*. Urbana: University of Illinois Press.

———. 1990. From the Mountains to the *Maquiladoras*: A Case Study of Capital Flight and Its Impact on Workers. In *Communities in Economic Crisis: Appalachia and the South,* eds. John Gaventa, Barbara Ellen Smith, and Alex Willingham, Philadelphia: Temple University Press, 85-95.

———, Barbara Ellen Smith, and Alex Willingham, eds. 1990. *Communities in Economic Crisis: Appalachia and the South.* Philadelphia: Temple University Press.

———, Helen Lewis, and Susan Williams. 1992. Disposable Communities: Picking Up the Pieces After the Company Leaves

Town. *Dollars & Sense* (May): 12-14, 22.

Gilbert, Pamela and Susannah Goodman. 1992. In *Changing America: Blueprints for the New Administration*, ed. Mark Green. New York: Newmarket Press, 589-603.

Gilder, George. 1981. *Wealth and Poverty*. New York: Basic Books, Inc.

Gish, Pat. 1983. 1983 is a Lot Like 1968. *The Mountain Eagle*. (November 30): B11.

Glasmeier, Amy, Amy Keys, and Jeffrey Thompson. 1993. *When Low Wages Aren't Enough Anymore: Prospects for Remote Branch Plant Regions in the International Economy*. Washington, D.C. Appalachian Regional Commission.

Goetz, Stephen J., Thomas W. Ilvento, and Ronald D Eller. 1992. Unemployment Rates as Measures of Economic Distress: How Reliable Are They and What Are the Alternatives? Lexington: Appalachian Center of the University of Kentucky (November).

Gray, Peter. 1992. Nuclear Weapons: Build Down/Clean Up. In *Changing America: Blueprints for the New Administration*, ed. Mark Green. New York: Newmarket Press, 273-82.

Green, Mark ed. 1992. *Changing America: Blueprints for the New Administration*. New York: Newmarket Press.

Greenhouse, Steven. 1992. Income Data Show Years of Erosion for U.S. Workers. *The New York Times* (September 7): 1ff.

Greenstein, Robert. 1992. Reducing Poverty. In *Changing America: Blueprints for the New Administration*, ed. Mark Green. New York: Newmarket Press, 415-430.

——— and Scott Baranick. 1990. *Drifting Apart: New Findings on Growing Income Disparities Between the Rich, the Poor, and the Middle Class*. Washington, D.C.: Center on Budget and Policy Priorities.

Greider, William. 1992. *Who Will Tell the People: The Betrayal of American Democracy*. New York: Simon & Schuster.

Gugliotta, Guy. 1993. War on Poverty: Three Decades and No Victory. The Washington Post (December 23): 1ff.

Gund, Agnes. 1992. Arts and Culture. In *Changing America: Blueprints for the New Administration*, ed. Mark Green. New York: Newmarket Press, 472-79.

Hall, Bob and Kerry, Mary Lee. 1991. *1991-1992 Green Index: A State-by-State Guide to the Nation's Environmental Health*. Washington, D.C.: Island Press.

Hall, V. Aileen. 1984. *Poverty and Women in West Virginia*. Charleston, WV: Women and Employment, Inc.

Harrington, Michael. 1962. *The Other America: Poverty in the United States*. New York: Macmillan.

Harrison, Bennett and Bluestone, Barry. 1988. *The Great U-Turn: Corporate Restructuring and the Polarizing of America*. New York: Basic Books, Inc.

Heilbroner, Robert L. 1986. *The Essential Adam Smith*. New York: W.W. Norton.

Hodges, Harriet. 1994. Presentation at the Seventeenth Annual Appalachian Studies Conference. Blacksburg, Va. (March 12).

Hoerr, John P. 1988. *And the Wolf Finally Came: The Decline of the American Steel Industry*. Pittsburgh: University of Pittsburgh Press.

Horton, Bill. 1989. Review of *Highlander: No Ordinary School, 1932-1962*. *Appalachian Journal* (16): 368-70.

——– and Frank Einstein. 1982. *Appalachia in the Eighties: A Time for Action*. New Market, TN: Appalachian Alliance.

Johnson, Fenton. 1992. In the Fields of King Coal. *The New York Times Magazine* (November 22): 30ff.

Johnston, William B. 1987. *Workforce 2000: Work and Workers for the Twenty-first Century*. Indianapolis: Hudson Institute.

Jordan, Mary. 1991. Business is Booming to Fill a Grim Order. *The Washington Post National Weekly Edition* (Jan. 14-20): 18.

Kamarck, Elaine. 1992. In *Changing America: Blueprints for the New Administration*, ed. Mark Green. New York: Newmarket Press, 443-56.

Katz, Michael B. 1989. *The Undeserving Poor: From the War on Poverty to the War on Welfare*. New York: Pantheon Books.

Keesler, William. 1991. Jobs and Economic Development: Meeting the Needs of the Appalachian People. Lexington: University of Kentucky, Appalachian Civic Leadership Project.

Kilborn, Peter L. 1992. Union Shows How to Fight in West Virginia. *The New York Times* (May 8):A12L.

Kuttner, Robert. 1991. *The End of Laissez-Faire: National Purpose and the Global Economy After the Cold War*. New York: Alfred A. Knopf, 286-87.

———. 1992. Labor Policy. In *Changing America: Blueprints for the New Administration*, ed. Mark Green. New York: Newmarket Press, 154-69.

Lav, Iris J., Edward Lazere, and Robert Greenstein. 1993. *The States and the Poor: How Budget Decisions Affected Low Income People in 1992*. Washington, D.C.: Center on Budget and Policy Priorities.

Lewis, Helen and eds. 1978. *Colonialism in Modern America: The Appalachian Case*. Boone, N.C.: The Appalachian Consortium

Press.

Little, Arthur D. Inc. 1982. *Regional Economic Development in Appalachia*. Washington, DC: Appalachian Regional Commission.

Littlefield, Nick. 1992. In *Changing America: Blueprints for the New Administration*, ed. Mark Green. New York: Newmarket Press: 457-471.

MacFayden, J. Tevere. 1984. *Gaining Ground: The Renewal of America's Small Farms*. New York: Holt, Rinehart and Winston.

MacLean, John N. 1992. Focus on Steel: Industry has Recast Itself. *Richmond Times-Dispatch* (August 1): C1.

Maggard, Sally Ward. 1993. From Farm to Coal Camp to Back Office and McDonald's: Living in the Midst of Appalachia's Latest Transformation. Paper presented at the Annual Meeting of the Appalachian Studies Conference. March 21. Johnson City, TN.

Marlin, John Tepper. 1992. In *Changing America: Blueprints for the New Administration*, ed. Mark Green. New York: Newmarket Press, 249-60.

Marmor, Theodore and Michael S. Barr. 1992. Health. In *Changing America: Blueprints for the New Administration*, ed. Mark Green. New York: Newmarket Press, 399-414.

Marris, Peter and Martin Rein. 1967. *Dilemmas in Social Reform: Poverty and Community Action in the United States*. New York: Atherton Press.

Marshall, Ray. 1983. *Work and Women in the l98Os: A Perspective on Basic Trends Affecting Women's Jobs and Job Opportunities*. Washington, D.C.: Women's Research and Education Institute.

Marshall, Will and Martin Schram. 1993. *Mandate for Change*. New York: Berkley Books.

Masnick, George and Mary Jo Bane. 1980. *The Nation's Families: 1960-1990*. Cambridge, MA: Joint Center for Urban Studies of MIT and Harvard University.

McDonald, Charles. 1992. U.S. Union Membership in Future Decades: A Trade Unionist's Perspective. *Industrial Relations* 31:1 (Winter): 13-30.

McIntyre, Robert S. 1992. Tax Policy. In *Changing America: Blueprints for the New Administration*, ed. Mark Green. New York: Newmarket Press: 29-45.

Merrifield, Juliet. 198O. *We're Tired of Being Guinea Pigs! A Handbook for Citizens on Environmental Health in Appalachia*. New Market, TN: Highlander Research and Education Center.

Metzgar, Jack. 1983. Would Wage Concessions Help the Steel Industry? *Labor Research Review*. Chicago: Midwest Center for

Labor Research (Winter): 26-37.

Micou, Ann McKinstry and Birgit Lindsnaes. 1993. *The Role of Voluntary Organizations in Emerging Democracies: Experience and Strategies in Eastern and Central Europe and in South Africa*. New York: Institute of International Education.

Murray, Charles. 1984. *Losing Ground: American Social Policy 1950-1980*. New York: Basic Books.

Myrdal, Gunnar. 1944. *An American Dilemma: The Negro Problem and Modern Democracy*. New York: Harper & Row.

National Research Council. 1982. *Toward Safer Underground Coal Mines*. Washington, D.C.: National Academy Press.

Newman, Katherine S. 1988. *Falling from Grace: The Experience of Downward Mobility in the American Middle Class*. New York: Vintage Books.

Norwood, Janet. 1987. The Future of Employment: Demography and Work. *Current History* (May): 18-23.

O'Brien, Timothy. 1993. Pride of Ownership: Making Entrepreneurs of the Poor May Lift Some Off Federal Aid. *The Wall Street Journal* (January 22): A1ff.

O'Hare, William, Taynia Mann, Kathryn Porter, and Robert Greenstein. 1990. *Real Life Poverty in America: Where the American Public Would Set the Poverty Line*. Washington, DC: Center on Budget and Policy Priorities.

Osborne, David and Ted Gaebler. 1990. *Reinventing Government*. Reading, MA: Addison-Wesley.

Passall, Peter. 1994. Public Schools for Profit, Phase 2: The Sales Pitch. *The New York Times* (January 19):B9L.

Pear, Robert. 1992. Ranks of U.S. Poor Reach 35.7 Million: The Most Since '64. *The New York Times* (September 4): 1 ff.

Phillips, Kevin. 1990. *The Politics of the Rich and Poor: Wealth and the American Electorate in the Reagan Aftermath*. New York: Harper Perennial.

Porter, Kathryn H. 1988. *Poverty in Rural America: A National Overview*. Washington, D.C.: Center on Budget and Policy Priorities.

Raitz, Karl B. and Richard Ulack. 1984. *Appalachia--A Regional Geography: Land, People, and Development*. Boulder, CO: Westview Press.

Ralston, Jeanne. 1993. In the Heart of Appalachia. *National Geographic* 183:2 (February): 112-37.

Reich, Robert B. 1982. Take the Money and Run. *The New Republic* (November 15): 28-32.

———. 1991. *The Work of Nations: Preparing Ourselves for 21st-Century Capitalism.* New York: Alfred A. Knopf.

———. 1992. On the Slag Heap of History: Review of *Homestead. The New York Times Book Review* (November): 15-16.

Reutter, Mark. 1988. *Sparrows Point: Making Steel--The Rise and Ruin of American Industrial Might.* New York: Summit Books.

———. 1991. The Raider and the Coal Town. *Southern Exposure* (Summer):48-55.

Richmond Times-Dispatch. 1992. One in Four Lacks Health Insurance. (June 25): A13.

Ross, Malcolm. 1933. *Machine Age in the Hills*. New York: Macmillan.

Rural Virginia, Inc. 1984. *Harvesting Our Choices: A Study of the Virginia Food System.* Richmond: Rural Virginia, Inc.

Saks, Daniel H. 1983. *Distressed Workers in the Eighties*. Washington, D.C.: National Planning Association.

Salamon, Lester. 1981. Rethinking Public Management: Third-Party Government and the Changing Forms of Government Action. *Public Policy* 29:3 (Summer): 266-72.

——— and Alan J. Abramson. 1982. *The Federal Budget and the Nonprofit Sector*. Washington, D.C.: Urban Institute Press.

Saunders, Robert J. n.d. *The Spatial Concentration of Industry in Appalachia: An Analysis of the Potential for Import Substitution.* Washington D.C.: Appalachian Regional Commission.

Sawhill, Isabell V. 1988. Poverty in the U.S.: Why Is It So Persistent? *Journal of Economic Literature* 26 (September): 1073-1119.

Schlesinger, Tom, John Gaventa, and Juliet Merrifield. 1983. *Our Own Worst Enemy: The Impact of Military Production on the Upper South*. New Market, TN: Highlander Research and Education Center.

Schorr, Lisbeth B. 1988. *Within Our Reach: Breaking the Cycle of Disadvantage*. New York: Doubleday.

Seminario, Margaret M. 1992. Workplace Safety and Health. In *Changing America: Blueprints for the New Administration*, ed. Mark Green. New York: Newmarket Press, 578-88.

Serrin, William. 1992. *Homestead: The Glory and Tragedy of an American Steel Town*. New York: Vintage Books.

Shapiro, Henry D. 1978. *Appalachia on Our Mind: The Southern Mountains and Mountaineer in the American Consciousness, 1870-1920*. Chapel Hill: University of North Carolina Press.

Shapiro, Issac. 1989. *Laboring for Less: Working but Poor in Rural America*. Washington, DC: Center on Budget and Policy Priorities,.

———. 1992. *White Poverty in America*. Washington, DC: Center on Budget and Policy Priorities.

——— and Robert Greenstein. 1988. *Holes in the Safety Nets: Poverty Programs and Policies in the States--National Overview*. Washington, D.C.: Center on Budget and Policy Priorities.

——— and Robert Greentein. 1991. *Selective Prosperity: Increasing Income Disparities Since 1977*. Washington, DC: Center on Budget and Policy Priorities.

——— and Marion E. Nichols. 1991. *Unemployed and Uninsured: Jobless Workers, Unemployment, Insurance, and the Recession*. Washington, DC: Center on Budget and Policy Priorities.

Shapiro, Robert. 1992. Fiscal Policy. In *Changing America: Blueprints for the New Administration*, ed. Mark Green. New York: Newmarket Press, 74-87.

Shifflett, Crandall A. 1991. *Coaltowns: Life, Work, and Culture in Company Towns of Southern Appalachia, 1880-1960*. Knoxville: University of Tennessee Press.

Smith, Adam. 1937rpt. *An Inquiry into the Nature and Causes of The Wealth of Nations*. Modern Library edition. New York: Random House.

Smith, Michael. 1989. *Behind the Glitter: The Impact of Tourism on Rural Women in the Southeast*. Lexington, KY: Southeast Women's Employment Coalition.

Social Policy. 1989. Democratic Dilemma: From Local Victories to National Impact? Parts I and II. (Spring) 22-40 and (Summer): 34-57.

Spencer, Scott. 1992. Hope and Hard Times. *Rolling Stone* (April 30):44-52.

Steinbrunner, John. 1992. Conventional and Nuclear Defense. In *Changing America: Blueprints for the New Administration*, ed. Mark Green. New York: Newmarket Press: 231-48.

Soboda, Frank. 1992. Tomorrow's Factories, Putting Their Future on the Line: They will offer good jobs--to a qualified few. *The Washington Post National Weekly Edition* (August 10-16):19-20.

Summer, Laura. 1992. *Number of Uninsured Rises*. Washington, DC: Center on Budget and Policy Priorities.

Thornton, Grant. 1990. *Eleventh Annual Grant Thornton Manufacturing Climates*. Chicago: Grant Thornton.

Toch, Thomas. 1993. Whittling the Future Schools. *U.S. News and World Report* (August 16):50-53.

Thurow, Lester. 1981. *The Zero-Sum Society: Distribution and the Possibilities for Economic Change*. New York: Penguin Books.

Troy, Leo. 1993. Big Labor's Big Problems. *Business and Society Review* 87 (Fall): 49-52.

U. S. Department of Commerce, Bureau of the Census. 1993. *Current Population Survey, 1990.* Washington, D.C.: U.S. Government Printing Office.

U. S. Department of Commerce, Bureau of the Census. 1994. *Poverty in the United States, 1991.* Washington, D.C.: U.S. Government Printing Office.

U.S. Department of Commerce, Bureau of Economic Analysis. 1971. *Local Area Personal Income, 1969.* Washington, D.C.: U.S. Government Printing Office.

U.S. Department of Commerce, Bureau of Economic Analysis. 1981. *Local Area Personal Income, 1979.* Washington, D.C.: U.S. Government Printing Office.

U.S. Department of Commerce, Bureau of Economic Analysis. 1991. *Local Area Personal Income, 1989.* Washington, D.C.: U.S. Government Printing Office.

Virginia Tech. 1987. The Future of Agriculture, Forestry, Food Industries and Rural Communities in Virginia: Report on the Western Region (unpublished). Blacksburg: College of Agriculture and Life Sciences, Virginia Polytechnic Institute and State University.

———. 1987a. The Future of Agriculture, Forestry, Food Industries and Rural Communities in Virginia: Report on the Western Region (unpublished). Blacksburg: College of Agriculture and Life Sciences, Virginia Polytechnic Institute and State University.

Waller, Altina A. 1988. *Feud: Hatfields, McCoys, and Social Change in Appalachia, 1860-1900.* Chapel Hill: University of North Carolina Press.

Walls, David. 1978. Internal Colony or Internal Periphery? A Critique of Current Models and an Alternative Formulation. In *Colonialism in Modern America: The Appalachian Case*, Helen Lewis, et al. eds. Boone, N.C.: Appalachian Consortium Press.

William T. Grant Foundation. 1988. *The Forgotten Half: Non-College Youth in America*. Washington, D.C.: William T. Grant Foundation Commission on Work, Family and Citizenship.

Wilson, William Julius. 1987. *The Truly Disadvantaged: The Inner City, the Underclass, and Public Policy*. Chicago: University of Chicago Press.

World Bank. 1991. *World Development Report 1991*. New York: Oxford University Press: Table 30.

Index